CANADIAN JUSTICE, INDIGENOUS INJUSTICE

Canadian Justice, Indigenous Injustice

The Gerald Stanley and Colten Boushie Case

KENT ROACH

McGill-Queen's University Press
Montreal & Kingston • London • Chicago

© McGill-Queen's University Press 2019

ISBN 978-0-7735-5638-6 (cloth)
ISBN 978-0-7735-5644-7 (ePDF)
ISBN 978-0-7735-5645-4 (ePUB)

Legal deposit first quarter 2019
Bibliothèque nationale du Québec

Printed in Canada on acid-free paper that is 100% ancient forest free
(100% post-consumer recycled), processed chlorine free

This book has been published with the help of a grant from the Canadian
Federation for the Humanities and Social Sciences, through the Awards to
Scholarly Publications Program, using funds provided by the Social
Sciences and Humanities Research Council of Canada.

Funded by the   Financé par le
Government   gouvernement
of Canada   du Canada

Canada Council   Conseil des arts
for the Arts   du Canada

We acknowledge the support of the Canada Council for the Arts, which last year
invested $153 million to bring the arts to Canadians throughout the country.

Nous remercions le Conseil des arts du Canada de son soutien. L'an dernier,
le Conseil a investi 153 millions de dollars pour mettre de l'art dans la vie des
Canadiennes et des Canadiens de tout le pays.

Library and Archives Canada Cataloguing in Publication

Roach, Kent, 1961–, author
Canadian justice, Indigenous justice : the Gerald Stanley and Colten Boushie case /
Kent Roach.

Includes bibliographical references and index.
Issued in print and electronic formats.
ISBN 978-0-7735-5638-6 (cloth). – ISBN 978-0-7735-5644-7 (ePDF). –
ISBN 978-0-7735-5645-4 (ePUB)

1. Stanley, Gerald (Farmer) – Trials, litigation, etc. 2. Boushie, Colten – Trials,
litigation, etc. 3. Trials (Murder) – Saskatchewan. 4. Trials (Manslaughter)
– Saskatchewan. 5. Self-defense (Law) – Saskatchewan. 6. Rural crimes –
Saskatchewan. 7. Discrimination in criminal justice administration – Saskatchewan.
8. Criminal justice, Administration of – Saskatchewan. I. Title.

HV6535.C32S28 2019   345.7124'0252308997323   C2018-905012-8
                                                   C2018-905013-6

This book was typeset in 10.5/13 Sabon.

Contents

Foreword

Justice has proven to be illusive for Indigenous Peoples in Canada. The Supreme Court of Canada has called this a crisis. Over the past forty years, dozens of official reports have confirmed this fact. The death of Colton Bushie and the trial of Gerald Stanley provide a concrete lens through which to examine this calamity. In this book Professor Roach delves deeply into the criminal "injustice" system as it relates to Indigenous Peoples. He highlights the significant challenges involved in addressing this issue through an examination of the Gerald Stanley case.

I have known Professor Roach for over twenty-five years. He has long worked to remedy injustice by ensuring that vulnerable people's rights are considered and upheld. His influential work on national security, the role of the courts, wrongful convictions, and Indigenous over-representation in Canadian criminal law processes demonstrate this commitment. His advocacy has garnered national and international attention. He was teaching and writing about these issues when I was a law student back in the late 1980s and he has never stepped back from this important work. He has worked with major Canadian Commissions of Inquiry and has appeared as counsel on many landmark cases before the Supreme Court of Canada. He is a member of the Order of Canada and a recipient of Canada's major academic awards. He is an uncommonly bright individual who works hard to understand both the intricacies of law and its broader societal context.

More importantly, Kent Roach is one of the most reasonable people I know. He is kind, civil, fair, and has sound judgment. He has a great respect for others, which is probably why he works so hard to have people and systems follow their highest professional standards. He labours diligently to help Canadians be their best selves and this book follows this path. This book leads us to reflect and to attempt to change.

One of the unique elements of this book is that Professor Roach considers the potential role of Indigenous treaties to address justice issues. This is a promising line of inquiry because treaties between Indigenous Peoples and the Crown are foundational agreements. They formed our country on the Prairies and beyond. They are also our highest law because they are constitutionally recognized and affirmed.

Each numbered Treaty in Saskatchewan contains a "peace and order" clause which has significant implications for justice issues explored in this book. Each Treaty says, with slight variations:

> The undersigned chiefs, on their behalf and on behalf of all other Indians inhabiting the tract within ceded do hereby solemnly promise and engage to strictly observe this treaty and also to conduct and behave themselves as good and loyal subjects of Her Majesty the Queen. They promise and engage that they will in all respects obey and abide by the law; *that they will maintain peace and order between each other, and also between themselves and other tribes of Indians or whites*, now inhabiting or hereafter to inhabit any part of the said tract, or that they will not molest a person or property of any inhabitants of such ceded tract or the property of Her Majesty The Queen, or interfere with or trouble any person passing or travelling through the said tract or any part thereof, and that *they will aid and assist the officers of Her Majesty in bringing to justice and punishment any Aboriginal offending against the stipulations of this treaty or infringe the laws in force in the country so ceded.*

The promise that Indigenous Peoples would play a role in maintaining peace and order within Canada has not yet been realized. Professor Roach urges us to implement these provisions and his book points out in great detail where we have fallen short.

When Indigenous Peoples formulate, apply and enforce their own laws within their communities, and aid Canada more generally in making its law more just, the Treaties will provide an important resource for improving our relationships in the justice field.

Fifteen years ago I wrote a report for the Treaty Commission of Saskatchewan which discussed the peace and order clauses from an Indigenous perspective. I learned that in the Cree language, the Treaties' "peace and order" promise is understood by the word *miyo-wicehtowin*. *Miyo wichetown* asks, directs, or requires people to conduct themselves in a manner that creates positive and good relations in all their relationships. Similarly, *pastahowin*, interpreted as "crossing the line," was another important provision relating to peace, order and justice treaties. It means that certain things cannot be done without experiencing bad consequences. Moreover, *wah-kohtowin* is an important part of the meaning of the peace and order provisions because it conveys the idea that laws and duties must be followed to have good relationships. In the Dene language similar concepts are described as *soholya* and *sugha eghena*, and they are embodied in the promises relating to justice under the Treaties. When Indigenous Peoples signed treaties and secured promises from the Crown relative to justice, these and similar teachings were present in the hearts and minds of the chiefs and headmen who entered into these sacred agreements.

As the courts have long recognized, treaties must be understood by reference to their written text and the oral understandings of these agreements. The written sources are often biased, being written in English, not the Indigenous language of the negotiation. Furthermore, the Treaties use technical legal words and their transcription was usually in the hands of non-Indigenous parties. The limitations of the written word mean that oral traditions and perspectives must be taken into account to determine the meaning of the treaties. These perspectives point citizens toward a more relational, less polarized approach when it comes to Indigenous justice issues. This should have implications for considering the Stanley case, as Professor Roach indicates.

Treaties are a key to our future in the criminal justice system because they speak to the need for mutual respect, aid and assistance in maintaining peace and harmony among peoples in Canada. They are significant sources of authority for the promotion of law and order because of how they were formed, what they stand for, and what they protect. They are built on one of the firmest of foundations: mutual consent. As such, their legitimacy is supportable under both the Indigenous and larger Canadian political and legal orders. Their existence saves the people of Canada from having to go through a costly, divisive search for new options to overcome the pressing problems that exist in relation to Indigenous Peoples and the Canadian legal system. Treaties have the widespread support of the Indigenous Peoples in the province where the Stanley trial occurred, and non-Indigenous Peoples are already party to its terms. The peace and order principles the Treaties articulate for creating fair and just relationships are logical, reasonable, and realistic.

As the Office of the Treaty Commissioner of Saskatchewan wrote in a 1998 report (*Statement of Treaty Issues: Treaties as a Bridge to the Future* [Saskatoon: Office of the Treaty Commissioner 1998], 74.):

> The people of Saskatchewan can benefit from learning more about the historical events associated with the making of the treaties as they reveal the mutual benefits and responsibilities of the parties. There is ample evidence that many people are misinformed about the history of the Canada-Treaty First Nations relations, and about the consequent experiences of Treaty First Nations communities and individuals. Until recently, the perspective of many Canadians has been to view treaties as remnants of antiquity, with little relevance to the present. Treaties were seen as frozen in time, part of Canada's ancient history. Some no doubt still hold this view of treaties as primarily "real estate transactions" modeled on business contracts and British common law. Non-Aboriginal Canadians forgot that they, too, gained rights through treaty – rights to the rich lands and resources from which they have benefited greatly. They also forgot about the partnership formed at the time of treaty-making. *The benefits of the treaties were to be mutual, assisting both parties. The wealth generated from these lands and resources has provided little benefit to Treaty First Nations* [emphasis mine].

Regarding the Treaties as agreements that create mutual obligations that alternately constrain and benefit both parties to the relationship is an important interpretive lens through which to view justice issues. It allows Indigenous and non-Indigenous Peoples to equally participate in the process of justice reform. While there is much in Professor Roach's wide-ranging text which follows, that identifies challenges and opportunities for addressing criminal justice failures, the need for mutual respect and action is one of the strongest messages I take from this book.

At the risk of trying the reader's patience in this foreword, I include a list of recommendations arising from the work with the Office of the Treaty Commission of Saskatchewan that I completed all those years ago. It is an unpublished report from 19 September 2003 entitled: *Peace and Order: Describing and Implementing Treaty Justice in Saskatchewan.* As you read through Professor Roach's text I hope you will conclude that they are as relevant today as when they were written over fifteen years ago. These are my own recommendations, after having listened to the elders discuss the peace and order clauses over a two-year period when I worked with them. These recommendations do not represent the views of the Treaty Commission, Canadian or provincial governments or First Nations at the time the report was prepared, though I tried to be faithful to their diverse views. I offer them in the spirit of learning and healing, to foreshadow some of the work that lies ahead, as raised in this book (the numbers after the recommendations correlate to pages in the report).

1 Indigenous languages should be used to understand the principles underlying the Treaties' peace and order clauses (16).
2 First Nations peoples are not the only beneficiaries under the Treaties. Non-Indigenous Peoples also have treaty rights. Treaties should be interpreted and implemented with this mutuality in mind (17).
3 At the time the Treaties were negotiated, the Elders said it was intended that both parties be equal, such that both parties would get benefit from the land, resources, and relationships (21).
4 Police protection was promised at time the Treaties were negotiated, to protect against other's encroachments (22).
5 Treaties have an "international flavour." First Nations made treaties to affirm that their own ideas of justice, embodied in the Cree words: *wahkohtowin, miyo-wihcetowin, pastahowin, ochinewin* and *kwayaskitotamowin* (21–27).
6 The Crown made treaties to affirm their own criminal justice jurisdiction (29).
7 There may have been ambiguity about how the Crown communicated criminal justice jurisdiction, or about how this communication was received (29–44).
8 When discussing the Treaties, the Elders and Federation of Saskatchewan Indian Nations representatives insisted that justice should not be limited to criminal justice. Justice under the

Treaties should not be equated with the criminal justice system, and justice under the Treaties should deal with larger societal and family relationships (46–51).

9 Despite the insistence that justice should not be limited to criminal justice, criminal justice should not be ignored because of its detrimental impact on Indigenous Peoples. Indigenous People are over-represented in conflicts with the criminal justice system in numbers extremely out of proportion to their numbers in the general population (51–58).

10 Colonization has broken both the Treaty and Aboriginal law and cultural teachings and should be reversed (58–62).

11 Indigenous Peoples have also broken their own law under the Treaty, and should return to respect their laws once again (62–65).

12 Despite the need to focus on larger issues of justice, there can be discussions to improve criminal justice as long as these discussions are contextualized within broader principles of justice (49).

13 In an earlier criminal justice report Justice Linn examined criminal justice in Saskatchewan and made helpful recommendations to improve the criminal justice system that could be implemented today. Among her suggestions were:

a. designing better data collection systems for Aboriginal involvement in the justice system;
b. establishing Youth Justice and Community Adult Liaison Justice Committees;
c. implementing and increasing employment equity for Aboriginal Peoples at all levels of the justice system (probation offices, parole officers, police, clerks, lawyers, judges);
d. providing cross-cultural training and sensitivity to those involved with Aboriginal peoples the system;
e. establishing court-worker programs to act as cultural and language interpreters for Aboriginal peoples involved with the criminal justice system;
f. creating more appropriate police services for Aboriginal peoples in the RCMP and municipal police forces;
g. designing and implementing mediation, diversion, and reconciliation programs;
h. making corrections more culturally sensitive (66).

14 Judge Cawsey's recommendations, in his earlier report about criminal justice in Alberta, could also be implemented (or further extended if already present in Saskatchewan). These include:

    a. creating legal aid education programs, pamphlets, service goals, etc., for Aboriginal peoples;

    b. establishing an Aboriginal lay justice of the peace program;

    c. developing language interpretation programs at the government level;

    d. involving Aboriginal communities in bail release programs;

    e. reforming the National Parole Board to incorporate Aboriginal concerns;

    f. establishing treatment centres and counseling for alcohol and other substance abusers;

    g. addressing and overcoming the socio-economic deficits faced by Aboriginal peoples;

    h. eliminating gender-bias against Aboriginal women in the justice system;

    i. creating an ongoing-process to monitor the state of Aboriginal justice in the province (86–69).

15 The recommendations of the Manitoba Aboriginal Justice Inquiry could also be implemented (or extended if already in existence). These ideas include:

    a. reforming the current court structure and administration through unification;

    b. holding trials in communities where the offence was committed;

    c. eliminating joint circuit travel with judges, lawyers and court personnel arriving together;

    d. actions being taken to make juries more representative of Aboriginal communities;

    e. reforming sentencing regimes;

    f. re-establishing gender harmony and equality by amending the *Indian Act*;

    g. creating special programs in mediation, sentencing, and corrections;

h. by Aboriginal leadership taking more responsibility for any role they play in abuse;

i. revising how Aboriginal child welfare is carried on in province by amending *Child and Family Services Act*;

j. supporting Aboriginal parents with their children through culturally appropriate service delivery;

k. amending the *Young Offenders Act* to create alternatives for removal, incarceration, supervision, replacing non-Aboriginal police forces with Aboriginal police forces in Aboriginal communities;

l. controlling liquor trade more sensitively through statute and administration;

m. amending the *Provincial Police Act* to create an Aboriginal Police Commissioner;

n. reconstituting the public complaints processes regarding police (70–71).

16 The Royal Commission on Aboriginal Peoples recommendations could also be implemented (or extended). These ideas include:

a. creating alternative justice initiatives funded on a long term basis that are community driven, have an appropriate development phase, and regard Indian status as irrelevant, and recognize the distinctive nature of Indigenous Justice initiatives;

b. recognition by the federal and provincial governments of an Aboriginal right to create justice systems;

c. recommending that the parties address *Charter* rights in the development of Aboriginal justice systems;

d. recommending that Aboriginal appellate structures be created;

e. recommending that an Aboriginal Justice Council be implemented to facilitate development, financing, and implementation of Aboriginal justice systems (72).

17 In implementing the Treaties' peace and order clauses in Saskatchewan, it is recommended that the choice not be viewed as being between separate or reformed systems (74).

18 It is recommended that the peace and order promises should only be implemented by focusing on the relationship of mutual

aid and assistance. The authority that people should look to in implementing justice should stem from a common source: the Treaties (74–75).

19 It should be recognized that both the Crown and First Nations could pass discrete laws under the Treaties that would only apply within their sphere, for the purposes of assistance and cooperation. There should be a vast area of joint law-making responsibilities to work for mutual assistance and respect to bring peace and order to the justice system in Saskatchewan (74–75).

20 It is recommended that the parties should not simply re-form the way in which the criminal justice system operates. They should work towards transformation: changing the way the system operates at all levels to take account of the Treaty relationship (76).

21 Jurisdiction over justice in the province should flow from one law, the Treaties (83).

22 Differentiation under the Treaties between Indigenous and non-Indigenous Peoples should be recognized as a mechanism to achieve equality (85–88).

23 Jurisdiction concerning justice should be shared, and the responsibility for administration divided between Indigenous Peoples and the Crown (88–94).

24 A Treaty Office should be established, and the Office of the Treaty Commission abolished (96).

25 To recognize the treaty-based nature of each government, each government should take action to proclaim these historic foundations. They should explicitly proclaim, enact into law, and celebrate the idea that they exist in the shared space known as Saskatchewan because of the Treaties (101).

26 Alternative initiatives such as the Cree court should be expanded throughout the province, in both rural and urban settings (107).

27 Justice should be enhanced, by Cree, Saulteaux, Dene, Dakota/Lakota/Nakota being spoken with more frequency at all levels of the criminal justice and other systems (107).

28 Courts should become more accessible by being held more frequently in communities where people are charged (108).

29 A much greater investment in therapeutic resources is needed in the courts, schools, families etc., with an Indigenous focus (109).

30 The creation of a *Justice and Healing Lodge* with a *Tribal Court Chamber* should take place (111–120).

31 The idea of *treaty-based* community policing should be further articulated and implemented (120).

32 Police should have a greater presence in communities by: participating more thoroughly in community events; speaking in schools; being visible role models; participating in circles. Conversely, others should recognize the difficulty of their jobs. (121–124).

33 Stable funding is needed for education, good governance, homes and recreation centres, drawing on the expertise of Indian people. Social justice is an important element of peace and order and the Elders were firm in stating this was necessary to create peace and order (125–128).

34 Families should be supported in their roles and responsibilities in teaching *wahkohtowin*. Precepts such as forgiveness, love, laughter, emotionally lifting, listening, patience, participation, communication and creativity, etc., should be taught in the home with the assistance of other people and organizations (128).

35 Communities should address the family, clan, and kinship conflicts that exist (128).

36 It should be recognized that women played a central role in the treaty process, and they should play a central role in implementing the Treaties' promises in contemporary settings (130).

37 Ceremonies should be performed to promote respect between men and women (131).

38 Women's shelters should be built to assist abused women (132).

39 Marriage and family break-down should be addressed using traditional teachings in light of contemporary circumstances (133–136).

40 Children should receive better treatment in the home, and should have greater support from Child Welfare Agencies when their home life breaks down (136–138).

41 Circles should be more extensively used to facilitate understanding of treaties, and implement the promises the Treaties contain (142–153).

John Borrows
Canada Research Chair in Indigenous Law,
University of Victoria Law School

CANADIAN JUSTICE, INDIGENOUS INJUSTICE

I

Introduction

On 9 February 2018, a jury in Battleford, Saskatchewan acquitted Gerald Stanley, a fifty-six-year-old white cattle farmer, of the intentional murder and negligent manslaughter of Colten Boushie, a twenty-two-year-old Cree man from the Red Pheasant First Nation. Why write a book about this case?

The Saskatchewan prosecution decided not to appeal the acquittal. The jury that rendered the verdict cannot under Canadian law explain why it acquitted Stanley either in open court or subsequently to the media. Some argue that it is unfair to question a jury's verdict.

But the Stanley/Boushie case will not and should not go away. It has resulted in proposed legislation to abolish the peremptory challenges that allowed Stanley's lawyers to keep five visibly Indigenous people off the jury. Such a reform will only partially address concerns that the Canadian justice system too often results in injustice to Indigenous people, whether they are crime victims or the accused.

BASIC FACTS

Colten Boushie was one of five Indigenous young people who came onto the Stanley property thirty miles north of Biggar, Saskatchewan in the early evening of 9 August 2016. The others were Eric Meechance, Cassidy Cross, Belinda Jackson and Kiora Wuttunee. They were returning to the Red Pheasant First Nation after a summer's afternoon spent drinking and swimming. They were driving a grey Escape sports utility vehicle that had developed a flat tire some time after the occupants had gone swimming. There was also a loaded .22-calibre rifle in the car though Gerald Stanley testified that he did not know this until after Boushie was dead.

Cross was driving the grey Escape with Meechance in the front seat. The two exited from the grey Escape after they drove onto the Stanley farm. They attempted to start an all-terrain vehicle parked near a shed on the Stanley farm. They had also tried to start another vehicle at a neighbouring farm. Cross and Meechance re-entered the grey Escape and started driving along a path on the farm after Gerald Stanley and his twenty-seven-year-old son, Stanley Sheldon, ran towards them. Sheldon Stanley used a hammer to break the windshield of the grey Escape. The grey Escape, driven by Cross, shortly after collided with the Stanley's blue Escape before coming to a stop some distance away, close to where Leesa Stanley, Gerald's wife, was mowing the lawn.

After the collision, Cross and Meechance exited the grey Escape and ran away from the farm. At some point, Colten Boushie went from the back seat, where he had been sitting with Belinda Jackson and Kiora Wuttunee, to the front seat where he would be shot.

Gerald Stanley retrieved an old pistol from his shed and loaded it with what he thought were two rounds of old ammunition. He testified he fired two warning shots after leaving the shed and when he was near his damaged blue Escape. Sheldon Stanley testified he heard those warning shots as he entered the family's bungalow to get his truck keys. As he emerged from the house, he saw his father walking towards where the grey Escape had come to a stop close to where Leesa Stanley had been mowing the lawn.

Unable to see Leesa, Gerald Stanley ran in fear to the front of the grey Escape to see if she had been run over by it. This was not the case. Gerald Stanley then went back to the driver's side where Colten Boushie was now sitting in the driver's seat. Gerald Stanley tried to turn the vehicle off because it had a revving engine and he feared being run over by it. He tried to do this with his left hand while holding his pistol in his right hand. The pistol discharged behind Colten Boushie's left ear, killing the twenty-two-year-old.

Stanley testified that the gun discharged accidentally and that he did not pull or have his finger on the trigger after firing the first two shots when he was close to his blue Escape. This was a controversial hang fire defence, suggesting that there was a delay between the pulling of the trigger and the exit of the bullet from the gun. This was to become the subject of both expert and lay evidence at trial.

The only other witness who said she saw what happened was Belinda Jackson. She was seated in the back of the grey Escape directly behind Boushie. Kiora Wuttunee was also in the back seat, but she would testify that she was asleep and did not see what happened. Jackson testified that she saw Stanley shoot Boushie twice. The autopsy indicated that Boushie was only shot once. While she was arrested, Jackson told the RCMP that she did not know who shot Boushie.

After Boushie was shot, Belinda Jackson and Kiora Wuttunee opened the driver's door of the grey Escape in an attempt to assist their friend, Colten. Boushie's body fell out of the car, along with a .22-calibre rifle. Both Jackson and Wuttunee said Leesa Stanley made a comment to them to the effect that's what you get for trespassing. After this, Belinda Jackson admitted she punched Leesa Stanley. Charges were laid against both Jackson and Wuttunee for assaulting Leesa Stanley, but were eventually dropped.

At the request of his mother, Sheldon Stanley called 911 using a cell phone he had in his back pocket. The three members of the Stanley family went into the house and made coffee to await the arrival of the RCMP. When the RCMP arrived, they initially detained everyone, but released Leesa and Sheldon Stanley at the scene. Meechance and Cross were charged with theft, but these charges were also eventually dropped.

Gerald Stanley was charged with second-degree murder and manslaughter by way of an assault or careless use of a firearm. He was acquitted of all charges on 9 February 2018 by a jury that did not include any visibly Indigenous people.

A DIVISIVE CASE

The Stanley case bitterly divided Canadians. A poll taken shortly after the verdict found 32 per cent of the respondents viewed the verdict as "flawed and wrong," but that 30 per cent believed it was "good and fair." The remaining 38 per cent were unsure. The picture was substantially different in Saskatchewan, where 63 per cent of respondents thought the verdict was "good and fair," but only 17 per cent – about the same number of Indigenous people in the province – concluded that it was "flawed and wrong."[1] These results affirm the need to be particularly attentive to local context, history and polarization when examining the case.

OUTLINE OF THE BOOK

Chapter 2 will provide the historical context to the Stanley case. This starts with Treaty 6 which applies to the territory where the events happened. I will examine the record of discussions between representatives of Canada and Indigenous nations when Treaty 6 was negotiated in 1876 with particular attention to discussions and some misunderstandings between the two sides about matters involving criminal justice. This will be supplemented by some more recent comments by Treaty 6 Indigenous Elders about their understanding and hopes for the Treaty. This chapter will also examine the mass hanging of eight Indigenous men at Battleford in 1885 after unfair trials in which the accused did not receive translators or defence lawyers. The role of all-white juries in various trials, including those arising from the 1885 uprisings led by Louis Riel against the Canadian government, will also be assessed. Finally, it will be seen how Indigenous people were punished for the uprisings by the increased use of residential schools and the introduction of the pass system to restrict their ability to leave reserves.

Chapter 3 will explore the social, economic and political background to the case. This includes economic disparities between Indigenous and non-Indigenous people in Saskatchewan. This chapter will also examine politicized and racialized debates about rural crime, self-defence and guns. These debates resulted in 2012 legislation that expanded the right to self-defence and defence of property and eased some restrictions on guns. This chapter will also examine a series of divisive Saskatchewan criminal cases that help set the context for the racial polarization and distrust seen in the Stanley case. They include the Carney Nerland/Leo Lachance case where police and prosecutors accepted that a neo-Nazi had accidently shot a Cree trapper who had come into his pawn shop. Nerland pled guilty to manslaughter and was sentenced to four years' imprisonment, but a subsequent inquiry raised concerns that the police and prosecutors had not adequately explored the role of racism in the case.

A few days after Colten Boushie's death, Saskatchewan premier Brad Wall made an extraordinary intervention because there had been "racist and hate-filled comments on social media." He pleaded that they "must stop" and warned about the existence of laws against hate speech. Wall also argued, "None of us should be jumping to conclusions about what happened. We should trust the RCMP to do their work."[2] One of the few things that the Stanleys and Boushies agreed on, however, was their dissatisfaction with the RCMP investigation. This investigation and other preliminary proceedings, including the decision to grant Stanley bail or pretrial release, to commit him for trial on second-degree murder charges, and not to allow cameras in the courtroom, will be examined in chapter 4.

The selection of an all-white jury to hear the Stanley case even though it involved an Indigenous person was not an aberration. Chapter 5 will discuss jury selection in the Stanley case in the context of Canada's complex process of jury selection – which differs in important respects from that used in the US and the UK. Indigenous people are under-represented on juries for a variety of reasons including socio-economic and geographic factors. These make it difficult for many Indigenous people to attend jury trials in centres such as Battleford where the Stanley trial was held. An additional obstacle is their alienation from the Canadian criminal justice system.[3] In 2015, a majority of the Supreme Court of Canada accepted dramatic Indigenous under-representation on juries so long as reasonable efforts were made and there was no deliberate exclusion. It concluded that addressing "historical and systemic wrongs against Aboriginal people" through jury selection would make it "virtually impossible" to select a jury and would deliver "a devastating blow to the administration of justice."[4] This, however, begs the question of how many more Stanley cases – with no Indigenous representation on the jury – can be repeated without the administration of justice suffering a devastating blow: one that will be absorbed by Indigenous people?

Indigenous under-representation on juries makes it something of a minor miracle that five visibly Indigenous prospective jurors were called to be on the Stanley jury. These five people were, however, subject to peremptory challenges by Stanley. Peremptory challenges give both the accused and the prosecutor a limited number of challenges – in this case fourteen each – without reasons having to be given. Attempts to control the discriminatory use of peremptory challenges have failed in the US. Such challenges are much less frequently made in Canada, but they also have failed. Such failures had led to calls for the abolition of peremptory challenges. The Justin Trudeau government accepted such calls in Bill C-75 which was introduced for first reading in Parliament two months after Stanley's acquittal. Another problem with the Stanley jury was that prospective jurors were not asked, through a challenge for cause procedure, if racist bias towards Colten Boushie or extensive pretrial publicity, both in traditional and social media, would prevent them from being impartial. This occurred despite Premier Wall's recognition of racism surrounding the case and several prospective jurors volunteering that they were biased in favour of Stanley.

One of the most controversial issues in the Stanley trial was his defence that he did not pull the trigger after he fired the warning shots and that the bullet that discharged into the back of Boushie's head was a delayed hang fire. Although this was dubbed a "magic gun"[5] defence, both prosecution and defence experts admitted that a hang fire was possible, especially given that Stanley used an old gun with old ammunition. This issue will be discussed in chapter 6, in the larger context of the growing knowledge of how shortcomings in forensic science, and its communication to judges and juries, have contributed to wrongful convictions. The Stanley case did not, of course, result in a wrongful conviction, but this book will suggest that research about the multiple causes of wrongful convictions can be applied to a wider range of miscarriages of justice. Specifically, there is a danger that both expert and non-expert evidence heard by the jury in the Stanley trial conflated the thirty to sixty second safety guidelines adopted to minimize damage caused by rare "hang fires," with the observed and measured length of less than half a second in experimentally induced "hang fires." The timing issue is critical to the facts of the case given the jury's interest in this question and Gerald and Sheldon Stanley's testimony about what happened between Stanley pulling the trigger for the first two shots and the fatal third shot.

Fact-finding, including determinations by judges and juries of the credibility of witnesses, raises uncomfortable questions about who is being judged and who is judging. It can be resistant to regulation by legal standards or by appeal court judges. Miscarriages of justice often result from errors in fact-finding. Chapter 7 will discuss how Stanley's lawyer successfully challenged the credibility of the Indigenous witnesses by introducing their criminal records or accusing them of lying. Even the prosecutor, in his closing address, told the jury that he would not rely on the evidence of Belinda Jackson – the only Indigenous witness to testify that she saw Stanley shoot Boushie. The challenge to the credibility of other Indigenous witnesses in this trial will be compared to the flawed fact-finding by the all-white jury that wrongfully convicted Donald Marshall Jr, a seventeen-year-old Mi'kmaq man, of murder in 1971 and a panel of five appellate judges who, in 1982, wrongfully convicted him of robbery and perjury even while they overturned his murder conviction. In all of these cases, there were suggestions that fact-finders had been influenced by racist stereotypes associating Indigenous people with lies, theft and violence.

Although Stanley said he would not rely on self-defence or defence of property to attempt to justify his killing of Boushie, chapter 8 will examine how implicit or phantom ideas of defence of property and self-defence permeated much of the trial. They explain why so much trial time was devoted to the actions of Eric Meechance and Cassidy Cross on the Stanley and a neighbouring farm. These events were relevant to the racially charged debate about rural crime and the expanded self-defence and defence of property rights discussed in chapter 3, but not so much to the murder and manslaughter charge that Stanley faced. The jury was told to consider whether Stanley had any "lawful excuse" for careless use of the firearm, but was never told that Stanley's perceptions that his own and his wife's life were threatened by Boushie and his friends should also be reasonable. The Stanley jury was never told by the judge about a reasonableness requirement in the Canadian law of self-defence and defence of property. This requires that the accused's perception and response to threats be reasonable and has the potential to combat the bias which may arise from racial fears and stereotypes, though this, perhaps, should be bolstered by law reform explicitly addressing the unacceptability of racist stereotypes.

The jury's acquittal of Stanley of both murder and manslaughter angered many Indigenous people and their supporters. Despite analogies being made to the Rodney King case, where an acquittal resulted in riots in Los Angeles in 1992, the response was peaceful, dignified and constructive. Canada has indeed been fortunate that the vast majority of protests by Indigenous people have been so peaceful. Chapter 9 will examine the aftermath of the Stanley verdict, including the controversies over Prime Minister Justin Trudeau's statements that we must do better. It will assess Bill C-75's proposed reforms to jury selection, including the abolition of peremptory challenges. The decision of the Saskatchewan attorney general not to appeal the acquittal will be critically assessed as will Saskatchewan's refusal to call an inquiry or appoint a coroner's inquest to examine the case. Finally, a few subsequent cases with similar dynamics to the

Stanley case will be examined, including the Peter Khill/Jon Styres cases in Ontario which resulted in a jury acquitting a white man charged with killing an Indigenous man. Unlike in the Stanley case, jurors were questioned in this case about possible racist bias and the prosecutor decided to appeal the acquittal, in part, on the basis of alleged errors in what the trial judge told the jury about self-defence.

The final chapter will explore whether "we can do better." The denial of history and racism evident in the Stanley trial, as symbolized by the refusal to ask prospective jurors whether they could be impartial in light of the fused issues of racism and pretrial publicity, are major barriers to change. The Stanley case should not be viewed as an aberration, but in the context of injustices suffered by Indigenous people in Saskatchewan at least since the 1885 trial and hangings of the Battleford Eight. Bill C-75 responds to the jury selection discrimination in the Stanley case by abolishing peremptory challenges, but it falls far short of radical jury reforms such as mixed juries composed of six Indigenous and six non-Indigenous persons, the use of volunteer jurors from the Indigenous community, or even more searching questioning of prospective jurors about possible racist bias.

As Justice Frank Iacobucci stressed in his 2013 report,[6] Indigenous under-representation on juries is a symptom of larger problems of systemic and colonial discrimination. Indigenous people mistrust the Canadian justice system and for good reason. Stereotypes about Indigenous people – whether they be accused, witnesses, or victims – need to be named and confronted. The focus of concern in the Canadian criminal justice system has been on protecting the accused against racist discrimination, but Indigenous crime victims and witnesses need similar protection. Eric Meechance and Cassidy Cross were charged with theft and Belinda Jackson and Kiora Wuttunee were charged with assault. These charges were eventually dropped, but the Indigenous witnesses were effectively put on trial by Stanley's lawyer. Self-defence laws may require reform to ensure that they are not influenced by racist stereotypes and fears and to ensure that they do not encourage the unnecessary and disproportionate use of force and guns in self-defence and in defence of property. The need for increased gun control will also be briefly examined.

Although the Canadian justice system has too often led to Indigenous injustice, a few areas of possible common ground for Indigenous and non-Indigenous people will also be explored in the

last chapter. These include the need to reform policing, including the
RCMP, to make it more responsive to the concerns of all communities and to meet the many challenges of policing rural, remote, and
diverse areas. There is also a need to try to make the criminal justice
system more accurate to avoid miscarriages of justice, whether they
be wrongful convictions or wrongful acquittals, both of which disproportionately affect Indigenous people. Finally, common ground
might once again be discovered in the Treaties, but only if there is
better appreciation and respect of Indigenous laws and perspectives.

METHODOLOGY

This book relies upon public sources including the full transcripts
of the preliminary inquiry held between 4–6 April 2016 (page references marked at PT) and the trial held between 29 January and
9 February 2018 (page references marked as TT). The sources take
account of the jury selection, trial, closing addresses of the lawyers,
and the judge's charge to the jury in the Stanley case. I have tried my
best to write this book so that it is accessible to non-lawyers as well
as those who study law. There are extensive endnotes, but they are
not of a narrative variety.

This book also examines media coverage of the case and a few relevant social media sites. I have deliberately not attempted to interview
those personally involved in the case, in part, because of concerns
about increasing the trauma they already have experienced. This book
does not attempt to tell the personal stories of either the Boushie or
Stanley families: those stories are for them to tell. My focus is on
the public record because I am primarily concerned about what the
case tells us about Canadian law, politics, and society. In particular, I
will focus on how the Stanley trial reveals the potential for injustice,
especially in cases involving Indigenous people as accused, victims or
witnesses. I will attempt to place the Stanley/Boushie case in its larger
historical, political, social, and legal context.

Like my previous work, this book uses a criminal process approach.
This means examining the role of the police, forensic experts, prosecutors, defence lawyers, trial judge, the media, and the jury. The criminal
process is part of a larger legal process approach to scholarship that
is attentive to the respective roles of courts and legislatures. There
is a danger that the minimum standards of the *Charter*, as defined
by the Supreme Court, on issues like jury selection can become *de*

facto maximum standards in the absence of Parliamentary activism. For example, I will criticize Bill C-75 for not imposing more robust equality standards on assembling panels of prospective jurors than the Supreme Court did in a 2015 case that accepted dramatic Indigenous under-representation on juries as consistent with the *Charter* rights of an Indigenous accused.[7] Jury selection, like so many matters affecting Indigenous people, is a frustrating mix of provincial and federal jurisdiction, one that makes effective reform difficult.

The legal process approach is also attentive to a broad range of legal instruments such as coroners' inquests, civil trials, and inquiries. The Boushie family has commenced civil litigation against both the Stanleys and the RCMP. A coroner's inquest with Indigenous jurors could examine the case and ways to prevent similar deaths in the future as might a public inquiry.

My approach also attempts to be attentive to the interaction of the Stanley trial with Indigenous laws and Treaties including discussing some instances where Cree laws appear not to have been recognized or fully respected during the Stanley trial and by considering the relevance of Treaty 6 to a number of matters raised by this trial including those related to the role of the RCMP and the jury in the case.

This book also explores some of the historical background to the case starting with negotiations and signing of Treaty 6 in 1876 by representatives of Canada and some First Nations. It also examines a number of controversial historical trials arising out of the 1885 uprising led by Louis Riel and the Métis against the Canadian government. My previous work with the Truth and Reconciliation Commission has opened my eyes to the impossibility of reconciliation unless there is a full accounting of the truth, and specifically, the multi-faceted and multi-generational harms of colonialism on Indigenous people. Thus matters that took place more than a century ago can still be relevant to understanding a trial process that took place between 2016 and 2018. I am also aware that truth can be both painful and divisive. It may be a barrier to reconciliation. Nevertheless, the truth of the injustices suffered and lived by Indigenous people must be faced and acknowledged by non-Indigenous people if there is any hope that they will not be repeated in the future.

The book also draws on my interest in wrongful convictions. In the last thirty years, there has been an explosion of knowledge and awareness of wrongful convictions. Many wrongful convictions depend not on fine points of law debated in appellate courts, but on erroneous fact-finding by police, lay and expert witnesses, judges, and juries. The Stanley case raises similar questions. Why did many of the justice system participants reject Belinda Jackson's testimony? How did the jury make determinations of credibility and might they have relied on racist stereotypes? Was the expert and lay evidence on hang fire presented to the jury in a clear and scientifically accurate way? Or did it manifest some of the same shortcomings in the practice and communication of forensic science that have contributed to wrongful convictions? What do the lessons learned from wrongful convictions tell us about other possible miscarriages of justice, including wrongful acquittals?

Fact-finding, whether by a judge or jury, plays a critical but underexamined role in the criminal justice process. Research on wrongful convictions and sexual assault prosecutions have both pointed to the centrality of fact-finding to the trial process and with it the role of fact-finders whether they be judges or jurors. It demonstrates that criminal trials are an all-too-human process.[8] This is also true in the Stanley/Boushie case. Canadian law[9] prohibits interviews with jurors so researchers can only rely on inferences and speculations when it comes to understanding the verdict of a jury. Some argue that jury verdicts should simply be accepted and not questioned. In my view, in a democracy we are all entitled to question public exercises of power even by twelve anonymous fellow citizens who are conscripted to do a difficult job.

The analogies to wrongful convictions raise the question of why the Canadian criminal justice system has traditionally favoured the risk of wrongful acquittals to wrongful convictions. Although some question this preference, I do not. Still, all preventable errors in justice should not be tolerated – especially when the consequences of these errors fall disproportionately on Indigenous people and other disadvantaged groups. The Stanley case will be considered in the context of both the historical and contemporary failure of the Canadian criminal justice system in relation to Indigenous people who are dramatically over-represented among both prisoners and crime victims.

Canadians were divided, sometimes bitterly, about the Stanley/ Boushie case both before and after the jury's verdict. Almost equal numbers concluded that the acquittal was "flawed and wrong" and "good and fair" with 38 per cent of respondents not sure.[10] This book will explore how such polarization may affect our law, politics, and social relations. In earlier work, I have outlined the concept of the new political case as one that promoted polarization of public and elite opinion. The traditional political case pitted the accused's rights against the state. This continues in the new political case, but because of increased concern about crimes against women, children, various minorities, and Indigenous people, the new political case also pits the accused against rights claims made on behalf of victims or groups of potential victims.[11]

The Stanley/Boushie case fits into the new political case framework, but with some additions. Different perspectives on justice mean that the Canadian justice system has, almost from the start, often resulted in injustice for Indigenous people. This polarization is longstanding, dating back to when the Europeans first came to this land.

But there are also modern pressures. Fragmented social media and increased partisan mobilization around criminal justice issues, including self-defence and gun laws, have placed additional pressures on the new political case. For example, the social media response to the Boushie killing was so great that Saskatchewan premier, Brad Wall, attempted to intervene and warn people about laws against the spreading of racial hatred.

Canada is not immune from racially charged debates about crime, self-defence, and guns that are so pervasive and polarizing in the United States. Ongoing Canadian debates about rural crime reveal real problems. Recent data confirm higher per capita reporting of crimes to the police in rural as opposed to urban areas. This places demands on those who police rural areas in addition to the inherent challenges of policing large areas.[12] At the same time, however, the rural crime debate also can consciously or subconsciously invoke racist fears and stereotypes about Indigenous people as dangerous and likely to steal and/or engage in violence. Such debates ignore that Indigenous people are much more likely than non-Indigenous people to be crime victims including of the most serious crimes.[13]

Some of Stanley's supporters echoed themes which have been presented in American "stand your ground" expansions of self-defence and gun rights as well as in the more moderate changes the Harper Conservative government made to the defence of property, self-defence, and gun laws. Prime Minister Harper's comments during the 2015 election campaign, about rural property owners using guns for their own safety, are also relevant. In turn, Prime Minister Justin Trudeau's remarks about "doing better," made immediately after the

Stanley verdict, were equally as controversial and polarizing. The Stanley/Boushie case received significant attention, in part, because it reflected so many of these milder but still significant Canadian versions of "red" and "blue" state political polarization seen in the US.

A criminal trial is inherently polarizing without the added challenges of social and political polarization and the frequently different world views of Indigenous and non-Indigenous people about justice. The challenges are great but we must use our reason, empathy, knowledge of history and current realities, compassion, and respect to help us overcome polarization. We must try to find common ground when it is available and respect differences where they exist. It is in this spirit that I seek to better understand the Stanley case.

2

From Treaty to "The White Man Governs"

INTRODUCTION

As a non-Indigenous person, I have learned much from the commentary, discussions, and advice that Indigenous colleagues have provided on the Stanley case. Almost without exception, these have started with a reference to history.

Saskatoon writer, Paul Seesequasis, and Darcy Lindberg of the University of Victoria both started their discussion of the case with memories of the eight Indigenous men who were hanged at Fort Battleford in 1885, very close to where the Stanley trial was held.[1] Jean Teillet, a leading Métis lawyer, started her account by outlining how little has changed in Canada's criminal justice system since an all-white jury convicted Louis Riel of treason.[2] Gina Starblanket and Dallas Hunt have noted "the continuing link between trading forts and individual farmers' castles," in reference to both the so-called "a man's home is his castle" doctrine in self-defence and Stanley's lawyer's argument to the jury that "your yard is your castle."[3] (TT 606)

Although the Stanley case was a modern one heavily influenced by social media, it cannot be understood without reference to the particular history of the Battleford area, north of Saskatoon, including its often troubled and even violent relations between Indigenous and non-Indigenous people. That said, history and specifically the Treaties that First Nations and the Canadian government agreed to can also provide foundations and lessons for making things better in the future.

TREATY 6

Treaty 6 was signed in 1876, in part, because the Canadian government wanted to expand European settlement, communication, and transportation on the Prairies, and to avoid wars with Indians that were consuming $20 million a year in the United States at a time when the entire budget of the Canadian federal government was $19 million.[4] Many, but not all, Indigenous leaders recognized the need to adjust their way of life in response to the decline of the buffalo herds that once populated the Prairie in such abundance. This led some of them to make Treaty demands that would help ensure food in times of famine and provide their Tribes with ploughs and cows that would allow them to farm. Both the physical hunger of Indigenous people and the colonial government's fears about possible conflict with them were factors in the negotiation of Treaty 6.[5]

The text of Treaty 6 agreed to provide the Indigenous tribes with farming equipment, medicine chests, schools, and relief during famines. As Cree Elder Gordon Oakes has explained, the Queen promised, "education, health, housing, school, blankets, farm implements: what the Indian can use to make a living. These are the things that were promised."[6] Many of these promises were broken. This Treaty, however, can still provide benefits for both Indigenous and non-Indigenous people. It is a foundational constitutional document that provides a basis for governing with consent, respect and harmony, as opposed to coercion, force and polarization.

MISUNDERSTANDINGS FROM THE START: OF HANGINGS AND ROPES ABOUT NECKS

The Treaty process should not, however, be romanticized as a perfect meeting of the minds of both sides. As John Borrows notes in his foreword to this book, the English text of the Treaty failed to capture what the First Nations thought they were agreeing to and the written historical record left by Europeans may not provide a full account of what was discussed before the Treaty was signed. Even respecting those limits, what follows cannot provide a full history of Treaty 6, which applies in the area where both Gerald Stanley and Colten Boushie lived. Rather, my focus will be on the available record as it touches on matters related to criminal justice. Alas, even this limited record reveals European stereotypes that associated Indigenous people with crime. It also demonstrates a failure by the European settlers to appreciate the importance of Indigenous laws and governance systems to the First Nations. These misunderstandings at the time when the Treaties were signed continue. They may help to explain why Canadian justice has so often been experienced as Indigenous injustice.

"dread the rope to be about my neck"[7]

Mistahimaskwa, the renowned Cree leader more frequently known as Big Bear, and Alexander Morris, the Chief Commissioner representing the Crown, failed to understand each other.

Big Bear joined the negotiation of Treaty 6 at Fort Pitt in 1876 late because he had been out hunting. He told Morris that what he dreaded most was having "the rope to be about my neck."[8] Big Bear likely used the Cree word *ay-saka-pay-kinit* which meant "led by the neck" in reference to the way that a wild horse loses its freedom. There was much packed into Big Bear's fears. The importance that Big Bear placed on freedom likely embraced not only physical freedom, but continued self-governance. Big Bear may have feared being led by ropes in the form of colonial laws and orders. In any event, Big Bear's fear that the Treaty and expanded European occupation of the Prairies would threaten his and his people's freedom was not far-fetched. Many Europeans saw the Treaty as a real estate transaction that would limit the First Nations to small reserves. Because of its fear and anger at Indigenous people after the 1885 uprising led by Louis Riel and the Métis, the Canadian government would attempt to confine First Nations to reserves through a pass system.

"No good Indian has the rope about his neck"[9]

Commissioner Alexander Morris, a lawyer who had trained with John A. Macdonald, did not understand Big Bear's concerns about dreading the rope to be around his neck. The Cree word used by Big Bear may have been mistranslated as *ay-hah-kinit*, a word that could be interpreted as hanging by the neck. This mistranslation makes sense if the translator and Morris thought of Big Bear and his people as potential criminals.

Morris replied to Big Bear in a manner that confirmed his commitment to English justice including capital punishment. He told Big Bear, "No good Indian has the rope about his neck. If a white man killed an Indian, not in self-defence, the rope would be put around his neck. He saw redcoats, they were here to protect Indians and whites. If a man tried to kill you, you have the right to defend; but no man has a right to kill another in cold blood, and we will do all we can to punish such. The good Indian need never be afraid; their lives will be safer than before."[10]

As with Big Bear's statement about dreading losing his freedom by having a rope around his neck, there was much to unpack in Morris's comments. On the one hand, Morris told Big Bear that he would be subject to colonial criminal law and possible hanging if he kills another "in cold blood." On the other hand, Morris promised that this law would apply equally to both settlers and Indians and that settlers would not be immune from the criminal law or hanging if they were to kill an Indigenous person not in self-defence. The rule of law would be the rule of English law, but it would apply to all.

Big Bear might not have been expecting a lecture about capital punishment. Morris's own records suggests that Big Bear responded to Morris's comments by stating, "What we want is that we should hear what will make our hearts glad, and all good people's heart glad. There were plenty of things left undone, and it does not look well to leave them so." This likely was an attempt by Big Bear to change the subject away from capital punishment. His reference to "plenty of things left undone,"[11] also reflected Big Bear's reluctance to sign the Treaty.

Morris, however, was anxious to seal the Treaty 6 deal that would make colonial expansion and the building of the railway easier. He replied, "I do not know what has been left undone."[12]

Big Bear had been offended twice: first by a mistranslation which had raised the issue of capital punishment and, second, by being told that the Treaty negotiations so far had covered everything. At this point, the Cree chief reiterated his original concerns, "I have told you what I wish, that there be no hanging."[13] This was likely said in reference to his concern about his people having their freedom constrained and being restricted to reserves, and by colonial laws and orders.

"Why are you so anxious about bad men? The Queen's law punishes murder with death and what you ask cannot be granted."[14]

Once he thought the subject of criminal justice had been raised, Morris was defensive and aggressive. He bluntly told Big Bear,

"What you ask will not be granted. Why are you so anxious about bad men? The Queen's law punishes murder with death, and your request cannot be granted."[15]

Morris's comments demonstrate some of the same rigid attitudes seen by some who have defended the Canadian criminal justice system, the jury, and its verdict in the Stanley/Boushie case. It amounted to an argument that colonial law is the only law and that it must be accepted by Indigenous people. Morris also appealed to a dichotomy between good and bad people that is rarely seen in Indigenous understandings of justice.

Given Morris's blunt refusal to concede to Big Bear's expression of concern about "hanging," it is not surprising that Morris left Fort Pitt without Big Bear's signature on Treaty 6. Big Bear would sign an adhesion to Treaty 6 in December 1882, but only after he and his people were close to starvation, in part, because of the government's refusal to honour some of the promises in Treaty 6 in relation to land and agriculture and the provision of food during times of famine.[16]

Big Bear was not hanged, but he did end up in prison. He was convicted of treason-felony by an all-white Regina jury that deliberated for fifteen minutes in the wake of the 1885 uprising. He was sentenced to three years' imprisonment at Stony Mountain Penitentiary. He told the court that he "did not so much as take a white man's horse. I always believed that by being a friend to the white man, I and my people would be helped by those who had wealth ... Now I am in chains and will be sent to prison."[17] He was released after two years. He returned to a reserve where the pass system restricted his and all other First Nations people's movements. The rope he had originally feared was hanging around his neck. He died a year after his release from prison.[18]

THE RULE OF LAW OR DISCRIMINATORY JUSTICE?

"If a white man killed an Indian, not in self-defence, the rope would be put around his neck"[19]

Treaty 6 was signed after the negotiations at Fort Pitt, albeit without Big Bear's signature. It contains provisions and promises that are still relevant in understanding the Stanley/Boushie case.

Morris's promise that English law would be applied to white men who killed Indians had a special meaning associated with the ideal of the rule of law, celebrated in English common law, that binds everyone equally. Morris explained that after American traders had shot "a party of Assiniboines, men, women, and children … we reported the affair to Ottawa; we said the time has come when you must send the red-coated servants of the Queen to the North-West to protect the Indian from fire-water, from being shot down by men who know no law, to preserve peace between the Indians, to punish all who break the law, to prevent whites from doing wrong to Indians, and they are here to-day to do honour to the office which I hold."[20] The idea that the redcoats and the law would "prevent whites from doing wrongs to Indians"[21] had paternalistic overtones, but it was also a promise of the equal protection of the law, something that many Indigenous people believe was denied to them by the Stanley verdict.

Morris made similar statements indicating his commitment to the rule of law, that would apply to all equally, when negotiating Treaty 4 which also covers part of what is now Saskatchewan. He stated:

> In this country, now, no man need be afraid. If a white man does wrong to an Indian, the Queen will punish him. The other day at Fort Ellice, a white man, it is said, stole some furs from an Indian. The Queen's policemen took him at once; sent him down to Red River and he is lying in jail now; and if the Indians prove that he did wrong, he will be punished. You see then that if the white man does wrong to the Indian he will be punished, and it will be the same if the Indian does wrong to the white man. The red and white man must live together, and be good friends, and the Indians must live together like brothers with each other and the white man.[22]

The rule of law is one of the central values of English common law and one that the Supreme Court has elevated to one of Canada's guiding constitutional principles.[23] The rule of law is the anithesis of what Elder Joe Crowe in 2002 described as "discriminatory justice" of which today many believe that the Stanley case is an example. Elder Crowe describes discriminatory justice as, "Just because you're an Indian you come under another justice in white man's court. And if you're a white man you could get away with it. But the Indian, you've got to suffer their judgment. Discriminatory justice."[24]

THE REDCOATS

The rule of law for Morris was not some abstract concept or one limited to the courts. The law is not meaningful if not enforced and as such Morris made frequent references to the "redcoats" or the North-West Mounted Police (NWMP) that had been formed by Prime Minister Macdonald in 1873. One hundred "redcoats" accompanied Morris to negotiate Treaty 6. Morris saw them as an "emblem and evidence of the establishment of authority in the North West."[25] He told those at Fort Pitt, "Our Indian Chiefs wear redcoats and wherever they meet the police, they will know they will meet friends."[26]

"The Police are the Queen Mother's agents and have the same laws for white as they have for Indians."[27]

Some Indigenous leaders looked to the redcoats with favour. For example, Mistawasis, a chief of the Plains Cree, stated, "The Police are the Queen Mother's agents and have the same laws for whites as they have for Indians.... There is no law or justice for the Indians in Long Knives' county [the US]. The Police followed two murderers to Montana and caught them but when they were brought to the Montana court they were turned free because it was not murder to kill an Indian."[28]

The references by both Morris and Mistawasis to the "redcoats" adds a Treaty dimension to the complaints, discussed in chapter 4, that the Boushie family have made about how they were treated by the RCMP during the case. It suggests that any failure by the RCMP to respect and protect the Boushies may also be a violation of Treaty 6.

More recently, Elders have explained how the promise of assistance by the RCMP would combine with and not displace Indigenous law. Elder Jimmy Myo of the Moosimin First Nation, Treaty 6 explained, "And at the time of the Treaty-making we were told that I will give you the police to protect you. But you will make your own laws, I will help you and I will provide anything that you want as far as the law is concerned on your reserve. I will help you if you want to do the policing on the reserve I will train you my way and we will train your way and my way to police the reserves. And that's what was promised."[29] The Treaty vision of mutual assistance and respect between Indigenous and non-Indigenous people on justice matters has not been realized. As will be seen in chapter 3, Indigenous people have raised concerns that they have been inadequately consulted over Saskatchewan's response to rural crime. Stanley's lawyers depicted the involvement of the Federation of Sovereign Indigenous Nations' (FSIN) special investigation unit in interviewing the Indigenous witnesses as a potential interference with the RCMP's investigation. (TT 319, 433, 446) In chapter 10, ways to make the RCMP more accountable to Saskatchewan communities will be explored.

A TREATY CONCERN WITH MISCARRIAGES OF JUSTICE

Mistawasis contrasted the Queen's law that could be applied to settlers who harmed Indigenous people with that in the United States where two murderers had been acquitted by a Montana court because "it was not murder to kill an Indian."[30] Morris would also have seen British justice as superior to the more populist style of justice in the United States that frequently saw juries nullifying laws when African Americans or Indigenous people were killed. The American system was experiencing aggressive and frequently racist interpretations of self-defence that suggested that "true men" – white men – could use guns, often against Indigenous and African American men, in order to protect their property and their women.[31] Wrongful acquittals of white men charged with killing Indigenous people, based on spurious claims of self-defence, were seen by both sides of Treaty 6 as a miscarriage of justice, prevalent in the United States but to be avoided in Canada.

"they will maintain peace and good order ... they will aid and assist the officers of Her Majesty the Queen"[32]

Like many of the Numbered Treaties, Treaty 6 contained the following peace, order, and mutual aid and assistance clause:

They promise and engage that they will in all respects obey and abide by the law, and they will maintain peace and good order between each other, and also between themselves and other tribes of Indians, and between themselves and others of Her Majesty's subjects, whether Indians or whites, now inhabiting or hereafter to inhabit any part of the said ceded tracts, and that they will not molest the person or property of any inhabitant of such ceded tracts, or the property of Her Majesty the Queen, or interfere with or trouble any person passing or travelling through the said tracts, or any part thereof, and that they will aid and assist the officers of Her Majesty in bringing to justice and punishment any Indian offending against the stipulations of this treaty, or infringing the laws in force in the country so ceded.[33]

The peacekeeping clause promises that the signatories will themselves "maintain peace and good order" and "aid and assist the officers of Her Majesty in bringing to justice and punishment any Indian" who violates the Treaty or the law. If Treaties are to retain their legitimacy and the benefits they provide for all of us who share this land, it is important that they be understood not simply on the basis of their written English text, but also on the basis of Indigenous expectations and understandings.

A literal interpretation of the text could suggest that the peacekeeping clause is only operative when the accused is Indigenous, but the spirit of reciprocity and equality implicit in the signing of the Treaty suggests there existed a common concern about all who were to violate the Treaty or the laws. In any event, it will be suggested in chapter 8 that the Indigenous witnesses in the Stanley trial and, by implication, their friend, Colten Boushie, were on trial with much of Stanley's trial being devoted to their alleged wrongdoing. The exclusion of visibly Indigenous people from the jury, however, constituted a failure to obtain the aid and assistance of Indigenous persons in maintaining peace and good order, or justice in this case. This arguably violated the intent, if not the letter, of Treaty 6.

University of Saskatchewan law professor, James (Sa'ke'j) Henderson, has documented the very different understandings about the peacekeeping clause by its colonial and Indigenous signatories. Commissioner Morris sometimes described the clause as a promise to obey colonial law. At the same time, the First Nations chiefs who signed the Treaty believed it contemplated the preservation of Indigenous justice systems through nation-to-nation interactions with the settlers over justice issues that affected them both.[34] Such misunderstandings continue to this day. They hinder good relations between the Indigenous and non-Indigenous signatories to the Treaty.

INTER-SOCIETAL LAW MAKING,
AID AND ASSISTANCE, AND MIXED JURIES

Symposia devoted to the Elders and others involved in Saskatchewan criminal justice, were convened in 2001 and 2002, by Professor
John Borrows of the Chippewa of the Nawash First Nation and the
University of Victoria. The Elders at these symposia made frequent
comments about the Treaty, their understandings of justice, and the
intent of the peacekeeping clause in particular.

Elder and Senator of the Federation of Sovereign Indigenous
Nations (FSIN), Joe Crowe of the Kahkewistahaw Band, Treaty 4
noted, "If the white man has any right to be in this country then the
treaty is the source of that right."[35] He described the Treaty as having
an "international flavour"[36] somewhat like extradition processes that
apply between nations negotiating possible transfer of criminal sus-
pects. If an Indian broke the law off the reserve, the RCMP could ask
for their return from the reserve. This would involve an investigation
by an Indigenous headman to determine if the person had committed
the offence and should be surrendered to the RCMP. As will be seen in
chapter 7, the involvement of the FSIN special investigation unit in the
interviewing of the Indigenous witnesses in this case was depicted by
Stanley's lawyer as an interference; whereas, it followed practices that
predated and were contemplated by the Treaty.

Elder Danny Musqua of Keeseekoose First Nation, referring to
Treaty 4, explained, "And so the old people tell us in their justice system, their justice system had to be a conscious knowledge that you
broke somebody's law; not necessarily your law. When you went into
somebody's territory or country you were more aware of the laws that
you were going to face in that territory and it was your purpose and
your very essence to understand those people's law so that you would
not break their law, because your law no longer applied. You have to
endeavour to understand how those laws were understood."[37]

Both of the above accounts by Elders describe processes of over-
lapping jurisdiction that could, in some cases, see both Indigenous
(Cree and Saulteaux) and English laws apply. One possible method
for achieving inter-societal law-making – albeit one that the Elders
did not discuss and one that was not spelled out in the Treaty – would
be a jury containing six Indigenous and six non-Indigenous persons.

A Saskatchewan court in 2014 rejected the idea that Treaty 4's
peacekeeping, order and assistance clause required a mixed jury of

Indigenous and non-Indigenous persons to be selected in any case involving an Indigenous accused. The judge stressed that the text of the clause made no reference to juries or mixed juries.[38] Chapter 5 will discuss the historical context of mixed juries, originally composed of equal numbers of Jewish merchants and citizens and, later, of non-citizens and citizens. Their long history in the English common law will also be explored. Mixed juries of half English and French speakers were also used in Quebec and Manitoba into the 1970s. Like the Treaties, a mixed jury of equal numbers of Indigenous and non-Indigenous people would recognize both different perspectives and understandings of justice, but also the possibility for consensual agreement on some issues.

Some might be inclined to dismiss mixed juries as a medieval relic, but what would the outcome of the Stanley/Boushie case have been if it had been decided by a jury of six Indigenous and six non-Indigenous persons? In order to reach a verdict, there would have had to be a genuine appreciation of both Indigenous and non-Indigenous perspectives about what happened on the Stanley farm: a meeting of the minds that has been all too infrequent after the Treaties were signed and, sometimes, even while they were being negotiated.

SUMMARY: TREATY (IN)JUSTICE?

Treaty 6 provides a guide for judging the Stanley/Boushie case and a foundation for doing better in the future. It also warns of the dangers of misunderstandings about justice that can contribute to miscarriages of justice.

The peacekeeping, order, and mutual assistance clause in Treaty 6 contemplated a degree of self-policing and reciprocity, respect and assistance with respect to justice issues that affected both Indigenous and non-Indigenous people. It should also be understood in light of the Cree concept of *miyo-wicehtowin* or having good, peaceful, and respectful relations.

What happened on the Stanley farm on 9 August 2016 was a violation of the Treaty and its emphasis on *miyo-wicehtowin*. That the trial proceeded without the assistance of any Indigenous persons was also a violation of the Treaty. Concerns that the RCMP did not respect the Boushie family and that the jury's acquittal may have been a miscarriage of justice that denied the Indigenous victim the equal protection of the law also have Treaty dimensions given Morris's promise that the law and the redcoats would protect Indigenous people equally.

The Treaties and their spirit of "mutual respect, aid and assistance in maintaining peace and harmony among peoples in Canada"[39] can be a guide for improvements in the future. The long list of recommendations made by John Borrows in 2003 and contained in the foreword of this book are Professor Borrows' own recommendations, but they have been inspired by the Treaties that apply in Saskatchewan and, in particular, Elders' understandings of them. They include greater use of Indigenous languages to understand the Treaties, greater respect for the Treaties by both Indigenous and non-Indigenous people, recognition of ambiguities about what the Treaties say about criminal justice, the need for mutual aid and assistance by both Indigenous and non-Indigenous people on a range of justice issues including social justice. They also include a recommendation to make juries and justice systems more representative of Indigenous communities, something that was manifestly not done in the Stanley trial tried by an all-white court party and an all-white jury. As will be seen in the next section, the approach taken to Canadian justice in the Stanley trial has a long history of producing Indigenous injustice.

THE 1885 UPRISING AND MORE MISUNDERSTANDING

Big Bear was discontented with how Treaty 6 was implemented and he sought to build alliances among the Cree to secure more land. Although many settlers assumed and feared that Big Bear and other First Nations people would join the Métis uprising led by Louis Riel, this was often not the case. Many of the First Nations chiefs, including Chiefs Big Bear and Poundmaker, took their agreement to the Treaties seriously. To the extent that they had grievances with the Canadian state, it was often based on a failure to honour the Treaties including the provision of food during famines. Nevertheless, the official record of Canadian justice suggests otherwise. Both Chiefs Big Bear and Poundmaker, along with many other First Nations men, were convicted of treason-felony after the Métis-led rebellion was put down with military force.[40] These convictions again suggest that Canadian justice was experienced by many Indigenous people as injustice. There are ongoing attempts to reverse the unjust convictions.[41] History remains very relevant today.

The Killings at Frog Lake

Big Bear was present at, and is believed to have tried to stop, the violence at Frog Lake in April 1885 that resulted in Indigenous men killing nine settlers including a farm instructor, two priests, and Thomas Quinn, an unpopular Indian agent. Indian agents controlled almost every aspect of the lives of Indigenous people, confirming Big Bear's fear about losing freedom. Quinn was notorious in his harsh treatment of Indigenous people.

The violence at Frog Lake is believed to have been triggered by a range of factors. These include grievances against the Indian agent, stolen alcohol consumed by some of the Indigenous men, broken Treaty promises in relation to the provision of food during the famine of the 1884–85 winter, some support for Riel, Big Bear's loss of influence among the younger members of his tribe, and the fact the NWMP had left the settlement. The Frog Lake killings were widely reported and discussed in Parliament.[42] These killings were avenged before the end of the year, by a mass hanging of eight Indigenous men at Fort Battleford, after trials before all-white juries and a biased judge. Even today, the killings at Frog Lake seem to haunt rural Saskatchewan.

"An imagined siege"[43]

Another historical misunderstanding that is relevant to the Stanley trial is what University of Saskatchewan historian, Bill Waiser, has called "the imagined siege"[44] of Fort Battleford in April and May 1885. The European settlers, who were a minority in the territory at the time, assumed that First Nations would join the Métis uprising, led by Louis Riel, even though many First Nations took their Treaty commitments seriously and remained loyal to the Crown. Especially after the Frog Lake killings, the settlers were very afraid of the First Nations.

Cree Chiefs Poundmaker and Little Pine came to Fort Battleford "to declare their allegiance to the Queen and to secure rations for their hungry bands" in April and May 1885. The Cree made no attempt to attack Fort Battleford; nevertheless, the settlers were afraid and abandoned the town and retreated to the Fort. There was no Cree attack on the Fort, but the Cree were later condemned by the settlers as "pilfering like rats"[45] when, eventually, they took provisions from the abandoned stores and homes. Elements of the siege mentality and fear of Indigenous people continue to exist in some of the contemporary debates about rural crime. They were also evident in the very heavy security that the RCMP supplied for Stanley's court appearances in Battleford and North Battleford.

THE 1885 REGINA TRIALS

The 1885 Regina trials, especially of Louis Riel, have attracted much scholarship and will only be briefly discussed here.[46] Riel, the Métis leader, was convicted of treason by a jury of six white Protestants. His appeals focused, in part, on arguments that if he had not been tried in Regina, he would have been entitled to a twelve-person as opposed to a six-person jury. If Riel had been tried in Manitoba, where he was originally sent after his capture, he would have been entitled to a mixed jury of six French speakers and six English speakers.[47] His lawyers would have preferred a mixed jury composed of half French, and most likely Catholic people, as these were perceived to be more sympathetic than the six-person, all-Protestant jury Riel faced.[48]

If Riel had not been charged with treason (the only charge that English courts had excluded from the jurisdiction of the mixed jury[49]), as an American citizen, he should have been entitled, under the common law, to a mixed jury of equal numbers of British subjects and American citizens. Just like the Stanley case, it is intriguing to think what the results of Riel's trial would have been had a mixed jury decided the case. A jury with half French speaking people or half Métis would likely have been more sympathetic to Riel, but so too might a jury with half American citizens. For example, the American consul in Winnipeg wrote to Washington that Riel's hanging would be "a hideous miscarriage of justice."[50] In any event, Riel's appeals were rejected with the courts stressing that Parliament had the unquestioned authority and supremacy to depart from the English common law and create a six-man as opposed to a twelve-man jury for the colonies.[51]

Riel was convicted and hanged, but the treatment of the only two white men charged in relation to the uprising did not sit well with Alexander Morris's 1876 promise of equal justice under the rule of law. Riel's secretary, Will Jackson, a white convert to Catholicism, was found not guilty on the basis of insanity despite telling the court, "As far as responsibility of mine about what you call a rebellion, I have always declared myself perfectly responsible, that is to say, as Riel's secretary, and I wish to share his fate whatever that may be."[52] Riel's lawyer had raised the same defence on his behalf, but it was rejected. The Regina juries also acquitted Tom Scott, the only other white man accused of assisting Riel. His lawyer played the race card by arguing that his client was "as loyal a man as sits on the bench" in reference to the white judge and that Scott was being subject to "political persecution" because the government feared it "must convict a white man or we are gone at the next elections." This argument was successful. The gallery cheered when the jury acquitted Scott.[53]

"Before such a jury, you cannot expect an impartial judgment"[54]

The minister of justice promised Prime Minister Macdonald that the prosecutions would be "well done. Any want of thoroughness in this respect would be unpardonable."[55] In all, forty-six Métis men, eighty-one First Nations men and two white men were charged. Many of the Métis received sentences of seven years, but fourteen of them were discharged. All but one of the First Nations men were convicted.[56] As mentioned, one white man was acquitted and the other found not guilty by reason of insanity.

The Indigenous defendants selected trial by jury. This may have been a mistake. Father André, who observed the trials, complained in a letter to a colleague that the jurors were "all Protestants, enemies of the Métis and the Indians, against whom they hold bitter prejudices. Before such a jury you cannot expect an impartial judgement, as we have seen in the case of One Arrow and Poundmaker. If there were two innocent people in the world, it was assuredly these Indians against whom nothing has been proven if not that they were well-disposed towards the whites."[57]

"Let us show that we really are superior to the unhappy race to which he belongs."[58]

Only one First Nations man, the Sioux chief, White Cap, was acquitted at Regina. One of the reasons for the acquittal may have been his defence lawyer's desperate attempt, after losing all his prior cases, to name and shame the jurors for their racist prejudice. The defence lawyer, Beverly Robertson, told the jury that after Big Bear's conviction, "It seemed to me that it was only necessary to say in this town, there is an Indian, and we will put him in the dock to convict him. But perhaps in feeling that, I did an injustice to the jury men of Regina. I hope so."[59] Robertson then attempted to use racism to the accused's advantage by arguing, "Let us show that we are really superior to the unhappy race to which he belongs. Let us not disgrace our race by any hasty condemnation of another because he is of a different race."[60] The jury acquitted White Cap, but only White Cap.

The charge of treason-felony faced by One Arrow was translated by the court interpreter into Cree as the equivalent of knocking off the Queen's bonnet and stabbing her in the behind with a sword. Not surprisingly, this caused One Arrow to ask the court interpreter whether he was drunk. More seriously, it demonstrated the difficulties that Indigenous and non-Indigenous people had communicating about the abstract and emotive subject of criminal justice. One Arrow's defence was that he had simply been present under duress during the battles at Duck Lake and Batoche. Like other accused at the time, One Arrow was not allowed to testify even though he told the court that he wanted to speak to the charges. Robertson told the jury he did not know his client and that he simply had to ask for their leniency. It was not forthcoming. The all-white jury convicted One Arrow after ten minutes' deliberation.[61]

It took the jury thirty minutes to convict Chief Poundmaker. He was sentenced to three years in Stony Mountain Penitentiary. The Chief was allowed to speak before being sentenced. He told the judge, "I am not guilty.... Everything I could do was to prevent bloodshed. Had I wanted war, I would not be here with you but on the prairie. You did not catch me. I gave myself up. You have me because I wanted peace.... You may do with me as you wish. I am done."[62] He also said, "I would rather prefer to be hung than to be in that place."[63] He died in 1886 after being released.

In another case, Judge Richardson echoed Commissioner Morris's 1876 promise that the law would apply equally to all by stressing that the First Nation accused "is to be measured by the same law that anybody else is to be measured by."[64] Despite this formal commitment to a rule of law, the refusal to convict the two white accused in Regina and the conviction of First Nations men who did not play an active role in the uprising suggest that the judge and jury were administering discriminatory justice.

Although today these trials are increasingly recognized as miscarriages of justice, the press, at the time, derided the sentences imposed on the First Nations and Métis men as being too lenient. They stated that the prisoners would be provided "with board" unless their "admirers" could induce the government to provide "a first-class hotel in Winnipeg."[65] Stony Mountain, alas, was far from a first class hotel. It did not have a proper sewage system. It became over-crowded as forty-four First Nations and thirty-six Métis prisoners started arriving in October 1885.[66]

THE 1885 BATTLEFORD TRIALS AND HANGINGS

The Battleford trials were even more unfair than those held in Regina. The Indigenous accused did not have counsel or a transla-tor. The presiding judge, Charles Rouleau, was a stipendiary mag-istrate that some settlers had first thought had been "too liberal by giving the prisoners the benefit of doubts that presented themselves in their favour."[67] This would change after his Battleford home and law books burned during the uprising. He then believed it was "high time" that "Indians should be taught a severe lesson."[68] Although an attempt was made to remove him as a judge in these cases because "he was a heavy loser pecuniarily in the Indian outbreak in Battle-ford," this was not successful.[69]

"a vindictive man" [70]

The sentences Judge Rouleau imposed at Battleford for felony trea-son were generally six years, double the time that Judge Richardson awarded for this frequently charged offence in Regina. Perhaps reflect-ing his own experience, Rouleau punished arson even more harshly, awarding sentences of fourteen and ten years for setting fire to a Cath-olic Church and a government building at Frog Lake.[71] Father André stated he would rather "see our people" judged by Judge Richardson than Judge Rouleau who he described as "a vindictive man and a ser-vile instrument in the hands of the government."[72]

One of the Indigenous men accused of one of the Frog Lake mur-ders, Kah-Payamahchukways or Wandering Spirit, pled guilty. He had already tried to kill himself in custody. Itka was found guilty of killing a farm instructor, but it appears that no one was charged with killing the white farm instructor's Indigenous wife and child.[73] This raises concerns, ones that will be discussed frequently throughout this book, that not all victims were equal in the eyes of the law as Alexander

Morris had originally promised in his defence of the rule of law when negotiating Treaty 6. At the same time, there was a formal and superficial commitment to the rule of law. For example, Judge Rouleau echoed Morris's rhetoric when, in sentencing Wandering Spirit to death, he said, "As far as murderers in cold blood are concerned, the Government has no pity on them. If a white man murders an Indian, he must hang, and so must an Indian if he kills a white man."[74]

Pah Pah-Me-Kee-Sick or Walking the Sky, Manchoose or Bad Arrow, and Kit-Ahwah-Ke-Ni or Miserable Man were found guilty after calling no evidence, perhaps reflecting the lack of both defence representation and translation to assist the Indigenous accused. This again illustrates how the rhetoric of the rule of law was false and what happened at Battleford was discriminatory justice.

On 9 October 1885, A-Pis-Chas-Koos or Little Bear was found guilty of murdering George Dill even though he testified that when he fired on Dill at Frog Lake, he intentionally missed.[75] Miserable Man claimed he was not present when Charles Gouin was shot. Nevertheless, he was convicted. After being sentenced to death by Judge Rouleau, he replied, "*Aquisee, mahga*," translated by some as a sarcastic "hear, hear."[76] Nahpase or Iron Body claimed that he shot, but did not kill, the Indian Agent Quinn. He argued, "I understood it was a murderer that the law would deal so severely with, so I went to Prince Albert and gave myself up, and now I am accused of murder."[77] He was also convicted and sentenced to death.

Ignorance of Indigenous Law

During the two and half weeks of sitting in 1885, Judge Rouleau also convicted three Indigenous men who had been authorized by their community to kill She Wins, an Indigenous woman who was seen to have become a *wendigo* or cannibal. Judge Rouleau was not willing to consider, or perhaps was not even aware of, Indigenous law that may have authorized the killings. Colonial law would recognize self-defence, but not the Cree law as it related to *wendigo*.[78] This reflected Commissioner Morris's belief in 1876 that colonial law was the only form of law and it must apply to all. Judge Rouleau also demonstrated the common commitment at the time to assimilation and cultural genocide of Indigenous people when he had said, when sentencing Wandering Spirit to death, that "the government did not wish to destroy the Indians, but they wish to help them live as white men."[79]

Rouleau convicted Charlebois and Dressy Man of murder and sentenced them to death. He convicted the third, Bright Eyes, of manslaughter and sentenced him to twenty years, presumably because he used a gun whereas the other two had used a sword and club to kill She Wins.[80] The death sentences of the two, unlike the death sentences of the eight for killing white settlers and priests at Frog Lake, were commuted.[81] Commutation of death sentences by the executive was a frequent and typical form of compromise at this time that avoided the extremes of an acquittal, on the one hand, and a hanging on the other. These commuted death sentences, like some manslaughter convictions in the killing of Indigenous victims that will be examined in the next chapter, raised concerns that the colonial state valued the lives of Indigenous victims less than those of the settlers killed at Frog Lake.

Hangings that "ought to convince the Red Man that the White Man Governs"[82]

Prime Minister Macdonald instructed the deputy minister of justice to charge those involved in the Frog Lake killings with murder because it carried a mandatory death penalty.[83] A week before the hangings, he contemplated that the public hangings "ought to convince the Red Man that the White Man governs."[84]

On 27 November 1885 the eight Indigenous men were hanged together, publicly, at Fort Battleford even though public hangings were no longer legal.[85] Special efforts were made to ensure Indigenous people were in attendance and to emphasize Indigenous criminality.[86]

There were also 350 armed men, including two full divisions of the NWMP, present at the hangings to keep order. One of them, a NWMP officer, reported that "no very cordial feeling could be looked for" among the spectators who included "the whites [who] had lost friends and relatives in the past unpleasantness" and "the different tribes of Indians" that had been "practically exterminated."[87] The heavy security supplied by the RCMP at all aspects of Stanley's Battleford trial had a historical precedent.

William Cameron, who had been shot at Frog Lake when the other settlers were killed, served on the coroner's jury that certified the deaths of the eight Indigenous men. He commented that before the deaths "all but Wandering Spirit smiled, sang and shouted short, shared war-cries." One urged the crowd "to show their contempt for the punishment the government was about to inflict upon them."[88] It is difficult to respect discriminatory justice.

Accounts of the Frog Lake killings were widely published in Canada. This included a best selling book written by two settler women held hostage for two months in Big Bear's camp who argued "the Indians are ... vicious, treacherous and superstitious" and "have no grievances and complaints to make."[89] According to historian Sarah Carter, publicity about the Frog Lake killings had the effect of keeping "in people's mind the idea of a peaceful community of innocent settlers, and the inexplicable, sudden outburst of savagery."[90] As will be seen, settler fears and racism played a role in the rural crime debate that formed a backdrop to the Stanley case.

The bodies of the eight Indigenous men hanged in Battleford were not released to their Tribes for burial according to Indigenous law. Rather they were buried in unmarked graves. The graves were capped in concrete in 1954 though they now have a more respectful marker.[91]

Up to 300 Cree responded to the unjust spectacle of the trials and mass hangings by moving to Montana.[92] This was contrary to the hopes that Commissioner Morris and some First Nations leaders had, less than a decade earlier, that Indigenous people would be safer under Treaty 6 than they would be in the United States.

THE WHITE MAN GOVERNS THROUGH THE PASS SYSTEM AND RESIDENTIAL SCHOOLS

Assistant Indian Commissioner, Hayter Reed, considered Indigenous people to be the "scum of the Prairies."[93] He would eventually become Deputy Minister of Indian Affairs. In August 1885, Reed proposed a series of punitive measures based on fears, and often erroneous assumptions, that many of the First Nations had supported Riel's uprising. The measures included denying payments under the Treaty, seizing firearms, breaking up tribes, and requiring some to move to the United States.

With Prime Minister Macdonald's approval, Reed implemented a system where Indians would have to obtain permission from the Indian agent to leave their reserve. Reed acknowledged that this pass system was "hardly supported by any enactment." It was never codified in the *Indian Act*, but would serve as a model for apartheid in South Africa. Reed argued that the pass system was "supported by common sense and by what may be for the general good." He sent the police "out daily" and they sent "any Indians without passes back to their reserves."[94] Farming was restricted and Indians had to secure the Indian agent's permission to sell any crops.[95] Big Bear's dread of being confined by having a rope about his neck was realized.

A residential industrial school for Indigenous children had opened in Battleford in 1883. Like all residential schools, it was poorly funded and did not have proper facilities to educate the Indigenous children or keep them physically healthy. After visiting the Battleford school, the stern Hayter Reed complained that "discipline is not what it should be, neither is proper regard to have the students speak English."[96] Other officials were more complementary, but on the basis that "Indianness is excluded"[97] from the activities of the schools.

After the 1885 uprising and the Frog Lake killings, the NWMP and Indian agents took special efforts to increase and enforce enrolment of Indigenous boys in the Battleford school.[98] By 1886, Indigenous parents resisted sending them to the Battleford school because they "did not like the way the boys were treated ... one died soon after and the other had been expelled on account of being a bad boy."[99] In 1891, an Indian agent commented that it was "a great mistake" to give Indigenous parents "a pass for any extended period of time to visit the school"[100] because they made complaints after visiting the school and more children ran away.

From its opening in 1883 until 1892, 19 of the 156 children at the Battleford residential school died and four others could not be accounted for. Only 25 of the 156 children during this time were discharged or graduated.[101] When the Battleford school closed in 1914, its principal informed Indian Affairs in Ottawa that there was a graveyard in the school where 70 to 80 people, many of them students, were buried. Like the graves of the eight hanged in 1885, it was left unmarked.[102]

CONCLUSION

Some might question the relevance of Treaty 6 signed in 1876 and the 1885 Regina and Battleford trials and hangings to the Stanley/Boushie case that started in 2016 and ended in 2018. But history lives on. It lives on in the multi-generational harms of residential schools, discrimination and other symptoms of colonialism. It lives on in stereotypes and fears associating Indigenous people with crime. It lives on in misunderstandings between Indigenous and non-Indigenous people about justice that mean that Canadian justice is often Indigenous injustice and a denial of Indigenous law and justice systems.

More fortunately, history also lives on in the Treaties which, while not free of misunderstandings, provide a foundation to reclaim common ground on the basis of mutual consent and assistance. What happened on the Stanley farm on 9 August 2016 was a violation of the Treaty and especially its emphasis on *miyo-wicehtowin* or peaceful and respectful relations between Indigenous and non-Indigenous people. The way that the investigation and trial proceeded without Indigenous assistance was also a violation of the Treaty. Better understanding and respect for the Treaty will be important if we are to do better in the future.

Colten Boushie's ancestors might have been one of those Cree families who fled to Montana after Canada's first prime minister had used the criminal justice system to show "the Red Man that the White Man governs" by hanging Riel and the Battleford Eight while also implementing a pass system and increasing the use of residential schools. In any event, it is known that Colten Boushie graduated high school in Billings, Montana. He won an award as a junior historian in 2011. His brother, William Boushie, explained, "the racism, it's different in Saskatchewan. In Billings, it's not like that. I didn't believe it, until we came here. And this happened to my brother."[103] Five summers after he won a junior historian award, Colten would lie dead on a Saskatchewan farm, in part, a victim of that province's history.

Racialized and Politicized
Rural Crime and Self-Defence

INTRODUCTION

The Stanley/Boushie case should be understood not only in its historical context, but in its larger economic, social, legal, and political context. Writer Thomas Hayden recalled that he grew up in Saskatoon "without knowing a single Aboriginal family."[1] In his 2004 report on the Saskatoon police's "starlight tours" that examined the police's abandonment of Indigenous men on the outskirts of town during the winter and the subsequent inadequate investigation of their deaths, Justice Wright observed, "Our two communities do not know each other and do not seem to want to."[2]

Differences between rural and urban Canada also came into play in the Stanley/Boushie case. There are rural grievances that urban Canada does not understand rural realities including longer police response times and higher gun ownership. Unfortunately, racist fears of crime by Indigenous people that have roots in the 1885 killings at Frog Lake, discussed in the last chapter, at times were evident. The rural crime debate was politicized when the Harper government expanded powers of citizen's arrest, self-defence and defence of property, and relaxed restrictions on guns. Rural crime needs to be understood in the context of rising gun crime rates in Canada, particularly Saskatchewan, and higher rates of Indigenous people being crime victims.

This chapter will end by examining a series of historical cases that are not well known outside of Saskatchewan, but that help explain the lens through which many Indigenous and non-Indigenous people in the province viewed the Stanley/Boushie case. These cases raise real concerns about discrimination against Indigenous crime victims. Some of the cases also help explain why many non-Indigenous rural residents are so fearful of crime and associate it with Indigenous people.

THE CONTRASTING WORLDS OF
RED PHEASANT AND GLENSIDE

One of the unexplored questions in the Stanley trial is how Colten Boushie and his four friends came to be on the Stanley farm on 9 August 2016. Why did they have a .22-calibre shotgun in their car? Why did the Stanleys have seven rifles and shotguns and two handguns on their farm? Stanley would eventually plead guilty to improper storage of some of these weapons, receive a $3000 fine and accept a ten-year firearm prohibition. His lawyer explained, "Mr Stanley wishes he never owned a gun … Mr Stanley has no desire ever to hold a gun again."[3] It is understandable that Gerald Stanley came to this realization; nevertheless, a gun culture still persists in rural Saskatchewan.

Gerald Stanley's cattle farm, including its four-bedroom bungalow, barn, and shed, is located in the rural municipality of Glenside. Stanley's farm has 150 acres and was listed for sale before the trial for $399,000. It was described as an "excellent equine estate,"[4] likely reflecting that it is too small for agriculture given the increasing large sizes of economically viable farms. Stanley's farm is a thirty to forty minute drive from Biggar, Saskatchewan where the nearest RCMP detachment is located.

After he moved from Montana, Colten Boushie lived with his family on the Red Pheasant First Nation. There are concerns about housing conditions and lack of employment and recreational opportunities on the reserve.[5] The Boushie family lived in a trailer with sewage and other problems.[6]

Red Pheasant has a young population. The median age is 23.2 years.[7] The Glenside rural municipality, where the Stanley farm is located, has a median age of forty-eight years.[8] The unemployment rate in Red Pheasant is 26.3 per cent compared to a 6.1 per cent unemployment rate in Glenside. In 2015, the average after-tax household income in Glenside was $59,904, compared to $25,280 in Red Pheasant. None of the Red Pheasant residents reported farming as their source of income. Only 500 of 50,000 farmers in Saskatchewan are Indigenous despite promises in the Treaties to support Indigenous agriculture.[9]

Women earn much more than men on Red Pheasant. In 2015, the average total income had increased to $16,506 with females making $21,216, but males making only $12,412.[10] This meant that Colten Boushie, Eric Meechance, and Cassidy Cross, the three male occupants of the 2003 grey Escape with close to 200,000 kilometres on it, did not have particularly bright economic prospects. As will be seen, they were also perceived by Gerald Stanley to be a threat to his family's safety. (TT 687) The two females in the car, Belinda Jackson who was visiting and training to be a nurse, and Kiora Wuttunee from Red Pheasant, had better economic prospects. They were not considered to present the same level of threat and were described by Sheldon Stanley as "two girls huddled in the backseat" of the grey Escape (TT 258) even though it was Belinda Jackson who engaged in the only physical confrontation with the Stanleys. (PT 308) There were gender and class as well as racial dimensions to the case.

Saskatchewan's Demographics

The economic divide between Indigenous and non-Indigenous populations in Glenside and Red Pheasant holds true throughout Saskatchewan, albeit somewhat mitigated by the higher earnings of urban residents, both Indigenous and non-Indigenous.[11]

The Indigenous population is 16.3 per cent of Saskatchewan's total population.[12] Such a significant population creates expectations, ones frequently frustrated in controversial cases, that Indigenous people would be represented on juries. North Battleford had just under 5,000 Indigenous people, the fourth largest concentration behind Saskatoon, Regina, and Prince Albert.[13] First Nations constitute 10.7 per cent, or 114,570 people, of Saskatchewan's population with Métis constituting the remainder. Just under half of the First Nations population live on reserves and 42.5 per cent of the Indigenous population is under the age of nineteen.[14]

Those who live in rural Saskatchewan earn less money than those in urban areas, with average earnings declining the farther one moves from cities. There is significant outmigration of youth and young adults. Only about a third of Saskatchewan residents live in rural areas, down from 70 per cent in 1951.[15] Gerald Stanley testified that both of his sons live in Alberta.[16] (TT 661)

An exception to rural depopulation is the 27 per cent increase of the Indigenous-on-reserve population during 2001 and 2011.[17] This has caused anxiety among some non-Indigenous people. For example, a rural high school student (who had no Indigenous students in his class) told a reporter about his concerns that "Saskatchewan is going to be turned into one big 'rez.'"[18] Such statements highlighted some of the racism and racial tensions that would affect both the rural crime debate and the Stanley trial.

RURAL CRIME:
GUNS, VICTIMIZATION, FEAR AND RACISM

The issue of rural crime has a long history on the Prairies. Before the 1885 uprisings, the NWMP would often refuse to enforce laws against cattle stealing. Historian Sidney Harring has explained, "Narrow law enforcement concerns gave way to policy considerations favouring good relations between the Mounties and the tribes."[19] This was to change after 1885 and a "new wing (partially built by Indian prison labour) at Stony Mountain Prison in Manitoba ... was kept filled with Indians after the early 1890s, mostly on charges of cattle theft."[20] There were attempts to regulate and restrict gun ownership after 1885 in the wake of the Frog Lake killings discussed in the last chapter.

Guns and Victimization

The fact that there were guns involved in the events that lead to Colten Boushie's death reflects larger trends. There is higher gun ownership in rural areas and this contributes to higher homicide rates than in the city. Possession of restricted firearms, such as the handgun that killed Boushie, is increasing in Canada with a 5.5 per cent national annual increase in 2016. Saskatchewan had a 9.3 per cent increase, the second highest provincial increase.[21] Saskatchewan was armed.

Saskatchewan also had the highest provincial rate of increase in firearm-related violent crime of 83 per cent between 2013 and 2016, producing a rate of 56 victims per 100,000 population.[22] Nationally, there were 30 victims per 100,000 people of firearm-related violent crime in rural areas compared to 25 per 100,000 in the south. In Saskatchewan, 6 of 10 violent gun crimes happen outside the city.[23] Saskatchewan had the highest rate of homicides among all the provinces in 2016 and its highest number since 1961.[24] Saskatchewan was armed and dangerous.

Data on Rural Crime

Police-reported crime statistics indicate that rural crime is a problem. About 17 per cent of Canada's population is policed by rural police services. In 2017, however, they dealt with 25 per cent of reported violent crime and 18 per cent of reported property crime. The rural crime rate in Saskatchewan was 36 per cent higher than the urban crime rate, though there were even higher rates of rural crime reported to the police in Manitoba and Alberta.[25] There is also some data suggesting that farms face higher rates of theft than metropolitan businesses. This is facilitated by the high price of fuel and other items commonly stolen from farms combined with less use of private security on farms than in cities.[26] Those who police rural and remote areas face challenges presented by higher crime per capita reported to them and by policing large areas. The concerns expressed by many Stanley supporters about rural crime were supported by the available data.

Data on (Indigenous) Victimization

The fact that an Indigenous man, Colten Boushie, was killed on the Stanley farm also reflected larger patterns of victimization even though this fact is hardly visible in the rural crime debate. Indigenous men were victims of homicide in Saskatchewan in 2016 at a rate of 31 per 100,000 population compared to 7.2 per 100,000 for Indigenous women and 1.94 per 100,000 for non-Indigenous people.[27] Saskatchewan was particularly dangerous for Indigenous men.

All Indigenous people in Canada are more frequently victims of crime than non-Indigenous people. In 2014, almost 30 per cent of Aboriginal respondents reported that their household was victimized by crime in the last year compared to 19 per cent of non-Aboriginal respondents. Residents of Saskatchewan also report higher rates of violent and property victimization than residents of the eastern provinces, but lower violent victimization rates than Alberta and B.C.[28]

As will be seen, rural crime has become and remains a salient political issue discussed in the federal Parliament and the media. At the same time, the greater victimization of Indigenous people by crime is much less frequently discussed, at least outside the context of missing and murdered Aboriginal women. One of the recurring concerns in debates about victims' rights is that not all victims may be treated as equal. Some may be seen as more deserving than others.[29] This is another example of the promise of a rule of law that protects all equally degenerating into discriminatory justice.

Fear of Crime, Rural Anxieties, and Racism

Fear of crime and of violence may help explain what happened on the Stanley farm. Canadians generally feel safe, but residents of Saskatoon, Prince Albert, and Moose Jaw report some of the lowest rates of being satisfied with their safety.[30] Those living in rural areas feel even less safe. A 2012 telephone survey of 1,750 randomly selected Saskatchewan residents, with an average age of fifty-three years of age, revealed that 69.6 per cent of rural respondents thought their community was "unsafe" as opposed to only 30.4 per cent of urban respondents. The 680 rural respondents were also more likely to favour reinstating capital punishment than the urban respondents.[31] Rural Saskatchewan was afraid and angry as well as armed.

One of the consequences of both high rates of crime reported to the police and high levels of fear and concern about crime in the province is that Saskatchewan imprisons more people per capita than other provinces. Saskatchewan has, by far, the highest per capita provincial sentenced custody rate of 114 per 100,000 compared to 77 per 100,000 in Manitoba and 31 per 100,000 in Alberta. Saskatchewan is especially punitive with respect to youth. It has 19 per 10,000 youth, aged twelve to seventeen years, imprisoned compared to 4 per 10,000 in Alberta.[32] Saskatchewan sees young people as particularly dangerous.

Who is in prison? In 2016–17, 74 per cent of adult admissions to custody in Saskatchewan were Indigenous, down from a 78 per cent admission rate in 2006–7. 85 per cent of female admissions were Indigenous. The youth prison population is almost completely Indigenous with 92 per cent of male youth and 98 per cent of female youth, sentenced to custody, being Indigenous.[33] Crime in Saskatchewan is impossible to separate from race. With 116 deaths in custody being recorded in Saskatchewan between 1995 and 2013, Indigenous persons in custody were not safe. Sherene Razack has argued this demonstrates "a deep disregard for Indigenous life."[34]

In 2004, students in a grade twelve class in rural Saskatchewan were interviewed by a reporter. This is hardly a scientific study, but it did reveal possible linkages between the rural crime issue and racist stereotypes and cultural fears of Indigenous people. As mentioned above, one of the students expressed concerns that "Saskatchewan is going to be turned into one big 'rez.'" Another said he was outraged by a bumper sticker he saw in Saskatoon saying, "Keep working White Man – I need a new truck." The reporter concluded that, as a group, the students "are convinced that the exaggeration on the bumper sticker is not that far from the reality they know."[35]

University of Saskatchewan sociologist Harley Dickinson referred to race as the "elephant in the room" with respect to the rural crime issue, adding, "It is a pretty visible elephant. It just isn't spoken about."[36] Professor Dickinson's point was underlined when unnamed farmers were quoted in the same September 2016 article, "Everybody is scared of being called a racist, but we don't have a race problem – we have a crime problem here.... Unfortunately it is a certain segment of the population that is responsible for most of the crime."[37]

The Stanley/Boushie case brought together many of the socio-political factors examined above: the economic disparities between the Indigenous and non-Indigenous populations of rural Saskatchewan; fear of crime; fear and lack of understanding of Indigenous people; and beliefs that the use of guns in self defence are necessary to defend land and people.

PANIC AND POLITICALIZATION OVER CITIZEN'S ARREST AND RIGHTS TO DEFEND PROPERTY

It would be unfair to suggest that concerns about rural crime were exclusively a Saskatchewan issue. It had national dimensions. As the welfare state has eroded, crime has become a more salient political issue in all western democracies including Canada.

The Harper government between 2006–15 made crime a signature issue, enacting close to one hundred pieces of crime-related legislation, many with snappy titles such as *Protection of Communities and Exploited Persons Act*[38] and the *Tougher Penalties for Child Predators Act*.[39] Such laws played on a growing fear of crime and concerns that Canada had been too lenient towards criminals. *The Citizen's Arrest and Self-Defence Act, 2012*[40] was rare because it was designed to decrease the use of the criminal sanction by increasing rights to make a citizen's arrest and to engage in self-defence and defence of property. At the same time, it was consistent with the messaging seen in the rural crime debate, namely, that Canadians had reasons to fear crime and to respond forcefully to it.

Although the jury in the Stanley case was never specifically told about the 2012 laws, Stanley made implicit appeals to them that will be examined in chapter 8. In addition, the similar Peter Khill/Jon Styres case, examined in chapter 9, that resulted in Khill's acquittal for killing an Indigenous man, made direct appeals to the expanded rights of self-defence that no longer require Canadians to only use as much force as was necessary in self-defence or defence of property.

The David Chen Case

The precipitating issue for the 2012 law involved David Chen, the owner of the Lucky Moose store in Toronto's Chinatown. In 2009, Chen was charged with assault, forcible confinement, possession of a weapon (a knife), and kidnapping after he detained a person who he had seen stealing plants from his grocery. Chen apprehended the man a few hours after the theft because he was unable to do so at the time the crime was committed. The Chen case received national publicity, most of it negative. For example, *Globe and Mail* columnist, Margaret Wente, stated, "Like me, almost everyone in Toronto wants to give Mr Chen the keys to the city. Obviously they do not understand how very un-Canadian that would be."[41] Wente, like others, was opposed to the fact that Chen had even been charged.

Although the Chen case came from Toronto, links were drawn to the rural crime issue. The Saskatoon *Star Phoenix* ran an anonymous story arguing, "Whether it's a shopkeeper such as Mr Chen who is trying to protect his livelihood, or whether it's a farmer in rural Saskatchewan or Alberta who is trying to defend his family and property from intruders or thieves when he knows immediate help from police simply isn't an option, ordinary citizens need some legal avenue to do what's required."[42] The *Calgary Herald* ran another anonymous story suggesting that the African Canadian person detained by Chen was lucky Chen did not hand out "Prairie justice" with a gun.[43] Others argued that Canadians had "absolute ... individual rights" both to "private property and to self-defence, up to and including the right to kill an attacker or burglar ... that existed before government and, so, cannot be extinguished by government."[44]

Even though it did not result in a conviction, the Chen case generated outrage that he was charged, and subsequently a change in the law to expand a property owner's powers of citizen arrest.[45] The more serious charges were dropped by the prosecutor and Chen was acquitted of the remaining charges. The judge who acquitted Chen warned that the case could be a "canary in the coal mine" with "Chen's community sending a message of vulnerability in the face of police inaction" only to end up "with a sense of betrayal" when the police arrived and laid charges in a "perceived heavy-handed reaction"[46] to self-help. Although written about Toronto merchants, the judge could also have speaking about farmers concerned about rural crime. Many farmers believed that the police failed adequately to protect them, but then added insult to injury by charging them when they used guns to defend themselves and their property.

The Chen case was national news. He was a crime victim who mattered. He was lauded in the press while the person he detained was vilified as a habitual criminal with racialized references to his being an immigrant from the Caribbean.[47] Prime Minister Stephen Harper instructed the Department of Justice to change the law to ensure that someone in Chen's position would no longer be charged. Harper even visited Chen at his store and purchased maple syrup from him, a somewhat strange choice, but nevertheless emblematic of Canadian identity. His minister of justice, Rob Nicholson, accompanied him. He also purchased maple syrup. But support for Chen crossed party lines. Both Toronto Liberal MP Joe Volpe and NDP MP Olivia Chow introduced private members bills that also were designed to make it easier to make a citizen's arrest.[48] There was an all-party political rush aided and abetted by the press to embrace David Chen as a hero, or at least a martyr, because he was criminally charged for defending his property.

Much less attention was paid to a Winnipeg case around the same time. A twenty-nine-year-old Indigenous women, Geraldine Beardy, died after a grocer attempted to prevent her from stealing a can of meat, apparently for friends who were homeless. When manslaughter charges were dropped against the north-end grocer, Kwang Soo Kim, because of the unavailability of a witness, the victim's cousin, David Harper, grand chief of Manitoba Keewatinowi Okimakanak, declared that the justice system "always failed the aboriginal community."[49] His statements reflected the deep distrust that many Indigenous people have of the Canadian criminal justice system including its commitment that all should receive equal protection of the criminal law.

THE CITIZEN'S ARREST AND
SELF-DEFENCE ACT, 2012

Sensing possible political advantage, both in the city and the country, the Harper government introduced bills both before and after the 2011 election that would eventually become *The Citizen's Arrest and Self-Defence Act.*[50] In a partisan environment, where the government enacted many crime bills, both the NDP and the Liberals were unwilling for this to become a wedge issue. Both opposition parties supported the new law. There was little political appetite to champion existing self-defence and defence of property laws that placed restraints on the accused relating to the need to use no more force than was necessary or to ensure proportionality in the use of self-help.

In introducing the bill, the minister of justice's parliamentary secretary explained, "To discourage vigilantism and to ensure that citizens only use a slightly expanded power of arrest in cases of true urgency, Bill C-26 also includes a requirement that the arresting person reasonably believes that it is not feasible in the circumstances for a peace officer to make the arrest. These are reasonable and responsible reforms and all members are urged to support them."[51]

Warning Shots

Not all of the debate about the bill was, however, reasonable and responsible. Brian Jean, then a rural Alberta Conservative member of Parliament, questioned whether "firearms shot in the air or shot around people (trespassing)" could be reasonable. Minister of Justice Rob Nicholson answered by stating, "I think it is." He added, "What is reasonable in a remote community in Nunavut in terms of turning that person is not reasonable in downtown Ottawa."[52] Jean echoed the Minister's comment stating, "Shooting a rifle over someone's head in Toronto is not acceptable. But on a farm in the middle of Alberta or thereabouts, (it) would probably constitute some sort of normalcy or reasonableness."[53] Eight other Conservative members of Parliament, representing rural ridings in western Canada, spoke in Parliament in favour of the bill. They linked the law to their concerns about rural crime, long police response time, and charges against farmers who defended their property.[54] The law may have started with a Toronto case, but it also spoke to a rural audience.

The minister of justice's comments about warning shots resulted in political controversy. When asked in Question Period about the danger that warning shots might kill innocent people, Nicholson replied, "Mr Speaker, we have to love the Liberals. If people are coming onto our property to set fire to our car, breaking into our house or attacking our family, those are the bad guys. Why can the Liberals not figure that out? How come they cannot figure out who the real victims are and stand up for them for a change?"[55]

Although the law made it more difficult to charge and convict people, it was part of the Conservative's pro-victim/anti-criminal agenda. Conservative Vic Toews sought to distinguish the government's approach from the opposition as one based on the idea that "when someone is arrested, by a citizen or police officer, there are consequences to breaking the law."[56] Conservative Kellie Leitch similarly argued, "Our government is committed to putting real criminals behind bars. Canadians who have been the victim of a crime should not be re-victimized by the criminal justice system."[57] The government's concern about victimization was selective: the "real" victims – those who mattered – were what were often described as law-abiding and tax-paying Canadians who used force to defend their property and not those actually harmed. In other words, not people like Geraldine Beardy or Colten Boushie.

It was not, however, only the Liberals who were concerned about the minister of justice's remark about warning shots. Eric Gottardi, of the Canadian Bar Association, cautioned that a missed warning shot could result in a murder charge. Tom Stamatakis, President of the Canadian Police Association, similarly observed that warning shots "may end up" where they were not intended and harm people.[58] Others, such as Tony Bernardo of the Canadian Shooting Sport Association, argued that "firearms are used in self-defence hundreds of times every day in Canada.... When there's a barrel pointing at you, it's amazing how sobering that can be." He also advised, "We do not advocate firing a firearm any place you don't know where the bullet is going to go."[59] All of these comments foreshadowed aspects of the incident that left Colten Boushie dead.

Despite the controversy over Minister of Justice Nicholson's comments, the bill remained popular and was supported by the NDP and Liberals. This response was similar to the overwhelming consensus seen when Florida expanded self-defence in 2005.[60] The opposition parties were sensitive to being placed at political disadvantage by questioning the popular reform.

The 2012 law said nothing about guns or warning shots. It was a milder version of Florida's controversial 2005 "stand your ground" law because it abolished a section of the *Criminal Code* that required an accused, who provoked an assault, to retreat before being able to claim self-defence.[61] With respect to other parts of self-defence and defence of property, the 2012 law dropped previous requirements that the accused use no more force than was necessary and, in the most serious cases, that the accused has "no alternative course of action open to him" in "situations of last resort."[62] Instead, the 2012 law stressed open-ended provisions that acts done in self-defence or defence of property must be "reasonable in the circumstances."[63] Such phrases would leave judges and juries much discretion. Proportionality was only one of many factors to be considered in determining whether self-defence was reasonable. It was not even mentioned in defence of property, even though the courts had stated clearly that the taking of life was not proportionate to defence of property.[64] The trial judge in the Stanley/Boushie case would tell the jury, twice, that Stanley was justified, under the 2012 law, in retrieving his pistol and firing two warning shots in the air. (TT 893, 898)

The 2012 law was a much-needed simplification of the complex laws that the courts had advised were almost impossible to explain to a jury. At the same time, however, it was also a more moderate Canadian version of an American-led populist revolt against proportionality requirements in self-defence and an expansion of the ability to use force for self-defence and defence of property.[65] Like many of those reforms, it was, in part, motivated by a sense that the laws restricting self-defence and defence of property were ill-suited to a world where people could and should no longer rely on the police and government to protect them.[66] Candice Hoeppner, a Conservative member representing a rural Manitoba riding, explained that simplifying the law of self-defence was all the federal government could do to respond to those "Canadians who are rightly concerned about many reported incidents of charges laid against Canadians who were doing nothing more than trying to defend themselves, their homes and their property."[67] The new Canadian law meant that Canadian judges and juries would have more discretion in determining whether self-defence or defence of property was reasonable and hence justified in the particular circumstances. It may have presumed a societal consensus on the use of firearms in the defence of property or in self-defence that no longer existed.

GUN CONTROL AND GUNS FOR SELF-DEFENCE

The debate about rural crime and the defence of property was also linked with debates about gun control. In 2012, the Conservative government enacted the *Ending the Long Gun Registry Act*[68] reversing requirements that had been extremely unpopular in rural Canada and had been subject to an unsuccessful constitutional challenge by the government of Alberta.[69] Some commentators linked increased gun regulation and charges against those defending their property with increases in rural crime.[70]

At the same time, Indigenous groups also expressed concerns about the long-gun registry raising some possible common ground on this issue. Both farmers and Indigenous people are more likely to own guns, and use them for hunting and protection from animals, than urban residents. The Stanleys had many guns at their farm and there was a .22-calibre long-gun in the car with Boushie and his friends that had been used for hunting.

> *"Gun ownership wasn't just for the farm.*
> *It was also for a certain level of security"*[71]

Prime Minister Stephen Harper raised the rural crime issue and linked it with guns while campaigning in Saskatchewan during the 2015 federal election. He stated, "My wife's from a rural area.... Gun ownership wasn't just for the farm. It was also for a certain level of security when you're a ways from immediate police assistance."[72]

> *"the idea that you could use guns ... in defence of your property ... is*
> *really at odds with the basic fundamentals of our Canadian law"*[73]

Like the 2012 warning shots comments, Harper's comments caused considerable controversy and polarization. Thomas Muclair, then the leader of the opposition, argued, "There's something frankly surprising when a prime minister tries to say to people they should use their guns to protect themselves."[74] Criminal lawyers and criminologists also opposed Harper's comments. This may have been exactly what the government wanted. Harper's former chief of staff had singled out both criminal lawyers and criminologists as vocal critics of the government's crime legislation whose opposition helped solidify support among the Conservative base. He also noted that such an approach sometimes made an evidence-based debate about new criminal laws unnecessary.[75]

Eric Gottardi, chair of the Canadian Bar Association's criminal justice section, argued, "The idea that you could use guns to threaten or indeed shoot at somebody in defence of your property – whether it's a tractor or your home itself – is really at odds with the basic fundamentals of our Canadian law."[76] Criminologists Irvin Waller and Michael Kempa (the latter himself running for the Liberals) argued that most gun homicides were gang related "which by definition do not occur on our typical rural communities." They warned that Harper's comments were more than a "misinformed but harmless election ploy" because by "loading up more guns, Canadians can expect to have more innocent victims killed."[77] This opposition may have unintentionally created a backlash and raised greater awareness among Canadians that you could use guns to defend property.

"what responsible and safe farm families have known for years"[78]

Harper's statement had many supporters. Saskatchewan-based commentator, John Gormley argued that in rural Canada "police response times are measured in half-hours" and that all Harper did was "acknowledge what responsible and safe farm families have known for years," something that was lost on "Harper deranged Toronto reporters."[79] David Bercuson, director of military and strategic studies at the University of Calgary, similarly argued that "where I live, it could take the RCMP forty-five minutes or longer to respond to an emergency call … if someone living in a rural area believes that their family members' lives are in danger, they might well be justified in using a firearm in self-defence."[80] Sheldon Clare of the National Firearms Association called Harper's remarks "long overdue" noting that prosecutions of those who use a gun in self-defence or defence of property, meant "the process becomes the punishment" for those "who have experienced violence in their homes and it's not just in rural areas."[81] The *National Post* concluded that Harper's statement was "not only supported by common sense – in a rural area, the closest cop is likely to be further away than in the heart of a large city – but by the law."[82] This statement linked Harper's comments about the use of guns in rural areas with the 2012 law that expanded self-defence and defence of property.

Harper's comments and the Conservative government's attempts to use guns as an election and fund-raising issue generated opposition, but one that was somewhat exaggerated and may have created unnecessary polarization. Soon after his 2015 comments, the prime minister made clear that he was not advocating vigilantism. Nevertheless, the attempt to merge the gun issue with the rural crime debate, with its implicit appeal to rural identity, helped set a rather combustible stage for the Stanley/Boushie case.

Although social media sites such as Farmers with Firearms featured American-style rhetoric about rights to have firearms and to stand-one's-ground, neither the 2012 self-defence and defence of property reforms or the 2012 and 2015 changes to gun regulations went nearly that far.[83] In addition, Saskatchewan courts consistently rejected arguments that people had a common law or *Charter* right to possess guns.[84] This disjuncture between more moderate Canadian law and politics and the more extreme aspects of right-wing American gun culture that has gained ground in Canada,[85] helped fuel the social media polarization seen both in the Stanley case in Saskatchewan and the similar Peter Khill case in Ontario.

Farmers with Firearms

The link between rural crime and the use of guns was made by the Facebook group "Farmers with Firearms." It was co-founded, a month after Boushie was killed in August 2016, by a man who farms about forty minutes from Gerald Stanley's property. Its original description on Facebook was, "We will protect our belongings and fight if need be! If the RCMP response time is delayed in anyway we will take matters in our own hands!"[86] The Facebook group's current "about" description states in more measured tones, "Farmers with Firearms is a community group for tracking and informing our neighbours of rural crime as an online Neighbourhood Watch. We believe in the natural right of all persons to protect their family and property by all reasonable means."[87] The Facebook group tracks rural crime often posting pictures of stolen trucks and other property. As of May 2018, it had over 10,500 followers and just under 10,000 likes.

Although the Facebook site has been policed by its moderators for racist comments, with about twenty of its members being removed for making a racist post, it still had evidence of the racial overtones of the rural crime debate. Its co-founder has stated, "In our area, it don't matter what colour you are. There's theft for every ethnic group."[88] Nevertheless, a number of disturbing posts were accessible from the site when accessed in May 2018. They include:

Some of the Indigenous usually on drugs never work also the government protect them and I guess the farmers are the racists. Holy moly ... The comment is made by my personal experience.

Does anyone know real reason they do not go on reservations to arrest or search?

You want to establish good relationships between garmers [sic] and aboriginals? Stop trespassing on, vandalizing, and stealing the farmer's property, and you won't get shot at. Allowing criminals to steal from you while they threaten and intimidate you is absolute nonsense. I've had my property stolen and vehicles vandalized and insuramce [sic] screwed me over time and time again, and the police did nothing. If there were to be a next time I would forsake the formalities of alerting a sluggardly police force and just use enough force to decisively end the theft of my property on my premises. And just how much force is that? Enough that the culprits will never even dare think about stealing from anyone in the face of God's green earth.[89]

These comments are not just about rural crime, defence of property and guns. They are about attitudes to race. American commentators have noted that the merger of opposition to gun control with aggressive self-defence laws is not "gender neutral or color blind." It often results in white males seeing Black, Brown, and Red males as reasonable threats.[90] Canadians like to think that they are immune from such politics especially in the Trump era, but they are not. Social media surrounding the rural crime issue has distinct anti-Indigenous elements that also reflects both historical and contemporary fears and racism. In the next chapter, the eruption of this racism after Stanley killed Boushie – one that resulted in Premier Brad Wall's intervention – will be described.

Other comments on the Farmers with Firearms site focused on the use of self-defence as a form of self-reliance, often expressing a lack of trust in the RCMP as well as hostility towards government and a desire for American-style "stand your ground" laws and gun laws to make it easier to use weapons. They included some chilling comments such as, "Better to be judged by 12 than carried by 6"; "Shoot shovel and shut up"; "It is not the police's job to protect us. It is up to each and every one off us to defend ourselves and our neighbours, with whatever force is needed." Also:

> I hope these thieving bastards knock it off but I suspect they won't. The RCMP can't possible cover all the ground out there so that leaves precious little alternative. Maybe one or two of these assholes need to disappear before they'll get the picture. Helping yourself to something that people busted their ass off to earn is bullshit and people are fed up. This is one area where the US has it right. If someone enters your property looking to harm your family or rob you blind you should be able to defend your family and your property because waiting 30–45 minutes for the RCMP to show up is simply not an option. It would be nice if the RCMP and lawmakers would concede that the public needs legislation introduced to protect them and would stop protecting the scum of the earth.[91]

The idea that "the US has it right" on gun rights and more permissive self-defence laws underlines how some who posted on the website were influenced by American gun and "stand your ground" culture.[92] The idea that the thieves were "the scum of the earth" has echoes of how Hayter Reed, who introduced the pass system, thought of Indigenous people.[93]

Farmers with Firearms also posted a link to a funding site for Stanley's family, in the wake of his acquittal, urging followers to donate. The comments on that post featured statements such as, "I don't see anyone calling for justice for the rest of the group who drink and drive with loaded stolen weapons."[94] One farmer, who lives thirty kilometres from the Stanley farm, explained that he gave $1,000 because "it could have been me. There was no respect for him or his property." In the wake of the verdict, one of the organizers of Farmers with Firearms told a reporter, "We have a problem here. It's not a race problem. It's a criminal problem."[95] Despite such denials of racism, the rural crime issue on sites such as Farmers with Firearms was at times defined explicitly in racial terms. In more mainstream media and politics, the rural crime issue was more often defined implicitly in racial terms.

RURAL MUNICIPALITIES CALL FOR ADDITIONAL EXPANSIONS OF SELF-DEFENCE

In March 2017, the Saskatchewan Association of Rural Municipalities (SARM) passed a number of resolutions related to rural crime. The one that received the most publicity provided, "Whereas crime has increased in rural communities and whereas individuals do not have sufficient rights to protect themselves and property; Be it resolved that SARM lobby the Federal Government to expand the rights and justifications for an individual to defend or protect himself, herself and the person under their care and their property."[96] The resolution ignored that the federal government had, as discussed above, already expanded self-defence and defence of property in 2012 with rural members of Parliament from western Canada making connections between the new law and rural crime. Nevertheless, the reforms provided by the Harper government were not enough for the SARM delegates: 93 per cent of them supported the resolution calling for more rights of self-defence and defence of property. Such continued dissatisfaction was fuelled by examples of more extreme reforms in the US. It promoted polarization and conflict between citizens and governments over the emotive self-defence and defence of property issue.

One of the supporters of the SARM resolution referred to "out of control" rural crime and warned that those who used force will "spend a lot of time and money on legal battles" even though "you have a good chance of winning your case, but you are going to be punished by the courts for protecting your property, your home and your family."[97] Canada's stricter laws and less politicized processes of prosecuting than the United States have resulted in prosecutions of those who used guns to defend their property. The SARM delegate correctly noted that even if a person was ultimately acquitted on the basis of self-defence or defence of property that it would be expensive for property owners to defend themselves in court. Many supporters of Gerald Stanley and Peter Khill fundamentally objected to the fact that the men had been charged for using weapons to defend their property or themselves. Such supporters would not be completely satisfied with either man's acquittal.

The SARM resolution was denounced by the Federation of Sovereign Indigenous Nations (FSIN), Saskatchewan's leading First Nations advocacy group. They warned that it could lead to "more violent confrontations and deaths of more innocent people."[98] This reflected the reality of the victimization data discussed above that indicated that Indigenous men were most vulnerable to firearm-related deaths. The FSIN also linked the SARM resolution to the Stanley case and saw it as implicit approval of Gerald Stanley's actions.

POLICING RURAL AREAS

Media coverage focused almost exclusively on SARM's resolution on self-defence laws, often characterizing it as a call for American "stand your ground" laws and linking it with the Stanley case. Unfortunately, it largely ignored another SARM resolution providing that, "Whereas cases of agriculture theft often go without resolution due to a lack of RCMP resources" that SARM, along with cattle groups, should "lobby the RCMP to dedicate resources to deal with agricultural related thefts."[99] There was indeed evidence of underfunding of rural policing. Provincial funding for law enforcement in rural municipalities was $63.93 per capita compared to close to $400 per capita in Regina and Saskatoon.[100] In chapter 10, it will be suggested that there may be some common ground among non-Indigenous and Indigenous people on the need for better resourced, better governed, and more responsive policing in rural areas.

In August 2017, Saskatchewan announced the creation of a Protection and Response Team (PRT) of 258 officers including 120 municipal and RCMP officers, 98 provincial conservation officers and 40 commercial vehicle enforcement officers. The 2017 funding only allocated $1 million from provincial revenues with more money coming from the provincial auto-insurer for the arming of transportation inspectors. This announcement was almost as controversial as the SARM resolution earlier in the year.[101] The opposition criticized it as a "shell game" backed by limited increases in funding and SARM called for more RCMP officers.[102] Vice Chief Heather Bear of the FSIN argued, "More authorities with more guns means more Indigenous people in jail."[103] She also raised concerns that conservation officers (who were already armed) did not have sufficient training in Treaty rights and that there had been a lack of consultation on the initiative. The government was not pursuing the intent of the mutual aid and assistance clause found in the Treaties that contemplated Indigenous groups assisting her Majesty's officers in keeping peace. Instead of including Indigenous people in dealing with rural crime, Saskatchewan's response suggested that more armed police officers were the answer.

SUMMARY: RURAL CRIME, GUNS, AND SELF-DEFENCE

Concerns about rural crime are backed by the available data especially with regards to higher rates of violent crime reported to the police and firearm-related homicide in rural as opposed to urban areas. The rural crime issue gained political salience at both the national and provincial level. It was linked with issues involving guns and self-defence and provided part of the political context for the Stanley trial.

Rural municipalities, as represented by SARM, and Indigenous people, as represented by FSIN, clashed over the resolution to allow even more ready use of force under the *Criminal Code* and Saskatchewan's use of armed conservation and transportation officials to respond to rural crime. This is unfortunate because both farmers and Indigenous people in rural Saskatchewan are dissatisfied with the policing services they receive. Both are concerned about crime and criminal victimization and the evidence is that Indigenous people are the most frequent crime victims including with respect to firearms related homicides. The promises made in Treaty 6 that the "redcoats" would protect Indigenous and European settlers equally and effectively and that Indigenous people would assist in the maintenance of peace, order, and enforcement of the law were ignored in the rural crime debate. The politicalization of the rural crime issue, both in the 2012 laws expanding self-defence and defence of property and Prime Minister Harper's 2015 campaign comments, linking the use of guns with the "security" concerns of rural residents, provided some of the broader social, political, and legal context that influenced the Stanley/Boushie case.

DIVISIVE SASKATCHEWAN CASES
PREDATING THE STANLEY/BOUSHIE CASE

Because they result in a guilty verdict or an acquittal, criminal trials are particularly amenable to polarization. During Stanley's 2018 trial, Indigenous people would sit on one side of the court while those in support of Stanley, including many of his rural neighbours, would sit on the other side.[104] The Stanley trial, however, was far from the first in Saskatchewan that resulted in such polarization or a white accused being acquitted under questionable procedures and circumstances for killing an Indigenous victim. Some of these cases starkly and uncomfortably raise the question of whether all-white juries nullified or refused to apply the law because of antipathy or lack of empathy towards Indigenous victims. They also raise echoes of what I have referred to elsewhere as the "new political case" which pits the accused's rights against rights claims made on behalf of crime victims, including groups disproportionately victimized by crime, notably Indigenous people.[105] Some of these cases reflected the racialized politics surrounding the rural crime debate examined earlier in this chapter. A few of these cases raised concerns in some quarters that Indigenous people had not been punished severely enough for crimes committed against white farmers. All of these cases suggest that the Stanley/Boushie case did not arise in a vacuum and should be seen in the larger context of a number of similarly divisive cases in Saskatchewan.

Allan Thomas

In 1963, Allan Thomas was killed in a village north of Battleford. He was Saulteaux and his case attracted media attraction including a *Macleans* feature by Peter Gzowski with the provocative title, "This is our Alabama." Gzowski described "race prejudice in North Battleford" that was "an ugly and, in some ways, frightening thing to behold." He added that it was "the race prejudice of gentle, friendly people" who minimized their contact with Indigenous people.[106]

Nine men, described as farmers and businessmen, were arrested and charged with the non-capital murder of Allan Thomas. The prosecution proceeded slowly because of a successful challenge by the accused to the Supreme Court of Canada which ruled that they could not be forced by the coroner to explain their role in Thomas's death.[107]

Even before the enactment of the 1982 *Charter*, it was recognized that accused people could take advantage of their right to silence.

Only three of the men were tried for manslaughter, not murder. All three, aged forty-eight, forty-one and twenty-two, were acquitted in 1966 by an all-male, all-white jury that deliberated for four hours. The Crown called twenty-two witnesses and the defence called none. The presiding judge, Justice Tucker, stated after the jury's verdict, "I hope nothing like this ever happens in this part of the province again" and that he did not want the verdict to be taken "as approval of racial prejudice of any kind."[108]

Justice Tucker's comments could be interpreted either as an implicit criticism of the jury for engaging in an act of jury nullification, fuelled by racial prejudice against the Indigenous victim, or as a defensive denial that the verdict had anything to do with racial prejudice that had attracted negative publicity for Battleford and Saskatchewan. Either explanation is disturbing. The Allan Thomas case could be a racist act of jury nullification quite similar to those that were occurring at the time in Alabama and other parts of the American south.

Leo Lachance

In 1991, Leo Lachance was shot in the back by Carney Nerland, a neo-Nazi who owned a pawn shop in Prince Albert. A year earlier, Nerland was video-recorded both in Nazi and KKK dress while burning a cross. He had at that time referred to the use of guns to defend private property as, "Native birth control."[109]

After having shot Lachance, Nerland refused to allow a bystander to make a 911 call for Lachance saying he was closing up his shop. He was in his store drinking with Russell Yungwirth and Gar Brownridge. All three men left the pawn shop shortly after Lachance was shot. They all maintained that they did not know that Lachance had been shot and was in fact bleeding on the sidewalk. After he was arrested, Nerland told a police officer, "If I am convicted of shooting that Indian I should get a medal and you should pin it on me."[110]

An Accidental or a Racist Killing?

Nerland claimed the killing was an accident and that he did not know there was a bullet still in a chamber when, after firing two shots in the floor, he fired a third shot at Lachance who was leaving his store.[111] This was remarkably similar to the claims of accidental shooting and a lack of knowledge of having bullets still in his gun that would successfully be made by Gerald Stanley at his trial.

Both Brownridge and Yungwirth gave their first statements to the police "from the Popescul law office."[112] They had initially not reported what happened to the police and sought legal advice from Martel Popescul's law office when they did eventually inform the police. Martel Popescul would subsequently represent the RCMP at an inquiry into the Nerland/Lachance case and successfully make claims that the inquiry should not delve into matters that could identify police informants. Appointed to the bench in 2006 and appointed as Chief Justice of the Queens Bench in 2016, he would also be the trial judge in the Stanley case.

Brownridge and Yungwirth were criticized by the inquiry for their "callous disregard for the fate of Lachance."[113] They both supported Nerland's claim of an accidental shooting with Yungwirth saying that Nerland had told him, "Well I-I checked the gun. I was – it was empty."[114] A day after these interviews, Nerland was charged with manslaughter and the police stopped investigating his white supremacist background or its possible relevance to the case.[115]

A subsequent inquiry criticized the police and prosecutors for "quickly embracing the probable accidental shooting theory" that Yungwirth and Brownridge proposed. It accepted the evidence of a RCMP firearm expert that Nerland's gun "could not be fired accidentally since it takes 16 ½ pounds to pull the trigger" and also agreed with testimony that "you should never point a gun at anybody, whether it's loaded or unloaded."[116] The inquiry also criticized the police for not investigating Nerland's white supremacist activities and expressed concerns that more forensic investigation might have helped to determine if Lachance had been shot within the pawn-shop or, as Nerland claimed, when he was outside the pawn shop. Such additional forensic information could have helped determine whether the shooting was intentional or accidental.

Justice Frank Gerein accepted a joint submission from the prosecution and the defence that Nerland receive four years' imprisonment for manslaughter on the basis of an accidental killing. He also made a special recommendation that Nerland be allowed to serve his time in a provincial prison. He found that Nerland had said that he should get a medal for "shooting that Indian." Nevertheless he concluded that "it would not necessarily follow that these feelings

or attitudes were operative at the time of the offence."[117] Justice
Gerein found that there was no evidence to suggest that Nerland's
manslaughter offence "was motivated in any way by [his] political
beliefs" and that he had "put completely out of [his] mind [Nerland's]
involvement with espousal of the beliefs of any white supremacist
organization"[118] when sentencing Nerland less than three months
after the shooting.[119]

Contrary to Justice Gerein's factual findings that racism did not play
a role in the shooting of Leo Lachance, a subsequent inquiry, chaired
by Justice Ted Hughes with Saskatchewan law dean Peter Mackinnon
and Cree lawyer Delia Opekokew, found that racism did play a role in
the killing. Although it did not fault Justice Gerein, the inquiry found
that the judge's conclusion "might have been different had the question of racial motivation been more fully investigated and developed
by those responsible for bringing Nerland to justice."[120]

The inquiry also recommended that the police should receive
cross-cultural training on racism and that Cree speaking officers
should always be available in Prince Albert. A Cree speaking officer could have learned more about the shooting if one had been
available to speak to Lachance before he eventually died from the
gun shot wound in a Saskatoon hospital.[121] The inquiry concluded
that the denial of a racist motivation by justice system participants
was a problem. The police and prosecutors "did not understand ...
the ways that racism may have explained Nerland's behavior ... the
experience of Indian and Métis people is that the criminal justice
system discriminates against them. The historical record supports
their view. If they do not see justice done, they have good reason to
believe that it has not been done."[122]

Was Nerland also a RCMP Informer?

At the subsequent inquiry into Leo Lachance's death,[123] the RCMP
successfully obtained an order prohibiting the inquiry from disclosing the identity of police informants.[124] The RCMP's lawyer, Martel Popescul, called for the Saskatchewan department of justice to
"look into" the Prince Albert Tribal Council after it subsequently
announced that Nerland was an RCMP informer.[125]

The inquiry was unable to make determinations of whether
Nerland was indeed a RCMP informer and whether this had an
impact on how the case was investigated and prosecuted and made

no comment on the issue. With an inability to examine or disclose information that could identify a police informer, the report left the *Globe and Mail* with "the troubling feeling of justice half done."[126]

Nerland was released from jail in late 1993. He was reportedly placed into the RCMP's witness protection program,[127] suggesting that he may have been the informer that the RCMP told Prince Albert police and the prosecutor about shortly after Nerland's arrest.[128]

The Carney Nerland/Leo Lachance case was a particularly divisive case. It would have been remembered and related to the Boushie/Stanley case even if it did not involve a claim of an accidental shooting of an Indigenous man remarkably similar to the claim raised by Stanley. This case also reveals how police, prosecutors, and Justice Gerein were quick to deny that Nerland's vile and blatant racism was relevant: a conclusion that a subsequent inquiry questioned. Although lawyers, and lawyers who become judges, should not be associated with their former clients, Martel Popescul's involvement at multiple stages of the Nerland/Lachance case raises questions about whether he was the best judge for the Stanley trial.

Pamela George

In 1995, Pamela George, a twenty-eight-year-old Saulteaux woman and mother of two, was found dead in a field near the Regina airport. Two white men, twenty-year-old Steven Kummerfield and nineteen-year-old Alexander Ternowetsky, were charged with first-degree murder. They admitted they beat George after one of them had picked her up while the other hid in the trunk of a car. They argued that they were not guilty of murder, in part, because of intoxication and, in part, because Pamela George had consented to sex and was alive when they left her in a field. The two men were acquitted of first-degree and second-degree murder. Like Nerland, they were convicted of manslaughter.

Representatives of the FSIN protested the manslaughter verdict arguing that "if you put an Indian on the part of the accused, he is treated more harshly. And when you put him in the part of the victim, justice is never seen to be done." It was also reported that one member of the all-white jury had flirted with one of the accused.[129] Kummerfield and Ternowetsky were sentenced to six and a half years each. An appeal by the prosecutor to the Court of Appeal was unsuccessful with the Court of Appeal concluding that the trial judge's and counsel's reference to Pamela George as a prostitute "were not made for the purpose of conveying a negative view of the victim to the jury."[130]

The Tisdale Sexual Assault Case

In 2003, three white men, aged twenty, twenty-four, and twenty-five, were charged with the sexual assault of a twelve-year-old Indigenous girl near Tisdale, Saskatchewan. They were granted bail, resulting in one of the girl's relatives arguing that "you would never see Indian men accused of doing this to a white girl released without bail, they still be in jail." One of the lawyers for the accused defended the bail decision because one of the accused "comes from a highly regarded farming family and another is well thought of at his workplace." One of the investigating officers responded "absolutely not" to the charge that racism may have played a role in the bail decision.[131]

Only one of the three men, twenty-six-year-old Dean Edmondson, was convicted. He was sentenced to two years' house arrest with the judge suggesting that the twelve-year-old victim might have been a "willing participant" or even "the aggressor."[132] The president of the Law Society of Saskatchewan defended the judge after the press noted that the judge had previously represented one of the men convicted of killing Pamela George. He made the valid point that a lawyer should not be identified with his client, but he also made more questionable arguments that the press should not have "editorialized" that the George case inflamed racial tensions and that critics of the decision should not "personalize the issue by concluding the judge – and, therefore, the 'system' – must be 'racist.'"[133] A reluctance to acknowledge the existence of racism would also affect the selection of the jury in the Stanley case.

The two other men were not convicted by all-white juries. The jury pool in their Melfort trial had over one hundred people, but only one person who was visibly Indigenous. The vice chief of the FSIN called the all-white jury "outrageous ... There was not one First Nations member of that jury ... This exemplifies why First Nations are calling for a total revamping of the justice system."[134]

Saskatchewan's two leading newspapers denied that racism played a role. The *Regina Leader Post* editorialized that the justice system had worked and "there's no evidence that racism played any part in the verdicts,"[135] something that should be impossible to discover given the *Criminal Code*'s ban on jurors disclosing their deliberations. The *Saskatoon Star Phoenix* published an op-ed arguing, "To slander twelve people as racists defies both probability and reality. To suggest that aboriginal jurors would have convicted simply because they were aboriginal is to demean an entire race and present an even-more-threatening scenario."[136] These defensive reactions suggest that all-white juries were normalized in Saskatchewan and that representatives of the legal profession and the media would react negatively and defensively when allegations of lack of representative juries or racism were made.

William Kakakaway

In 2001, an all-white jury acquitted Ryan Miller of the murder of William Kakakaway, a twenty-two-year-old member of the White Bear First Nation. Miller admitted he threw a tire iron that killed Kakakaway, but argued self-defence. Kakakaway and his cousin were pursued by ten to twenty people after they had smashed windows of cars. Kakakaway's uncle concluded that, "my nephew was killed for breaking a window."[137]

Miller was granted bail on conditions that he stay away from the White Bear and Caryle communities where the event took place.[138] The jury acquitted Miller of both murder and manslaughter after less than two hours' deliberation.[139] This case was prosecuted by Bill Burge who also prosecuted the Stanley case. Like the Stanley case, it also resulted in a decision by Saskatchewan attorney general not to appeal the acquittal suggesting that the factual determinations of juries were not amenable to appeal.

As in the Stanley case, the victim's family complained about how the RCMP handled the case, but the RCMP dismissed the complaint as unfounded. The case raised racial tensions in the area. A white man was convicted of uttering threats against the victim's family and an Indigenous man was convicted of breaking windows in three police cruisers after he learned that the case would not be tried in the local community but in Estevan, 120 kilometres away from where the events happened.[140] One proposed recommendation to increase Indigenous representation on juries is to have jury trials in the communities where the crime is alleged to have been committed. As examined in chapter 5, courts have rejected such requests and the recommendations have not been implemented in Saskatchewan or in most provinces.[141]

Divisive Cases Involving Indigenous Accused
and Non-Indigenous Victims

Settler concerns about rural crime go back to the 1885 Frog Lake killings. There are a number of more recent cases that were also well-publicized with some expressing concerns that Indigenous offenders were treated too leniently. A notable feature of these cases, however, is that none of them resulted in an acquittal of the Indigenous accused. Rather, controversy arose when Indigenous accused were convicted of manslaughter. In other words, Indigenous accused were not benefiting from possible jury nullification that allowed them to walk free.

William Dove

In 1992, a seventy-three-year-old man, William Dove, left his cottage 150 kilometres east of Regina to help three males from the Sakimay First Nation fix a flat tire. He was abducted and his badly beaten body and burned-out car was discovered a few miles outside of Regina. A passing man suspected that Dove might be in danger and phoned the RCMP, but they did not immediately pursue the complaint because they were "busting up parties."[142]

The three Indigenous men were charged with first-degree murder because of the kidnapping, but they pled guilty to manslaughter with the two adults receiving an eight-year and a four-year sentence and the third person, a young offender, receiving three years' closed custody. The wife of the deceased denounced the plea bargain commenting, "I think it is a dirty shame. I can't see why they don't bring the death penalty back." The Saskatchewan justice department defended it on the basis that the accused men's intoxication would be a barrier to establishing the fault for murder.[143]

Linda Unger, a freelance writer from Melville, Saskatchewan, wrote that after the Dove case, the "white community looked suspiciously at every dark face, reinforcing prejudices unjustly placed on the whole instead of the individuals involved. Motorists drove by stranded vehicles on cold Saskatchewan highways." She also reflected on the impact of fear of crime on beleaguered rural communities by concluding, "We learn to live with most things here. We can live on half our past incomes on the farms, deal with jobs that vanish and friends that move to other provinces. Now we must learn to be callous, suspicious, and uncaring. After all, kindness might kill us."[144]

John Sorgenson

John Sorgenson was beaten to death by four males and one female a few weeks later, in 1992, at his farm in the Kamsack area. The accused used knives and a tire iron and stole $800. They were drinking beer and had stolen gas from a neighbouring farmer. One of the accused, Charles Gordon, was convicted of second-degree murder and sentenced to life imprisonment with nineteen and a half years ineligibility for parole.[145] He later died in Drumheller penitentiary either of a murder or a suicide.[146]

Another accused unsuccessfully challenged his murder conviction on the basis that one of his relatives had overheard one juror asking another juror, "Well are they guilty?" after the opening address and then both jurors laughed. The Court of Appeal held the conduct of the jurors did not reveal a reasonable apprehension of bias.[147]

The two young offenders in the case, one aged fifteen and the other seventeen, were also convicted by a jury of murder and sentenced to life imprisonment with no parole for ten years. This period of parole ineligibility was subsequently reduced to seven years on the basis that the trial judge had not considered their background as Indigenous offenders.[148] The sentence remained quite severe because the judge ordered the young offenders to serve their sentence in the Prince Albert penitentiary as opposed to a youth facility.[149]

Bryan Kipp and Gordon Tetarenko

In 1994, two farmers who lived near the Stanley farm, Bryan Kipp and Gordon Tetarenko, were murdered execution-style. Ron Caldwell pled guilty to shooting both farmers in a botched attempt to steal gas from them – a typical rural crime complaint. Colin Leonard Baptiste was convicted of manslaughter in a trial by judge alone. Both men were reported to having been drinking heavily and to have been on the Red Pheasant reserve shortly before the killings.[150]

Baptiste received a five-year sentence causing the families of the slain farmers to say, "Our justice system has failed the victim again ... those people who do these things like this are still running around. You just don't know anymore."[151] The prosecutor successfully appealed the five-year sentence. The Court of Appeal added three years on the basis that the trial judge had wrongly held Baptiste only responsible for the death of one and not both farmers.[152] Colin Leonard Baptiste is a distant cousin of Debbie Baptiste, Colten Boushie's mother.

One might be tempted to conclude that the 1994 murders of Kipp and Tetarenko, like the Leo Lachance case, are matters of history and of no relevance to Stanley's case. To be sure, a criminal trial should not be the site for the settling of historical grievances and injustices. Nevertheless, connections were made. As will be discussed in greater detail in chapter 8, the 1994 murders of Kipp and Tetarenko were one of the reasons given by Gerald Stanley in his testimony about why he feared Boushie and his friends. (TT 687–688)

CONCLUSION

The economic circumstances faced by Colten Boushie and his friends on the Red Pheasant First Nation were markedly different than those faced by Gerald Stanley and his family. Extremely high unemployment rates and low earnings, especially for males on the Red Pheasant reserve, helped to create conditions conducive to abuse of alcohol and the commission of property crime. The social, economic and political distance, and mutual fear and distrust between the Indigenous and non-Indigenous population, often manifested in debates about rural crime, may also have affected the encounter between Boushie and his friends and the Stanleys.

The political context is equally as important. Prime Minister Harper and his government linked rural crime, guns and self-defence. Statements by Minister of Justice Rob Nicholson that the use of guns to fire warning shots could be justified under the new defence of property provision, were opposed by representatives of the Canadian Bar Association and the Canadian Police Association. Nevertheless, these statements had consequences. Chief Justice Popescul would tell the jury twice that Gerald Stanley would have been justified in defending his property, in retrieving and loading his pistol, and firing warning shots in the air. (TT 893, 898) The political rhetoric over rural crime, defence of property, and guns had real-life implications.

Although they had some common interests on the gun and policing issues, the rural crime issue and the Stanley case divided Indigenous people and farmers even more. The FSIN objected to calls by SARM, in March 2017, to make it even easier to use force in self-defence and defence of property. The FSIN also criticized the Government of Saskatchewan's subsequent announcement that it would arm transportation enforcement officers in an attempt to deal with rural crime noting that there had been a lack of consultation with them by the government. The Treaty promises of mutual aid and assistance in peacekeeping were not honoured. The common interests of all those living in rural areas to have better financed and more responsive policing were not realized.

In April 2017, Boushie's cousin, Jade Tootoosis, commented that Colten's "death reveals a deep divide that exists between many within this province … we, Colten's family, hope that this preliminary hearing and the issues that it raises about our relationships with each other will generate further discussion and dialogue to help us to bring our communities together."[153] Unfortunately Tootoosis's gracious plea for better relations was not realized as the case progressed. A few months later, Tootoosis seemed to be losing faith in the justice system. She explained that Saskatchewan just seems to be "a very well connected province, especially with it being so farmer based" and called for the appointment of out-of-province investigators and prosecutors in the case.[154] Colten Boushie's mother, Debbie Baptiste, reflected this polarized environment when, before the trial, she warned, "If it's an all-white jury, I don't think we have a chance."[155] Her comments are supported by the Allan Thomas and William Kakakaway cases where all-white juries acquitted white men charged with killing Indigenous men. On the other hand, the well-known 1992 cases, where the white cottager William Dove and the white farmer John Sorgenson were killed, provided some support for settler fears of violence that dated back to the 1885 Frog Lake killings that led to the mass hanging of eight Indigenous men at Fort Battleford. Fears and suspicions have long been harboured between non-Indigenous and Indigenous people.

It can be argued with justification that criminal trials should be focused on specific allegations and not on distant or even recent history and grievances. Nevertheless, Gerald Stanley was able to testify that he was thinking about the 1994 killing of Bryan Kipp and Gordon Tetarenko on a farm nine miles from the Stanleys just before his fatal encounter with Colten Boushie (TT 688–89) even though Stanley did not formally claim self-defence. The discussion of this case, however, created an imbalance in the historical record of grievances. Even if the prosecutor had objected and Chief Justice Popescul had prevented such a historical case from being discussed before the jury, the history of the troubled relations between Indigenous and non-Indigenous people would still have cast a large shadow over the Stanley case. In rural Saskatchewan, as in Faulkner's Mississippi, "the past is never dead. It's not even past."[156]

4

The Investigation, Polarization, and Preliminaries

INTRODUCTION

The controversy, polarization, and racial tensions that beset the Stanley trial had roots in the distant and near past as discussed in the last two chapters. Significantly, their sources also lay in a variety of actions taken in the week after Colten Boushie was killed on 9 August 2016.

As in some wrongful conviction cases, questionable early investigative decisions influenced the case. They included decisions not to retain the grey Escape that Boushie was killed in or to call a blood splatter expert to the scene. The initial statements that the RCMP took from Belinda Jackson, Kiora Wuttunee, Cassidy Cross, and Eric Meechance may have been influenced by the fact that they were under arrest and facing charges at the time. In any event, the witnesses departed from their initial statements as the trial process continued. The RCMP's initial press release, which mentioned a related theft investigation, and the way they informed Boushie's mother about her son's death, raised concerns that the Indigenous victim and his companions would be placed on trial just as much as Gerald Stanley.

Social media placed a twenty-first century spin on historical tensions between Indigenous and non-Indigenous people and inflammatory social media may have poisoned the jury pool.[1] Five days after Boushie's death, Saskatchewan premier, Brad Wall, made an extraordinary plea for racist and hate-filled social media to stop. By the end of that first week, the decision to release Gerald Stanley on bail raised issues about how to maintain public confidence in the administration of justice when the public was so polarized. This, combined with the publicity and strong views about the case, created predisposing circumstances for a miscarriage of justice not altogether different from those often seen in cases of wrongful convictions.[2]

Both the bail and preliminary inquiries were held with heavy security even though the crowds supporting the Boushie family were peaceful. This raised questions of whether another "imagined siege"[3] was taking placed in Battleford based on unwarranted and irrational fears of Indigenous people. The last pretrial hearing concluded with Chief Justice Popescul rejecting an application by the media, including the Aboriginal People's Television Network, to allow cameras in the courtroom. In itself the ruling was not exceptional as cameras are not generally allowed in Canadian trials. But the motion to televise proceedings was supported by the Boushie family who had reasons to be distrustful of a process that would continue not to involve Indigenous participants in the justice system. The media's motion was opposed by both the accused and the prosecution, and rejected by the trial judge.

THE RCMP INVESTIGATION

The RCMP apparently had difficulties finding the Stanley farm, but Sheldon Stanley, who had called 911 after Boushie was shot, was able to direct them. They eventually arrived with six or seven cars. (PT 84) On the one hand, this reaffirmed rural concerns about the difficulties of policing large areas, but it also demonstrated that the RCMP could appear in full force when necessary.

The RCMP promptly arrested and handcuffed everyone they found on the Stanley farm. They released Sheldon Stanley and his mother at the scene, but detained Eric Meechance, Belinda Jackson, and Kiora Wuttunee, as part of a theft investigation. They continued to search for Cassidy Cross who had been able to get a lift back to the Red Pheasant First Nation.

Belinda Jackson, who along with Kiora Wuttunee was in the back seat of the grey Escape when Boushie was killed, expressed resentment that she was held by the RCMP for nineteen hours on theft charges. While detained in the back seat of a RCMP cruiser, she was also taken on a high speed chase when the RCMP suspected two cars of suspicious activity when they drove by the Stanley farm. (PT 329) The RCMP determined that taking Jackson on a chase was contrary to policy, but explained that the constables had forgotten that she was in the back seat.[4] It is not known whether Belinda Jackson feared for her safety during this time. However, such fears would be understandable given a Human Rights Watch study, based on six weeks of fact-finding in the first half of 2016, that documented sixty-four alleged cases of violent abuse of Indigenous women by police in Saskatchewan, including sexual harassment.[5]

Colten Boushie's body was covered by a tarp, but left where it had fallen out of the car after Jackson and Wuttunee had tried to come to the aid of their friend. His body was left on the ground while the RCMP obtained a *Criminal Code* warrant to search the site. The heavy rain of forty-four millimetres during the evening of 9 August (TT 13) washed away blood and foot-prints. The RCMP decided that it was not necessary to send a blood splatter analyst to the scene. A former homicide investigator, however, has criticized the investigation as "sloppy … someone should have had the wherewithal to get a tarp of some sort to protect the car. For a blood splatter expert to come and look at something like this, what would be the point? It's been contaminated – the blood pattern, everything has been washed away."[6]

"I can't say anything more" and "You'll find out"[7]

Gerald Stanley was arrested and advised of his right to counsel at 6:53 p.m. on 9 August. He was able to speak to counsel both at 8:16 p.m. and 10:43 p.m. He was not interviewed at that time, but he was awoken at 2:09 a.m. on 10 August to have his hands swabbed for gunshot residue and his clothes retained as evidence.

Stanley was interviewed by RCMP Constable Gullacher during the afternoon of 10 August 2016. After he indicated to the Constable that he "knew nothing about the law" and did not "want to do something stupid,"[8] Gullacher allowed Stanley to make a third call to his lawyer, but she was not available. Shortly thereafter, he received his fourth call from Scott Spencer, who would be his lawyer at trial.

Upon his return from that call, Stanley told Gullacher, "I'd like to get it over as bad as you but I've got to do what he says."[9] Over the next hour, Stanley refused to say anything substantive about what happened. Given the advice he likely had received from his lawyer and the jeopardy he faced, Stanley sensibly exercised his right to silence. At the same time, no one seemed to expect Jackson, Wuttunee, Meechance or Cross to exercise their right to silence even though they were also in custody and eventually charged with theft or assault.

A "Friendly"[10] Conversation between Gerald Stanley and the RCMP

Although he unsuccessfully challenged the interrogation as a violation of his *Charter* rights and as oppressive, the hour-long conversation between Stanley and Constable Gullacher was described by Chief Justice Popescul as "friendly in tone" and "relaxed and cordial."[11] Stanley was apologetic about not being able to tell Gullacher anything more. He chatted about other matters, observing that Gullacher was close in age to one of his sons.[12]

Much more interesting than Stanley's non-statements were those made by Constable Gullacher in his unsuccessful attempt to get Stanley to tell his side of the story. Gullacher discussed legal issues with Stanley including the differences between murder and manslaughter as well as the defences of accident and self-defence.[13]

Where did these early ideas for Stanley's defence come from? At the time of the interview, the RCMP was drafting a warrant that contained references to Leesa Stanley saying "something about property," possibly in reference to claims that her husband had acted in defence of property. The reference by the RCMP officer to self-defence in Stanley's interview reflected the discovery of a loaded .22-calibre rifle near Boushie's body. The warrant also made reference to Sheldon Stanley's statement to the RCMP that his father told him he was just trying to scare the young people and the gun "just went off."[14]

A "Tactical"[15] Approach to Informing Debbie Baptiste that her Twenty-two-year-old son was Dead

If the conversation between Gerald Stanley and Constable Gullacher was friendly, the way the RCMP informed Debbie Baptiste of her son's death was anything but.

A large number of RCMP officers, some with weapons drawn, approached Baptiste's trailer on the Red Pheasant First Nation. They entered the trailer and asked her if Colten Boushie was her son. When told that she was his mother, they replied, "He's deceased." Debbie Baptiste alleged in a complaint against the RCMP that an officer also told her, "Ma'am, get yourself together," and asked whether the distraught mother had been drinking. A subsequent RCMP investigation into the complaint found that none of the officers recalled making such comments. It is not, however, disputed that a significant number of RCMP officers searched Debbie Baptiste's home causing her to ask, "What did we do? Why are all these officers on us? My son was the victim. But I thought we did something wrong."[16]

The RCMP were searching for Cassidy Cross, one of the people who had been in the grey Escape with Colten Boushie. The RCMP's investigation into the Boushie family's complaint concluded that "given the safety risks involved ... the approach the RCMP had to take was tactical in nature and in this situation it was acceptable."[17]

But why would the RCMP combine the task of informing a mother that her son had been killed with the "tactical" search of a house for a suspect who was eventually charged with theft? The RCMP did not ask for assistance from the community with either the difficult task of informing a mother about the death of her twenty-two-year-old son or in discovering the whereabouts of Cassidy Cross even though such assistance is contemplated in Treaty 6 as discussed in chapter 2. The RCMP's rejection of the Boushie family complaint has been appealed with Debbie Baptiste stating, "How are we to trust the RCMP when they treat us like criminals when we are the victims?"[18]

RCMP *Press Release*

The RCMP issued a press release on 10 August 2016. It stated that "one adult male associated with the property was arrested at the scene without incident. Three occupants from the vehicle including two females (one being a youth) and one adult male were taken into custody as part of a related theft investigation. Another male youth is being sought; his identity is not being confirmed at this time." It also noted that no charges had been laid in this "complex investigation" and that the investigation was continuing "into the events leading up to the arrival of the vehicle in the yard, the circumstances involving the death, and the actions following."[19]

The FSIN responded with its own press release stating that the RCMP news release "contained just enough prejudicial information for the average person to draw their own conclusions that the shooting was somehow justified." In reference to the rural crime debate, it added that the "messaging in a RCMP press release should not fuel racial tension."[20]

The press release seemed to give equal weight to the theft investigation as it did to the investigation of Colten Boushie's death. This set a pattern that was replicated later at trial where much time was devoted to whether Eric Meechance and Cassidy Cross had been attempting to steal vehicles even though by that time the charges against them had been dropped.

An RCMP internal investigation of a complaint by the Boushie family concluded that the news release followed protocol, but the Superintendent who wrote the report stated, "Regardless, I apologize if you felt the media releases depicted your son as a thief, and caused your family further anguish, as that was never the intent."[21] This complaint would only be subject to independent review after an internal police investigation. Significantly, the way this complaint was handled did not reflect the special obligations and role of RCMP under the Treaty including its emphasis on respectful and good relations.

Early Polarized Narratives

It was not long after Colten Boushie's death that the media started reporting on the tragic event that had occurred on Stanley's farm. The early media reports, with some exceptions, reflected stories told by Eric Meechance that denied attempted theft of a vehicle on the Stanley property. This contributed to the early polarization of opinion that would continue to dog the case.

On 11 August 2016, a story quoted Colten Boushie's uncle, Alvin Baptiste Sr, that Boushie's companions "pulled into that farmer's yard to see if they could get any help with the vehicle."[22] The next day, the press reported Eric Meechance's statements that they were looking for help with a flat tire and that "running is probably what saved our lives, you know, because if he is going to shoot one, he probably would have shot us all."[23] This early press which was at odds with the reference in the RCMP press release to detaining three people and seeking a fourth in a "related theft investigation," probably helped to ignite the social media firestorm that pitted Boushie supporters, who believed the initial press reports, against those who viewed the RCMP's reference to a theft investigation through the lens of their concerns about rural crime and, perhaps, their fear of Indigenous youth.

One example of the social media backlash to the early press was a post on a GoFundMe page for the Stanleys (subsequently removed) that stated, "These dirty Indians off the Rez stopped in at our farm and tried to steal our vehicles and when they couldn't, they vandalized it. After our farm pitstop, they carried on to Gerrys where things got out of hand."[24]

Some of the early press, however, hinted at the possibility of threats from the Indigenous people more serious than theft. The self-defence narrative that had been put to Stanley in his RCMP interview started to emerge in the mainstream media. On 12 August 2016, the CBC ran a story entitled, "Deadly Shooting near Biggar Sask Sparks Debate over Right to Defend." It featured a statement by a criminal defence lawyer that "when there doesn't appear to be any reasonable alternative, lethal force is no doubt permitted."[25] The CBC story also discussed a recent case where Saskatoon police did not lay charges against a woman who killed an intruder in her home. For Stanley supporters, this raised questions about why Stanley had been arrested, detained, and charged. At the same time, it also raised the notion of self-defence without any factual foundation, perhaps reflecting negative stereotypes about Indigenous people as often drunk and dangerous. There were twenty-four complaints about the CBC story and the CBC ombudsperson subsequently found that the story prematurely declared that self-defence would be a matter before the courts.[26] Although Stanley did not formally claim self-defence at the trial, it will be suggested in chapter 8 that he made implicit appeals to self-defence.

A 13 August 2016 press story repeated reports that the "natives stopped in the farmyard to seek help with a flat tire." It also painted a picture of polarization by juxtaposing Cree and subsequent Boushie family lawyer Eleanore Sunchild's comments about "100 years of stereotypes and racism" and the Battleford's "particular history" with statements that many local farmers are "raising money online and scheduling a steak night" in support of the Stanleys. An employee of the hotel, where the steak night was to be held, stated that the Stanleys "are awesome people. We want to help as much as we can. Nobody should have died, but we knew it was going to come to this. Things are out of control."[27] The idea that "things are out of control" played into the rural crime narrative which, as discussed in the last chapter, was freighted with racial overtones.

The planned steak night to support the Stanleys captured the public imagination. It invoked images of cowboys versus Indians. It reflected the comparative wealth of the non-Indigenous population compared to the Indigenous population. The Boushie family urged that the steak dinner be cancelled, but *National Post* columnist

Colby Cosh argued, "[h]elping to provide a legal defence for a friend – or just a fellow creature in deep trouble – ought to be acceptable." He noted that his retired parents raise cattle in the region and "like Stanley, they live outside the immediate range of law enforcement, and they are armed.... There is an omnipresent tension between reserve natives and non-native farmers."[28]

Premier Brad Wall Intervenes: "Racism has no place in Saskatchewan"[29]

Premier Brad Wall posted on Facebook on Sunday, 14 August to respond to the social media comments. As the post is quite extraordinary and is no longer on Facebook, it will be quoted in full as taken from a screen shot in media coverage:

> Racism has no place in Saskatchewan. In the wake of the shooting near Biggar, there have been racist and hate-filled comments on social media and other forums.
>
> This must stop. These comments are not only unacceptable, intolerant and a betrayal of the very values and character of Saskatchewan, they are dangerous. There are laws that protect citizens from this kind of hate may be enforced. They will be enforced.
>
> I also have every confidence that the circumstances of Colten Boushie's death will be fully investigated by the RCMP and that appropriate charges will be laid and prosecuted, based on the evidence. None of us should be jumping to conclusions about what happened. We should trust the RCMP to do their work.
>
> I call on Saskatchewan people to rise above intolerance, to be our best and to be the kind neighbours and fellow citizens we are reputed to be.[30]

Wall's comments deserve praise for calling out and denouncing racism. It is surprising that they were not introduced at trial as evidence of a realistic possibility that some potential jurors may be biased both because of the pretrial publicity and the racist and hateful views expressed in some of the social media postings.

At the same time, Wall did not express sympathy to Boushie's family or his community. He did not name the racism at play as anti-Indigenous. Indeed, the CBC reported a number of social media comments that painted the non-Indigenous majority as the victims of racism, including, "I've been called more names by Natives than I can count." Also, "Wanna stop racism? Revamp those obsolete treaties and make every adult in Saskatchewan pay taxes. A society that treats people differently because of their race is an unjust society."[31]

Wall reminded people about criminal offences against the wilful promotion of hate propaganda and the RCMP echoed Wall's comments about laws against hate speech. Such offences are notoriously difficult to prosecute. Saskatchewan's most famous hate-speech prosecution involved two trials of Indigenous leader David Ahenakew for anti-Semitic remarks, the first resulting in a conviction reversed on appeal and the second resulting in an acquittal. This may also have fuelled the idea that there was hate and racism on both sides. The false equivalence between Stanley's murder charge and the theft and assault charges that Boushie's friends faced was echoed in a false equivalence between long engrained anti-Indigenous racism and Indigenous attitudes towards settlers of various origins and races.

"we should trust the RCMP *to do their work"*[32]

Wall's comments that "we should trust the RCMP to do their work" did not address the history of distrust of the RCMP by many Indigenous people. The RCMP appropriately respected Stanley's *Charter* rights allowing him several opportunities to talk to lawyers, but they informed Debbie Baptiste of her son's death during a "tactical" search and issued a press release that twinned the investigation of Colten Boushie's death with a related theft investigation.

In any event, Wall's intervention did not stop some of the vile social media commentary. Ben Kautz, a municipal councillor in Browning, Saskatchewan, posted to the Saskatchewan Farmers Group on Facebook that "in my mind his only mistake was leaving witnesses." A screen shot of the post was widely circulated. Kautz received threats, apologized for the post, and subsequently resigned his elected position.[33]

It is difficult to know exactly what effect the social media explosion after Boushie's death had on attitudes among potential jurors. The Canadian justice system takes pains to impose publication bans on bail hearings and preliminary inquiries because of concerns about tainting the jury pool, but it is less experienced with dealing with prejudicial pretrial social media. In any event, no questions would be asked of prospective jurors to establish if they had been exposed, or had participated, in the social media firestorm that erupted after Colten Boushie's death. Prospective jurors were not questioned about social media even though a few court decisions recognized "the reality of the new internet world" and allowed potential jurors to be questioned about their social media use in order to determine if they could be challenged as not being impartial.[34]

BAIL

Gerald Stanley was detained for ten days before being released on bail. A two-hour bail hearing was held on Thursday, 18 April 2016. The North Battleford courtroom was filled to capacity with about one hundred spectators and about the same number outside. Some had signs that said "Justice for Colten" and "Indigenous lives Matter." The latter mirrored the Black Lives Matter movement that started in the wake of the 2013 acquittal of George Zimmerman for killing seventeen-year-old African American, Trayvon Martin. This underlined how competing claims of self-defence and racial justice would also be present in the Stanley trial. Both those who championed the use of guns in self-defence and those asserting that Indigenous lives matter were influenced by American developments. This cross-border migration of ideas and grievances contributed to a Canadian version of the polarization and conflict seen south of the border.

The spectators at the bail hearing chanted "Justice for Colten" as Stanley was led into the courtroom in handcuffs and with an orange t-shirt covering his head. Proceedings were temporarily halted because the stenographer could not hear due to the sound of drumming outside the court.[35] This would not be the last time that courtroom procedures and Indigenous traditions would make an awkward fit.

Because Stanley was charged with murder, he faced a reverse onus that meant that he, not the prosecutor, had to establish that continued detention was not necessary to ensure his attendance at trial, to protect the public safety or to maintain confidence in the administration of justice.[36]

The prosecution conceded that Stanley's detention was not necessary either to ensure his attendance at trial or for public safety. Justice Gabrielson noted, "The accused has only a dated record which includes no acts of violence. He owns property in the community and steps can be taken to ensure that he remains on his property."[37] The reference to ownership of property was a legitimate consideration, but it raised questions about how someone from the Red Pheasant reserve would be treated in the same situation.

"It was a sudden confrontation between two groups"[38]

The critical issue at the bail hearing was whether Stanley's detention was necessary to maintain public confidence in the administration of justice. The case for continued detention had been strengthened by a recent Supreme Court of Canada decision. The Supreme Court suggested that in cases of overwhelming evidence of a violent crime against a vulnerable victim, bail should usually be denied. The Court emphasized that the controversial public confidence ground for denying bail should not be used sparingly. The decision suggested that public confidence should be measured by what a reasonable and well-informed person and not a legal expert would conclude.[39] Public confidence was the key factor, but this only raised the difficult question of how to determine public confidence given the racial tensions and polarization that had already developed around the case. Some of Stanley's supporters opposed the fact that he even had been charged while nothing short of detention would be sufficient for some Boushie supporters.

The *Criminal Code* and the Supreme Court's decision mandated the judge to pay special attention to four factors. The first was the strength of the prosecution's case. Justice Gabrielson tersely observed, "The Crown's investigation is only at a preliminary stage and the statements of the witnesses vary greatly."[40] The next two factors favoured the denial of bail because Stanley was charged with second-degree murder and faced a lifetime imprisonment sentence. Justice Gabrielson acknowledged that a second-degree murder charge was "extremely grave," but stressed that Parliament had not precluded bail in such cases and that second-degree murder "might not be the charge which the accused is convicted of."[41] The last mandatory consideration also seemed to work against Stanley because it required the judge to consider the circumstances under which the alleged offence was committed "including whether a firearm was used."[42] Here Justice Gabrielson commented that "the circumstances of this offence are confusing and the evidence is conflicting.... It was a sudden confrontation between two groups. A firearm was used but the intent to use it has not been determined."[43] The judge, like the media, hinted that self-defence might have been in play.

Despite most of the enumerated factors pointing towards the denial of bail, Justice Gabrielson decided that Stanley would be granted bail. At the same time, Stanley was released under these strict conditions: he would need to be electronically monitored; he could possess no firearms; he would make no contact with Boushie's family or anyone else at Red Pheasant; no contact would be made with potential witnesses, except his son and wife; and bail was set at $10,000.

As discussed in chapter 3, the grant of bail in other cases involving Indigenous victims, including in the Tisdale sexual assault case and the killing of William Kakakaway, had been controversial with concerns raised by some Indigenous people that an Indigenous person would be unlikely to be granted bail in similar circumstances. FSIN Vice Chief Kimberly Johnston commented on the Stanley bail decision, "This isn't the result we wanted but I am calling for calmness and peace in the face of what feels like injustice."[44] At the same time, denial of bail and imprisonment of a person before a trial is always a serious matter and the public confidence ground for the denial of bail is rightly controversial. In any event, Canadian justice in the form of granting Stanley bail seemed to be perceived as Indigenous injustice.

PRELIMINARY INQUIRY

The preliminary inquiry started on 3 April 2017 with the RCMP again taking extensive security measures including having officers posted at all the approaches to the North Battleford courthouse.[45] Given the peaceful nature of all the demonstrations at the courthouse in support of Boushie, this recalled "the imagined siege"[46] of Fort Battleford discussed in chapter 2.

The court made an overflow room available for additional spectators. Judge Bauer of the Saskatchewan Provincial Court started proceedings by warning spectators that the Deputy Sheriff "has the power to remove anyone if they do cause a disturbance. So good morning to you all." (PT 1) It was not only the RCMP that seemed to anticipate potential disturbances and disorder.

The RCMP officers provided new information when they testified. A .22-calibre rifle found five to eight feet from the grey Escape had five live rounds in the magazine and one in the chamber. It also had a broken handle. (PT 12, 36) The RCMP could not find the bullet that killed Boushie, but they did find a discarded cartridge with a bulge on the passenger side of the car. They also found Stanley's revolver that had been returned to its storage box. (PT 19, 22)

The RCMP had emailed photos to a blood splatter expert in Calgary, but she determined that it was not necessary for her to attend at the scene on the basis that the splatter had been contained by Boushie's hood and hat. (PT 43) The grey Escape that Boushie had been killed in had been released by the RCMP on 14 August 2016, only five days after the killing (PT 45), and before Stanley had even been granted bail. The prosecutor recognized that Stanley's lawyer had expressed concerns about this, but told the court "there is nothing we can do" (PT 3). This acknowledged the dominant and largely independent role that the RCMP played in the investigation, but also hinted that prosecutors should perhaps play a more active role in criminal investigations to ensure that adequate evidence was collected and retained. A number of Canadian inquiries have found that wrongful convictions are frequently the product of police "tunnel vision" that fails to collect evidence that does not fit into the initial police hypothesis about the case.[47]

Gerald Stanley's twenty-seven-year-old son was the first civilian witness called by the prosecutor. He testified that the grey Escape came onto the Stanley farm and that some of the males approached several vehicles on the farm including a quad four-runner. They re-entered the vehicle when he and his father "began yelling and running." (PT 70) When the grey Escape came closer, Sheldon Stanley hit the windshield of their grey Escape with a hammer. The grey Escape next collided with the Stanley's blue Escape and went a further distance before coming to a stop. Sheldon Stanley then went into the house to retrieve his truck keys. He heard "one gunshot and then another" (PT 73, 76) as he was climbing the stairs to his house to get his keys, presumably so that he could chase the grey Escape should the need arise. Upon emerging from the house, he saw his father walking toward the grey Escape that was occupied by Boushie, Jackson, and Wuttunee. He stated "four or five seconds, probably" later, as he was walking down the steps from his house with his keys (PT 78), he heard, but did not observe, a third shot. The timing issue would be critical to the hang fire defence at trial.

All four young people who were with Colten Boushie testified. Eric Meechance said that he "was positive those two shots were at me," (PT 111) in reference to the first two shots that Stanley would testify at trial were warning shots in the air. The RCMP seemed not to believe Meechance's statement because Stanley was never charged with any offence in relation to the first two shots. This may suggest something about the operating assumptions in the RCMP investigation.

The trial judge would later tell the jury that if they found that Stanley's first two shots were indeed warning shots, they were justified as defence of property. (TT 893, 897) This reflected concessions made by the prosecutor, but was also consistent with statements that Minister of Justice Rob Nicholson had made when questioned by a rural colleague about the effects of the 2012 amendments to defence of property.[48]

Meechance admitted on cross-examination that he did not tell the media about the .22-calibre rifle that was in the grey Escape. (PT 127) Cassidy Cross, who had just turned eighteen-years-old, testified that the rifle was Meechance's. With reference to the live and spent bullets in the grey Escape he explained, "Res vehicles – they're always full of bullets ... everyone goes hunting ... because it is legal on a Reserve. You don't have to have a license." (PT 254) Cross admitted to drinking alcohol, adding, "When people are smashed they are a different person" (PT 230) and that he should not have been driving but that he was "probably the safest one there." (PT 251)

"I wouldn't kill a guy for trying to steal – that's dumb"[49]

Like Meechance, Cross was subject to extensive cross-examination by Stanley's lawyer, Scott Spencer. At one point, Cross stated, "I wouldn't kill a guy for trying to steal – that's – that's dumb." (PT 238) Like Meechance, Cross testified about Sheldon Stanley's actions in breaking the windshield of the grey Escape. He thought that Sheldon had used an axe rather than a hammer. This helps explain the following exchange with Stanley's lawyer:

Q: Did you consider, hey guys, flat tire here need some help?
A: I didn't consider it because they're coming at me with an axe. I seen them. (PT 241)

Kiora Wuttunee, eighteen-years-old and Boushie's girlfriend, also testified. This would be the only time that she testified. She admitted that she had been "drinking for a week" (PT 265) at the time of the incident. She repeatedly testified that she was asleep when

Colten was shot. (PT 271–72, 275, 289) She denied knowledge of the gun, bullets, and shell casings found in the grey Escape (PT 290) and denied assaulting Leesa Stanley.

She also explained an altercation between Leesa Stanley and Belinda Jackson after Colten had been shot. It started when Leesa Stanley said "something like her property or trespassing. So I think that got Belinda mad." (PT 280) Wuttunee said she had persuaded Belinda Jackson to walk away from the farm because "I thought they would have shot us if we did something." (PT 280) Both Indigenous women had been charged with assault though the charges had been dropped by the time of the preliminary inquiry. (PT 292)

> *"you can't really expect me to be truthful with these police who are like racist and thinking that I am on that farm to steal"* (PT 329)

Belinda Jackson was perhaps the most critical but also the most controversial witness both at the preliminary inquiry and the subsequent trial. She was the only one of the four people with Colten Boushie who testified that she saw Stanley shoot Colten. Eric Meechance and Cassidy Cross both admitted that they were running away from the farm at the time of the shooting while Kiora Wuttunee said that she was asleep.

Belinda Jackson testified that she saw Gerald Stanley fire two shots at Boushie from the passenger side window. (PT 306, 322) The prosecutor, Bill Burge, knew that Jackson's testimony of two shots was neither consistent with the coroner's report that Boushie was killed with one shot nor with the theory that Stanley came from the driver's side. Nevertheless, Burge made no attempt to explain these discrepancies or relate them to Jackson's statement that "I was scared. I was in shock" (PT 329) after having seen Colten Boushie fatally shot in the back of the head. Jackson also testified that Sheldon Stanley had retrieved a gun from the house (PT 304), something that Sheldon Stanley denied while acknowledging that he had brought two weapons on this visit to his parents. (PT 84)

Jackson was subject to aggressive cross-examination about why she had not told the RCMP that she saw Stanley shoot Boushie. She had read her initial statement to the RCMP and admitted "none of it makes sense. I'm aware of that. I know that." (PT 325) She explained "I was scared. I was in shock." (PT 329). She elaborated, "I was held there for nineteen hours. I didn't sleep, I didn't eat, as they were expecting me to." (PT 313) She added, "You can't really expect me to be truthful with these police who are like racist and thinking that I am on that farm to steal." (PT 329) She could not understand, "Why am I being put in handcuffs, I just watched somebody die? And he said. Well you're being arrested for theft." (PT 331)

Jackson was particularly upset that she had been detained and charged with theft when she only exited the grey Escape after Boushie was shot. She admitted to assaulting Leesa Stanley, explaining that Mrs. Stanley had told her "that's what you get for trespassing.... She stood there with her arms crossed, watching us cry and scream." (PT 308)

Stanley's lawyer, Scott Spencer, challenged Jackson's statements that the RCMP was racist asking "what part of it is unreasonable and racist to take you into custody and charge you with assault when you assaulted somebody, and then ask you for a statement in relation to a death?" (PT 332) Spencer apparently did not appreciate Jackson's anger about the stereotypical assumption that she was involved with theft when she did not leave the vehicle until after Boushie was shot. The judge eventually had to intervene telling Spencer, "You've told her a number of times that – why you think she shouldn't think that they're racist, that she continues to think they are, and I'm not sure we are going to get anywhere by continuing to go down this road." (PT 334) The polarized views about racism outside the courtroom had entered the courtroom with Jackson complaining that the RCMP had made racist assumptions that she was involved in theft and Spencer, questioning Jackson's allegations.

Committal for Trial

On 6 April 2017, after three days of testimony, Judge Bauer committed Stanley to face trial on second-degree murder. The judge indicated that he had "a limited role. I'm not here to weigh evidence at this point." Judge Bauer based his decision solely on Sheldon Stanley's evidence that he "observed his father with a gun and heard gunshots and saw his father walking back from the car with a gun." (PT 385) The judge did not mention Belinda Jackson's evidence that she saw Stanley shoot Boushie twice. This was telling because a judge at a preliminary inquiry is not supposed to evaluate the credibility or truthfulness of witness testimony, but leave that task to the jury at the trial. The attack on Jackson's credibility seemed to have succeeded even at the preliminary inquiry. It would again be successful at trial.

NO CAMERAS IN THE COURTROOM

There was one more preliminary matter before the selection of the jury and the start of the trial. In January 2018, a number of media outlets, including the Aboriginal Peoples Television Network, applied to have cameras in the courtroom. They relied not only upon the *Charter* protection of freedom of expression, but also the support of the Boushie family. After unsuccessfully asking for out-of-province investigators and prosecutors to be appointed, the Boushie family wanted as much transparency as possible so that people could see for themselves whether the trial was fair. This also echoed the George Zimmerman/Trayvon Martin case that had been televised in the US, but not the Canadian practice of not allowing trials to be televised.

Chief Justice Popescul was concerned that the media's motion was even reported in the press. He ordered a publication ban and raised concerns about "tainting or influencing potential jurors."[50] This recognized that pretrial publicity could have an effect on the jury pool, but one would have thought Premier Wall's intervention about racist and hate-filled social media would have been more of a concern. In any event, courts can control the pretrial publicity they generate much easier than the privately governed world of social media.

Both the prosecutor and Stanley opposed the motion to allow cameras. Stanley expressed concerns that the media's "fragmented" coverage had created "widespread anger and division within the province" and that broadcasting counsel's arguments "creates the risk of further division and anger within the province."[51] Stanley's written brief noted, "large-spread anger and division across the province, largely as a result of the media's inaccurate portrayal of the events of that day and the alleged motives behind the shooting" including Premier Wall's intervention. This recognized the tense racial dynamics and polarization in the case including the extensive pretrial publicity. All of this suggested that Stanley might want to challenge prospective jurors for their exposure to pretrial publicity.[52]

Stanley's written brief argued, "Saskatchewan is a province that values cohesion and community.... The media reporting to date has done more than enough damage to the 'societal interests' of Saskatchewan and Canada."[53] This defensive argument raised the question of how inclusive Saskatchewan's "cohesive" community was. Specifically, what place did the Boushie family and other Indigenous people who distrusted the justice system have in that community? Stanley's brief played into an us versus them dynamic that was a fertile ground for implicit or subtle forms of bias and that would be replicated, a few months later, when Stanley used peremptory challenges to keep Indigenous people off the jury.[54] The media was portrayed as a form of out-of-province interference that had been unfairly critical of Saskatchewan. By implication, Stanley's argument also placed the Boushie family outside the circle of Saskatchewan's "cohesive" community, given both that they supported the media's motion and because they themselves had previously requested the appointment of out-of-province investigators and prosecutors. Although they had roots in Saskatchewan, the Boushie family had also fairly recently moved to the province from Montana.

Stanley's brief also questioned the Boushies' status in the proceedings by arguing "to have a 'victim' you must have a finding of guilt."[55] This reflected the reality that while the system pays greater attention to crime victims and their families, it generally does not grant them participatory rights in the criminal trial until after a finding of guilt and sentencing.[56] This meant that all victims have to rely on the prosecutor to represent their interests. This provides a special challenge for crime victims who may distrust the criminal justice system.

In the end, Chief Justice Popescul concluded that a departure from the usual policy of not allowing cameras in the courtroom had not been justified. He stressed, "The jeopardy faced by Mr Stanley is of the most serious in Canada, and the risks that could result from allowing such an experiment could undermine the integrity and administration of our justice system."[57] His decision was similar to that reached by other Canadian courts in other high profile trials, but it assumed a level of trust in the system that Indigenous persons, perhaps especially in Saskatchewan, did not have.

The no-cameras-in-the-courtroom ruling had an unfortunate effect of suggesting that the court, the defence, and the prosecutor all had common interests not shared by the press or the Boushie family. Broadcasting the proceedings might have convinced many of the fairness of the trial process. Similar arguments were made about the Jian Gomeshi sexual assault trial.[58] Some might have reached opposite conclusions especially if it was possible to televise the jury selection process where five visibly Indigenous people were excluded from the jury. In any event, televising jury selection would have been challenging given concerns about protecting the privacy of jurors. Alas, we will never have the benefit of a televised version of the

Stanley trial. Like most Canadian trials, it can only be judged on the basis on a written transcript and media reports.

CONCLUSION

There are many unanswered questions about the RCMP's investigation. Would covering and retaining the car and having a blood splatter analyst examine it at the scene have produced additional evidence about the nature of the shooting? Was the RCMP investigation unduly influenced by its early awareness of Stanley's possible defences of accident and self-defence? The literature and the Canadian inquiries on wrongful conviction have frequently pointed to police tunnel vision as having a distorting effect on investigations and one that has, at times, been influenced by negative attitudes towards Indigenous people. A recent study has found that problematic police investigations have contributed to almost 40 per cent of seventy discovered wrongful convictions in Canada. Racial prejudice, almost always against Indigenous persons, has contributed to 10 per cent of discovered wrongful convictions.[59] Both of these findings raise the possibility that other police investigations may be affected by similar phenomena.

Would Belinda Jackson's statements to the RCMP have been different if she had not been detained and charged with an offence? Was she exercising a similar right to silence as Gerald Stanley did? There has been much writing in the wrongful conviction literature about the dangers of testimony of incentivized witnesses, often those who are detained or facing charges. The reality is that Jackson, Wuttunee, Cross, and Meechance all had incentives to be cautious in talking to the RCMP given the charges they faced at the time. In addition, the trauma of seeing Boushie killed before her eyes, and her sense of grievance about how the RCMP treated her, may have played a role in Jackson's initial statement to the RCMP.

The preliminary inquiry provided hints that one of the defence's strategies would be to attack the credibility of the Indigenous witnesses. The prosecution made no attempt to explain why Belinda Jackson's testimony about Stanley firing two shots differed from that of the other witnesses or the autopsy evidence that Boushie had only been shot once. Some possible explanations came out in response to aggressive cross-examination by Stanley's lawyers when Belinda Jackson said that she was "scared. I was in shock" (PT 329) when she made her original statements to the RCMP while under arrest. In the absence of any explanation for the discrepancy between Jackson's account and the physical evidence of Boushie being killed by one shot, even the judge, who committed Stanley to stand trial for murder, avoided relying on her testimony.

Gerald Stanley effectively exercised his right to silence after he spoke multiple times to lawyers while detained by the RCMP. He was also able to establish that bail should be granted and that his pretrial release under strict conditions was consistent with the maintenance of public confidence in the administration of justice despite the seriousness of the murder charge he faced and his use of a firearm. Although it is a problematic ground for pretrial detention, both the *Criminal Code* and the Supreme Court had authorized judges to deny bail if necessary to maintain confidence in the administration of justice. The public confidence ground begged the question of what elements of polarized public opinion about the case should be given the most weight.

Many factors contributed to the quick and continuing polarization of opinion around the case. Meechance told the press that they had simply asked the Stanleys for help with a flat tire while the RCMP, having discovered the .22-calibre rifle that had been in the grey Escape, indicated in a press release that Boushie's companions were being detained in a related theft investigation and asked Stanley whether he was acting in self-defence. The differing and sometimes false stories invited, and almost required, the public to select sides: was Stanley a cold-blooded and likely racist killer or a person protecting his property and family from rural crime?

Premier Wall's early intervention to tell people that "racist and hate-filled comments on social media ... must stop"[60] was extraordinary. Sitting premiers rarely feel compelled to make comments about either social media commentary or ongoing criminal investigations. His comments, combined with Chief Justice Popescul's concern when denying a motion to allow cameras in the trial about "tainting or influencing potential jurors,"[61] suggested that racism and the extensive pretrial publicity would have to be addressed when a jury was selected for the trial. Alas, that was not to be the case.

5

Jury Selection

INTRODUCTION

It was the Boushie family that made the selection of an all-white jury and Stanley's use of five peremptory challenges to exclude all visibly Indigenous jurors a national controversy.[1] The idea that there is an all-white jury and that it can be problematic is based on a lay understanding of the law.[2] In Canadian law, a juror is qualified by being a Canadian citizen who understands the language of the trial and has no disqualifying criminal convictions of one year or more.[3] The *Criminal Code* is colour-blind.

Judges have not taken kindly to questions about the racial composition of juries. The Saskatchewan Court of Appeal decided that a trial judge was justified in removing an Indigenous accused from the courtroom because he was going to complain that he was being tried by "an all-white jury." It reasoned, "To suggest the jury was tainted by bias, simply by virtue of racial composition, was a direct challenge to the legitimacy of the court as constituted."[4] The Court of Appeal was not wrong to conclude that such a claim challenged the legitimacy of the justice system: the real question is whether the legitimacy of the justice system in cases dealing with Indigenous people should simply be assumed. Canadians appear divided on the issue. In the wake of the Stanley verdict, 59 per cent agreed that jury selection procedures should be reformed, but 41 per cent of respondents believed that juries render good verdicts regardless of the way they were selected.[5]

Most of the divisive cases examined in chapter 3 were identified by Indigenous groups and the media as involving all-white juries.

The Manitoba Aboriginal Justice Inquiry identified the jury in The Pas that convicted one white man and acquitted another of the murder of a young Cree woman, Helen Betty Osborne, as an "all-white" jury. It found that the accused had used six peremptory challenges to exclude visibly Indigenous people in a racially charged case and in a district that, like the Battleford district in Saskatchewan, had about a 30 per cent Indigenous population.[6] The inquiry, co-chaired by Justices Alvin Hamilton and Murray Sinclair, concluded that the "exclusion of Aboriginal people from the jury fuelled public concern that racism might have played some part in the trial.... We do not believe that this should be allowed to continue. Whether it is the accused or the victim who is Aboriginal, the perception of a fair trial will be enhanced if Aboriginal persons are properly represented on juries. They are, after all, very much affected by the outcome of trials in their communities."[7]

Another infamous Canadian case involving an all-white jury was the 1971 wrongful conviction of Donald Marshall Jr, a seventeen-year-old Mi'kmaq man. The commission concluded that, "Native concerns are not unreasonable: would a white person facing a Native prosecutor, defence lawyer, judge and jury, have some apprehension whether he would get as fair a hearing as if everyone were white?"[8]

Juries are used less frequently in Canada than in the US or the UK. In the US, prospective jurors can be questioned extensively about their attitudes and non-discriminatory rationales must be given for peremptory challenges. In contrast, Canadian judges carefully vet any questions that lawyers ask of prospective jurors. In Canada, prosecutors and defence lawyers do not have to provide non-discriminatory justifications for their use of peremptory challenges to exclude jurors. British judges also tightly control the questions that can be asked of prospective jurors to determine if they can be impartial, but the UK abolished peremptory challenges in 1988.

After a brief introduction to jury selection, this chapter will examine how attempts to challenge Indigenous under-representation in pools of prospective jurors have almost universally failed. Courts have refused to require proportionate representation of Indigenous people or other racialized groups. They have, with few exceptions, been quite defensive of their juries.

Jury reform has tended to come from the legislature and not the judiciary. Building on old English traditions of mixed juries composed of six citizens and six foreigners, the Saskatchewan legislature amended its *Coroner's Act*[9] to allow for the representation of specific racial and cultural groups. In 2014, however, a Saskatchewan court rejected a claim by an Indigenous accused that the Treaties required a Regina jury in a criminal trial to be composed of six Indigenous and six non-Indigenous jurors.[10] Some dismiss mixed juries as a medieval relic, a futile and endless search for a perfectly proportionate jury, and manifestly not suited for criminal trials. But this discounts the merits of such juries. A mixed jury of six Indigenous and six non-Indigenous people would have to agree on a verdict. Its members could be challenged for cause if there were a realistic possibility that they would not attempt to decide the case impartially on the basis of the evidence they heard in court.

There was no questioning of prospective jurors as part of a challenge for cause process to determine whether they could be impartial in light of the pretrial publicity and racism that was evident since the day after Colten Boushie was killed. A single question about whether prospective jurors could be impartial because the victim was Indigenous was asked in the Peter Khill case in Hamilton, Ontario – a case with similar racial dynamics and polarization as the Stanley case. Canadian courts generally only allow prospective jurors to be asked a blunt and single question about racism. The effectiveness of this question is unknown, in part, because Canadian jurors are prohibited by the *Criminal Code* from speaking about their experiences.[11] More searching challenges for causes may be necessary to reveal deep seated racism and to promote public confidence in juries.

The use of peremptory challenges will be examined in the final section. The courts have long accepted that both the accused and the prosecutor can exercise a limited number of peremptory challenges on a subjective basis. Although courts have indicated that a racially discriminatory use of peremptory challenges by the prosecutor can be challenged, such challenges are very rare. When made, they have failed. Even fewer courts have addressed discriminatory use of peremptory challenges by the accused. Courts have doubted that *Charter* standards of equality can be applied to the accused or even that the accused can be required to justify their use of peremptory challenges. Canada has not developed the extensive jurisprudence seen in the United States in an attempt to prevent discriminatory uses of peremptory challenges. This may be a good thing, however, because many have concluded that American attempts to require both prosecutors and defence counsel to provide non-discriminatory reasons for the use of peremptory challenges have failed. The tough but optimal solution may be that adopted in Bill C-75, introduced in response to the Stanley case: abolish peremptory challenges.

Although juries are generally only used in the most serious cases in Canada, they are here to stay. As retired Supreme Court Justice Frank Iacobucci suggested in his 2013 report on Indigenous under-representation in juries, this under-representation is a symptom of a much deeper problem in Canada's colonial relations with Indigenous people. He recommended a range of jury-specific reforms including expanding the pool of prospective jurors, the use of volunteer jurors from Indigenous communities, and prohibiting discriminatory uses of peremptory challenges. Consistent with his awareness that Indigenous under-representation on juries was only a symptom of a larger disease, he suggested that governments must work with Indigenous peoples in a more respectful and nation-to-nation manner to respond to systemic and colonial discrimination in the criminal justice system.[12] Jury selection is important, but it is also a symptom of much larger problems of colonialism and racism.

THE COMPLEX PROCESS OF JURY SELECTION

Like so many other public policy issues affecting Indigenous people, jury selection involves a baffling interplay of provincial and federal jurisdiction. To simplify: the provinces are responsible for getting prospective jurors to court. At that point, the federal *Criminal Code* takes over and establishes the procedure for determining which twelve people will be on the jury.

The Provincial Role

The provinces have responsibility for the administration of criminal justice. This includes preparing lists or rolls of prospective jurors, summoning people for jury service, and paying jurors. Saskatchewan's approach to these issues was reformed after a 2004 commission of inquiry raised concerns about the under-representation of Indigenous people on juries.[13]

Saskatchewan uses random selection from provincial health cards to compile jury lists. This may still under-represent Indigenous people, but it includes more Indigenous people than the approach taken in some other provinces which still use less inclusive voting or property tax lists. Ontario still uses the latter but supplemented by *ad hoc* attempts to obtain lists of those who reside on reserves. Some concerns have been expressed that a second random selection from the Saskatchewan health card lists by court services was not done in the Stanley and many other cases,[14] but it is not clear what a second random screen would have accomplished.

Saskatchewan has increased the pay that jurors receive to $80 a day, more than many other provinces. There are, however, still concerns about how Indigenous people may be deterred from jury duty because of transportation, accommodation, and child care costs.[15] The provincial *Jury Act*[16] only excludes people from jury service if they are actually serving a sentence of imprisonment rather than having been convicted in the past. This is more generous and more inclusive of the Indigenous population than the *Criminal Code* that prohibits anyone sentenced to one-year imprisonment or more from ever serving on the jury.[17] Saskatchewan's approach to jury selection is more inclusive than that of many other provinces.

Three Forms of Challenges under the Criminal Code

Once prospective jurors, not excused by the province, arrive for jury duty at the courtroom, the *Criminal Code,* enacted by the federal Parliament which has exclusive jurisdiction over criminal procedure, takes over. It allows for the prosecutor or the accused to make three different types of challenges.

The first challenge is based on what the *Criminal Code* has described, since 1892, as "partiality, fraud or wilful misconduct" by provincial officials in creating the panel of prospective jurors.[18] No such challenge was made in the Stanley case, even though it is likely that Indigenous people were under-represented among the 178 prospective jurors out of the 750 people who were summoned who were available in the community centre in Battleford where the actual jury was selected in one day. (TT 1–19) As will be seen, however, such a challenge to the panel of available prospective jurors would almost certainly have failed courtesy of a 2015 Supreme Court decision that stressed that provinces only have to make reasonable efforts to summon a representative cross selection of the population and not deliberately exclude people in order to comply with the *Charter* right to a jury. The Court also concluded that provinces need not make special efforts to target Indigenous people for inclusion on juries and it rejected any right to a panel of prospective jurors that proportionately represents any sub-group of citizens.[19]

The second challenge relates to the unlimited number of challenges that either the prosecutor or the accused can make of prospective jurors "for cause," generally on the basis that the juror "is not indifferent between the Queen and the accused."[20] Canadian courts only allow a party to question a prospective juror if there is a realistic possibility of partiality because of an articulated factor such as pretrial prejudice or racial prejudice. Canadian courts have traditionally rejected, as being too American and invasive of juror privacy, wide-ranging questions about the experiences or attitudes of prospective jurors including towards the alleged crime.[21] If a juror is challenged for cause, two jurors, not the judge, decide whether the person is impartial and can sit on the jury. No challenges for cause were made in the Stanley case despite the extensive pretrial publicity and Premier Wall's intervention about racist and hate-filled social media commentary.

The third possible challenge relates to peremptory challenges. Both the accused and the prosecutor had fourteen peremptory challenges in Stanley's case.[22] The trial judge in the Stanley case explained the peremptory challenge process to the jury as follows, "As each number is read out, each lawyer will say 'content' or 'challenge' without saying why. If any lawyer says 'challenge' when your number is called, you will not be a person who sits on the jury." (TT 59) No objection was made by the prosecutor or the trial judge about Stanley's exercise of five of the thirteen peremptory challenges he made to exclude visibly Indigenous jurors.

NO CHALLENGE TO THE LIKELY UNDER-REPRESENTATION OF INDIGENOUS PEOPLE ON THE PANEL OF PROSPECTIVE JURORS

A 2004 survey by the Saskatchewan Ministry of Justice found that distrust of the justice system, travel, financial difficulties, and unfair elimination of Aboriginal people in the jury selection process were the top four reasons why Indigenous people in Saskatchewan did not respond to jury summons.[23] As indicated above, Saskatchewan has responded to some of these concerns by increasing the pay of jurors. Nevertheless,

many of the reasons for Indigenous people not being able or not wanting to be jurors may still have contributed to less Indigenous people
making themselves available in the Battleford Community Centre than
were among those 750 people summoned for jury service.

The Battleford Jury Panel

Because the jury system is colour-blind, it is not known with certainty how many of the 178 prospective jurors, of the 750 summoned, (TT 1–19) who were available in the Battleford community
centre on 29 January 2018, were Indigenous. It is likely that Indigenous people were over-represented among those who did not appear,
or were excused by provincial authorities, on the basis that they
were disqualified for jury duty. Hence Indigenous people were likely
under-represented among the 178 potential jurors in relation to their
percentage in the adult population of the judicial district.

One factor explaining the under-representation is the hard fact of
Canada's vast geography and the costs and difficulties of bridging
long distances. The Stanley trial was held in Battleford in the winter.
Although nearby North Battleford has a substantial Indigenous population, most First Nations persons in the Battleford judicial district
live north of that city on reserves. Many Métis people live in cities
that are 300 to 500 kilometres north of Battleford, a judicial district that extends to the border with the Northwest Territories. They
would be much farther away from Battleford than Saskatoon, which
is about 140 kilometres away.

Travel barriers to jury service are aggravated by the custom of holding jury trials in courthouses, like the Battleford courtroom, that are
located in what is often the largest town (usually with the best hotels
and facilities) in the district. This practice makes it more difficult for
Indigenous people who live far away to serve as jurors. As will be seen,
the holding of trials in the communities where crimes are alleged to
have been committed has been recommended as one way of increasing Indigenous representation on juries, but this recommendation has
not been implemented in Saskatchewan and many other provinces.

Press reports suggest that about a dozen visibly Indigenous prospective
jurors, who were in the Battleford community centre, were excused by
the trial judge from serving for hardship reasons.[24] Jury selection can
replicate the socio-economic disparities, discussed in chapter 3, both
at the stages of potential jurors not receiving or responding to their

summons or being excused from jury duty on hardship grounds either by provincial officials or by the trial judge.

Three prospective jurors were also excused by the trial judge because they were related to Colten Boushie. (TT 48–49) Another five Indigenous jurors, who did not request a hardship dispensation, were subject to peremptory challenges by the defence.[25] This suggests that at least 20 of the 178 or about 11 per cent of the people available to serve on the Stanley jury may have been Indigenous. This would significantly under-represent the approximately thirty per cent Indigenous population in the judicial district. Nevertheless, and as will be seen, courts have rejected challenges to far more dramatic examples of Indigenous under-representation on panels of prospective jurors.

Defensive Judicial Reactions to Indigenous Under-Representation on Jury Panels: "The Imposition of Inequality"[26] and "Racial Profiling"[27]

There has been only one reported successful challenge to the jury panel assembled by provincial authorities, on the basis of Indigenous under-representation, that has been sustained on appeal. In that case, the sheriff admitted on the last day of trial that he deliberately did not summon Indigenous people for jury duty because of concerns about their reliability.[28] Without such a smoking gun of intentional and deliberate discrimination, attempts to challenge Indigenous under-representation on panels of prospective jurors have all failed.[29]

Not only have the attempts to challenge Indigenous under-representation failed, but judges have in several cases expressed anger at the fact that they were made. One judge characterized an accused, who challenged the exclusion of Mohawks living on a Quebec reserve from jury duty because they did not pay property taxes, as "flying false colours because this is clearly not a case of racial discrimination."[30] A Manitoba judge rejected a challenge to a jury panel that had 2 Indigenous persons out of 148 prospective jurors by arguing that "there is no need to Balkanize the citizenry of this country for the purpose of jury selection."[31] His colleague added that proportional representation would "mean the imposition of inequality."[32] More recently, the Manitoba Court of Appeal rejected a similar challenge by concluding that polling the jury "on racial grounds" would be "offensive" and that "racial profiling" is not "required."[33] These comments are even more striking when it is considered that they were written by appellate judges and not delivered orally in the heat of a trial.[34]

Disqualifications from Jury Service that
Contribute to Under-Representation

The exclusion under the *Criminal Code* of those who have been sentenced to imprisonment for one year or more may have the effect of disproportionately excluding Indigenous people from jury service since there is well-documented evidence of Indigenous over-representation in jails. Despite this, an Alberta court concluded in 2016 that an even broader exclusion under the *Jury Act* of Alberta was not discriminatory and "serves to promote impartiality." The judge concluded that the disproportionate impact on Indigenous people "does not affect the reasonableness of the exclusion." The case involved a murder trial of a Cree accused in Edmonton where not one of 178 prospective jurors was Indigenous.[35]

Judges have also upheld requirements that jurors must be Canadian citizens even though such requirements disproportionately exclude visible minorities in Toronto who have permanent resident status, even though we do not require lawyers to be citizens.[36] In all these jury-selection cases, judges have embraced formal understandings of equality. They have ignored the disproportionate adverse effects that identical treatment of all individuals have on Indigenous people and other racialized groups who are themselves over-represented among those accused and convicted of crime as well as among victims of crime.

Gross Indigenous Under-Representation is Consistent with the Charter

Even if the prosecutor had brought a challenge to under-representation of Indigenous people on the panel of prospective jurors assembled for Stanley's trial, it would have been unsuccessful. In 2015, a majority of the Supreme Court in *R. v. Kokopenace* rejected a challenge, by an Indigenous accused in Kenora, to a less inclusive Ontario system that relied on incomplete and dated lists of reserves to supplement a basic list based on property tax assessments. The Court upheld a panel of prospective jurors where only 8 of 175 people were Indigenous people living on reserve even though 30 per cent of the population lived in the judicial district in northern Ontario on reserve.[37] If the Kenora panel passed constitutional muster, Stanley's panel, that seemed to have at least 20 Indigenous persons out of the 178 prospective jurors, would have survived *Charter* review even though such a figure would also significantly under-represent the thirty per cent Indigenous population in the Battleford judicial district.[38]

In the controversial 5:2 decision, Justice Moldaver decided that the Ontario system did not violate the *Charter* rights of an Indigenous accused because Ontario had made "reasonable efforts to: compile the jury roll using random selection from lists that draw on a broad cross-selection of society and to deliver jury notices to those who have been randomly selected."[39] Ontario's efforts, "while not perfect" (including some omitted and dated lists and high non-delivery rates of juror questionnaires), were nevertheless reasonable.[40] As long as there was no "deliberate exclusion,"[41] the results of dramatic under-representation on the Kenora jury panel did not seem to matter. An attempt to argue for an Indigenous-specific approach was rejected on the slippery-slope basis that it would open the door to inefficient and futile attempts to ensure perfect proportionality of every possible group.[42]

No Need or Standing to Consider Equality

The majority of the Supreme Court ruled there was no need to consider equality rights because the Indigenous accused had not "clearly articulated a disadvantage" despite the dramatic under-representation of Indigenous people on the panel of prospective jurors. The accused was not allowed to assert the rights of Indigenous people who may never have received their notice of jury duty.[43] Consideration of equality rights is critical in cases with Indigenous victims like the Boushie family who are not represented in the trial. It would be unrealistic to expect prospective Indigenous jurors to challenge their exclusion from serving on a jury, something that because of the time, stress, and financial sacrifice involved, many people want to avoid. The brief dismissal of the relevance of equality in *Kokopenace* symbolizes the Court's aversion to substantive equality reasoning when it comes to the jury.

No Need to Consult with Indigenous People
or Apply Gladue to Jury Selection

Justice Moldaver also concluded that the honour of the Crown, which generally requires consultation with Indigenous people, did not apply to the obtaining of lists of reserve residents under Ontario's jury selection system. He also determined that *Gladue* principles that have recognized systemic and colonial discrimination against Indigenous people in the justice system and require special attention to the circumstances of Indigenous people did not apply to jury selection.[44] He held that the Ontario Court of Appeal's consideration of both of the above factors wrongly made jury selection "a vehicle for repairing the long-standing rupture between Aboriginal groups and Canada's justice system. In doing so, it raised the bar Ontario was obliged to meet to satisfy its representativeness obligation."[45] The guiding rule was to treat everyone the same under rules of random selection even though the *Juries Act* singled out reserve residents because they were excluded from the base property tax list.

"crippling, the ability to proceed with jury trials
throughout the country"[46]

Justice Moldaver avoided the specific history of Indigenous under-representation on juries and colonialism despite the fact that the Court had just a few years earlier reiterated that judges should take judicial notice of it when sentencing Indigenous offenders.[47] Instead, he raised the spectre of a search for a perfectly representative jury that would reflect religion, ethnicity, sexual identity, and age. He predicted that this would result in defence challenges on the basis that the jury "roll is unrepresentative of *any group's* rate of inclusion does not approximate its percentage of the broader population," thus "compromising, if not crippling, the ability to proceed with jury trials throughout the country."[48] This is a familiar theme in the defensive jury-selection jurisprudence, but one that avoided confronting Canada's unique and colonial treatment of Indigenous people.

Justice Moldaver concluded that it would be a "radical departure" to use jury selection "to address historical and systemic wrongs against Aboriginal people." If jury selection became "a public inquiry" into such wrongs and "damaged relationships," it would be "virtually impossible" to select a jury thus providing "a devastating blow to the administration of justice."[49] Inquiring into the identities of prospective jurors would be "a radical departure from the way jury selection has always been understood in Canada" and it would "impermissibly"[50] invade the privacy of prospective jurors. He also implicitly criticized one of the recommendations of the Iacobucci report by suggesting that if "special rules" allowed "Aboriginal people to volunteer for jury duty," this could "destroy the concept of randomness vital to our jury selection process in criminal trials."[51] His criticism of volunteer jurors could prevent the extension of modest jury reforms which, in Ontario, have seen volunteer jurors used as part of coroner's juries and in Saskatchewan have allowed coroners' juries in appropriate cases to have a specific racial composition.

The Court's 2015 decision confirmed the many previous cases that suggested that when it came to jury composition, the courts had elevated random selection that treated everyone the same over substantive equality that was attentive to disproportionate impact and substantial Indigenous under-representation on juries. The Court's approach to jury selection failed to recognized what Cree lawyer Don Worme observed in 1994, "There is nothing so unequal as the equal treatment of unequals."[52]

In dissent, Justice Cromwell found the Ontario process of using old and incomplete lists from reserves and mailing juror questionnaires through general delivery violated the *Charter*. Foreshadowing the Stanley case, he warned, "Unintentional yet substantial under-representation ... casts a long shadow over the appearance that justice has been done."[53] He also argued that a representative jury panel was more likely to produce juries that can avoid often "unconscious effects of racism"[54] that, since 1998, the Court had recognized could impact the impartiality of prospective jurors. At the same time, Justice Cromwell, joined in dissent by Chief Justice McLachlin, also confirmed that the right to a representative roll of prospective jurors did not mean a right that the jury chosen to hear the case "proportionally represents the population. Nor is there a right to be tried by a jury whose members belong to the same group, race or gender as does the accused."[55]

Since the Court's 2015 decision, Indigenous under-representation in Ontario juries continues to be a problem. In 2016, only 650 Indigenous persons responded to 6023 jury questionnaires. Moreover, 356 of the 650 were found ineligible for a variety of reasons including disability, language, and criminal record. In 2017, there were only 553 returns on 6131 questionnaires with, again, a majority of the returnees, 294, being found ineligible.[56] Gross under-representation of Indigenous people on juries in Ontario continues, but is consistent with the *Charter* at least under the Supreme Court's decision in *Kokopenace*.

Judicial Resistance to Affirmative Provincial Action
to Increase Indigenous Representation

There is one case where a prosecutor successfully challenged the panel of prospective jurors that the province had compiled. It did not, however, provide a precedent for the prosecutor in the Stanley case to have challenged the panel on the basis that Indigenous people were under-represented compared to their population in the judicial district. Rather, it suggested that provincial attempts to increase Indigenous representation on juries are themselves vulnerable to challenge.

The case involved Milton Born with a Tooth who was charged with weapons offences committed on the Peigan or Piikani Indian Reserve while he was protesting against the building of the Oldman Dam. The provincial sheriff responded to concerns raised by an inquiry and prior litigation about Indigenous under-representation on Alberta jury lists which were taken from voters lists (which had traditionally excluded Indigenous people).[57] The provincial sheriff added 52 names of Indigenous people living on reserves to the 200 names of prospective jurors taken from voters' lists. The prosecutor, however, objected to the addition of the 52 reserve residents and convinced the judge that the sheriff's actions were an impermissible form of "affirmative action" that departed from "random" selection.

In the typically strong language found in jury selection cases, the judge concluded that the sheriff's attempt to ensure that some Indigenous reserve residents were present as prospective jurors would lead to "the demise of the jury system." He suggested that the "calculated inclusion of members of one distinct group" would lead to "the express exclusion of those other groups."[58] The judge concluded that "[a]rtificially skewing the composition of jury panels to accommodate the demands of any of the numerous distinct segments of Canadian society would compromise the integrity of the jury system."[59]

This approach reduced Indigenous people who had signed the Treaties to just another of "numerous distinct segments of Canadian society." It ignored that Indigenous people (at least those not prepared to renounce their identity as Indigenous) had been denied the vote federally until 1960, and provincially in Alberta until 1965, and that the voting lists were still used as the basis for jury lists in Alberta. Given consistently defensive judicial attitudes on this issue, the judge was correct about one thing: jury-selection reform, especially if departing from random selection, "should only be made by legislation."[60]

Milton Born with a Tooth was found guilty, but only when the judge dismissed a motion to declare a hung jury after the one Indigenous person on the jury said, "I don't know" and "you don't understand" when the jury was polled to affirm its initial verdict of guilt. The judge dismissed a motion by the accused for a mistrial and sent the jury back for more deliberations. After an additional seventy-five-minute deliberation, the jury unanimously convicted the accused with the defence lawyer stating that the Indigenous juror was in a very difficult position.[61] The judge sentenced Born with a Tooth to sixteen-months' imprisonment for firing two warning shots in the air at construction workers building the dam.[62] In contrast, the judge in the Stanley case told the jury that Stanley was justified in firing two warning shots under the defence of property (TT 898) that, as discussed in chapter 3, Parliament expanded in 2012.

Local Juries?

Another means proposed to increase Indigenous representation on juries is to conduct jury trials in the local community where the crime is alleged to have been committed. For example, Born with a Tooth's trial might have been held in the community and not in Calgary, as it was. Alas, courts have rejected arguments by Indigenous accused to have jury trials in their northern communities rather than in the district centres of Prince Albert, Saskatchewan; Thompson, Manitoba; and Kenora, Ontario.[63] Again, this suggests that change must come from the legislature and is unlikely to occur through the courts. The issue of local juries will be discussed again in chapter 10.

Summary: The Judiciary's Resistance to Challenges to Indigenous Under-Representation

Justice Moldaver's majority judgment in *Kokopenace* shows how little has changed since Cynthia Petersen, in 1993, concluded that Canadian jury selection was resistant to substantive equality and should be reformed to ensure respect for the rights of both accused and complainants from disadvantaged groups.[64] What did this mean for the Stanley case? Even if the prosecutor had been inclined to raise concerns about possible under-representation of Indigenous people on the panel of prospective jurors, his challenge would have been dismissed.

Going forward, it suggests that more radical jury reform would have to come from legislatures and not the courts. Even then, such reforms could be challenged as violating requirements of random selection and identical treatment that the Court had read into the accused's *Charter* right to a jury. It is unfortunate that the Court has done this when it has rightly abandoned such formal and weak approaches to equality as requiring the same treatment of everyone in every other aspect of Canadian law.[65]

MIXED JURIES

It is an interesting thought experiment to think how the Stanley case might have changed if it had been decided by a mixed jury composed of six Indigenous and six non-Indigenous people. This means that the five Indigenous people that Stanley peremptorily challenged would have been on the jury and one more. Whatever the ultimate verdict of such a jury, its reception would have been very different.

Before mixed juries are dismissed out of hand as an unworkable attempt at social engineering or extreme multiculturalism, their long history should be appreciated. As discussed in chapter 2, Louis Riel might have been entitled to a mixed jury – one composed of half French and half English speaking jurors if he had been tried in Manitoba as opposed to Saskatchewan. As an American citizen, he might also have been entitled to a mixed jury with half non-citizens if he had not been charged with treason, the only crime for which English courts, since 1577, did not allow mixed juries.[66] It is impossible to know whether the results of Riel's controversial trial would have been different had a mixed jury been used. It is, however, certain the results of the trial would have been considerably less divisive.

Thomas Flanagan has questioned whether a mixed jury would have made a difference in the Riel trial arguing, "Those who criticize the composition of the jury seem to assume that a fair trial is impossible unless the jurors are some microcosm of the some larger population. This principle is highly dubious and has never been enshrined in Canadian law, except for the existence of bilingual juries in Quebec and Manitoba."[67] His comments deny the long use of mixed juries in the English common law. They also ignore the controversy over the Riel trial and his hanging, which played a role in Quebec nationalists being elected, and eventually led to Quebec supporting the Laurier Liberals. Consistent with his other writings,[68] Professor

Flanagan's arguments implicitly reject the idea that Indigenous persons have distinct and Treaty-based claims that others in Canada do not have: specifically, in this context, to a mixed jury.

It is glib to criticize the mixed jury as one that necesarily sacrifices impartiality. One Canadian case rejecting arguments for a representative jury suggested that, "[t]o permit aboriginal members of the panel to take a place on the jury without being subjected to the challenge for cause and to peremptory challenges, just for the sake of appearance, would fly in the face of the right of an accused to an impartial and independent fact-finder."[69] An 1870 American case, rejecting juries that would require some African American representation, raised a similar spectre that a mixed jury "would not be a honest or fair one" but rather one in which "the prejudices of one race were set off against the prejudices of another."[70] Contrary to the suggestions in the above cases, however, there is evidence that jurors in a mixed jury could not serve if they had an interest in the matter or were not otherwise impartial.[71] Similarly, a volunteer juror from an Indigenous community could be subject to a challenge for cause if there were grounds to believe that he or she would not impartially decide the case on the basis of the evidence. Moreover, even if the prejudices and experiences of different groups were initially set off against each other in the jury room, there would have to be some appreciation of the other perspectives and collective deliberation if the jury was to reach a unanimous verdict.[72] The different perspectives in mixed juries were a starting point not an end point.

Hard and fast contrasts between demands for representative juries and demands for impartial jurors are often made, but they are not particularly helpful. Mixed juries may represent different perspectives, but they need to appreciate all perspectives in order to agree on a verdict. Jurors on a mixed jury would not swear an oath to represent their group but rather to decide the case on the basis of the evidence heard in court. But a mixed jury would recognize that on some issues, especially those related to race, gender, police, and stereotypes, that jurors inevitably bring their life experiences to their deliberations. As Justice Thurgood Marshall, the first African American to serve on the United States Supreme Court explained, the exclusion of minorities from the jury removes "from the jury room qualities of human nature and varieties of human experience, the range of which is unknown and perhaps unknowable. It is not necessary to assume that the excluded group will consistently vote as a class in order to conclude, as we do, that its exclusion deprives the jury of a perspective on human events that may have an unsuspected importance in any case that may be presented."[73]

The Common Law Mixed Jury

The mixed jury, sometimes known as the *Jury de Mediete Linguae*, was originally created in 1189 in England to allow juries composed half of citizens and half of Jewish merchants in cases involving a Jew and a non-Jew. The King was responding to anti-Semitic violence and fears that Jewish merchants would take their capital and leave. The deliberations of the mixed jury were likely influenced by Jewish law that was applied by Jewish courts in England to cases involving Jews[74] though the mixed jury would have been instructed by the judge to apply English law.

By 1354, the mixed jury was extended to include a right of any non-citizen to have a mixed jury including fellow non-citizens. The potential for a mixed jury was threatened in 1414 when residence requirements were imposed on all jurors, but a 1429 statute[75] exempted non-citizens from such requirements because many foreign merchants had refused to do business in England if they did not have the option of a mixed jury should legal disputes arise.

One justification for the mixed jury in England and in Canada is that it helped ensure that some jurors would understand witnesses who did not testify in English. Marianne Constable has, however, argued that a "more fundamental" rationale for the mixed jury is "that a person be judged by the laws and members of that person's community."[76] I agree, but would add that part of the genius of the mixed jury was that it did not allow one group to impose its approach on the other. There had to be a meeting of minds, and perhaps compromise, if the jury was to reach a unanimous decision that would result in a verdict. By including "the other" in the jury and requiring that their views be respected in order to reach a verdict, the mixed jury could work towards the difficult task of true impartiality as a collective institution.[77] The late Andrew Tazlitz argued that the exclusion of African Americans from American juries created a danger of "racial blind-sight"[78] where there was a lack of understanding of the reasonable fear that African Americans have of the police. Other commentators have suggested that the lack of diversity in both the juries that acquitted Los Angeles police of beating Rodney King in 1992 and O.J. Simpson, may have led people, perhaps unfairly, to conclude that the jury's verdict was simply the product of racial bias and solidarity.[79]

Mixed juries could be of particular importance in cases involving Indigenous people. New historical accounts have complicated the story of early European-Indigenous relations and have found that the jurisdiction of European courts were often resisted, sometimes successfully. Before 1675, mixed juries of six Algonquian and six English persons were used in some North American colonies.[80] In 1844, New Zealand provided for mixed juries in cases where the liberty or property of a Maori person was at stake.[81]

Depending on context, mixed juries can be a threat to Indigenous law and justice systems or a means to ensure that Indigenous perspectives are respected in European systems. The mixed jury of half Europeans and half Maori were used infrequently partly because of other provisions that allowed for the Maori to apply their own laws including the importance of compensation to victims in cases where British colonial law would emphasize punishment.[82] This reveals a dilemma for Indigenous people between retaining their own Indigenous systems of justice or having some influence over European justice systems through the mixed jury. Indigenous people may require both given the reality of cases like Stanley's which involve both Indigenous and non-Indigenous people.

The Decline and Fall of Mixed Juries

In 1862, New Zealand abolished the mixed jury in criminal cases so that all-European juries would be used in cases with a Maori accused.[83] Although this change allowed all Maori juries to continue to be used in cases of intra-Maori disputes,[84] it abandoned the potential of inter-societal law-making or mini treaties inherent with mixed criminal juries. Mixed juries including six Indigenous Hawaiians were abolished with the American take-over of the Islands in 1898.[85] All-settler juries could have led to the sort of injustice that was described in chapter 2 in the trials of Métis and Indigenous people who had participated in the 1885 uprisings.

Mixed juries for aliens in England were abolished in 1870[86] at a time of resurgent British identity and imperialism. One parliamentarian overconfidently argued, "It is stigmatizing ourselves as a nation very unjustly to assume that the prejudice against foreigners is such that an alien on his trial will not have a fair trial before British subjects."[87]

After the Civil War, the United States Supreme Court banned formal exclusions of African Americans on juries, but rejected arguments that having African Americans on a jury were required for the equal protection of the law.[88] Again, this approach ignored the role that informal and formal exclusions played in suppressing African American representation on juries. If African American participation had been mandated on juries, the history of the United States after its Civil War might have been quite different. At the very least all-white juries could not have as easily nullified criminal laws by refusing to convict white accused of violence against African Americans including 3,220 lynchings of African Americans between 1877 and 1930.[89]

Aliens retained the right to mixed juries in many colonial states. Professor Ramirez of Northeastern Law School aptly summarized the lessons from the gradual abolition of mixed juries as, "when minorities are powerful ... or serve vital functions ... they will receive the protection of a mixed jury," but mixed juries will be abolished "when the majority can safely ignore the minority."[90]

Alas, there is little enthusiasm in the common law world for the revival of the mixed jury. The New Zealand Law Reform Commission rejected it in 2001 concluding that "once an exception is made for one group there is no reason in principle why it should not be made for all other ethnic minorities and any other group."[91] This unfortunately ignores the distinct case that could be made for mixed juries in cases involving Indigenous people as both a requirement of Treaty and a commitment to mini-Treaty-making and inter-societal law-making going forward. As will be seen, such a Treaty argument was made in Saskatchewan shortly before the Stanley case, but was rejected.

One modern example of the use of mixed juries has been seen in some Argentinian states where the jury is required to have six men and six women. In at least two states, there are also mixed juries of six Indigenous and six non-Indigenous people in cases involving Indigenous people.[92] There are also arguments that requiring mixed juries, or some guarantee of minority and gender representation, may be more efficient and effective than attempting to control possible prejudice and discrimination through extended challenges for cause, litigation about whether pools of prospective jurors are fairly compiled, and challenges to alleged discriminatory uses of peremptory challenges.[93]

Despite their long history under the common law, the contemporary use of mixed juries would be seen as radical jury reform, one that, if introduced, might even be challenged under the *Charter* and the principles of treating everyone the same through random selection celebrated in much of the Canadian jury jurisprudence. Nevertheless, they are worthy of consideration as a possible way to ensure that excluded perspectives are represented on the jury.

A Mixed Jury as a Treaty Right?

Stony Lee Cyr, a member of the Pasqua First Nation, argued that an aid and assistance and peacekeeping clause in Treaty 4, (almost identical to the 1876 Treaty 6 clause discussed in chapter 2), required the use of a mixed jury of half Indigenous persons and half non-Indigenous persons for a criminal trial in Regina.

Cyr called no evidence from Elders and others in support of his argument. It is not clear whether Indigenous people would support mixed juries, especially if the alternative is an Indigenous justice system. Instead, Cyr relied on common law precedents of mixed juries of citizens and foreigners and mixed French and English speaking juries in Quebec and Manitoba as discussed above.

The Saskatchewan attorney general sent four lawyers to argue that the Indigenous accused was relying on "nothing more than a hodgepodge of legal history spanning 200 years and two continents with nothing tying it to the negotiation of Treaty No. 4."[94] This argument was accepted by the trial judge who concluded in 2014 that nothing in the text of the Treaty referred to juries or mixed juries and that even a generous approach to Treaty interpretation could not justify requiring a mixed jury. A mixed jury of six Indigenous and six non-Indigenous persons might be challenged under the *Charter* as a departure from random selection, but it could be protected from *Charter* invalidation if recognized as a Treaty right or defended as action designed to ameliorate the conditions of a disadvantaged group.[95]

A mixed jury might have prevented the controversy surrounding the Stanley case. To be sure, each group represented on a mixed jury could voice their distinctive perspectives (without necessarily the danger of being the lone person to do so as was the case with the one Indigenous juror in Milton Born with a Tooth's trial). At the end of the day, however, there would have to be a sharing of experiences and a meeting of minds if the jury was to agree on a verdict. A mixed jury might also reveal a diversity of Indigenous and non-Indigenous perspectives and create space for frank discussion of racism and stereotypes that might otherwise be avoided even if relevant to the jury's evaluation of the evidence.

Although he was not commenting about a mixed jury of six Indigenous and six non-Indigenous people, Elder Danny Musqua of the Keeseekoose First Nation, Treaty 4, contemplated the possibility of a meeting of minds that could occur in a mixed jury's deliberations when he said in 2002, "In order for justice to take place (speaking in Saulteaux) you must come to a situation where there are commonalities, common understandings of what it is that these two could come to agreement on. And that is when we say a settlement has taken place, or a peace venture is taking place."[96]

The judge in the Cyr case indicated that the mutual aid and assistance clause in the Treaty "should at the very least, be interpreted as imposing an obligation on the Crown to work with the native signatories on criminal justice issues" and "not to shut the First Nations out of the criminal justice process."[97] The discriminatory use of peremptory challenges to exclude visibly Indigenous prospective jurors in the Stanley case arguably had this shutting-out effect. As discussed in chapter 3, Saskatchewan's response to rural crime also did not draw on the aid and assistance that might be offered by the First Nations who signed the Treaties.

An Unsuccessful Saskatchewan Challenge to Indigenous Under-representation on the Jury Panel

Having lost his Treaty argument for a mixed jury, Stony Cyr made an alternative argument that the under-representation of Indigenous people on the panel of prospective jurors violated his *Charter* rights. Like others that had made such arguments, he lost.

A former sheriff, who had been summoning jurors in the Regina district since 1996, "was unable to recall any trial where a First Nations person sat on the jury in circumstances where the accused was also First Nations."[98] Such a result likely reflected Indigenous under-representation on the panel of prospective jurors and perhaps prosecutorial use of peremptory challenges. The judge, however, stressed that Saskatchewan's use of provincial health cards was the most comprehensive way to compile lists of jurors and there was no statistical evidence that Indigenous people were less likely to receive jury notices even though they were sent to the post offices in the town or village nearest to a reserve.[99] The fact that the sheriff was not able, over almost two decades, to recall Indigenous jurors on a Regina jury involving an Indigenous accused is shocking. It recalls the trials of Indigenous and Métis accused in 1885 in Regina before all-white juries. The all-white jury in the Stanley case was not an aberration.

CHALLENGE FOR CAUSE AND THE REALISTIC POSSIBILITY OF BIAS ON THE BASIS OF RACISM AND PRETRIAL PUBLICITY

No attempt was made on the public record by either the prosecutor or the accused to ask prospective jurors questions about bias based on racism or pretrial publicity despite the racially charged and extremely well-publicized lead up to the Stanley trial. The trial judge would have had to find that there was a realistic possibility that jurors might be partial as between the Queen and the accused. As discussed in chapter 3, there was plenty of evidence of both prejudicial publicity and racism including Saskatchewan premier, Brad Wall's extraordinary statement that "there have been racist and hate-filled comments on social media and other forums. This must stop. These comments are not only unacceptable, intolerant and a betrayal of the very values and character of Saskatchewan, they are dangerous."[100] The lead up to the case could have been the subject of evidence or judicial notice indicating a realistic possibility of widespread partiality in the community.

The focus of any challenge for cause would have been on race and pretrial publicity. It could not have been on the nature of the crime because of the unwillingness of Canadian courts to allow prospective jurors to be questioned about their attitudes towards certain crimes.[101] The failure of either the prosecutor or the accused to seek permission from the judge on the basis that there was a realistic possibility of bias seems to have been premised on a denial of racism in the face of much evidence to the contrary. Later in 2018, an Ontario prosecutor, with judicial approval and no challenge from the defence, required prospective jurors to be asked about whether their ability to decide a case impartially would be impaired because a white accused, Peter Khill, was charged with murdering an Indigenous man, Jon Styres. To be sure, such a single question was not a guarantee that racist stereotypes relating Indigenous people to theft and violence would play no role in the jury's deliberations. Nevertheless, even the blunt single question resulted in a few jurors in the Ontario case being excluded from the jury for cause.[102] Not only were there no challenges for cause, but Chief Justice Popescul made no reference to pretrial publicity or racism in his generic instructions to the pool of prospective jurors that they must be impartial and not have personal experience with similar crimes or associations with anyone involved in the case. (TT 24–26)

Challenges for Cause in Cases with Indigenous Accused and Victims

Since its 1998 decision in R. v. Williams, the Supreme Court has recognized the need to ask prospective jurors whether racial prejudice against an Indigenous accused would influence their deliberations.[103] This decision was immediately applied in Saskatchewan with one judge, after hearing expert evidence, concluding, "Widespread anti-aboriginal racism is a grim reality" that exists both "openly and blatantly in attitudes and actions of individuals" but also "privately in the fears, in the prejudices and stereotypes held by many people."[104] In 2003, the Saskatchewan Court of Appeal stressed the importance of such questions in ensuring the fairness of a trial of an Indigenous accused before a jury without Indigenous people in Estevan.[105] As Victor Williams, the Indigenous accused in the Supreme Court's landmark 1998 case stated, his lawyers had explained that it was very unlikely that any Indigenous person would be on his jury, but he hoped that "the 12 people that try me are not Indian haters."[106]

The Supreme Court has stated that asking questions about racial bias "eliminates from the panel potential jurors who cannot, in good conscience and under oath, give a negative answer to the question. It also brings home to the other jurors the potentially insidious effect of racial stereotyping and, thirdly, it provides the accused (and members of visible minorities generally) palpable assurance that the law takes seriously the overriding objective of empanelling an impartial jury."[107] Such goals of non-discriminatory and impartial justice are important. They were not achieved in the Stanley case where the question was not asked of prospective jurors.

There are legitimate concerns that the single question approved twenty years ago in Williams and based on a question first approved over twenty-five years ago[108] may not be sufficient to reveal deep-seated racist stereotypes and implicit bias.[109] One of the reasons why defence counsel have frequently defended peremptory challenges is that they can be exercised after an unsuccessful challenge for cause including ones where prospective jurors quickly deny that they would be affected by the race of the accused or the victim. Defence lawyers have been frustrated by the restraints that judges often place on their questioning of prospective jurors. This underlines the need to understand how the various parts of jury selection interact with each other.

The Supreme Court has denied challenges for cause on the basis of concerns about the nature of the crime alleged in a sexual assault case[110] and on the basis that the victim was East Indian.[111] The latter case, however, allowed questions about racist bias with respect to an African Canadian accused. In other words, the issue of possible racism was already being aired and the Court held it was a matter of judicial discretion whether the questions for possible bias referred to the interracial nature of the crime.[112] That case did not involve the long history of racial tensions presented by having a white accused and an Indigenous victim as in the Stanley/Boushie case. Nevertheless, it confirms how courts have tended to be conservative and concerned that allowing more questions might lengthen jury selection, invade juror privacy, and bring Canadian jury selection closer to American practices.[113] Again, this suggests that we should look more to Parliament than the judiciary for reform.

Although most of the focus in the challenge-for-cause jurisprudence has been on the risk of racist discrimination against Indigenous and other racialized accused, many of the same stereotypes about violence and lack of credibility apply in cases with Indigenous victims and witnesses. They can effectively be placed on trial with allegations that they have been involved in criminal conduct and are not as credible as white witnesses. In the Stanley case, it was the prosecutor who had the most incentive to seek judicial permission to challenge prospective jurors for cause on the basis of racist bias.

The Star Light Tour Precedent

The experienced prosecutor and Queen's Counsel in the Stanley case, Bill Burge, had previously encountered issues involving racist bias against crime victims. Over the objections of one of two white police officers charged with the forcible confinement and assault of a Saulteaux man, Darrell Night, in one of Saskatoon's infamous "starlight tour" cases that he prosecuted in 2001, Burge successfully convinced a trial judge in Saskatoon to allow jurors to be questioned about whether their "ability to judge the evidence in this case without bias, prejudice, or partiality be affected by the fact that the persons charged are white and the complainant is aboriginal?"[114]

Like the Stanley case, the Night case was racially charged, where "supporters on each side screamed racial insults at one another." Like the Stanley case, the use of peremptory challenges by the accused police officers resulted in an all-white jury, but the questions asked of each prospective juror when selecting the jury at least attempted to eliminate those who were prepared to admit to racial bias.[115] The Saskatchewan Court of Appeal noted that the challenge for cause, including questions about the accused being white and the victim being Aboriginal, were permissible when it dismissed the officers' appeals from their convictions for forcible confinement of the Indigenous victim. It ruled that the question also helped justify a lack of change of venue from Saskatoon.[116]

*"racism will be at work as soon as the victim
is described as Aboriginal"*[117]

A second precedent that Burge could have relied upon was an Ontario case that allowed the prosecutor to question prospective jurors about racism towards the Indigenous victim on the basis that:

> racism will be at work on the jury panel as soon as the victim is described as an Aboriginal.... I don't agree with defence counsel's submission that the question proposed would be counterproductive because it would inject racial overtones into a case where none previously existed. A question directed at revealing those of the panel whose bias renders them partial does not 'inject' racism into the trial but seeks to prevent that bias from destroying the impartiality of their deliberations.[118]

Stanley's lawyers might have opposed the prosecutor's request to ask prospective jurors about possible racism against Boushie, as did the accused's lawyer in the above Ontario case.

"race has nothing to do with the proper outcome of Gerry's trial."[119]

In a rare public statement shortly before jury selection, Stanley's lawyer, Scott Spencer, argued that "Gerry's trial is not a referendum on racism" and "race has nothing to do with the proper outcome of Gerry's trial."[120] At the same time, he conceded that "racial tensions existed in Saskatchewan, and across Canada, before the Boushie tragedy and they continue today. It will take a lot of time and effort to mitigate those tensions. It is dangerous to deny them, but it is perhaps equally dangerous to allege racism where it does not exist." He added, "It is truly unfortunate that the original narrative set off the vile exchange of uninformed comments, which in many instances were racist. Unfounded declarations of a hate crime and death threats are also serious."[121]

Spencer, on behalf of Stanley, might have objected to the challenge for cause question for injecting race into the case, but his own pretrial comments recognized the racial tensions as well as the extensive, and at times inaccurate, pretrial publicity surrounding the case. It is possible that Stanley and his lawyers might have assumed that their use of fourteen peremptory challenges could ensure an impartial jury. Nevertheless such a strategy, if taken, would have been risky because they would have no basis other than the prospective juror's appearance and address when deciding whether to make a limited number of peremptory challenges. The use of the challenge for cause procedure would have allowed the lawyers to ask prospective jurors judicially approved questions. They also could have asked the last two jurors or triers to exclude any number of prospective jurors on the basis that they were not impartial.

The decision of both Burge, the prosecutor, and Spencer, for Stanley, not to seek to question prospective jurors for a possible challenge for cause is curious. It meant that the issue of racism would remain unspoken in the trial. The failure to seek to ask any questions essentially denied that racism existed and could influence prospective jurors notwithstanding Premier Wall's intervention. Spencer, on behalf of Stanley, had expressed concerns about inaccurate pretrial publicity that was prejudicial to his client. To be sure, asking jurors blunt questions about whether they had made up their minds about the case because of racism or pretrial publicity might not have weeded out all biased jurors, but it would have at least tried.

Prospective Jurors in the Stanley Trial who Volunteer Bias

It is difficult to deny that there was a realistic possibility that racism and pretrial publicity could influence a prospective juror given the lead up to the Stanley trial, including Premier Wall's statement that plenty of racist and hate-filled comments had been made about the case. Such a conclusion is also supported by the fact that a few prospective jurors volunteered that they were biased towards Stanley in the actual jury selection process.

Juror 28 indicated that he or she is a farmer who "had difficulties with theft." (TT 41) Juror 54 stated "that I was raised on a farm just outside of town here." (TT 41) Unfortunately, there is no more detail in the transcript about the nature of the bias. With respect to both jurors 54 and 60, the transcript describes as "indiscernible" additional statements that they apparently made that may have elaborated on the nature of their bias. (TT 35, 54)

In all three cases where prospective jurors indicated that they had some bias, the trial judge did not remove them from the panel of prospective jurors. Rather, Chief Justice Popescul indicated that their bias could be addressed later if the prospective juror was called randomly to serve on the actual twelve-person jury.[122] This is contrary to the practice in the subsequent Ontario trial of Peter Khill, with similar dynamics to the Stanley trial, where the trial judge immediately excused prospective jurors who indicated that they might be biased because they had experienced break-ins.[123]

Fortunately, none of the three prospective jurors who volunteered their concerns about bias were called to serve on the actual jury. Nevertheless, the trial judge's failure to excuse them is troubling, especially when many other prospective jurors were immediately dismissed and removed from the panel after they told the judge that they had planned holidays, or had health concerns, or knew Stanley or Boushie, or were related to RCMP members. The three jurors who volunteered their bias would have remained with the other prospective jurors. The message sent may have been to indicate that such attitudes were not unacceptable or at least not an immediate disqualification from serving on the jury.

Summary

Much more than the failure to challenge likely Indigenous under-representation on the panel of prospective jurors, the failure to question prospective jurors about bias on the basis of racism and pretrial publicity in the Stanley case is disconcerting and even shocking. Prosecutor Bill Burge had convinced a court to allow prospective jurors to be questioned about possible racist bias against an Indigenous victim in a similar racially charged case in 2001. In that case Don Worme, who represented the victim Darrell Night, stated that the jury's conviction of forcible confinement "goes some way to restoring shaken confidence in the justice system generally."[124] The failure to question prospective jurors in the Stanley case about whether they had made up their minds before the trial because of racist prejudice and/or pretrial publicity meant that no similar statements could be made after the Stanley verdict. Although the courts have resisted demands for proportionate or mixed juries, they have prided themselves in their attempts to address racist bias among jurors. In 2005, the Supreme Court confidently declared, "The administration of justice has faced up to the fact that racial prejudice and discrimination are intractable features of our society and must be squarely addressed in the selection of jurors."[125] Such statements ring hollow when applied to the Stanley trial.

PEREMPTORY CHALLENGES

Both Stanley and the prosecutor were entitled to fourteen peremptory challenges. Stanley used thirteen peremptory challenges and the prosecutor used only four. University of Saskatchewan law professor Glen Luther correctly predicted, before jury selection, that it was likely that the accused would use peremptory challenges to exclude Indigenous jurors, but less likely that the prosecutor would use them to exclude non-Indigenous people in an attempt to have Indigenous representation on the jury.[126] This appeared to have happened with Stanley using five peremptory challenges to exclude visibly Indigenous and otherwise qualified prospective jurors.[127] The Stanley trial was added to the significant, but non-official, list of cases decided by all-white juries.

"If it's an all-white jury, I don't think we have a chance"[128]

Boushie's family was dismayed by the jury selection. Colten's mother refused to attend jury selection, but stated, "If it's an all-white jury, I don't think we have a chance."[129] Her statements underlined that the controversial acquittals and manslaughter verdicts by all-white juries in Saskatchewan, discussed in chapter 3, had a lasting impact. The majority of the Supreme Court decided in 2015 that jury selection should not be the vehicle for addressing historical grievances, but its conclusion discounted how some jury verdicts themselves contributed to these grievances.

Jade Tootoosis, Boushie's cousin, commented after the jury selection, "A lot of my family didn't come today because they already felt that a decision had been made and I came with hopes that it would be different. It was really difficult to sit there today and see every single, visible Indigenous person be challenged by the defence. It's not surprising but extremely frustrating and something that we feared would come true."[130] The Boushie family did not have standing in the trial, but they were directly affected by all aspects of it, including jury selection.

Peremptory Challenges and "Unaccountable Prejudices"

Peremptory challenges have long been a feature of British justice. William Blackstone defended them in the eighteenth century on the basis that they demonstrated the concern of English law for the accused and allowed the accused to act upon "sudden impressions and unaccountable prejudices." Quoting Blackstone with approval, the Supreme Court has described peremptory challenges as "purely subjective."[131] In 1982, a judge referred to peremptory challenges as "guess work" noting that they could be used even if the prosecution or the accused could not establish that a prospective juror was not impartial, but because they "may be suspicious of the views of a particular juror because of his or her age, occupation, appearance, place of residence, dress, nationality, race, religion and numerous other reasons."[132]

Peremptory challenges were abolished in England in 1988. Since 1986, the United States Supreme Court has attempted to prevent discriminatory uses of peremptory challenges by the prosecutor,[133] and since 1992, by the accused.[134] The American courts require a neutral non-discriminatory reason for using a challenge, but have often been unsuccessful in preventing the exclusion of African American jurors,[135] except in cases of a clear intent to discriminate.[136]

The Manitoba Aboriginal Justice Inquiry observed three trials in Thompson, Manitoba in 1989 and found that thirty-five of forty-one Aboriginal people called to serve on juries were rejected, often by the prosecutor, but sometimes by the accused.[137] It also documented how the two white men accused of murdering Helen Betty Osborne used six peremptory challenges to exclude all Indigenous people from the jury.[138] The Inquiry recommended that peremptory challenges should be abolished. In his 2013 report, retired Supreme Court Justice Frank Iacobucci warned, "First Nations jury service could still be significantly undermined through discriminatory use of peremptory challenges."[139]

Unsuccessful Challenges to Alleged Discriminatory Peremptory Challenges

A few unsuccessful attempts had been made in Canada to try to control discriminatory uses of peremptory challenges.

In one case, the prosecutor sought to prevent a white accused police officer from using peremptory challenges to challenge prospective jurors who were African Canadian in a case where the victim was African Canadian.[140] The judge noted, "As anyone who lives in the Metropolitan Toronto area well knows, there have been a number of incidents in recent years in which white police officers have shot usually-young Black males, which has caused understandable concern in Toronto's Black community."[141] Nevertheless, the judge decided that the accused's use of peremptory challenges was not subject to the equality rights of the *Charter*. Consistent with Blackstone's rationale that peremptory challenges primarily offer an adversarial advantage for the accused, the judge concluded, "In a criminal trial the accused is pitted against the state. In my opinion it is fanciful to suggest that in the selection of a jury he doffs his adversarial role and joins with the Crown in some sort of joint and concerted effort to empanel an independent and impartial tribunal."[142] This essentially condoned the race-based use of peremptory challenges by the accused. The accused police officer was acquitted by a jury of eleven white people and one Asian. The peremptory challenge issue was not appealed.[143]

Even trial judges, who have recognized that the prosecutor could challenge discriminatory uses of peremptory challenges by the defence, have concluded that the *Charter* would not assist such challenges. They have also reasoned that the accused's *Charter* right to silence would prevent the court from requiring the defence to justify their use of a peremptory challenge.[144] This is different from the American experience where the accused, like the prosecutor, must provide some non-discriminatory reason for the use of a peremptory challenges when racial discrimination may be in play.

Some courts have indicated that abusive use of peremptory challenges by the prosecution might be reviewable, but have not found such discrimination in cases where it was alleged.[145] The Supreme Court avoided the issue in a 1995 case where a prosecutor used a form of peremptory challenge to keep all males off the jury.[146] The courts subsequently rejected an allegation that the prosecutor had engaged in a discriminatory use of a peremptory challenge in a Yukon case, but the press reported that the prosecutor had explained he challenged the prospective juror, not because he was Indigenous, but because he worked for an Indigenous band.[147] This underlines the scepticism that often accompanies attempts to regulate discriminatory uses of peremptory challenges. It casts doubt on whether legislation that attempted to stop the discriminatory use of peremptory challenge would actually be effective.[148]

Also, the limited Saskatchewan experience does not suggest that challenges to discriminatory uses of peremptory challenges would likely have been successful. After Stony Lee Cyr lost his Treaty and *Charter* challenges to Indigenous under-representation on a Regina jury, his lawyer complained to the press that when "the opportunity came for a clearly aboriginal person to sit on the jury, the Crown chose to exercise their challenge." The Crown prosecutor replied that there were many reasons for using peremptory challenges, including criminal history, and that a person was not a right fit for the case. This demonstrates the range of excuses that can be made for the exclusion of Indigenous people and others from the jury. The forensic difficulties of proving a discriminatory use of a peremptory challenge were also underlined by the prosecutor's statements: "I don't even remember who I peremptorily challenged" and "it's difficult to say, based solely on last name or physical appearance, whether or not people are aboriginal."[149]

The trial judge declared a mistrial the next day, not on the basis of the prosecutor's alleged use of peremptory challenges to exclude an

Indigenous juror or that the aid and assistance clause of the Treaty prohibited First Nation persons being "shut ... out of the criminal justice process,"[150] but on the basis that the defence counsel's comments "strike to the very heart of the jury system as they imply that Mr Cyr cannot receive a fair trial based on the ancestry of the jurors which have been selected."[151] The judiciary's defensiveness about juries again resurfaced. No attempt was made in court to challenge what the accused alleged was a discriminatory peremptory challenge of an Indigenous prospective juror.

If the prosecutor had challenged the accused's use of peremptory challenges to exclude visibly Indigenous jurors in the Stanley trial, he might have faced an arduous task. We will never know, because the prosecutor made no objection as the accused used peremptory challenges to keep five visibly Indigenous persons, as well as seven other persons, off the Stanley jury. The trial judge was also passive in the face of these peremptory challenges and did not raise the issue on his own initiative.

"Do not take it personally. It is a normal part
of these types of trials."[152]

Chief Justice Popescul explained the peremptory challenge to the jurors with the following standard explanation:

> I want to stress to you that in exercising a right of challenge, the Crown and the accused are in no way casting any reflection upon the individual concerned, and such individual ought not feel embarrassed. Counsel know the type of case to be tried and from experience decide the type of person who would be best suited to be a juror in this case. A juror in one type of case may, for any number of reasons, be more suited for one type of case and less suited for another. This is why our *Criminal Code* provides for this procedure. (TT 60)

The judge seemed to anticipate that the peremptory challenge process might cause some offence, but reiterated, "Again, when the Crown and the defence use their rights that our law has given them to challenge jurors, they do not mean to offend anyone. Do not feel embarrassed if you are not selected. Do not take it personally. It is a normal part of these types of trials." (TT 60)

The idea that the parties have a "right" to use peremptory challenges suggests that an objection by one of the lawyers to the way that the other exercised their peremptory challenge might not have been viewed favourably. It is not clear that the prosecutor could have relied on the *Charter* to challenge discriminatory use of peremptory challenges by the accused or that the judge could require Stanley to justify his use of peremptory challenges.

Chief Justice Popescul's explanation of the peremptory challenge process was "colour blind." Nevertheless, it seemed to suggest that prospective jurors should not take their challenge "personally" or take offence by a process that, almost by definition, would be based on their appearance, including the colour of their skin. Nothing was said about race, but race and presumptions about Indigenous people were very much in play.

CONCLUSION

It is likely that Indigenous people were under-represented among those who showed up as prospective jurors for the Stanley trial. Saskatchewan had summoned about 750 people for the trial, but only 178 people were available for jury duty. (TT 1–19) Indigenous people were more likely to have been excused because of hardship, language, travel and accommodation difficulties, and past criminal sentences. They also were more likely simply to ignore demands that they participate in a justice system that fails them and their families, as seen in Indigenous over-representation among prisoners and crime victims, and that often excludes them from jury service through peremptory challenges without explaining why.

Given decisions by a Saskatchewan court in 2014 and the Supreme Court in 2015, a challenge by the prosecutor in the Stanley case that Indigenous people were under-represented among the panel of prospective jurors would, unfortunately, have been futile. The judiciary has rejected almost every reported challenge to Indigenous under-representation, often in defensive tones. They have been quick to depict such challenges as raising the spectre of demands that every group be perfectly and proportionally represented without giving due consideration to the unique experience of Indigenous people and their Treaty and Aboriginal rights.

Despite all of the above challenges to Indigenous people serving on juries, we do know, from reading press reports and the transcript, that at least twenty Indigenous persons, and perhaps more, were among the panel of prospective jurors assembled on 29 January 2018. We know that some of them were excused by the trial judge for hardship reasons and three were excused because they were related to Boushie. Five, however, were kept off the jury by Stanley's use of peremptory challenges. The jury selection process resulted in the selection of an all-white jury. The discriminatory use of peremptory challenges without objection from the prosecutor or trial judge understandably dismayed the Boushie family. It created a national controversy that, as will be examined in chapter 9, has resulted in Bill C-75 being introduced in Parliament to abolish peremptory challenges.

All prospective jurors should have been questioned about whether racist bias and pretrial publicity would prevent them from deciding the case on the merits. The prosecutor, Bill Burge, had convinced a judge to ask similar questions of prospective jurors in a similar case arising from the forcible confinement of an Indigenous victim as part of the Saskatoon's police infamous "starlight tours." It is difficult to understand why Burge did not attempt to persuade the trial judge to allow similar questions in the Stanley case. He could have asked the trial judge to take notice of Premier Brad Wall's extraordinary plea to his fellow citizens to stop engaging in racist social media posts about the case and to the extensive, and often inaccurate, pre-trial publicity in the case that Chief Justice Popescul had already cited as a reason not to allow cameras in the courtroom.[153] Three prospective jurors volunteered that they were biased in favour of the accused, but the trial judge did not immediately exclude them though none of the three sat on the actual jury.

Allowing questions of prospective jurors might have kept some self-admitted racists off the jury. A fuller list of questions, including less confrontational questions designed to elicit whether people subscribed to stereotypes associating Indigenous people with theft, violence, and lies, might have excluded more people. Such questions also may have sensitized the remaining jurors not to rely on such stereotypes to fill in gaps or to make inferences from the evidence they heard. Whether it would have made a difference in the verdict is impossible to determine. It would have, however, made clear that racist assumptions were illegitimate and should not be used in the trial process. Instead, the jury selection process in the Stanley case remained silent about race and racism even while it excluded five Indigenous people that had come to serve on the jury and were called to sit on the jury.

It would be unfair to blame the individual jurors who served on the Stanley jury for performing their difficult duties. They are legally prohibited from explaining their verdict and defending themselves. Nevertheless, the jury should have been selected differently. At a minimum, all prospective jurors should have been questioned as to whether pretrial publicity and racist bias would make it impossible to judge the case impartially. Stanley should not have been able to use peremptory challenges to exclude the five visibly Indigenous persons who were called to serve on his jury.

This chapter has raised the possibility of a more radical approach to jury selection, one that has precedents in both the common law and Canadian criminal law. Mixed juries of citizens and non-citizens were used for centuries under English common law and mixed juries of French and English speakers were long used in Quebec and Manitoba. The use of mixed juries might have made a difference in perceptions, if not the result, of Louis Riel's trial. An accused in Saskatchewan argued in 2014 that a mixed jury of six Indigenous and six non-Indigenous people was required by the aid and assistance clause found in both Treaty 4 and Treaty 6. If mixed juries had been accepted as a Treaty right, they should apply if the victim and not just the accused was Indigenous. This is especially so given the apparent desire of both sides of Treaty negotiations to avoid the American experience where juries had refused to convict white men of killing Indigenous people as discussed in chapter 2.

If the 2014 argument had been accepted, it would have given mixed juries of six Indigenous and six non-Indigenous jurors a constitutional status as a Treaty right that could not be overwhelmed by the Supreme Court's insistence that all prospective jurors be treated the same under principles of random selection. The Saskatchewan court, however, rejected such an argument. A mixed jury would have ensured that different perspectives were brought to bear on many of the issues raised at trial including Stanley's attack on the credibility of the Indigenous witnesses and his implicit rural crime appeal to self-defence and defence of property. This was not to be. The case would be decided by an all-white jury even though five visibly Indigenous people were called and prepared to serve as jurors. The unfair jury selection process in the Stanley case greatly aggravated the racial polarization that had beset the Stanley/Boushie case from the start.

6

Hang Fire?

INTRODUCTION

Other than jury selection, the most controversial part of the Stanley trial was the defence's theory that the shot that killed Boushie was a hang fire: an event in which there is a delay between the pulling of the trigger and the bullet exiting the gun. It is easy to be sceptical of the argument and dismiss this as a "magic gun" theory.[1] Nevertheless, the jury heard both expert and lay testimony that while hang fires are rare, they are possible. They are more possible if, as in the Stanley case, an old gun and old ammunition is used. The occurrence of hang fire and some malfunctioning of Stanley's old revolver, might also help explain why a cartridge from the bullet that killed Boushie had an unusual bulge. (TT 468, 578) The jury was also correctly instructed to give Stanley the benefit of a reasonable doubt. (TT 880–1)

The hang fire issue provides an opportunity to examine the Stanley trial in light of our growing knowledge about the role that expert and forensic evidence has played in wrongful convictions.[2] Although the justice system prioritizes the prevention of wrongful convictions, reasonable steps should be taken to avoid all justice errors. The inquiry into the shooting of Leo Lachance bemoaned the fact that additional forensic testing did not determine if Nerland shot Lachance while he was in the pawn shop, which would have suggested intent, or outside the pawn shop, which would be more consistent with Nerland's claim of accident.[3]

Canadians first became alive to forensic error when hair and fibre comparison evidence was found to have contributed to Guy Paul Morin's wrongful conviction. Fortunately, DNA testing was available to overturn the wrongful conviction. In most cases, the forensic science used in criminal trials, like the gun evidence presented in the Stanley trial, will not have the scientific pedigree of DNA. The Morin inquiry recommended that forensic experts use published research with more care, and employ quality control both with respect to their testing of material and the communication to judges and juries of their findings.[4]

Despite these recommendations, Ontario subsequently experienced a series of wrongful convictions, disproportionately involving Indigenous people, when pathologist Charles Smith testified that children died from unnatural causes, evidence that was subsequently found to be erroneous when it was reviewed by better trained forensic pathologists who, unlike Smith, did not believe that the job of an expert witness was to support the case of the party that called the witness. Justice Stephen Goudge, in his subsequent review of forensic pathology, suggested that trial judges should be stricter in qualifying and confining expert witnesses to their area of expertise and that expert witnesses should be better informed about their duty to be impartial and not provide opinions that were not supported by their scientific expertise.[5] He also recommended that more funding, research, quality control, and care be devoted to how scientific findings are communicated to judges and juries. He noted the importance of ensuring that proper death investigations were available in remote areas and for First Nations, and that steps be taken to ensure that both sides in the adversarial system had sufficient resources, knowledge and skills to call and challenge expert evidence.[6] Justice Goudge's findings also built on other reports that suggested that the scientific basis for much forensic evidence that is the bread and butter of criminal courts – fingerprints, fire analysis, ballistics and gun analysis – lack a rigorous scientific basis in research, peer review, quality control, and other tests to determine their reliability.[7]

The expert witnesses in the Stanley case seemed to have heeded the lessons of the Goudge commission. They did not act like "hired guns" for the side that called them. Although they were quickly qualified as experts without precise definition of their areas of expertise (TT 456, 551), neither expert did what Smith did by offering opinion evidence outside of their areas of expertise. Both experts appeared to have followed the scientific method by proposing various hypotheses to explain the physical evidence of the bulged cartridge. They also conducted experiments on weapons, including Stanley's pistol. In the end, neither expert would offer a definitive opinion about what caused the bulge or whether a hang fire occurred in the particular case. Their modesty followed best practices in forensic science. At the same time, however, it also left the jury with limited help in deciding the complicated hang fire issue.

A critical issue on the facts as presented at the Stanley trial was the possible length of a delay between pulling the trigger and the discharge of a bullet. The prosecution's expert testified, based on research which he consulted and brought to trial, that the delay between pulling a trigger and a hang fire bullet exiting a gun is about a "half second at most." (TT 519) The trial judge allowed, without objection from the prosecutor, two lay witnesses to provide anecdotal evidence about their experiences with longer hang fires. Moreover, he allowed both a lay witness and the defence expert to testify and introduce as evidence safety guidelines that guns should be held in a safe position for thirty to sixty seconds after last pulling a trigger. These guidelines might be justified as a safety precaution, but they had no scientific basis in the admittedly scant literature on the length of observed hang fires including the two articles that were the basis of the prosecution's expert opinion. These articles measured delays between the pulling of the trigger and the discharge of the bullet in hang fires as less than half a second. The prosecution's expert brought these articles to trial but, unlike the safety guidelines, these were not admitted as evidence in the trial.

We may never know whether the jury accepted or had a reasonable doubt about Stanley's hang fire defence and, if so, whether they thought that the delay in a hang fire could be as long as thirty to sixty seconds. The danger is that they conflated the issue of safety precautions taken in light of hang fires and the available information about the actual length of delay between pulling a trigger and a delayed discharge of a bullet from a gun. Such a mistake should have been avoided. It was similar to a distinction that the Supreme Court has drawn between practices that may be perfectly acceptable in the clinical treatment of a person but which neither the prosecution[8] or the defence[9] should be able to use in court for the very different forensic purposes of establishing facts in a court of law.

THE TIME LINE FOR THE HANG FIRE DEFENCE

It was generally accepted that hang fires rarely occur, but may be more likely when old ammunition was used. Assuming that the jury would give Gerald Stanley the benefit of a reasonable doubt about whether a hang fire was possible, the focus in this chapter will be on evidence that the jury heard, and that was readily available to it, concerning the length of the delay between the pulling of a trigger as an intentional act and the delayed discharge of a bullet from a gun as a possible accidental act.

Sheldon Stanley's Testimony

Sheldon Stanley testified that after he hit the windshield of the grey Escape with a hammer, and it collided with the Stanley's blue Escape, he went into the house to retrieve the keys for his truck. He testified, "As I went into the house, I could hear a second shot. I went into the house grabbed my keys, came back out ... I could see my father walk up – walking up beside – the grey Escape.... When – as I came back down the stairs, I remember looking into the back seat again and then back towards my truck, thinking that I needed to – to get to it still. And that's when I heard a third shot." (TT 258)

At the preliminary inquiry, he testified that he heard two shots as he was climbing the stairs to enter the house (PT 73, 76) and that there were "four or five seconds" between seeing his father "walking up the side" (PT 78) of the grey Escape and hearing the third fatal shot. Because he heard the first two shots before or while he was in the house, and because Gerald Stanley testified he stopped pulling the trigger shortly after the two warning shots, this would support the existence of a hang fire delay between his father's pulling the trigger for the first shots and the third shot of significantly longer than four to five seconds.

Gerald Stanley's Testimony: "boom, this thing just went off"[10]

Gerald Stanley testified at trial that he fired two warning shots "straight up" into the air, pulling the trigger "two or three times." (TT 691) He said he "brought the gun down. And the barrel was sticking out the end, as if it was empty.... As it has a hundred times before," (TT 693) and that he took the clip and magazine out of the pistol.

Stanley estimated that the grey Escape that contained Boushie and his friends came to a stop "twenty feet or more" from the blue Escape (TT 720) and on cross-examination extended this to between thirty and twenty-five feet. (TT 726) Stanley also indicated that he had fired the two warning shots while he near his blue Escape. (TT 700) This would mean that he would need time to cover the distance from the blue Escape to the grey Escape.

Stanley testified that he ran from the blue Escape to the front of the grey Escape "in pure terror" because he could not see his wife who had been mowing the lawn. He feared that she had been run over by the grey Escape after it had hit the blue Escape and before it came to a stop. (TT 700) He did not find his wife under the grey Escape, but he said that he feared that the grey Escape, which had its engine revving, might run him over. This caused him to go back to the passenger side window of the grey Escape and use his left hand to try to turn the ignition off while his right hand held the pistol that discharged into the back of Boushie's head. Gerald Stanley testified that his finger was not on the trigger; that he did not point the gun at Boushie and "boom this thing just went off." (TT 700)

Writing in the *Globe and Mail*, University of Saskatchewan criminal law professor Michael Plaxton noted that the prosecutor called the jury's attention to "a possible inconsistency between Mr Stanley's evidence and that of his son: whereas Mr Stanley testified that he 'ran' to the SUV to check on his wife, his son testified only that he walked. That doesn't sound like much of a difference, but it goes to just how much of a delay there was between the trigger-pull and the discharge. Clearly, the jury thought this was significant, since they specifically asked to hear the testimony of both Mr Stanley and his son as to what happened after the warning shots were fired."[11]

The hang fire between Stanley pulling the trigger repeatedly after the second shot and the third shot that killed Boushie was likely more than a few seconds given the distance between the blue Escape and the grey Escape and Gerald Stanley's testimony about the various actions he took, first at the front and then at the passenger side of the grey Escape. A time frame of more than a few seconds is also supported by Sheldon Stanley's testimony about hearing the second shot when he was still in the house (TT 258) or even before he entered the house to retrieve his keys (PT 73, 78) as well as Sheldon Stanley's testimony that he saw his father walking toward the grey Escape. (PT 78) (TT 258) Assuming that the jury gave Stanley the benefit of a reasonable doubt that the rare hang fire occurred, it is difficult to see how a hang fire of less than a half second is consistent with: the amount of distance Gerald Stanley covered; the activity he engaged in after pulling the trigger; Sheldon Stanley's testimony about the delay and Sheldon's own actions between the first two shots and the fatal third shot. If, however, the jury accepted that there could be a thirty to sixty second delay between pulling the trigger and the fatal bullet discharging, the hang fire theory becomes possible.

THE PROSECUTION'S FIREARM EXPERT

The prosecution's firearm expert was Gregory Williams, a civilian employee of the RCMP who works out of Ottawa. Like many who provide expert forensic testimony in criminal cases, he was trained after his undergraduate science physics education through an understudy program. He was qualified by the RCMP in 2014. He had testified in six trials before his testimony in Stanley's trial. (TT 460) Although relatively new at his job, there was much to admire in Williams's work and testimony especially at the trial.

At the preliminary inquiry, Williams explored hang fire as one of five testable hypotheses to explain the bulge in the cartridge found in the car occupied by Boushie. He noted that Stanley had used "old ammunition" (PT 379) that could have "malfunctioned in a way that's called a hang fire, what happens in a hang fire is the firing pin falls against the primer, but the primer doesn't explode like it normally would. Instead there's a delayed fire, and so in firearm safety training, when you take that course, they'll tell you if ever you fire, if you pull the trigger of the gun and it goes click, if it doesn't go bang, you should keep the gun pointed in a safe direction for about thirty seconds or a minute in case there's a hang fire, in case there's a delayed fire." (PT 353–4) At one level this was an admirably clear explanation of a concept that would be difficult for a lay audience, especially one that was not familiar with guns, to understand. On the other hand, Williams's reference to the thirty to sixty second waiting period, after clicking the trigger, falls into a trap, one that Williams would not repeat at trial, but others would, of conflating safety measures with available scientific evidence about the length of hang fires.

"hang fire ... doesn't go off in that first minute? A. Right"[12]

Williams testified that he had experienced misfires, in which no bullet exited the gun, when testing Stanley's pistol, but no delayed discharges or hang fires. Stanley's lawyer, Scott Spencer, asked how long Williams had waited between the misfire and unlocking the gun and Williams replied thirty seconds. Spencer then asked, "And as I understand it, the firearms training says you should wait for a minute to be certain that you do not have a hang fire?" (PT 366) Williams agreed with this proposition. Spencer repeated the question asking, "Am I right that a hang fire is as simple as I pulled the trigger, it doesn't go off, and then sometime in the next thirty seconds directly it does fire?" Williams replied, "Yes, that's a hang fire," (PT 373) seemingly accepting the thirty-second premise. Spencer pushed the timeline in a subsequent question asking, "Basically the only difference between the defective and hang fire, the misfire and hang fire, is that it doesn't go off in that first minute? A. Right." (PT 381) Given Spencer's knowledge of the testimony that Stanley and his son would provide about the chain of events, it seemed important to him to extend the hang fire delay as long as possible.

"it's not a long time. You click and then bang, not a ten-second and not a twenty-second delay, but less than half a second"[13]

Spencer had signalled his interest in a hang fire defence at the preliminary inquiry and Williams, to his credit, conducted additional research on hang fires before the trial. He read and brought to court two articles. Williams testified at trial that "based on what I've read, I would say the upper limit of that would be – to be generous, half a second … half a second at the most." (TT 519) He added that "it's not a long time. You click and then bang, not a ten-second and not a twenty-second delay, but less than half a second." (TT 474)

THE 1971 AND 1991 ARTICLES

Williams based his opinion on the length of hang fires on two articles that he had researched. He told the court, "I don't want to delay the proceedings, but if it would be useful for the – for the jury or the Court, I can provide these to have copies." (TT 529) Unfortunately, this offer was not taken up.

Could the 1971 and 1991 articles that Williams brought to court have been admitted as evidence? Even under restrictive approaches to such evidence, Williams could have been asked about the articles to the extent he adopted them as his own opinion evidence.[14] As will be seen, the court accepted without challenge the admission of evidence about the thirty to sixty second hunting and safety guidelines and it might similarly have accepted the two articles as evidence had the prosecutor tried to have them admitted into evidence. In the adversarial system, the court will generally only accept evidence that is offered by the parties. In some of the wrongful convictions caused by Charles Smith, the defence called no expert evidence at trial to challenge Smith's testimony. This failure to call evidence meant the court had no other scientific basis on to which to base its verdict. These wrongful convictions were subsequently shown to be erroneous when more evidence was obtained years later. We will never know what effect the two articles that Williams brought to court might have had on the jury because they were never accepted as evidence and exhibits for them to consider. As will be seen below, however, a hunting safety guide with the scientifically dubious thirty to sixty second safety guideline was accepted as evidence and an exhibit that the jury could consider. (TT 628)

The two articles that Williams had were dated and published in trade or guild journals that are typical of the under-developed science that exists behind most forensic sciences including gun analysis. They were based on a small sample of induced hang fires. Nevertheless, it is unfortunate that Williams's offer was not taken up because the articles, if read and understood by the jury, or even further explained in Williams's testimony, might have helped the jury understand that the thirty to sixty second safety guidelines that were entered into evidence had no scientific basis in the observed length of hang fires.

The 1971 article was written by Colonel Jim Crossman. It was published in the *American Rifleman* magazine that, since 1916, has been owned and distributed by the National Rifle Association. Given the NRA's primary role as a gun lobby, its magazine is not the optimal venue for vetting and publishing independent scientific research. This reflects a larger problem about the lack of scientific research and traditions of independence and peer review in many of the forensic sciences.

"I never had a 'hang fire' longer than 'click-bang'"[15]

In any event, the Crossman article estimated that most hang fires were forty milliseconds which the author analogized to a click of a camera. Crossman used his own experience and wrote that "over forty years and many millions of rounds," he had three hang fires that he measured at sixty milliseconds. He provided no information about how he measured these hang fires, but concluded, "I never had a hang fire longer than 'click-bang,' which measured at around sixty milliseconds. If the cartridge didn't fire in the 'click-bang' period, then it never did go."[16]

Crossman conducted some experiments in his research for the article. He was able to get more hang fires when he used defective ammunition from the 1940s that misfired more often than not. This was information that, if presented at trial, might have assisted Stanley, though Williams also agreed that hang fires were more likely with old and poorly stored ammunition such as that used by Stanley. There was, however, no evidence presented at the trial or in the published articles about the frequency of hang fires. The jury was simply left with testimony that hang fires were rare or exceedingly rare with no guidance about how they should relate the rarity of hang fires to the reasonable doubt standard.

Crossman measured the hang fires that he induced in an experiment. He wrote, "The longest – 280 ms – is still only about a quarter of a second, which really isn't very long!"[17] Other people quoted in the article also supported the short length of hang fires. One expert was quoted as stating that the "safety precaution" of thirty to sixty seconds, though "not burdensome," was not "based on experience"[18] with actual "hang fires." Another stated that "the practice of waiting fifteen seconds after a misfire is certainly a useless safety precaution, although relatively easy to observe."[19]

"the delays were estimated to be in the order of 1/4 to 1/5 of a second"[20]

The second article was written by Lucien Haag, a frequently published firearms expert. His article was published in the journal of the Association of Firearm and Toolmark Examiners (AFTE), which was founded in 1969. Haag explained that it was useful to study hang fires because the issues were subject to litigation in both civil and criminal cases, the latter in cases such as Stanley's when the accused claimed that a shooting was accidental.

In an attempt to build a research tradition, Haag referenced Crossman's earlier work. Unlike Crossman, he used modern ammunition and not older military ammunition that uses mercury based primers.[21] Haag reported that the hang fires "were all of short duration. The audio recording of these discharges were rerecorded and played back at half speed where, with the aid of a stopwatch, the delays were estimated to be in the order of 1/4 to 1/5 of a second."[22] Haag concluded, "The effective result of this work was a reaffirmation of Col Crossman's observations of twenty years ago.... If that very rare instance of a hang fire does occur, it will be of a very short duration (fractions of a second) and can generally be described as a 'click-boom' event."[23]

Had they been entered as evidence or explained more fully for the jury, the Crossman and Haag articles would have provided evidence that the thirty to sixty second safety guideline that was entered into evidence was not scientifically supported by evidence of the delay between pulling a trigger and a bullet leaving a gun in experimentally induced and observed hang fires.[24]

Law versus Science: "There is a lot of lore about hang fires ...
I wouldn't just trust Wikipedia"[25]

To be sure, the two articles did not reflect a robust or thoroughly scientific research tradition. They did, however, provide some evidence that observed and scientifically measured hang fires are very short, under half a second. The authors of the two articles performed and measured hang fires and Haag tested and examined Crossman's earlier work. There was some modest attempt to follow the scientific method in terms of testing hypotheses and observing experiments.

In his testimony, Williams stated, "There is a lot of lore about hang fires. People have sort of myths of these accounts of hang fires happening at the range ... and I think the best place to look for information on hang fires is scientific research ... I trust the sources I have – I have researched extensively ... I wouldn't trust just Wikipedia or outside sources for a scientific question about an experience." (TT 528) Williams's statement also reflected the idea accepted in both science and the law about the need for proper qualifications and expertise. Such an approach may appear elitist. In any event, it was challenged by Stanley's lawyers who attempted, without success, to cross-examine Williams on the basis of anecdotes about lengthy hang fires taken from posts on the website *Reddit*. As will be seen, however, Stanley had more success calling two lay witnesses to testify about hang fires even though he readily admitted that the two witnesses were not experts. (TT 615, 626)

The prosecutor Burge objected that using the *Reddit* website was "wrong on so many levels." The posts were "irrelevant hearsay that may be totally unreliable." (TT 530) The trial judge sustained the prosecutor's objections, but subsequently allowed Stanley to introduce evidence from two lay witnesses who, like the *Reddit* posters, testified about their past experience with long hang fires. The acceptance of such lay testimony can be seen as a form of populism that is distinct from the elitism of published and peer-reviewed research and expert opinion evidence. Lay testimony may have played better with a Battleford jury than testimony from Williams who was a qualified expert from Ottawa. (TT 456–57)

The acceptance of the lay testimony was also related to the lack of objection from the prosecutor and the tendency for trial judges to err on the side of the accused in order not to provide unnecessary grounds of appeal in the event of a conviction. The legal difference between the *Reddit* posts and the lay testimony was that Burge could cross-examine the two lay witnesses but not the *Reddit* posters. As will be seen, the cross-examination, in one instance about a forty-year-old hang fire, was, understandably, not particularly illuminating. From a scientific perspective, the added safeguard of being able to question the two lay witnesses was of dubious value: they both testified about one-off events and self-measurements of hang fires that could not be replicated.

THE DEFENCE FIREARM EXPERT

The defence's firearm expert was John "Sandy" Ervin. Like the prosecutor's expert, Ervin worked for the RCMP, but as a firearm instructor where he had thirty years' experience. Like Williams, Ervin conducted a number of tests on Stanley's pistol when it was made available to him under court order. Unlike Williams, he was able to produce hang fires, but ones that produced a slower exit of the bullet from the gun that produced no bang or "sonic crack." (TT 580) This was at odds with the evidence of the witnesses who all heard three shots (Belinda Jackson said there were four shots) and in tension with Stanley's testimony that he used the Tokarev pistol, in part, because it was "super loud" (TT 662) and helped scare coyotes away from his calves.

Ervin seemed to agree with Williams on most of the issues. He agreed that the bulge in the cartridge was likely a result of the bullet discharging partly out of the battery in the sense that the bullet was only partially in the pistol's chamber and the slide on the pistol was not locked. (TT 495, 578) Similar to Williams, he testified that, "It is my experience that hang fires are extremely rare and usually occur within seconds of the initial strike of the primer." (TT 579) The reference to "within seconds" was somewhat longer that Williams's testimony based on the literature of less than half a second even though Williams himself had doubled the time observed in the two articles.

"you can't ask the witness to guess"[26]

Spencer attempted to ask his expert Ervin to provide an opinion about a maximum hang fire. Prosecutor Burge objected that Spencer was simply trying another route to introduce the anecdotes from *Reddit* about long delays in hang fires that the judge had disallowed. The judge was sympathetic to the objection and told Spencer "you can't ask the witness to guess." Spencer then issued a revealing reply, "Well, but that's an opinion though." (TT 588)

Ervin's refusal to speculate about a maximum length of a hang fire was appropriate because he did not have information to support his opinion. Burge, the prosecutor, indicated that he had an objection and that the jury should leave. (TT 586) Chief Justice Popescul warned Spencer that he needed to lay an evidential and factual foundation for Ervin's opinion at the risk of the judge telling the jury to disregard or give less weight to Ervin's opinion evidence. (TT 589) This approach followed the increased attention paid in Canadian evidence law to the need for experts to support their opinions. It was consistent with best legal practices. But, as will be seen, both Ervin's and the trial judge's actions may have had counter-productive effects that may have left the jury confused about a central issue in the trial.

"that's the training. That's what we teach"[27]

In order to provide a basis for his expert's opinion about the length of hang fires, immediately after the jury returned, Spencer elicited evidence from Ervin about the thirty to sixty second safety guidelines as a basis for his expert opinion. (TT 590–591) This was an opinion that Ervin, as a firearms instructor, was amply qualified to give. The problem, however, was that the safety standard was just that: a precautionary standard that, as the articles that Williams brought to court revealed, had absolutely no scientific support in actual observed and measured lengths of hang fires.

Ervin's evidence was presented to the jury in a way that could have allowed them to conclude that hang fires of between thirty and sixty seconds were possible, perhaps even probable, if they were basis for safety guidelines promulgated by the government and observed by the RCMP. This danger is revealed by the following exchange between Spencer and Ervin:

Q: And, the – basically, it could still go off after a minute?
A: Yeah, it would be rare, but that's –
Q: – But –
A: – that's the training. That's what we teach. (TT 590)

Ervin's reply attempted to relate the sixty second range to "the training" or what Ervin described, on cross examination, as a "common rule of thumb." (TT 591) At the same time, however, Ervin could be understood by the jury as saying that a hang fire of sixty seconds "would be rare." (TT 590) But there was no evidence from Ervin or from Williams, or even from the two lay witnesses, that a thirty to sixty second hang fire delay between pulling a trigger and a bullet discharging was even possible though it might come closer to fitting the time frame provided by the testimony of Sheldon and Gerald Stanley. Spencer had gotten what he wanted from his expert. He abruptly stopped his examination within minutes of Ervin retaking the witness stand and the jury's return after the prosecution's objection. (TT 591)

Neither the prosecution or defence expert fit into the stereotype of the expert witness as a partisan gun-for-hire or as one who was prepared to go beyond their areas of expertise. At the same time, their appropriate modesty about the limited forensic science research on hang fires created a gap in the jury's knowledge. That gap may have been filled by both expert and lay testimony about the thirty to sixty second safety measure even though that standard was designed for a very different purpose and had no scientific support based on experimentally induced and recorded hang fires.

THE LAY WITNESSES

Two witnesses were allowed to provide testimony about their own personal experience with hang fires without formal objection from the prosecutor or the trial judge. They testified about their one-off and self-measured experience with longer hang fires of between seven and twelve seconds. This essentially allowed anecdotes, similar to those found on the *Reddit* website, to go before the jury, but with the important legal (but not scientific) difference that the prosecutor had an opportunity to cross-examine the lay witnesses.

Even more dangerously, the second lay witness was allowed to enter, as an exhibit, a hunting safety booklet that contained the thirty to sixty second safety guideline for hang fires. This focused the jury's attention on the longer times used for safety reasons compared to the much shorter delays that both experts had testified about and were scientifically measured in the two articles.

"because I knew I was going to be here today, I took the stop watch on my phone ... it was about ten to twelve [seconds] every time I did it"[28]

The first lay witness to testify was Wayne Popowich. Had the trial not been about such a serious and sad matter, his testimony might have provided comic relief. After saying he did not know Stanley, Popowich explained:

> Well, Saturday morning, I was having coffee at the kitchen table, reading the news, talking on the phone with my girlfriend, and just making small talk about the news. And I saw this gun expert evidence. There was a little news blurb there, and I was reading it through and I told her – I said, you know, I don't agree with this one statement the gun expert said, you know, a delayed fire couldn't cause a bulge in a cartridge. (TT 615)

Popowich went on testify that forty years ago, when he was "hunting gophers at the family farm south of Wynyard," he had a hang fire with his .22-rifle so that "bang, it went off. And my eyes were burning. My ears were ringing." (TT 616)

Spencer then asked him the critical question of how long the hang fire was and Popowich replied:

> Well, because I knew I was going to be here today, I took the stop watch on my phone, and I'd say from the first click, the very first click to the second time I pulled the firing pin, would be about seven or eight seconds ... then I did it again a few times from the second click to putting the gun down, getting the bullet,

and then pulling. And it was about ten to twelve every time I did it. (TT 616)

This is astounding testimony based on a forty-year recollection. It was a self-experiment with Popowich's memory and his stop watch. If accepted, it would have given the jury a sense that the delay between pulling a trigger and the discharge of the bullet could be between ten to twelve seconds.

The prosecutor did not object to the admissibility of Popowich's testimony which the defence readily admitted was not expert evidence and, in some respects, seemed more suited to a radio call-in show or *Reddit* than a court of law. Popowich was a surprise witness to the prosecution and the trial judge gave Burge a fifteen-minute break to prepare for cross-examination. (TT 616)

Burge then asked Popowich about the possibility that the gun or the ammunition was defective. He did not, however, question Popowich about how, over the weekend, he had apparently measured his forty-year-old hang fire at ten to twelve seconds. He also did not confront Popowich with Williams's expert testimony that measured experimental hang fires as less than half a second or compare Popowich's lack of expertise with those of the prosecution or defence experts. Popowich explained he was not familiar with guns and it was "just – like I said, .22 on the family farm" to which Burge replied, "Yeah – I – I – got you, sir." (TT 621)

"maintain muzzle control in a safe direction for at least 60 seconds."[29]

The second lay witness was Nathan Voinorosky. The trial judge raised the possibility of a challenge to the admissibility of his testimony by asking whether the jury should be removed, something that would happen before a formal hearing about whether the jury should hear his testimony. This had happened when Burge objected to attempts to have Ervin testify about the maximum length of a hang fire. With Voinorosky, however, prosecutor Burge did not make a formal objection instead stating, "Well, I guess we'll see where it goes, but I have – I'm starting to have some real concern." (TT 625) The prosecutor and the judge might have both been reluctant to exclude the testimony because it could give Stanley grounds for appeal if he was convicted.

Like Popowich, Voinorosky was also allowed to testify about his own experience with hang fire. He testified that he had experienced one "of approximately seven seconds" (TT 628) when he was using surplus ammunition with a semi-automatic rifle. This was quite similar to the information about one-off experiences with hang fires posted on *Reddit* that the trial judge had disallowed. The critical legal difference, however, was that Voinorosky was present in court and could be cross-examined. Again, however, the prosecutor only briefly cross-examined him without exploring how Voinorosky had measured the length of his hang fire.

As with Popowich, the defence readily admitted that Voinorosky was not an expert. He had learned about hang fires through a hunting safety course offered by the Wildlife Federation of Saskatchewan. Voinorosky read from a 2007 hunting safety book that noted that because hang fires can occur people should, after pulling a trigger, "maintain muzzle control in a safe direction for at least sixty seconds." (TT 626) In some respects, this was even better for Stanley than Ervin's testimony about the thirty to sixty second safety guideline because it could be interpreted as suggesting that sixty seconds was a minimum time. It may have left the jury with the impression that there could be a delay of more than sixty seconds between pulling a trigger and a bullet exiting a gun in a hang fire.

The prosecutor consented to entering the safety manual as an exhibit. (TT 628) The acceptance of this material as an exhibit demonstrates the same confusion discussed above between using knowledge for safety purposes, where the sixty second guideline may be justified, and using it for the very different purposes of trying to establish the length of a hang fire in the Stanley case. The Supreme Court has recognized a similar distinction in a number of leading evidence cases. These cases stress that just because techniques like hypnosis and penile measurement are used as forms of clinical treatment does not mean that they are reliable enough to be used as evidence either for the accused[30] or the prosecutor[31] to establish critical facts in criminal trials. They could have provided a basis for an objection to the introduction of evidence about the thirty to sixty second safety guideline.

CLOSING ARGUMENTS

*"We don't know how long. We know the
rule is thirty to sixty seconds."*[32]

In his opening address, Scott Spencer argued for Stanley that the shooting was "a freak accident. "Hang fires happen." He added, "That's why the guide book for hunting says you wait thirty seconds after a misfire in case it's a hang fire I think it says a minimum of thirty seconds. Sixty seconds – which is the testimony you heard – sixty seconds for a handgun. That's the reality. Hang fires happen. And that's what happened here." (TT 608)

In his closing address, Spencer repeated, "We don't know how long. We know the rule is thirty to sixty seconds." (TT 846) He then characterized Williams's testimony about duration of "split seconds" as "minimums." (TT 846) He added, "I would have liked the experts to come here and tell you exactly what happened. We don't know. We are never going to know." (TT 845) This invited the jury to fill the gaps in the expert and scientific evidence with their own inferences and perhaps also with the thirty to sixty second safety guideline.

In his closing address, Burge for the prosecution did not take the hang fire theory on except to note they are "extremely rare" (TT 860) and that "my friend said to you that both of the experts thought hang fires were – were – might – have been the explanation for this. Ladies and gentlemen, that's not my recollection. I ask you to please think about what you heard." (TT 865) He did not address the critical issue of length of hang fire or how it fitted into the facts of the case. He did not remind the jury that his own expert's testimony was that the delay between pulling the trigger and a delayed firing of a bullet was "half a second at the most." (TT 519)

Burge devoted a surprising amount of time in his closing address to Wayne Popowich – the gopher hunter of forty years ago – stating, "He pulled the trigger. Nothing happened. He pulled it again. Nothing happened. Then he decided to change the ammunition. He opened the bolt, started to pull it back, and at that point, … the cartridge then discharged, exploded. Caused a lot of grief for him." (TT 864) Burge may have intended this explanation to support his ultimate argument that Stanley pulled the trigger when the gun was in the grey Escape either intentionally or accidentally. (TT 865–6) Nevertheless, it may also have supported any impression the jury might have that there could be a substantial lag between Stanley pulling the trigger and a bullet exiting his handgun into Boushie's head.

Burge argued that Stanley was careless in not knowing how many bullets he had put in the gun; how many times he pulled the trigger; and in the way that he placed the gun in the car. (TT 857) This approach, however, played into arguments that Spencer made that it was not reasonable to expect Gerald Stanley to wait the recommended thirty to sixty seconds when he was faced with a "nightmare situation." (TT 854) The full force that this argument might have had with the jury may not be apparent until the next two chapters discuss how all the Indigenous witnesses were effectively placed on trial for various misdeeds and how implicit self-defence arguments were placed before the jury. With respect to the forensic evidence, Burge's carelessness argument even reminded the jury about the thirty to sixty second guideline (TT 865) and played into Spencer's arguments that it was not reasonable to expect Stanley to abide by safety guidelines in the dire circumstances he faced.

Rather than focus on the hang fire defence, Burge provided the jury with another theory about what happened. He argued Stanley's testimony was "demonstrably untrue" (TT 862) because Stanley's account of how he handled the gun would only make sense if there were no bullets in the pistol. This argument itself was difficult to follow, especially for someone not familiar with the particular gun. As Michael Plaxton has suggested, it may also have "pushed" the jury "into a corner"[33] that pointed towards a second-degree murder conviction, especially given that Stanley's lawyer told the jury "at no point I am going to suggest" that the "intentional use of lethal force" was justified. (TT 838) This raises the uncomfortable issue of possible jury nullification. This occurs when a jury refuses to apply the law to convict the accused because of its own view of the equities of the case.[34] Jury nullification will be discussed again in chapter 8.

Chief Justice Popescul told the jury, "Both experts testified that hang fires are exceedingly rare. Mr Williams testified that the delay in the hang fire would normally be less than half a second." (TT 894) He gave equal time to the two lay witnesses noting that the second had testified that he had experienced a seven second hang fire while using army surplus ammunition. Without distinguishing the forensic issues in the case from the safety issues, he also noted "that government gun safety regulations recommend that after a misfire, one should wait thirty to sixty seconds before extracting a bullet" and that "the publication was filed as a court exhibit." (TT 894) The timeline was left for the jury to decide.

The trial judge presented Williams's testimony of hang fires being under a half a second, the lay evidence of seven-second hang fires, and the safety guideline of thirty to sixty second as all equally valid for the jury to consider, even though only Williams's testimony was based on published research that was available, but alas not entered as evidence. This followed a view of strict judicial neutrality and deference to the jury's role as fact-finder. The judge's instructions, however, left the jury with little to help them distinguish Williams's evidence, which was backed by scientific research from anecdotes, or from a standard developed without a scientific basis for safety rather than forensic purposes.

CONCLUSION

Unless a juror breaches the law by revealing deliberations, we will never know whether the jury thought this was a hang fire case. If they did, we may never know whether they thought that the delay between pulling a trigger and a bullet exiting the gun could be thirty to sixty seconds or whether they thought it would only be half a second as Williams had testified based on the research.

The thirty to sixty second safety guideline received much more air time during the trial than the expert evidence about much shorter delays. This created a risk that the jury might have thought there could have been a thirty to sixty second delay between Stanley pulling the trigger when he fired the first two shots and the third shot killing Colten Boushie. Such an approach would have made it possible for Gerald Stanley to have travelled the distance from his blue Escape to the grey Escape where Boushie was and to have checked for his wife under the grey Escape. The thirty to sixty second safety guidelines might have provided the jury with "an answer for an easy question" without confronting "the difficult question of fact that is before the court," namely whether a hang fire was possible given the timeline suggested by Gerald and Sheldon Stanley's testimony. As Emma Cunliffe has observed, the substitution of readily available answers for easy questions when the court is actually confronted with much more difficult questions of fact may "lead to errors of judgment."[35]

If the two articles that the prosecution expert, Williams, brought to court were entered as evidence or even explained more fully to the jury, it would have been made clear to the jury that the thirty to sixty second safety guideline had no scientific support in observed and measured hang fires, a point that neither the prosecutor or the trial judge made clear to the jury. The safety standard was what the famed film director, Alfred Hitchcock, called a MacGuffin:[36] something that is obvious and attracts attention but is simply not relevant to the more difficult task at hand. The thirty to sixty second safety standard that received so much play at trial, and may have captured the jury's imagination, was not useful for them in deciding whether a hang fire actually occurred and was even possible given the testimony that the jury had heard from Gerald and Sheldon Stanley.

The treatment of the hang fire evidence reveals limitations of the adversarial system as a vehicle to determine the truth. This is also a theme in much of the literature about the causes of wrongful convictions. The articles that Williams relied upon in estimating scientifically measured hang fire delay between pulling the trigger and a bullet discharging were not considered by the jury or the judge because the prosecutor did not attempt to introduce them as evidence. Conversely, lay anecdotes about long hang fire delays were accepted as evidence because the defence introduced them and because the prosecutor was able to cross-examine the witnesses. The jury was a captive of the limited information it received. It was not placed in a position where it could easily assess the lack of a scientific basis for the thirty to sixty second safety guidelines. Stanley understandably made the thirty to sixty second safety guidelines the focus of his hang fire evidence and argument. It was not Stanley's role in an adversarial system to explore whether the safety guidelines had any scientific basis. In other words, any errors that the jury might have made in judging the hang fire issue can be attributed more to the limits of an adversarial system that relies on the parties to present and challenge evidence as opposed to any fault of the jurors.

Concerns generated in the wrongful conviction context about the lack of developed forensic science and its poor communication to legal decision-makers, who are not trained or comfortable in science, may also contribute to other forms of justice error including possible wrongful acquittals. The irony here is that both the prosecution's and the defence's expert witnesses acted appropriately in acknowledging the limits of scientific knowledge about hang fires. In addition, the trial judge acted appropriately in requiring the defence expert to lay a basis for any opinion evidence about the length of hang fires. The problem, however, was that the gap in scientific knowledge may have been filled, not by the modest research contained in the 1971 and 1991 articles and by the prosecution's expert witness's adoption of those articles, but by the thirty to sixty second safety guideline that both the defence expert and one of its lay witnesses testified about despite its lack of a scientific basis in measured hang fires. More scientific evidence might have prevented the jury from potentially conflating the thirty to sixty second safety guideline for holding weapons in a safe position after pulling the trigger with the existing, albeit limited, evidence that hang fires involve only less than a half a second delay. A diligent and attentive jury might have been confused about the difference between these issues that were, unfortunately, never explained to them, but which could have made the difference between an acquittal and a guilty verdict.

Indigenous Witnesses on Trial

INTRODUCTION

As discussed in chapter 5, no effort was made in jury selection to confront the danger that some jurors might be influenced by racist stereotypes about Indigenous victims and witnesses. Stereotypes and possible racism was relevant because Stanley's defence strategy effectively placed all the Indigenous witnesses on trial. Even though their evidence was of minimal relevance to the ultimate issue because they did not see Boushie get killed, much of the testimony of Eric Meechance and Cassidy Cross focused on how much they had been drinking; their knowledge of, and use of, a .22-calibre rifle in the grey Escape; and their actions in relation to vehicles on the Stanley and the neighbouring Fouhy farms. This testimony, along with the entry of their criminal records as evidence, played into anxieties about rural crime and stereotypes relating Indigenous people to alcohol, theft, and danger.

The testimony of Belinda Jackson was critical because she testified, both at the preliminary inquiry and the trial, that she saw Stanley shoot Boushie, twice. The problem was that the physical and autopsy evidence suggested that Boushie was shot only once. Jackson was subject to aggressive cross-examination by Stanley's lawyers. The trial judge and even the prosecutor also expressed concerns that Jackson did not tell the RCMP, when she was detained on 9 August 2016, that she saw Stanley shoot Boushie.

Borrowing again from growing research on wrongful convictions, I will suggest that Meechance, Cross, and Jackson can be understood as incentivized witnesses, defined by the inquiry into

Guy Paul Morin's wrongful conviction as anyone whose statements can be influenced by self-interest or other strong motivations not to tell the full story.[1] The most well-known incentivized witnesses are jailhouse informers who, for example, contributed to about fifteen known wrongful convictions in Canada, including those of Guy Paul Morin and Thomas Sophonow.[2] But an incentivized witness could be anyone under arrest and facing charges, just as Meechance, Cross, and Jackson all were when they gave their initial statements to RCMP. Another important human factor is that they were, in the words of Chief Clinton Wuttunee of the Red Pheasant First Nation, "traumatized beyond belief" by having their friend killed on the Stanley farm.[3]

The way that judges and jurors find facts, including their decisions about who is telling the truth and who is lying, are often critical contributing factors to miscarriages of justice. Comparisons will be made between fact-finding as it related to the credibility of Indigenous witnesses in the Stanley trial and the way that an all-white jury wrongfully convicted a seventeen-year-old Mi'kmaq man, Donald Marshall Jr, of murder in 1971. In this case, a five judge panel of the Nova Scotia Court of Appeal also wrongfully convicted Marshall of robbery and perjury even while it corrected his wrongful murder conviction in 1982. Some comparisons of the fact-finding by courts and inquiries will also be made in the context of Carney Nerland's killing of Leo Lachance discussed in chapter 3.

The treatment of the Indigenous witnesses also raises the question of whether the Canadian legal system can effectively accommodate Indigenous difference. Stanley's lawyers repeatedly suggested that there was something "odd" (TT 319, 413) about the fact that the Indigenous witnesses had spoken to the special investigative unit of the Federation of Sovereign Indigenous Nations (FSIN) after they spoke to the RCMP. Stanley's lawyer appeared to have confronted both Eric Meechance and Belinda Jackson with photos of the dead Colten Boushie, causing them serious distress and violating Cree laws and spirituality. The judge and the lawyers responded compassionately, but did not seem to appreciate why the witnesses may have reacted to the photo as they did. Finally, the trial judge inquired twice about an eagle feather that Indigenous spectators brought to court. (TT 336) On behalf of the jury, he asked Indigenous spectators not to wave the feather at perhaps the most critical juncture of the trial. (TT 704) The Indigenous presence in the courtroom appears to have been approached with, at best, a lack of understanding and, at worst, suspicion.

The Stanley trial was hardly the first time that Indigenous witnesses have been placed on trial in Canadian courtrooms. As Dalhousie Law Professor and Mi'kmaq lawyer Naomi Metallic has written, the Stanley case reminded her of "how Nova Scotia's Donald Marshall Jr, even after the Mi'kmaq man was completely exonerated, was blamed for his own wrongful conviction based on the questionable narrative that he, with a friend, had attempted to rob someone. This view was even shared by the Nova Scotia Court of Appeal, who commented that, "Any miscarriage [in the case was] more apparent than real."[4]

The All-White Marshall Jury: "It was like two dogs in the field"[5]

The Marshall case, like most wrongful convictions, turned more on fact-finding than the law. The all-white jury that wrongfully convicted Marshall of murder in 1971 chose to believe the evidence of three very young witnesses who had been bullied by the police into hesitantly testifying that they saw Marshall stab the victim Sandy Seale. The jury rejected Marshall's testimony that both he and Seale had been stabbed by a stranger they encountered in the park even though Marshall had been stabbed that night and he was the one to call the police.

We will never know how the Marshall jury arrived at their verdict after less than four hours' deliberation.[6] We do know that one of the jurors denied to a reporter that discrimination played any part in the verdict, but then added, "With one redskin and one Negro involved, it was like two dogs in the field – you knew one of them was going to kill another. I would expect more from a white person. We are more civilized."[7] Hopefully this juror did not voice similar vile and racist stereotypes in the jury room, but we will never know for sure. There is no suggestion that racist sentiments were expressed by any of the Stanley jury, but it is sobering that it was fifteen years after the verdict that one of the Marshall jurors revealed his racist thinking to a reporter.

Jury Secrecy and Racism

In 2001, the Supreme Court upheld the secrecy of jury deliberations even after a juror complained that other jurors had made racist comments and that she had been pressured into convicting.[8] Justice Arbour, for the Court, likened the jury deliberations to the reasoning process that judges engage in prior to releasing oral or written reasons explaining their decision, "A judge's written reasons only reveal the judge's ultimate rationale for deciding the case as he or she did. They do not necessarily reveal all the thought processes, the hesitations, the *quaeres* and the revisions leading up to those final written reasons."[9] This case demonstrates the same defensive reaction that Canadian judges have had when juries have been challenged as under-representing Indigenous people and other racialized minorities. As Chief Justice Popescul told the jury, "jurors are judges." (TT 901)

In the above case, the Supreme Court reasoned that there were enough other safeguards that it was not necessary to breach the secrecy of the jury's deliberations. Some of these safeguards – the ability to challenge jurors for cause,[10] and the ability of the accused to appeal a guilty verdict on the basis that it was unreasonable or a miscarriage of justice – were not engaged in the Stanley case. Consistent with feminist critiques of sexual assault prosecutions,[11] the fact-finding process in the criminal trial can be influenced by stereotypes that may relate to the victims or witnesses called by the prosecution. Attempts to increase legal regulation of fact-finding to prohibit stereotypes will be examined in chapter 10.

Fact-Finding by Nova Scotia Judges: "hardly capable of belief"[12]

Fact-finding by judges is more transparent than fact-finding by juries. For example, a Nova Scotia trial judge commented, when acquitting a young African Canadian of assaulting a police officer, that "police officers do overreact, particularly when dealing with non-white groups." The prosecutor challenged this remark, made by Nova Scotia's first African Canadian judge, as raising a reasonable apprehension of bias. The prosecutor lost, but a majority of the Supreme Court judges who heard the case suggested that the judge's remarks were either close to or over-the-line with only four judges being comfortable with the judge using the history of discrimination to assist her determinations of credibility.[13] As a result of this judgment, judges may have become more cautious about explaining how their view of the world shapes their reasoning process. The world view of the judge may still play a role, but, as is the case with juries, it would not be publicly articulated or explained.

In 1982, the Nova Scotia Court of Appeal heard two days of fresh evidence including testimony from Donald Marshall Jr before, with the prosecutor's consent, reversing his wrongful murder conviction. The five judges who sat on the appeal, however, were not done with Marshall. They unanimously concluded, "Marshall's evidence, old and new, if it stood alone, would hardly be capable of belief."[14] They stated Marshall had "committed perjury for which he still could be charged. By lying he helped secure his own conviction.... By planning a robbery with the aid of Mr Seale he triggered a series of events which unfortunately ended in the death of Mr Seale.... There can be no doubt but that Donald Marshall's untruthfulness through this whole affair contributed in large measure to his conviction."[15] They effectively convicted, of robbery and perjury, a man who had served eleven years in jail for a murder he did not commit.

The Court of Appeal did not explain why they thought Marshall was lying, but they were likely influenced by a 1982 statement Marshall made in Dorchester Penitentiary to RCMP officers who told him if he was to "have any hope of getting out of jail, he had better tell the officers a story they could believe; otherwise, they would walk away and he would never see them again."[16] Marshall had been in the high security prison since 1971. He knew that the real killer, Roy Ebsary, was admitting to friends that he killed Sandy Seale, but that Ebsary was also claiming that Seale and Marshall had been trying to rob him.

As he had from the start, Marshall affirmed his innocence to the killing, but stated that he and Seale had attempted to rob Ebsary. Like the Indigenous witnesses in the Stanley case, Marshall was an incentivized and vulnerable witness. The Court of Appeal failed to appreciate the desperate position in which Marshall found himself. Similarly, there is a danger that the Stanley jury did not fully appreciate the position the three Indigenous witnesses found themselves in especially when detained and charged by the RCMP.

The Marshall case dramatically underlines the fallibility of fact-finding. To the jury, who heard his case in 1971, Marshall was a liar and a murderer. To the Court of Appeal, who heard his case in 1982, he was a liar and robber. Stereotypes about Indigenous people may have played a role in both determinations. To the Commission of Inquiry, that reported in 1989, Marshall was a truthful witness who made a "low key, non-violent, non-criminal request"[17] to Ebsary for money.

Marshall, who spoke Mi'kmaq at home but English in school (before leaving after grade 6), testified to the commission in Mi'kmaq with an interpreter. Before the jury and the Court of Appeal, he testified in English. He was told twenty-nine times to speak up while testifying in English.[18] The three experienced trial judges who sat as commissioners and heard the translated testimony concluded, "Marshall's ability to express himself freely in his native language introduced a comfort level to the proceedings we sense was absent in his other court appearances." His testimony appeared more conversational and "replaced the direct and potentially antagonistic interchange between lawyer and witness" and helped obtain "the best evidence possible from the witness."[19]

It is not known whether any of the Indigenous witnesses in the Stanley trial would have been more comfortable testifying in Cree. The Cree language is relatively strong in Red Pheasant with 23 per cent reporting that an Indigenous language was the first language they learned and 20 per cent reporting that they used it at home.[20] Meechance, Cross, and, especially, Jackson were exposed to antagonistic cross-examinations by Stanley's lawyers. Even their examination by the prosecutor, who called them as witnesses, could not be described as particularly relaxed or conversational. For example, prosecutor Burge said "pardon me" ten times in his examination of Jackson apparently because he had not understood or heard her answers or was not satisfied with them. (TT 402–426) Fact-finding and credibility determinations by juries and judges lie at the heart of the criminal trial process. It is influenced by the way that witnesses use language, how they appear, and the way that judges and juries rely on their life experiences when drawing inferences.

Fact-Finding and the Carney Nerland/Leo Lachance Case

As discussed above, the Marshall Commission of Inquiry made very different factual findings about Donald Marshall's case than either the 1971 trial or the 1982 appeal.[21] Similar differences in fact-finding were also evident with respect to Carney Nerland's killing of Leo Lachance discussed in chapter 3.

The trial judge who sentenced Nerland for manslaughter found that Nerland's racism did not influence Nerland's killing of the Cree trapper, but a commission of inquiry three years later essentially reached the opposite conclusion. It stressed that the police had not adequately investigated Nerland's racist activities, including his prior reference to the use of firearms as a form of "Native birth control." The Commission placed greater weight than the trial judge on Nerland's past statements and activities. The Commission also drew inferences of racism because Nerland only mishandled a firearm when an Indigenous person was in his store.[22]

This was not the only difference in fact-finding. The police and prosecutor, relying in part on what Nerland's two companions told them, accepted that the killing of Lachance was accidental and thus charged him with manslaughter as opposed to intentional murder. In contrast, the inquiry rejected this claim of accident saying it accepted the evidence of a RCMP firearm expert that Nerland's gun "could not be fired accidentally since it takes 16 1/2 pounds to pull the trigger."[23] As in the Marshall case, the facts in the Nerland case were contested. Fact-finding, especially decisions about whether people are telling the truth or inferences about their intent, is a difficult and very human process. It can be influenced by the assumptions and life experience of the decision-maker.

"put yourself in Gerry's boots"[24]

We may never know what really happened on Stanley's farm on 9 August 2016. The lesson we need to take from wrongful convictions is that we should not be overconfident about fact-finding. The Marshall and Nerland cases reveal how a second look at the facts can sometimes result in different judgments.

Stanley's lawyer urged the jurors to, "Put yourself in Gerry's boots." (TT 840) The jury may well have done that in acquitting Stanley, but no one urged them to walk in the shoes of Belinda Jackson or the other Indigenous witnesses. As Justice Murray Sinclair has written, "Given the Aboriginal world view, where the relativity of truth is well understood," Aboriginal witnesses can appear untruthful even when they are simply acknowledging different perspectives on an issue.[25] Mary Ellen Turpel-Lafond, a retired Saskatchewan judge and University of British Columbia law professor, has similarly warned that for many Indigenous people "the reluctance to criticize others is greatly exacerbated by the trial process which is extremely intimidating and loaded with alien cultural baggage."[26]

There were differences between what Meechance, Cross, and Jackson first told the RCMP and what they later said in court. Meechance and Cross were more forthcoming at trial than with the RCMP about what they did with vehicles on the farms and the .22-calibre gun that was in the grey Escape. Jackson did not tell the RCMP that she saw Gerald Stanley shoot Colten Boushie, something that she would testify to both at the preliminary inquiry and the trial. The day after Cross and Jackson testified, Chief Justice Popescul told the jury in mid-trial instructions that "common sense tells you that if a witness says one thing in the witness box but has said something quite different on an earlier occasion, this may reduce the value of his or her evidence." (TT 488) He again pointed out the relevance of inconsistencies to the witness's credibility at the end of the trial (TT 886) with particular attention to those in Jackson's testimony. (TT 892) The jury was invited to decide whether these inconsistencies cast doubt on the truthfulness of their testimony without reference to the trauma that Meechance, Cross, and Jackson suffered on the Stanley farm or the difficult position they were in when detained and first questioned by the RCMP.

Both in the middle (TT 487) and end of the trial (TT 885, 892), the trial judge invited the jury to consider Meechance's and Cross's prior criminal records as "one of many factors" when deciding whether they were telling the truth. The trial judge also reminded the jury at the end of the trial that Jackson admitted "to assaulting" Leesa Stanley. (TT 892) All of these reminders could have triggered stereotypes suggesting the Indigenous witnesses were criminals who could not be believed and who may have presented a danger to the Stanleys.

Finally, the jurors were not questioned about whether they had negative stereotypes about Indigenous people at the start of the trial associating them with theft, violence, and deceit. Moreover, the trial judge's instructions to the jury about impartiality did not discuss the danger of racist stereotypes entering into jury deliberations. (TT 82–92, 878–881)

BELINDA JACKSON: TWO SHOTS?

Other than Gerald Stanley, Belinda Jackson was the most important witness at the trial. She testified both at the preliminary inquiry and at trial that she was in the back seat of the grey Escape and saw Gerald Stanley shoot Boushie, twice. As Stanley's lawyer told the jury, if they believed Jackson, Stanley could be convicted of murder. He went on, however, to accuse Jackson of telling "dangerous, malicious" lies in an attempt to convict Stanley of murder. (TT 850)

"I'm not comfortable in describing it, like, how he was shot"[27]

It is clear from the transcript that Belinda Jackson's testimony was difficult for her. The prosecutor asked her:

Q: Okay, please tell us what happened?
A: And he shot Colten in the head.
Q: Can you tell us in as much detail?
A: I'm not comfortable in describing it, like, how he shot him.
   (TT 408)

Jackson insisted that she heard four shots in total and that Colten was in the passenger's seat. (TT 411) The prosecutor knew that this testimony was inconsistent with the rest of the evidence, but never asked for or offered an explanation. Instead, Burge plowed on:

Q: Is there something making this difficult for you to remember?
A: Yeah, in a way.
Q: Pardon me?
A: Yes.
Q: What's that?
A: Just – I don't know – trying to remember everything all over again.
Q: Okay. Well, we have to go through these details, Ms Jackson. So I'm sorry, but we have to do this.
A: Yeah, I understand. (TT 412)

The prosecutor did not appear to have much empathy for Jackson and he eventually told the jury that he would place no reliance on her testimony. (TT 856)

"I'll be candid with you, I don't believe you're telling the truth"[28]

Belinda Jackson was subject to aggressive cross-examination by Scott Spencer both at the preliminary inquiry and at trial. In this, she shared some of the experience faced by sexual assault complainants who are subject to cross-examination at the two separate legal proceedings.

Spencer told Jackson at trial, "I'll be candid with you, I don't believe you're telling the truth." (TT 432) This earned Spencer a warning from the judge. Chief Justice Popescul told him with the jury not present, "Injecting your opinion into it is generally inappropriate. Not horribly wrong, but I would ask you to try to rephrase that it in different ways, if you would." (TT 450) As seen in chapter 4, however, Spencer's cross-examination of Jackson did seem to have some effect on the preliminary inquiry judge who committed Gerald Stanley for trial on the basis of Stanley's own son's testimony, but without reference to Jackson's far more damning testimony. It likely also had an effect on the jury.

*"why I am being put into handcuffs when
I just watched someone die?"*[29]

Spencer's cross-examinations of Jackson focused on why she did not mention Gerald Stanley's use of a handgun in her first interview when she told the RCMP she didn't know who shot Colten and that Mrs. Stanley might have had a gun. (TT 426–7) Jackson explained, "I wasn't comfortable speaking of what – you know – what I knew – it's not that I was lying to the police." (TT 427) She elaborated that the way the RCMP officer "was talking to me – it felt like he made it seem like I was – I did something wrong. So I didn't know how to answer him ... I didn't have a whole lot to say at that time." (TT 440–41) Jackson added that she did not have "any rest or sleep" and was "confused." She added, "it's not something I deal with every day, watching someone get shot." (TT 446) At the preliminary hearing, she explained, "You can't really expect me to be truthful with these police that are like racist and thinking that I was on the farm to steal ... why am I being put into handcuffs when I just watched someone die." (PT 329, 331)

In addition to her concerns about how the police treated her, Jackson might also have been influenced by the fact that the RCMP had arrested her in a criminal investigation and eventually charged her with assaulting Leesa Stanley. At the time she made her statements to the RCMP, Jackson was a suspect and might have thought it in her best interest not to tell the full story. As examined in chapter 4, this is precisely what Stanley did at the same time.

"I don't want to see"[30]

During his cross-examination, Spencer confronted Jackson with a photo of the deceased as he had already done the day before with Meechance. Jackson started to say, "I don't want to see." Chief Justice Popescul added, "She doesn't want to look at a picture of the deceased." Spencer's reply was, "Yeah, which concerns me a little bit that there's been some talking, but it doesn't have – it's – it's a pretty neutral picture." (TT 429)

Showing Jackson a picture of the deceased was a violation of Cree law with respect to a deceased's journey after death.[31] This did not seem to be appreciated by either the judge or Spencer, even the second time it happened at trial. Jackson stayed on the stand, but when asked the next question by Spencer, the judge told her "you are going to have to answer in words for me" (TT 430) suggesting that Jackson may have understandably been shaken by the experience.

Spencer's cross-examination of Jackson was successful in attacking her credibility before the jury. In his closing address, Spencer argued that Jackson's story was "made up" after a "collateral investigation.... Now fortunately for Gerry, it's also completely disproved ... pretty tough for me to tell you that two shots is an accident. So, you know, what do you do when a witness comes out and just outright maliciously lies, to talk about a murder that never occurred?" (TT 850)

In his charge to the jury, Chief Justice Popescul pointed out that Jackson's testimony that Boushie was shot twice "although this is entirely up to you to decide, is at odds with the autopsy report that definitely states that Mr Boushie died from a single gunshot" (TT 891) and that "in cross-examination, it became evident that she initially told police that she did not know who shot Boushie.... She denied she lied to the police but admits that she did not tell the whole truth." (TT 892)

"I don't intend to be relying on what she told you"[32]

In an adversarial system, Jackson could expect to be confronted by the accused and even have the judge direct the jury to inconsistencies in her various statements. At the same time, she may have been surprised when the prosecutor, who called her as a witness, told the jury that he would not rely on her testimony.

Burge told the jury that he had called Jackson as a witness because she was in "a special position," but that "for some of the reasons" that Stanley's lawyer had suggested "you might conclude she didn't always tell the truth. And there were a number of instances that could lead you to believe that, ladies and gentleman. I acknowledge that. And I intend to be pointing to evidence that, in my submission is reliable, and I – I don't intend to be relying upon what she told you. As I said, we called her because she was there. And you're the triers of fact. You can determine if she did her duty, and you may well decide she didn't." (TT 856) This was an extraordinary concession by the prosecutor that the Crown's key witness was not reliable. It made a murder conviction extremely unlikely.

Summary

If he believed that her testimony was not reliable, it is difficult to understand why the prosecutor Burge called Jackson as a witness even though "she was there."[33] (TT 856) Her trial testimony was not materially different from that she had given at the preliminary inquiry. Burge did not pursue the explanation, given by Jackson at the preliminary hearing, that Jackson assaulted Leesa Stanley after Mrs. Stanley had said "that's what you get for trespassing." (PT 308) The prosecutor never offered any innocent explanation for why Jackson may have mistakenly thought Boushie had been killed by two shots. He did not explore the effects on her of the trauma of seeing Boushie killed, the sound that a loud pistol might make in a vehicle, or the vulnerable position she was in when she made her first statement to the RCMP. Perhaps these possibilities were explored behind the scenes, but they were not explored when Jackson testified either at the preliminary inquiry or trial.

ERIC MEECHANCE

The prosecutor asked Meechance, as he did the others, about the amount and type of alcohol he drank on 9 August. (TT 292–3) Burge also brought out that there was a .22-rifle in the grey Escape and it was used for shooting targets and ducks. (TT 286–8, 314) This may have been a tactical decision to minimize the damage of cross-examination, but it also seemed to have placed Meechance on the defensive from the start.

On cross-examination, Spencer asked why Meechance did not tell the police that they were "armed" (TT 315) at the Stanley farm. Meechance explained that he did not tell the police because he was under "a gun ban" (TT 315) as a result of a firearm conviction, suggesting that he was an incentivized witness. Meechance elaborated, "I wouldn't say armed ... it's not like we went there in a stolen vehicle, not like we went there and whipped out a gun or nothing." (TT 321, 315) This is also consistent with Gerald Stanley's testimony that he was not aware of the gun when he approached the grey Escape. (TT 699)

Meechance testified that Gerald Stanley's first two shots were not warning shots and that he did not see Stanley shoot Boushie because "you get shot at, you're not going to – you hear a third gunshot, you're not going to turn around and start looking." (TT 306) It is likely that the police did not believe Meechance because Stanley was not charged in relation to his first two shots. The trial judge indicated to the jury that if they found that warning shots were fired, they were justified as defence of property. (TT 890)

Meechance's testimony about three shots (as opposed to the four shots in total that Jackson testified to) and not seeing the fatal shot, belies suggestions made by Stanley's lawyer during cross-examination that the Indigenous witnesses had colluded at Boushie's funeral or when they spoke to FSIN investigators. (TT 319, 433, 436)

"aren't we here today for Mr Stanley?"[34]

When cross-examined about what happened at the neighbouring Fouhy farm, Meechance replied, "But we are not here for that farm. We are here for Stanley's farm though ... aren't we here today for Mr Stanley?" (TT 321–2) His testimony in this regard is similar to the Donald Marshall Jr testimony, "I wasn't dealing with a robbery and I was afraid that one way or the other they would put the finger at me."[35] In both cases, Indigenous witnesses were effectively placed on trial for crimes that were not the subject matter of the trial.

CASSIDY CROSS

"I was terrified ... I was only thinking of myself"[36]

Cassidy Cross had just turned eighteen years of age when he testified at trial. He admitted he had not told the truth to the RCMP, the media, and at the preliminary inquiry. He stated that he was "willing to face the consequences" for doing so. (TT 356) He explained why he had not originally told the truth about the .22-calibre rifle and his attempt to steal vehicles, "I was terrified. I didn't know what to say. I was young. I was stupid ... I was being selfish at the time. I – I was only thinking about myself ... I was thinking about what was going to happen to me." (TT 356, 361, 358) This honest and brave testimony revealed what perhaps should have been obvious to all justice system participants: Cassidy Cross was an incentivized and vulnerable witness, especially when detained and charged by the RCMP.

At trial, Cross frankly admitted that his and Eric's "intentions were to go steal." (TT 356) They had tried to smash the window of a vehicle on the Fouhy farm, breaking the stock off the .22-rifle that Cross obtained by trading his dirt bike. (TT 351) Cross's honesty at trial distinguishes him from the young witnesses who, when threatened with perjury over their testimony at the preliminary inquiry, reverted to the lies that they told about seeing Donald Marshall Jr kill Sandy Seale and that resulted in Marshall's wrongful conviction.

Like Meechance, Cross was not a direct observer of what transpired between Stanley and Boushie because he was running away from the Stanley farm when the fatal shot was fired. He explained, "I was scared out of my mind. I didn't know what to do. I ran for my life."

Q: Why were you running for your life? You just smashed into
   their vehicle.
A: Yeah.
Q: Why were you running?
A: I just got a hatchet smashed on my window right on my face.
Q: Because your buddy was stealing?
A: Yeah.
Q: –the quad?
A: It wasn't my actions. (TT 389–90)

This exchange reflects the fear that the occupants of the grey Escape likely experienced after Sheldon Stanley broke their windshield with a hammer because, as he testified, "I was mad." (TT 254) It also reveals the defence's fixation on theft, implicitly running a rural crime and defence of property narrative, one that will be explored in the next chapter.

The defence's focus, and sometimes even the prosecution's, seemed more on what happened before the fatal shot than the circumstances of the fatal shot. This approach allowed the Indigenous witnesses to be questioned and effectively put on trial for matters such as their drinking or attempts to steal vehicles that were of very limited relevance to the ultimate issue of whether Stanley had intentionally or negligently caused Boushie's death. In contrast, Sheldon Stanley's actions in breaking the windshield of the grey Escape with a hammer, and Gerald Stanley's actions in firing the first two shots, went unquestioned at trial on the assumption that they were justified as defence of property. As will be seen in the next chapter, the defence was not formally pleaded at the trial, but it was very much present.

The trial judge, in his final charge to the jury, reminded them that Meechance and Cross's previous convictions had been entered into evidence and "you may use those convictions to decide how much or how little of their evidence you will believe or rely on." (TT 885) There was no apparent attempt to balance the value of the jury knowing about these convictions against the prejudice that they might cause. The trial judge also told the jury that "either Eric Meechance or Cassidy Cross, or both of them, tried to steal a quad runner" (TT 890) from the Stanley farm. He also pointed out Belinda Jackson "admits to assaulting the woman, presumably Ms Stanley." (TT 892) The charges that the RCMP originally laid against them may have been dropped, but the trial judge still told the jury that all of the Indigenous witnesses were associated with criminality.

THE INDIGENOUS PRESENCE IN THE COURTROOM

"you could see everyone in charge of our fate was white"[37]

Cree activist Erica Violet Lee attended the Stanley trial and recalled, "We looked up at the front of the courtroom and you could see everyone in charge of our fate was white." Lee continued, "And above it all, there is a picture of the Queen looking over the court-room. We realized this is not a system set up for us: this is not a system set up to keep us safe."[38]

"how come you have to have that body laying in front?"[39]

Stanley's lawyer, Scott Spencer, firstly confronted Eric Meechance, and then Belinda Jackson, with photos of Colten Boushie dead on the ground. Meechance told Spencer, "How come you couldn't take a picture just of that barrel? How come you have to have that body laying in front … I don't even want to look at it. But, yeah, I seen that barrel." (TT 329)

Chief Justice Popescul intervened asking Meechance, "Do you need a break, Mr Meechance?" He added, "maybe we should give him … a little bit of time." The judge then called for Victim Services to "come up and give him some comfort. We are adjourned until we are ready to go again." (TT 330) During a break, Spencer and Burge consulted and Spencer told the judge, "I think we can let this young fellow go." (TT 331) This was a humane and compassionate response to Meechance's distress by both the trial judge and the lawyers. Nevertheless, there was no evidence from the transcript that any of the participants were aware of why Meechance had reacted as strongly as he did to the pictures, nor of the prohibition on viewing the dead in Cree law.

Twice during the trial, Chief Justice Popescul inquired about an eagle feather that some Indigenous observers had brought into the courtroom. An "unidentified speaker" explained that it "represents truth and justice." (TT 334–5) The judge then explained to the jury that the feather was "honouring me and the jury." (TT 336) The judge mentioned the eagle feather a second time later in the trial. He was told by an unidentified speaker that the feather was for "the truth to be told" and to show "the Creator is here." (TT 703–4) This was perhaps indicative of a sense of justice that was not limited to man-made justice.

The second mention of the eagle feather came just before the jury returned for what was likely the most critical moment of the trial: the prosecution's cross-examination of Gerald Stanley. Chief Justice Popescul told the courtroom that the jury had "made an inquiry about the feather being waved in the courtroom." He then stated, "I want to respect culture, and I want to do what's fair. But I think to – to motion in the way you are doing it is distracting the jury, and I don't know if it's doing any good for anybody ... I would respectfully request that you not wave it at Mr Stanley. Okay. Is – is that fair?" (TT 703–4)

The judge also stated that "the jury has reported to the sheriff that they are hearing snickering from the gallery" (TT 704) and that the trial was not "a sporting event where we're rooting for one team or another. It – we have to be very – respect the sanctity of the courtroom." (TT 704) The jury's questions about the eagle feather and the snickering suggests that there may have been some tension between the all-white jury and the Indigenous spectators at the most pivotal moment of the trial.

There were other signs of possible tension and even fear by the jury. After the jury had started deliberations and were in court listening to evidence being read back, one of the jurors expressed concerns to the judge that one of the spectators might be taking photos of the jury even though the judge determined that this was not the case. (TT 919)

When other evidence representative of Indigenous identity entered the courtroom, it was greeted with suspicion. Both at the preliminary inquiry (PT 124–5, 145, 202, 313, 333) and at trial, Stanley's lawyers repeatedly suggested to the Indigenous witnesses that "there is something odd" that they spoke to investigators that were part of the Federation of Sovereign Indigenous Nations or FSIN's special investigation unit as part of a "separate" or "collateral" investigation." (TT 319, 433, 446) This allowed Stanley's lawyer to introduce the FSIN name before the jury.

The FSIN is the most prominent voice for First Nations issues in the Saskatchewan, but not one that is always popular especially with rural non-Indigenous populations.[40] As discussed in chapter 3, the FSIN had opposed the March 2017 Saskatchewan Association of Rural Municipalities resolutions on rural crime that had been supported by nearly all the rural delegates present.

The FSIN's special investigations unit was formed in 2000 in light of the "starlight tours" in which Indigenous men were taken by Saskatoon police to the edge of town in winter with some subsequently dying. It hears complaints by First Nations persons against the RCMP and municipal police. Since 2005, it has been included as an official police complaints agency under Saskatchewan's *Police Act*.[41] Despite having its budget cut 38 per cent to $108,000 in 2016,[42] it is a part of the Saskatchewan legal system. As suggested in chapter 2, its involvement was also consistent with an understanding of justice under Treaty 6 that would include Indigenous involvement as warranted and necessary in cases where Indigenous people interacted with the settlers' justice system. Despite all this, the FSIN involvement was portrayed by Stanley's lawyer as meddling and interfering. Any suggestion that the Indigenous witnesses colluded, however, was unwarranted. Meechance and Cross testified that there were three shots whereas Jackson testified there were four. Only Jackson testified that she saw Stanley shoot Boushie.

CONCLUSION

The Indigenous witnesses were, to varying extents, all placed on trial. Much of Meechance's and Cross's evidence was devoted to their conduct before Boushie was killed despite its limited relevance to the charges that Stanley faced. This caused Meechance to raise the valid point, "Aren't we here today for Mr Stanley?" (TT 321–2) Colten Boushie's cousin, Jade Tootoosis, made the same point, "Colten Boushie is not on trial here. Those four other youth are not on trial here. Gerald Stanley is."[43]

The most critical witness was Belinda Jackson. Both at the preliminary inquiry and trial, Jackson testified that she saw Stanley fire two shots at Boushie out of a total of four shots even though this was inconsistent with other evidence. The prosecutor did not explore in open court any possible innocent explanation for this discrepancy. We do not know whether Jackson's statements to the RCMP were influenced by her concerns about her arrest or whether her perception of two shots being fired could have been related to the trauma and/or auditory experience of being in the back seat when Boushie was shot. Perhaps these possible explanations were explored and rejected. What we do know is that in his closing statement, Burge told the jury that, "I don't intend to be relying on what she [Jackson] told you." (TT 856).

Fact-finding and credibility determinations were at the heart of the Stanley case, just as they were at the heart of Donald Marshall's wrongful convictions. The danger in both cases is that all-white juries, as well as non-Indigenous lawyers and judges, may lack the life experiences, knowledge, or empathy to try to understand why Indigenous witnesses testified as they did. They may be unable, as Stanley's lawyer successfully urged the jury to do for his client, to stand in the boots (TT 840) of Indigenous witnesses. Moreover, an all-white jury that was not challenged for cause on racist bias, or specifically instructed by the judge about the danger of such bias, might be more likely to rely on stereotypes associating Indigenous people with theft, violence, and deceit. As will be examined in the next chapter, these themes figured quite prominently in Stanley's defence.

8

Murder, Manslaughter, and Phantom Self-Defence

INTRODUCTION

The Stanley trial was sometimes sensationally reported as one where Stanley claimed that he could kill in order to defend his property. In fact, Stanley's lawyers told the jury that nothing in the case justified "the intentional use of lethal force" (TT 838) and that he did not know that there was a .22-calibre rifle in the grey Escape until after Boushie was dead. (TT 838) Stanley did not ask the judge to explain the law of self-defence or defence of property to the jury.

At the same time, concerns about rural crime, defence of property, and self-defence were hardly absent from the trial. Stanley's lawyers conducted a skilful defence that allowed them to have it both ways: the main defence was accident caused by a malfunctioning old gun and ammunition, but the defence also argued that the Stanleys faced a "nightmare situation" (TT 854) involving threats to both their property and themselves and that they "were on their own." (TT 844)

Stanley made implicit or phantom claims of self-defence and defence of property to the jury that effectively capitalized on concerns about rural crime, crimes against elderly women, a past and notorious crime in the area that involved a relative of Colten Boushie, and even fears that Boushie and his companions were acting as terrorists. This may all seem far-fetched, but as will be seen, they all find support in the trial transcript.

Although neither Stanley or the prosecutor asked the judge to tell the jury about self-defence or defence of property, judges have the legal duty to instruct juries about defences if they conclude that there is evidence that, if accepted by a reasonable jury, would support the defence.[1] Judges in an adversarial system, however, are often reluctant to intervene when not asked to do so by the parties. The Commission on Donald Marshall's wrongful conviction criticized the trial judge and the Court of Appeal for not being more proactive on Marshall's behalf.[2] Here neither the prosecutor or the accused asked the judge to instruct the jury about self-defence. In addition, they agreed that warning shots would be justified by defence of property. Nevertheless, instructions to the jury on both defences would have been helpful and responsive to Stanley's implicit or phantom defences. They might have helped regulate or discipline the jury's thinking about these emotive defences.

The jury might still have acquitted Stanley had the judge explained self-defence and defence of property to them. They were, after all, asked to determine whether Stanley had acted reasonably when deciding whether he was guilty of manslaughter. Nevertheless, it is possible that a formal judicial instruction on self-defence might have encouraged the jury to ask themselves whether Stanley's perceptions of threats to both his wife and himself were reasonable as is required even under the 2012 expansion of self-defence discussed in chapter 3. This raises the question of whether a reasonable perception of threat is one that is free of racist stereotypes associating Indigenous people with danger and violence.

PHANTOM DEFENCE OF PROPERTY

The rural crime issue was part of the social and political context of the case. Moreover, the judge told the jury, twice, that defence of property justified Stanley getting his pistol and firing two warning shots in the air, if the jury concluded that was what he did. (TT 893, 897) This judicial instruction to the jury reflected concessions that the prosecution had made (TT 805–06, 812), but it underlines that the jury was aware of defence of property.

Meechance and Cross

As discussed in the last chapter, much of Eric Meechance's and Cassidy Cross's testimony involved questions about their conduct in relation to vehicles on the Stanley farm and on the neighbouring Fouhy family farm. Some of this evidence was presented by the prosecutor in a possible attempt to mitigate some of the damage that would be caused by Stanley's lawyers on cross-examination, but the prosecution never attempted to contextualize this behaviour, either in light of the damaged car that Cross was driving, or life circumstances on the Red Pheasant First Nation. If Cross and Meechance were guilty of property crimes, there was no equivalent to the *Gladue*[3] analysis that is used at sentencing in an attempt to explain the many factors that bring Indigenous people before the court.

Gerald Stanley testified that there was "between 4000 and 5000" dollars' worth of damages to his blue Escape after the grey Escape collided with it in the immediate aftermath of Sheldon Stanley using a hammer to hit the front windshield of the grey Escape. (TT 701) Stanley's lawyers also called one of Stanley's neighbours to testify that "over $4,000 bucks damage" (TT 632, 647) had been caused on their farm. Spencer also argued in his closing address that the only reason Cross and Meechance did not steal a truck on that farm is "they didn't know how to drive a standard." (TT 839) This evidence was of limited relevance to the facts of the actual shooting of Boushie, but it would have had an impact on a rural jury that, while more prosperous than most of their Indigenous neighbours, were far from wealthy.

The Frightened Neighbours: "I was afraid they would come into the house and then what?"[4]

Stanley's lawyer ended the case for the defence by calling Glennis Fouhy from the neighbouring farm. The seventy-four-year-old alluded to the rural crime issue by mentioning that she had to call the RCMP at both the Warman and North Battleford detachments before someone at the Biggar detachment finally answered her call. (TT 648) She testified, "I was terrified. I was afraid they would come into the house and then what?" (TT 648)

Burge wisely did not cross-examine this sympathetic witness. (TT 649) Spencer, however, would cite her calls to the three detachments in his closing address arguing that while "it would be so great if you could – if you could have the police there right away," the Stanleys "were on their own." (TT 843–844)

PHANTOM SELF-DEFENCE

Stanley's lawyers readily admitted to the jury that defence of property could not justify shooting someone in the back of the head.

(TT 838) With some justification, the pro-Stanley forces could feel aggrieved when suggestions were made by pro-Boushie forces that Stanley was arguing that property was more valuable than life. That was not Stanley's formal and explicit legal argument. It was not even his implicit or phantom argument.

Stanley's phantom self-defence argument, or what his lawyer told the jury was "a self-defence factor," (TT 607) was in some ways more insidious and dangerous than the crude argument that a farmer's property trumps a thief's life. Although he admitted "Gerry wasn't aware of that in his panic," Spencer told the jury "Colten had a rifle between his legs, essentially pointing at Gerry." (TT 606) Stanley's implicit argument seems to have been that the Indigenous occupants of the grey Escape were drunk, dangerous, and prone to violence, with hints of even possible murder or terrorism.[5]

> *"I'm thinking about the news on and people using*
> *their vehicles to crash into crowds"[6]*

Gerald Stanley testified that after he retrieved his pistol from his shed and was walking toward the grey Escape, just before Boushie was shot, "I'm thinking about the news on and people using their vehicles to crash into crowds, and I'm thinking about when we first moved there, a couple of murders took place just down the road. It's always on your mind." (TT 687) This is quite an extraordinary statement. Stanley seems to be equating the actions of Boushie and the others to a terrorist, who less than a month before, had killed 86 pedestrians and injured close to 500 on the Promenade des Anglais in Nice, France. It may have been possible that Gerald Stanley had thoughts of the 14 July 2016 Nice terrorist attack on his mind on 9 August 2016, but that does not mean that his perception of such a threat from Boushie was reasonable. Boushie and his companions could not reasonably be thought to have been terrorists trying to run people down.[7]

> *"I'm thinking about when we first moved there, a couple of murders*
> *took place just down the road. It's always on your mind."[8]*

Gerald Stanley also said he was thinking about "a couple of murders" that took place "just down the road from us." (TT 687) Stanley's lawyers were allowed to follow up this reference, without objection from the prosecutor, by marking the site of two murders that happened nine miles away from the Stanley farm. The murders, however, occurred in 1994, twenty-two years before the incident in question. Chief Justice Popescul seemed to be aware of a possible objection by the prosecutor and stated, "Have you seen this, Mr Burge? Do you have any objection?" There was no objection. (TT 690)

No more details about the 1994 murders were discussed and it is not known if any of the jurors had a personal recollection of them. Hopefully they did not because the prejudicial effect of such recollections would have been great even though their relevance to the issues in the Stanley case was minimal.

The 1994 case, discussed in chapter 3, involved the killing of two farmers, Bryan Kipp and Gordon Tetarenko. Ron Caldwell pled guilty to shooting both farmers in the back of the head in a botched attempt to steal gas from them: a typical rural crime. Colin Leonard Baptiste was convicted of manslaughter. After the prosecutor appealed it, his sentence was raised from five years' to eight years' imprisonment.[9] Both Caldwell and Baptiste had, like Boushie and his friends, been on the Red Pheasant First Nation shortly before the events in question.

Criminal trials should not be a contest of historical grievances. But if they become one, there should be equality of arms. Stanley's lawyers were able to invoke the ghosts of Bryan Kipp and Gordon Tetarenko, but the competing ghosts of Indigenous victims discussed in chapter 3, such as Leo Lachance and William Kakakaway, were nowhere to be found.

Stanley might have had the Kipp and Tetarenko murders on his mind, but that does not make such perceptions any more reasonable than analogies to the Nice or other terrorist attacks. Boushie was killed in the driver's seat of the grey Escape likely trying to drive the immobilised vehicle away from the Stanley farm. He could not reasonably be thought to have been trying to shoot Stanley or his family in the back of the head. In fact, it was Stanley who shot Boushie in the back of the head.

The Closing Address to the Jury: "The Stanleys were on their own"[10]

In his closing address to the jury, Scott Spencer painted a horrifying picture of fear experienced by his client. He argued that by the time the grey Escape hit the blue Escape, matters had escalated from defence of property to self-defence, "You're now going from people stealing, stealing in broad daylight … Now you got them not leaving. They're – they intentionally crash. Where is your anxiety now? The roller coaster is going up like crazy. Up like crazy." (TT 843) In another veiled reference to the Nice and similar terrorist attacks, Spencer told the jury that the grey Escape was a "weapon" and Stanley "had to do what he had to. He had to stop that vehicle, that weapon. He had to shut that weapon off. He had to disarm that weapon. He had to." (TT 848–49)

Stanley told the jury that he got his pistol because he was "scared." (TT 722) He said he was in a state of "pure terror" when he could no longer see his wife. (TT 735) Just before his gun discharged, Stanley testified he thought the grey Escape "was going to run me over." (TT 697) Again this may have been Stanley's honest perceptions and fears, but that does not make them reasonable. There was other testimony that the grey Escape was immobile and "done" because of smoke coming from the radiator. (TT 299) The reasonableness requirement would have been made clear had the judge instructed the jury on the law of self-defence.

Spencer appealed to any anxiety that the jury might have had about rural depopulation that had seen many sons and daughters abandon the farm when he told them that "in some ways, it is fortunate that Sheldon, his son, happened to be home this day." (TT 840) He then skilfully appealed to any concerns the jury may have had about rural crime by telling them that because he lives in the city, "I've got the luxury of calling 911 and reasonably expecting the cops are going to be there in five minutes, ten minutes." (TT 843) In contrast, "the Stanleys were on their own." (TT 844) This mirrored some of the rhetoric discussed in chapter 3, surrounding the rural crime issue, including statements made by Minister of Justice Rob Nicholson in 2012 in relation to the new self-defence law and Prime Minister Stephen Harper's statement, during the 2015 election campaign, in reference to rural families using firearms for "security."

"a measured response"[11]

Spencer shrewdly addressed possible concerns, very much alive in the media, that Stanley's self-defence was excessive or based on a crude and manifestly disproportionate preference for property over life. He repeatedly stressed that Stanley engaged in a "measured response," (TT 842) something that would be relevant if the judge had instructed the jury on self-defence. He painted a picture of more excessive forms of self-defence that Stanley did not take by stating, "If he'd had loaded up with nine and come out shooting, well, that's a lot tougher, a lot tougher." (TT 845) He added, "Lots would have assaulted the driver, grabbed and hauled him out of there – got physical." (TT 849) This may have been quite effective with the jury because it distinguished Stanley's defence from crude ideas of vigilante action that had been featured in some commentary that was critical of Stanley and farmers who would employ self-defence.

Implicit concepts of race and gender influenced the threat that Gerald Stanley perceived. He told the jury he approached the grey Escape and looked under it because he was concerned about the safety of his wife. Spencer asked him, "Why were you concerned about your wife, at that point? A: Well, because I love her, that's why." (TT 735) He did not find his wife, but states, "she could have been in the bush." (TT 736) This alludes to a narrative of settler women at risk and scared of Indigenous men that is as old as the 1885 Frog Lake killings discussed in chapter 2.

"hoodies up"[12]

Gerald Stanley told the jury that he remembered that Meechance and Cross "had hoodies up" (TT 725) when they left the grey Escape even though his son Sheldon Stanley has described them differently as wearing respectively "a windbreaker" and "a black T-shirt." (TT 261) After Gerald Stanley had volunteered the reference to "hoodies up," Scott Spencer made sure this point was not lost on the jury by asking, "And you say they were all wearing hoodies? A: These two were wearing hoodies, right there." (TT 725) The reference to "hoodies" alluded to the Trayvon Martin case including stereotypical fears of violence from racial minorities and the iconic hoodie that the seventeen-year-old African American was wearing when killed by George Zimmerman in 2012. Hoodies were subsequently worn by many as a sign of protest and solidarity with the Black Lives Matter movement.[13]

Gerald Stanley also stated that Meechance and Cross did not start running away until after the first warning shot. Spencer in his opening argument stated "for farm people your yard is your castle" and argued what happened was "really in the nature of a home invasion" and "being terrorized." (TT 606-607) In his closing address Spencer told the jury that when Gerald Stanley retrieved his gun, he is thinking "one of my boys is taking on a group of three people" who were "adult males, young males, doesn't matter" who were "stealing and crashing." (TT 844) The reference to a "group" of three adult males alluded to the possibility of gang violence. Meechance and Cross were depicted as threats to the Stanleys' safety even though their actions – getting back into the grey Escape when Sheldon and Gerald Stanley ran towards them and subsequently fleeing the farm after their vehicle hit the Stanley's car and became immobilized – were the opposite of threatening or aggressive behaviour.

Ironically, the only recorded violence from the five Indigenous people on the farm was Belinda Jackson's admitted assault of Leesa Stanley, after Boushie was killed, something that Jackson testified was provoked by comments that Mrs. Stanley made about property and trespassing. Nevertheless, even Jackson's actions fit into social patterns where Indigenous women are even more over-represented in prison than Indigenous men or youth.[14]

THE JUDGE'S CHARGE TO THE JURY

One of the most important parts of any criminal trial is the trial judge's charge to the jury. It is the last thing the jury hears before it starts its deliberations. The charge to the jury is particularly important in Canada because the judge not only explains the relevant law to the jury but also summarizes the evidence.

The trial judge gave the jury only a brief and generic instruction to consider just the evidence they heard and not to consider "social media" or "public opinion." Consistent with the lack of inquiry into the danger of racist stereotypes at the jury selection, he only told the jury to avoid "passion, or sympathy or prejudice against the accused, the Crown, or anyone else connected with the case" (TT 879) without any reference to Boushie or the Indigenous witnesses or the dangers of stereotypes in relation to them.

The Murder Charge

Chief Justice Popescul told the jury that for a murder conviction, the prosecution must prove, beyond a reasonable doubt, that Stanley meant to cause Boushie's death or meant to cause him bodily harm that he knew was likely to cause death. (TT 895) As discussed in the last chapter, that position was supported by Belinda Jackson's testimony. The jury was unlikely to believe Jackson after the prosecutor told them he would no longer rely on her testimony. The trial judge also extensively outlined all the inconsistencies in her testimony noting that her testimony about witnessing two shots fired at Boushie was "at odds with the autopsy report that definitively states" Boushie died from a "single gunshot wound" and that she had not told the RCMP that she saw Gerald Stanley fire the two shots. (TT 891–2)

A murder charge could also be supported if the jury did not have a reasonable doubt about the hang fire defence. Chief Justice Popescul told the jury that, before considering whether Stanley had the intent required for murder, it first had to be convinced that Stanley had intentionally assaulted Boushie. (TT 903) This meant that the jury had to consider whether Stanley intentionally, "on purpose" and "not by accident," made a "conscious choice" to shoot Boushie in the head. He continued, "The Crown must satisfy you beyond a reasonable doubt that what happened to Mr Boushie was not an accident." (TT 889–90) If the jury got past that point, however, things did not look good for Stanley with the judge telling them, "Generally speaking, if you point a gun at the head ... of a person and fire the gun, you intend to cause his death." (TT 896)

The Manslaughter Charge by way of Assault

There were two different forms of manslaughter for the jury to consider. The first was manslaughter through the commission of the unlawful act of assault. The trial judge instructed the jury that Stanley would not be guilty of assault if they had a reasonable doubt that "what happened to Mr Boushie was an accident" which he defined as an "unintentional act" such as a driver who "unavoidably strikes" a person who runs onto the road between two parked cars. (TT 880–890) Criminal law doctrine focuses on whether the person was at fault at the moment of the fatal act even though much of the trial had been devoted to actions before that time including the attempts to steal property.

The trial judge noted the evidence in favour of Stanley's defence that the shooting was accidental, including Sheldon Stanley's testimony that after the shooting, his father told him, "I don't know what happened. It just went off. I just wanted to scare them." (TT 891) He discussed the hang fire defence, noting that the Crown expert, Williams, testified "that the delay in a hang fire would normally be less than one half a second." At the same time, he noted that one lay witness has testified to a delay of about seven seconds and that safety regulations recommend a thirty to sixty second wait and that they had been filed as a court exhibit that the jury could consider in their deliberations. (TT 894) It was up to the jury to decide whether a hang fire occurred, how long the delay between pulling the trigger and the discharge of the bullet might be, and whether it gave them a reasonable doubt about Stanley's guilt.

Manslaughter by way of Careless Use of a Firearm

Even if the jury accepted the defence of accident, based on an involuntary and accidental hang fire, the judge made clear (TT 894–5) that the jury should still consider whether Stanley committed manslaughter by a second and distinct unlawful act: the careless use of a firearm. Consistent with the ruling authorities, the trial judge explained that carelessness required proof beyond a reasonable doubt of "a marked departure from the standard of care that a reasonably prudent person would exercise in the same circumstances." (TT 898)

"you can't defend yourself by carelessly using a firearm."[15]

In his preliminary discussions of the charge he would give to the jury with the lawyers and without the jury present, Chief Justice Popescul suggested that it was difficult to see how someone could have a lawful excuse for careless use of a firearm. (TT 791, 798, 826) Stanley's lawyer, however, persistently argued that self-defence might be relevant. (TT 802, 822) He stressed that once Stanley became concerned about his wife's safety and then his own safety, the situation evolved "from a property concern to a safety concern." (TT 803) As such, "self-defence comes back into play." (TT 822, 823)

The trial judge was sceptical about this claim and concluded there was no air of reality that justified telling the jury about self-defence. (TT 831) He reminded Spencer that he had told the jury that self-defence would not be argued. He also asked, "What was Colten Boushie doing to your client at that point as he sits in the passenger – the driver's side with a blood alcohol level of .300?" (TT 825) This suggests that the judge had not heard evidence that Boushie was a threat to Stanley. He summed his concerns up, "You can't defend yourself by carelessly using a firearm." (TT 825) This approach made sense. It would have focused on Stanley's actions in bringing a weapon into the grey Escape in such close proximity to Colten Boushie's head. It might have provided a means to hold Stanley criminally accountable for the death, even if the jury had a reasonable doubt about hang fire or, in an act of jury nullification, was reluctant to convict him of murder.

Lawful Excuse or Subjective Self-Defence?

Despite his initial scepticism, about both self-defence and whether there was any lawful excuse to the careless use of a firearm offence, Chief Justice Popescul told the jury that they should consider whether Stanley had "a lawful excuse" to the careless use of a fire-arm charge. At one level, this simply followed the text of the offence as written in the *Criminal Code*.[16] But the trial judge provided little guidance to the jury about what was a lawful excuse. As discussed above, Stanley's own testimony implicitly addressed self-defence in his reference to his own subjective thoughts about terrorism and the twenty-two-year-old murders on a near-by farm.

Although he did not tell the jury about self-defence, the judge told the jury that Stanley would have been justified in firing warning shots:

> I have already told you that it is not disputed that Mr Stanley was legally justified in defence of his property, to retrieve his handgun and fire it into the air, if you find that is what he did, in light of what had gone on in his farmyard. However, you must now closely analyze whether his actions between that point and the shooting of Mr Boushie amount to careless use of a firearm and whether he had a lawful excuse. The elements of careless use and lawful excuse are somewhat intertwined. (TT 898)

The reference to defence of property reflected concessions that the prosecution had made in the open court discussion leading to the jury charge. (TT 805, 812) This followed from the judge's own suggestions to Spencer, "You might be stronger focussing on defence of property." (TT 803) It also implicitly factored in the rural crime issue because the judge indicated, "if I was in my backyard of my residence in Saskatoon, blasting a gun in the air ... I'd have some police at my doorstep pretty quick, taking my guns away." (TT 812–13)

The judge's brief reference to defence of property failed to make clear to the jury that the accused's perception of threat – not just the accused's response to a perceived threat – had to be reasonable for either defence of property or self-defence to apply.[17] Without such guidance, it is possible that the jury might have applied their own unexplained ideas of what constitutes a lawful excuse. They might have thought that Stanley's subjective fears of Boushie, including his thoughts about a 1994 murder and terrorism, were a lawful excuse even if such fears

were far-fetched as applied to the incident in question and hence unreasonable. The jury may have read in their own approach to self-defence
into the judge's undefined reference to lawful excuse.

The trial judge explained the defence theory, on the careless use
of the firearm issue, by noting Stanley "feared his wife was trapped
under the vehicle"; he "faced a crisis situation"; and he "did not have
the luxury of carefully counting out the recommended sixty seconds
and clearing the gun before he knew his wife was safe." (TT 900)
This again may have left the jury with the impression that Stanley
might have pulled the trigger of his pistol when firing warning shots
but that a bullet could discharge as much as sixty seconds later after
Stanley had ran or walked towards the grey Escape, checked for his
wife, and attempted to seize the keys of the vehicle.

There was no instruction that Stanley's fears would have to be reasonable, as would be required if the trial judge had instructed the jury
on self-defence. Without such guidance, the jury could have concluded
that Stanley's subjective fears were sufficient, even if based on irrational analogies to the 2016 Nice terrorist attack, the 1994 execution-style murders of Bryan Kipp and Gordon Tetarenko, or, perhaps,
even racist stereotypes that Indigenous males with "hoodies up" (TT
725) were dangerous even while running away. The jury's reasoning
about what was a lawful excuse for careless use of firearm was not
subject to judicial guidance. This allowed the jury essentially to act
as a legislator in determining what was a lawful excuse. As such, the
jury's decision on this point was unregulated by law.

A SUBJECTIVE APPROACH TO SELF-DEFENCE?

A concrete example of unregulated jury reasoning occurred when
a New York jury applied its own concepts of self-defence in acquitting Bernhard Goetz, the so-called subway vigilante, of shooting
four African Americans. Analogies to the Goetz case are not made to
suggest that Goetz and Stanley are the same, but because both cases
raise common issues about how much weight jurors may give to the
accused's subjective perceptions of danger compared to those that a
reasonable person would have in the same circumstances.

Based on interviews with jurors that are allowed in the United
States but not in Canada, Professor George Fletcher of Columbia discovered that the New York jury "placed the entire burden of their
analysis on subjective perceptions and motives"[18] which they believed

were inspired by Goetz's genuine and subjective fear that he was about to be mugged. This raises the question of whether the jurors in the Stanley case similarly might have given weight to Stanley's subjective fears of Boushie, including Stanley's testimony that he related what was happening on the farm to the 1994 murders of Bryan Kipp and Gordon Tetarenko and terrorist attacks with vehicles. (TT 687–8) Indeed the danger of jurors giving weight to the accused's subjective fears is perhaps greater in the Stanley trial than the Goetz trial because the Stanley jury was never told that Stanley's perception of threat and danger had to be reasonable. The Goetz jury was so instructed, though in the end it appears what mattered most to them was Goetz's subjective fears of the four African American men he encountered on the New York subway.

Subjective Understandings of Self-Defence and Racism

Like the Stanley trial, the Goetz trial was "on the verbal level at least, color blind."[19] Nevertheless, Fletcher found "covert"[20] appeals to racial bias and fears that were "hidden behind innuendo and suggestion."[21] This was also true in the Stanley case starting with the heavy courtroom security, the defence's use of peremptory challenges of all the visibly Indigenous jurors, repeated references by Spencer to the FSIN special investigation as a "collateral investigation" (TT 319, 433, 446) that may have resulted in witness collusion, the introduction of Cross and Meechance's criminal record, and references to Jackson's assault of Leesa Stanley after Colten Boushie was killed.

I agree with Professor Fletcher that while "criminal trials may not solve the problems of racial bias in our society," they "should not add to them."[22] As he notes, this will be no easy task because "racial fears invariably infuse routine judgments" about danger.[23] Self-defence laws such as Canada's, that require both the apprehension of threat and the responses to be reasonable, "may demand that we surmount racially based intuitions of danger."[24] As such, they may "force us to be better than we really are."[25]

I also agree with Fletcher that "[o]penly talking about racial fear in the courtroom" can help "the jury to deal more rationally with their own racial biases."[26] Here the Stanley trial completely failed. Racism was not discussed when the jury was selected. It was not discussed during the trial. It was not discussed by the trial judge in his instructions to the jury.

The fact that the judge did not instruct the jury about self-defence and defence of property also meant that the jury was never told that even if Stanley subjectively feared that Boushie and his companions were threats – potential terrorists or murderers – such a belief also had to be reasonable and not based on racist bias or assumptions. In the final chapter, I will suggest that self-defence law should be contextualized so as to name, and hopefully prohibit, racist fears and stereotypes.

ACQUITTAL ON ALL COUNTS: JURY NULLIFICATION AND IMPLICIT BIAS?

A number of commentators have raised concerns that the jury's verdict to acquit Stanley of both murder and manslaughter may have been a product of jury nullification. This occurs when a jury refuses to apply the law regardless of the strength of the evidence. Juries are not explicitly told by judges that they have this power. Chief Justice Popescul told the jury, "If I am wrong about the law, any error can be corrected by the Court of Appeal, because my instructions are recorded and will be available if there is an appeal. However, your deliberations are secret. If you wrongly apply the law, there will be no record of your discussions for the Court of Appeal to review. Therefore, it is important that you accept the law from me without question; you must not use your own ideas about what the law is or should be." (TT 879) This standard instruction told the jury to follow the law, but also indicated that their deliberations would be secret and not subject to possible appeal if they did not.

Jury nullification is most often associated with decisions not to enforce oppressive laws. The most famous Canadian example was the consistent refusals of juries to convict Dr Henry Morgentaler for violating Canada's former restrictive abortion law. In 2005, the Supreme Court implicitly preserved the right of jury nullification in a murder trial where a white accused was charged with killing an Indigenous victim in rural British Columbia. It ruled that the trial judge erred when he told the jury that they must convict the accused of the lesser included offence of careless use of a firearm. The court ordered a new trial after the accused was convicted by the jury of second-degree murder. The accused eventually pled guilty to manslaughter and was sentenced to eight years' imprisonment.[27]

Osgoode Hall law professor Benjamin Berger has argued that jury nullification remains part of the Canadian criminal justice system and can sometimes be used to bridge the gap between law and justice. Although Canadian courts have at times disapproved of and refused to encourage jury nullification, they also recognize and preserve the jury's *de facto* power to decide whether to acquit.[28] Perhaps the best rationale for nullification is that the jury can act as the community's conscience. As University of Calgary law professor Alice Wooley has noted, however, the Stanley jury failed to represent the entire community, namely Saskatchewan's significant Indigenous population.[29]

In the case where it struck down Canada's restrictive abortion law, Chief Justice Brian Dickson reasoned that lawyers should not be allowed to urge jury nullification because of the dangers that "a jury fuelled by the passions of racism could be told that they need not apply the law against murder to a white man who killed a Black man."[30] Chief Justice Dickson (who, as a trial judge, had a soft heart for Prairie juries that he presided over and never once encountered a challenge for cause to any prospective juror in Manitoba[31]) did not have to look to the American south for an example of racism-fuelled jury nullification. He could have looked to cases like the Allan Thomas case, discussed in chapter 3, where it appears as if the presiding judge may have had concerns that a jury may have simply refused to convict three white men from the Battleford area for killing an Indigenous man. The presiding judge, Justice Tucker, stated after the jury's verdict, "I hope nothing like this ever happens in this part of the province again" and that he did not want the verdict to be taken "as approval of racial prejudice of any kind."[32]

David Milward, who is a University of Victoria law professor and member of the Beardy's & Okemasis' First Nation in Saskatchewan, has raised the troubling hypothesis that the juries in both the Stanley and Tina Fontaine cases may have refused to apply the law because the victim was Indigenous. Professor Milward believes that such "racial injustice" should not be condoned.[33] University of Windsor law professor David Tanovich has argued that nullification is also connected with implicit racial bias that may be more complex than simple intentional racism. He suggests that implicit bias was "even more likely" after the defence used peremptory challenges to keep visibly Indigenous people off the jury suggesting "that Indigenous perspectives were irrelevant or could not be trusted. The 'us' versus 'them' racial dynamics of the case and any other preexisting racial bias would have been reinforced by this exclusionary process."[34]

The "us versus them" dynamic was also re-enforced by Indigenous and non-Indigenous spectators generally sitting on opposite sides of the court[35] and by the all-white jury having the judge request Indigenous spectators not to wave the eagle feather or snicker just before Gerald Stanley would be cross-examined. (TT 703–4) At the very end of his closing address to the jury on behalf of Stanley, Spencer argued, "You must acquit. Some people aren't going to be happy. Some people aren't going to be happy with – unless it's murder. And that's, in my respectful submission, not even a starter – a non-starter. But you have to do – all twelve of you ... what's right based on the evidence you heard in this courtroom. And based on the evidence you heard in this courtroom, you must acquit." (TT 854) On the one hand, Spencer properly called on the jury to base its decision on the evidence it had heard. On the other hand, his statement that "some people" would not be happy with an acquittal could have been seen by the jury as an "us versus them" statement given the racial tension and polarization surrounding the case and in the courtroom.

Professor Tanovich also notes that bias was more likely given the trial judge's refusal to confront the danger of the jury relying on racist stereotypes. Chief Justice Popescul did not follow the Alberta Court of Appeal's recommendation, arising from a 2017 murder case, by specifically telling the jury to "leave behind any assumptions" they might have about an Indigenous victim because they might be "unsound and unfair. Everyone in this country is entitled to have their actions assessed as an individual and not on the basis of assumptions attributed to them because of their gender, race, or class."[36] Jury research suggests that homogenous groups are less likely to discuss race even though racism is more likely to happen in groups.[37] It is possible that the silence about race seen in the trial might have carried over into the jury's deliberation. Such silence, however, does not mean that racist assumptions and stereotypes played no role in the jury's decision or that the jury did not think that the "some people" (TT 854) who would be unhappy with an acquittal would be Indigenous people. In any event, implicit bias research suggests an alternative to the type of intentional racism and nullification raised by Chief Justice Dickson.

Stanley's lawyer did not make any improper appeal for the jury to nullify the law. He made no direct criticism of Colten Boushie other than to suggest that Colten had been identified as checking a Lexus vehicle on the Fouhy farm. (TT 838) Spencer also argued that Gerald

Stanley identifying Eric Meechance as the person who tried to steal his quad meant Stanley was telling the truth because "Gerry would know that it would be better if it was Colten stealing the quad." (TT 841) Stanley's lawyer stressed that Meechance and Cross had criminal records and were trying to steal, and argued that Jackson was engaged in malicious lies. Such attacks on the character of the witnesses might have created an environment where the jury might have seen Colten Boushie as being less worthy by association. Spencer's closing argument for Stanley addressed the careless use of a firearm charge by implicitly comparing Stanley's actions to those of Cassidy Cross. Spencer told the jury, "You want dangerous use of a firearm? Well, try a loaded rifle and trying to smash into a truck," (TT 839) in reference to Cassidy's actions on the neighbouring farm. Spencer also played the "rural crime" card by stressing that the "Stanleys were on their own" in dealing with a "dangerous situation." (TT 844, 851)

Stanley mounted a multi-layered defence based both on the "freak accident" of a hang fire and the "self-defence factor." (TT 607) The jury may have had a reasonable doubt that Stanley had a lawful excuse to the careless use of the firearm based on self-defence, albeit without the guidance and discipline of the trial judge instructing them on self-defence, including the requirement that Stanley's fear of Boushie must be reasonable.

As Professors Milward, Wooley, and Tanovich all note, the jury nullification hypothesis cannot be proven or disproven. It may also have unconsciously entered into the jurors thoughts if they had problems with the hang fire defence because they would be "backed into a corner"[38] where a murder verdict was the most likely alternative. The judge's instructions to them made it fairly clear that if Stanley deliberately assaulted or pointed the gun at Boushie, then "generally speaking ... you intend to cause his death." (TT 896) A jury, perhaps aware of the Robert Latimer saga where a Saskatchewan jury's recommendation of one year's imprisonment was rejected after they convicted him of second-degree murder, might have concluded that it was unjust to label and punish Stanley as a murderer even though the trial judge gave them the standard instruction not to consider "possible penalties." (TT 879) It may be too much to expect a jury to ignore such questions.

Even if the jury was reluctant to convict Stanley of murder, this still fails to explain the jury's surprising decision[39] not to convict him of manslaughter by careless use of a firearm. Given the judge's instructions, they could have convicted Stanley of manslaughter by careless use of a firearm even if they had a reasonable doubt about the hang fire defence (perhaps one based, as suggested in chapter 6, on a conflation of a thirty to sixty second safety standard and the much shorter measured length of hang fires). Thus, troubling suspicions of jury nullification remain.

CONCLUSION

Given that even the prosecutor would not rely on her testimony, it was not surprising that the jury refused to convict Stanley of murder based on Belinda Jackson's testimony. It will never be known whether a more contextual and sensitive approach to her testimony might have made it more credible and whether there was some innocent explanation for why she believed Gerald Stanley fired two shots at Boushie instead of one. It is sobering to think that both Marshall's all-white jury in 1971 and five judges of the Nova Scotia Court of Appeal in 1982 were convinced that the seventeen-year-old Mi'kmaq man was lying, but they were wrong. Similar to many other cases of suspected miscarriages of justice, we may simply never know the full truth.

The trial judge's instruction to the jury made clear that even if they had a reasonable doubt about the hang fire theory of a delayed discharge of a bullet, they should still consider manslaughter by the unlawful act of careless use of a firearm. This was the charge on which many experienced observers predicted that the jury would convict and it would have resulted in a minimum sentence of four years imprisonment for Stanley. The judge told the jury that the "elements of careless use and lawful excuse are somewhat intertwined" (TT 898), but never told the jury that Stanley's subjective perceptions of threats and fears of Boushie must also be reasonable, as he would have done had he told the jury about the legal requirements for either defence of property or self-defence.

Without guidance from the trial judge on whether Stanley's fear of Boushie and the others must be reasonable, the jury was left free to define for itself what was a lawful excuse for careless use of a firearm. Again, we will never know how the jury defined lawful excuse and what, if any, weight they gave to conscious or sub-conscious racial fears and Gerald Stanley's subjective, but perhaps, unreasonable fears about the threat he and his family faced.

Acquittal, Decision Not to Appeal, and Aftermath

INTRODUCTION

For a case that had been labelled by the *Guardian* as Canada's "Rodney King" case,[1] where an acquittal had triggered riots in Los Angeles, the reaction to the Stanley acquittal was peaceful and dignified. The national debate after the verdict was, however, quickly sidetracked into a debate about whether Prime Minister Justin Trudeau had interfered with the administration of justice by promising "to do better." Trudeau's intervention allowed much of the legal profession to echo the judiciary's stubborn defence of non-representative juries, affirming that any reform would have to come from the legislature.

When that reform did come, less than two months after the acquittal in the form of the introduction of Bill C-75, many defence lawyers opposed the proposed abolition of peremptory challenges arguing, contrary to the facts of the Stanley case, that they were one of the few devices available to them to make juries more representative. In announcing its decision not to appeal the acquittal, a representative of the attorney general of Saskatchewan defended all of the justice system participants: the trial judge, the prosecutors, defence lawyers, and jury. He suggested that those who criticized them were uninformed or wanted the criminal process to reflect "a particular perspective" or to "send a message about inclusiveness."[2] There was no announcement that Saskatchewan would hold an inquiry or a coroner's inquest in an attempt to prevent a repeat of what had happened.

Despite Prime Minister Trudeau's promise to do better, similar problems continued. Soon after the verdict, farmers in both Saskatchewan and Alberta used firearms to defend their property with charges either not being laid or dropped. In Ontario, Peter Khill was acquitted of murdering Jon Styres of Six Nations in a case with similar dynamics to the Stanley case.

THE VERDICT

The verdict that Stanley was not guilty of both murder and manslaughter was delivered at 7:35 p.m. on 9 February 2018 after the jury had deliberated for less than fifteen hours, including almost four hours of testimony being played back to them. (TT 909–924) Both Stanley and the jury were rushed out of the court. This exhibited fears for their safety that had been evident in the presence of heavy security throughout all of the proceedings. Similarly, a juror had expressed concerns that a spectator was taking a picture of the jury after it has started deliberations, but had returned to hear Gerald and Sheldon Stanley's testimony re-read to them. (TT 919)

One person yelled, "You're a murderer" and was recorded on the official transcript. (TT 924) Others yelled, "The system is broken. There is no justice."[3] Debbie Baptiste, Colten's mother, told the crowd gathered outside the courthouse, "White people they run the court system ... Enough killing our people. We fight back ... That ain't no freak accident. Go to hell, Gerald Stanley. That's where you belong."[4] The Red Pheasant First Nation called the verdict "absolutely perverse." The FSIN said it was "disgusted and angry" and called for an immediate inquiry into what it described as "a gross miscarriage of justice."[5]

Despite this angry reaction, there was no violence. Doug Cuthand, a Cree columnist in Saskatchewan, eloquently explained the dignified, almost stoic response, of many Indigenous people to the acquittal, one that was followed less than two weeks later by the acquittal of a white man charged with the murder of Tina Fontaine, a fifteen-year-old girl from Sagkeeng First Nation:

> All across Indian country, people have been saying prayers and conducting ceremonies in support of the Baptiste family and the call for justice.
>
> The prayers don't call for revenge or harm to the Stanley family. Our people believe that it's not our place to ask the Creator to bring harm to others ...
>
> We First Nations people believe in natural justice. It's called karma in India. Our elders tell us to be patient because what

goes around comes around. Hatred and racism cannot correct what has happened.[6]

Many non-Indigenous people also joined with Indigenous persons to hold peaceful protests of the verdict in many Canadian cities including Saskatoon, Edmonton, Winnipeg, Toronto, and Montreal.

TRUDEAU AND WILSON-RAYBOULD REACT: "WE HAVE TO DO BETTER"[7]

Colten Boushie's uncle, Alvin Baptiste, commented that Prime Minister Justin Trudeau had "asked for reconciliation. North Battleford has destroyed that.... All the Indigenous nations throughout Canada felt that. They felt the injustice. Instead of taking two or three steps forward, now we're [set] back again. What do we do about this?"[8]

Speaking from the United States on the evening of the verdict, Trudeau stated, "I'm not going to comment on the process that led to this point today, but I am going to say we have come to this point as a country far too many times." He added, "I know Indigenous and non-Indigenous Canadians alike know that we have to do better."[9]

Justice Minister Jody Wilson-Raybould stated on *Twitter*, "My thoughts are with the family of Colten Boushie tonight.... I truly feel your pain and I hear all of your voices. As a country we can and must do better – I am committed to working every day to ensure justice for all Canadians." She elaborated, "Too many Indigenous and marginalized people are victims of crime. Too many are in jail. Too many find themselves asking why they are not serving on juries. As a country, we have to do better."[10]

These comments recognized that the Stanley case was not the first case with such polarized racial dynamics. They related it to the context of over-representation of Indigenous people among both crime victims and prisoners. Although the comments did not criticize the jury or any other justice system participant, they were incredibly controversial. They threatened to overshadow the verdict.

In their plea to do better, the prime minister's and minister of justice's comments went beyond those of the new premier of Saskatchewan, Scott Moe, who acknowledged "the pain felt by the Boushie family and all First Nations communities" and understood "their deep disappointment." They also went beyond those of the leader of the federal official opposition, Andrew Scheer, who said,

"It's appropriate to show concern and support ... for the family of the victim," but also "important that we remember that politicians don't decide these types of things."[11] Rob Nicholson, who as minister of justice, caused controversy in 2012 when he said that the use of firearms might be justified in remote areas, likewise expressed sympathy for the family, but argued that it was necessary to respect "the independence of the judicial process."[12]

National Post columnist Christie Blatchford argued that the comments from Trudeau and "especially from the justice minister, were outrageous, given the separation that is meant to exist between the legislative and judicial branches and which is the very foundation of judicial independence." She drew the same equation that courts had between judges and juries by arguing, "[w]hen government signals its unhappiness with particular verdicts, as this one did unmistakably, judges are but a step or two away from being at the mercy of politicians."[13] She shared the courts' scepticism about representative juries quoting Justice Moldaver's majority decision, examined in chapter 5, that jury selection cannot become "a public inquiry into historical and cultural wrongs" and concluded that "the notion that you can get justice only when the correct number of jurors looking back at you are the precise shade of your own skin colour – that only those of your race or culture are your true 'peers' – that's nonsense."[14]

Eric Gottardi, the chair of the Canadian Bar Association's criminal justice section, warned that "criticism of the jury's verdict becomes criticism of the jury itself" and "when elected politicians make comments like that, it can serve to undermine public confidence in the system." Canadian Council of Criminal Defence Lawyers argued the comments were "unprecedented, inappropriate and quite frankly dangerous" because they could be interpreted as criticism of the jury's verdict. In their view Trudeau and Wilson-Raybould had "rendered an incredible disservice to the jurors in this matter."[15] The Saskatchewan Trial Lawyers Association criticized "uninformed criticisms made by politicians, citizens and some members of the bar who have unfairly criticized the judge, jurors, prosecutor and defence counsel on the Gerald Stanley murder trial."[16]

International Attention

Although the Canadian debate got side-tracked into a debate about the propriety of Trudeau and Wilson-Raybould's statements, the international press remained focused on the impact of the verdict on Indigenous people.

The *New York Times* reported that the verdict would be added to the grievances in the Battleford area arising from the 1885 public hangings of eight Indigenous men and the use of the pass system "similar to South Africa's under apartheid." It quoted Cree lawyer Eleanor Sunchild questioning whether Saskatchewan had even "started on reconciliation ... both sides have to take responsibility and accountability for what got us in this situation."[17] It ran an op-ed by Gabrielle Scrimshaw who explained that she grew up "in a small Saskatchewan town two hours east of where Mr Boushie was killed. As a Dene girl of seven, I was accused of stealing.... When I was in college, a young man (whose father, brother and uncle were members of the Royal Canadian Mounted Police) declared one night that he wanted to be a police officer so that he 'could shoot' some Indians."[18]

The *Guardian* from the UK recorded the polarization around the verdict. It quoted a farmer who donated $1000 to the Stanleys because, "It could have been me." This was juxtaposed with a Métis writer who expressed shock at the donations received for the Stanleys and "the amount of malice" expressed in social media.[19] It also ran an op-ed arguing, "I am Colten Boushie. Canada is the All-white Jury that Acquitted his Killer."[20]

CONTINUED POLARIZATION

The polarization that had proceeded the trial continued after the verdict: Stanley's *GoFundMe* page raised just under $225,000 while Boushie's raised over $200,000.[21] Each funding page had to disable their comment functions because of the nature of some of the accompanying statements.[22] Kevin Joseph, a Cree writer, in the *Prince Albert Herald*, wrote thoughtfully about how he refused to engage with comments on social media. One said, "I wish I had an opportunity to kill one of these thieving Indians, too." Another stated, "ALL farmers are racist, it's just a matter of time before they kill us all." Joseph reasoned, "I can't calm fears. I can't stop hate. I can't erase 500 years of history in one column." He added, "We are all somewhat responsible for this current tense climate in this province I love."[23]

Canadians who had been engaging with the case over social media sent the federal minister of justice over 1,700 emails, some demanding change in light of the verdict, many of them asking for an immediate appeal. They included over 350 emails criticizing the minister of justice and the prime minister for commenting about the case.[24] Saskatchewan Justice received 1,000 emails and letters on the case between January and March 2018.[25]

A public opinion poll taken after the verdict found that 46 per cent of respondents believed Trudeau had inappropriately intervened, higher than the 30 per cent who defended the acquittal as "good and fair." The number who supported Trudeau's comments (32 per cent) were identical to those who opposed the verdict as "flawed and wrong."

Reactions to the verdict reflected gender, age, race, and partisan affiliation differences. Indeed, the Stanley case was a kind of "red state blue state" barometer of larger cleavages. Women and young people were more opposed to the verdict than men and older people. For example, only 24 per cent of female respondents and 20 per cent of those under thirty-five-years of age concluded the verdict was "good and fair" regardless of how the jury was selected. Young people and women also were more inclined to believe representational juries were necessary to justify the verdict. Of women aged eighteen to thirty-four, 50 per cent saw the verdict as flawed and wrong with only 16 per cent thinking it was good and fair.

There were also race differences with 41 per cent of visible minorities thinking the verdict was flawed and wrong compared to 30 per cent of non-visible minorities. At the same time, in both groups, there was considerable support for the verdict as good and fair (28 per cent and 31 per cent respectively). Unfortunately, the poll did not include Indigenous respondents.

There were regional differences with 63 per cent of respondents in Saskatchewan and 44 per cent of respondents in Manitoba and Alberta thinking the Prairie jury had rendered a good and fair verdict compared to under 30 per cent of respondents in the eastern provinces and 32 per cent in British Columbia.

Finally, there was also a partisan dimension. The vast majority (81 per cent) of Conservative supporters and 45 per cent of NDP supporters thought the prime minister's comments were inappropriate. At the same time 33 per cent of Liberal supporters thought Trudeau had crossed a line. Trudeau's comments were more polarizing than the verdict, with 54 per cent of Conservative voters, 24 per cent of NDP voters, and 20 per cent of Liberal voters concluding the acquittal was good and fair.[26]

THE PROSECUTION'S DECISION NOT TO APPEAL

Under the *Criminal Code*, the prosecution can appeal an acquittal only on the basis of an error of law. Unlike the accused, the prosecutor cannot appeal a conviction alleging a miscarriage of justice or an unreasonable verdict.[27] This means that a decision by a judge or a jury that there is a reasonable doubt about guilt is on its own not subject to appeal.[28] This reflects the criminal law's traditional priority for avoiding wrongful convictions. It may, however, produce a situation where legal understandings are in tension with lay understandings that may view wrongful acquittals as miscarriages of justice.[29]

The legal preference for limiting appeals by the prosecutor is not immutable. England changed its rule on double jeopardy in 2003 to value accuracy and victims' interests in cases where new and compelling evidence of guilt was discovered. This change was made, in part, in response to the Stephen Lawrence case when the acquittal of white men, charged through a private prosecution with the racist killing of a Black teenager, was seen by an inquiry as "an affront both to the Lawrence family and the community at large."[30] If there were increased understanding and concern about miscarriages of justice that result in acquittals, Parliament could amend the *Criminal Code* to allow the prosecutor to appeal on the basis of a miscarriage of justice.

The decision not to appeal Stanley's acquittal was announced by Saskatchewan's Assistant Deputy Attorney General Anthony Gerein, who was responsible for criminal trials and appeals in the province. He accurately stressed that the Crown could not appeal because of "a disagreement over the facts."[31] He defended the prosecutor, but without addressing Burge's failure to: challenge prospective jurors for racism or pretrial publicity; object to the use of five peremptory challenges to exclude Indigenous jurors; or to the testimony of lay witnesses about hang fire; or to request that the trial judge explain the law of self-defence to the jury; or his concession that warning shots would have been justified. The prosecutor's failure to make such objections meant that fewer legal decisions were made by the trial judge. Subsequently, this meant there were fewer available grounds for appeal.

Gerein went beyond attempting to justify the decision not to appeal to defending the entire justice system. He argued that "defence counsel should not be faulted for using procedures available to them" and that anyone, if charged with an offence, "would expect as much from their lawyer."[32] He made no reference to whether that person would expect their lawyer to challenge all persons who visibly appeared to be of a different race or the impossibility of an Indigenous accused using peremptory challenges to remove all non-Indigenous people from the jury. Gerein suggested critics of the verdict were un-informed stating, "To say something could have been better or differently with no specifics and without demonstrated knowledge about the case gives no cause to think anything was improper or inadequate."[33]

Gerein deflected the jury selection issue by stressing that whether jury selection should change was a matter for "elected officials." He prefaced these comments by quoting Justice Moldaver's judgment in the case of Kokopenace about jury selection not being "a mechanism for repairing the damaged relationships between particular social groups." This was consistent with the attorney general of Saskatchewan's vigorous and successful attempts in 2014 to defeat claims that lack of Indigenous representation on juries in Regina violated both Treaty 4 and the Charter. He also argued it was a "disservice" and suggestive of "an agenda" to suggest that the jury "acted improperly."[34]

Gerein was silent about how Indigenous organizations and people had responded to the case. Instead he spoke about the illegitimacy of appeals "because a particular perspective leads to the opinion that the verdict was unreasonable" or to "send a message about inclusiveness." He urged for "no one to be discouraged or distrust the system. We are all in this together and must be united against crime and in the search of justice."[35] These comments ignored how the Stanley case was perceived by most Indigenous people and how the Stanley case related to other similar Saskatchewan cases.

The decision not to appeal was controversial. Both Chris Murphy, one of the Boushie's family lawyers, and Professor David Tanovich, an evidence expert and experienced appellate counsel, argued that the admission of lay evidence about hang fire and the judge's failure to warn about or differentiate the lay witnesses' testimony about hang fires from the testimony of qualified experts were legal errors that could be appealed. Tanovich noted, however, that one of the challenges of the appeal was the prosecution's failure to object to the admissibility of the lay witnesses, the judge's charge to the jury or to the jury selection process.[36] As will be seen, the attorney general of Ontario has appealed a similar acquittal in the Peter Khill case. In that case the prosecutor alleges that the trial judge made legal errors by admitting lay evidence about Khill's military training and when instructing the jury about self-defence. In the Stanley case, the judge did not instruct the jury about self-defence or defence of property, thus limiting legal grounds for appeal.

After the Crown announced its decision not to appeal, Scott Spencer issued a statement that "on behalf of the Stanley family, and my team, I offer our unreserved condolences to the Boushie/Baptiste family. The Stanley family is relieved that the criminal process is now complete, but this is not a happy day. A young man died, that is a terrible tragedy. There is no going back; there is no making it right. We hope that with time the Boushie/Baptiste family can begin to heal."[37] Gerald Stanley subsequently pled guilty in April 2018 to the charge of unsafe storage of six rifles and shotguns and was fined $3,000 with a ten-year ban on possessing firearms.[38]

CONTINUED CONCERNS ABOUT RURAL CRIME

After the verdict, governments continued to grapple with the rural crime problem and, as will be seen, farmers continued to use firearms to defend themselves.

Saskatchewan's 2018–19 budget allocated just under $5 million to create thirty new police positions.[39] This may be justified, but Saskatchewan's focus on adding more armed state officials seems fixated on law enforcement as opposed to exploring more creative and constructive means of crime prevention. In any event, it appears to not have satisfied either the rural municipalities as represented by SARM or First Nations as represented by FSIN.

The Saskatchewan government expressed interest in SARM's proposal to change provincial trespass law so that owners would no longer be required to post no trespass signs to trigger provincial trespass laws. Saskatchewan Attorney General Don Morgan suggested landowners are "entitled to have their rights asserted; their rights protected," but without any reference to Treaty rights in the province.[40] There was no apparent recognition that changing trespass laws could cause concerns over Treaty relations and could trigger confusion and armed confrontations. The Saskatchewan government subsequently started a consultation on its trespass laws. Some proponents of no longer requiring "no trespassing" signs to be posted admitted that the Stanley/Boushie case was "in the back of everybody's mind." The SARM president acknowledged "the perception that First Nations people are singled out," but argued "that's not the case at all" and the new law would apply to all.[41] The Saskatchewan government's consultation document on the proposed change only briefly mentioned Treaties concluding that proposed changes would not affect hunting and fishing Treaty rights that would still be established by court decisions.[42]

The Alberta government announced a $10 million rural crime initiative featuring thirty-nine new RCMP officers, new prosecutors, and plans to use bait programs to arrest those who would steal farm equipment.[43] As with the Saskatchewan plan, the focus seemed more on law enforcement than crime prevention or working with the affected communities.

The United Conservative Party official opposition in Alberta issued a report on rural crime. In addition to calls for increased police, prosecutors, and restitution, it recommended amending the self-defence and defence of property provisions in the Criminal Code to include significant delay or non-response by the police, failure to leave when confronted, the number of trespassers, and whether they were intoxicated as factors to be considered when determining whether force was reasonable. It also recommended that rural crime be seen as an aggravating factor at sentencing.[44] The report did not mention the Stanley case, but seemed inspired by it.

Perhaps in an attempt to avoid some of the negative publicity that the Farmers with Firearms Facebook group had received, a new Farmers Against Rural Crime Facebook group was formed. One of its organizers explained, "We need to find a happy medium for what we can do to defend ourselves ... life over property isn't what we're looking for ... People claiming we're redneck racist farmers, wheeling our guns around our hip like it's the wild west, that's not what we're about."[45] The Facebook group quickly had over 16,000 followers. Its founder suggested more emphasis on crime prevention through the use of technology such as surveillance cameras and greater use of sentences where offenders "would be giving back to the community they have hurt."[46]

"I'm going to use something that's appropriate, even if I go to jail."[47]

The RCMP held a public meeting in Biggar, close to the Stanley farm. One farmer questioned the RCMP, "Have we got any rights to try and stop them?" He was correctly told by the RCMP that, "We are not able to give specific answers on what the victim of a crime can do because we don't know the exact circumstances." This caused the farmer, who asked the question, to say, "I don't know what's appropriate and what's not appropriate, but I am going to take measures into my own hands if it involves my family. I'm going to use something that's appropriate, even if I go to jail."[48]

About a month after the verdict, a farmer in Spiritwood, Saskatchewan fired shots in an attempt to prevent a break and enter. He was not charged, but an Indigenous man was charged with theft, break and enter, and weapons charges.[49] An Okotoks, Alberta farmer was charged with aggravated assault, pointing a firearm, and careless use of a firearm when he shot a trespasser who was charged with theft a few weeks after the incident. Over 150 people gathered at the courthouse to protest the charges. One protester alleged the RCMP were acting under "orders to lay charges because of all the other events and the political happenings. Our system is broken." Another had a sign, "Keep your city out of our country." Others criticized federal and provincial governments for not "changing the damn laws." As with Stanley, they contributed money to the farmer's defence fund because they could imagine themselves in the same position.[50] The charges were later dropped to applause from supporters in the court. The prosecutor explained new forensic evidence indicated that the trespasser had been wounded by a ricochet.[51] The result, however, continued to normalize the use of warning shots to protect property.

The concern about rural crime also resulted in police unnecessarily detaining Indigenous persons. Seraine Sunkawaste from the White Bear First Nation was handcuffed and detained by the RCMP for about thirty minutes on suspicion of break and entering shortly after his seventeen-year-old son, who has Down Syndrome, relieved himself on a rural road close to a farm. Sunkawaste said he was reluctant to stop near the farm in light of the Stanley/Boushie case, and told his son, "You cannot go on farm property." He was released after the farm owner reported nothing had been taken from the farm. He indicated he would make a police complaint to the special investigation unit of the Federation of Sovereign Indigenous Nations.[52]

Debates about rural crime and farmers' use of guns to defend their property continued in the aftermath of Gerald Stanley's acquittal. Both Saskatchewan and Alberta devoted more resources to rural crime, but the initiatives seemed focused on law enforcement and adding more officers rather than on crime prevention.

Racial tensions and the Stanley/Boushie case were present just below the surface as rural crime and changes to Saskatchewan's trespass laws were debated.

THE FEDERAL GOVERNMENT RESPONDS WITH BILL C-75: "THERE'S GOING TO BE CHANGE. MAYBE WE DO HAVE HOPE AFTER ALL"[53]

The Boushie family met with both Prime Minister Trudeau and Justice Minister Wilson-Raybould. After the meetings, the Justice Minister commented, "Those reforms are coming ... The reality of the Boushie family coming here and the elevation of the national consciousness on the challenges and systemic barriers that marginalized people face in the criminal justice system is very welcome."[54]

At the end of March 2018, less than eight weeks after the Boushie verdict, the federal government proposed changes to jury selection in a controversial omnibus criminal justice bill known as Bill C-75. It proposed to abolish peremptory challenges and give judges, as opposed to two jurors, the power to decide challenges for cause.[55] This would implement two of the recommendations of the 1991 Manitoba Aboriginal Justice Inquiry. Debbie Baptiste reacted positively stating, "There's going to be change. Maybe we do have hope after all."[56]

If implemented at the time of the Stanley trial, the changes proposed in Bill C-75 likely would have resulted in the presence of Indigenous jurors at the Stanley trial. At the same time, Bill C-75 does nothing to alter the cases examined in chapter 5: there is still no requirement for proportionate representation of Indigenous people in panels of prospective jurors or the actual jury.

The bill only proposed minor alterations to juror qualifications under the *Criminal Code*: under it people would be permanently disqualified from being jurors if they had been sentenced to two years' imprisonment, not, as at present, one year. Recent data from Ontario suggests that over half of Indigenous people who returned juror questionnaires in both 2016 and 2017 were disqualified for some reason. The disqualification of these Indigenous people is particularly unfortunate because they were among the small minority of Indigenous people who responded to jury notices by filling out the questionnaire sent to them by provincial authorities.[57]

The new Bill C-75 did not propose to change the *Criminal Code* standard for challenging panels of prospective jurors prepared by the provinces. Those challenging the representativeness of the panel would still have to establish "partiality, fraud or wilful misconduct" by provincial officials. In addition, the Supreme Court's majority judgment in *Kokopenace* would still set a minimal standard of reasonable efforts for including Indigenous people on juries with no requirement to single out for affirmative action Indigenous people and other groups under-represented on juries but over-represented in the justice system.

Bill C-75 could have taken a more aggressive approach to jury qualifications by following the Saskatchewan approach that only prohibited those serving actual prison sentences from sitting on a jury. At the same time, it is likely that Indigenous people would continue to be disproportionately exempted from jury service for various hardship reasons related to socio-economic and health disparities and travel demands. Taking steps to provide translation services for Indigenous languages, requiring trials to be held closer to, or in, remote Indigenous communities, and providing transportation, accommodation and child care for jurors would require consultation and provincial buy-in. There may not have been enough time for provincial consultation on these issues before Bill C-75 was introduced, but another option would have been to impose new standards on the provinces but delay their implementation until the provinces had time to make necessary adjustments to their systems of compiling jury lists and helping prospective jurors come to court.

Bill C-75 would also give judges the power to stand aside prospective jurors if they determined it was necessary to maintain confidence in the administration of justice.[58] The jury selection jurisprudence examined in chapter 5 suggests, however, that many judges may be reluctant to depart from principles of random selection that they have frequently equated with impartiality. The new public confidence grounded in Bill C-75 did not address the specific need to increase the representation of Indigenous people and others who have been over-represented as both the accused and victims in the criminal justice system, even though other parts of the Bill pointed out these realities. Without such explicit legislative guidance, many judges may be reluctant to use stand asides, as defence lawyers say they use peremptory challenges, to produce more diverse juries. This is important because judicial stand asides would effectively replace peremptory challenges by the accused and the prosecutor under Bill C-75.

Bill C-75 did not go as far as two UK commissions of inquiry that recommended, in cases where race was an issue either because of the identity of the accused or the victim, that judges should be able to ensure that three members of the jury were from a minority population.[59] These recommendations, however, have not been implemented in the UK. If they had been included in Bill C-75, they would have been criticized on the basis that they would depart from random selection[60] based on treating every prospective juror the same.

Bill C-75 also does not alter the traditional role of jury secrecy that might allow juries to explain their verdict. To be practicable and persuasive, juries would probably have to, as in some civil law countries, work with judges or be given their own legal advisors to be able to give collective reasons. The American practice of not prohibiting individual jurors from talking about their deliberations is more open than the Canadian practice, but fails to provide collective justifications for the jury's verdict. Given the anxiety about protecting the identity and safety of the jurors in the Stanley case (TT 919), it would be surprising if any of them spoke publicly. They would be risking criminal prosecution. In any event, they could only speak for themselves. The silence of the jury about the reasons for its verdict makes the process of jury selection even more important.

Opposition to the Proposed Abolition of Peremptory Challenges

Many defence lawyers criticized the proposed abolition of peremptory challenges. Most of their arguments avoided engaging directly with the fact that defence lawyers had used peremptory challenges in both the Stanley and Helen Betty Osborne cases to keep Indigenous people off the jury. Instead, defence lawyers frequently asserted that abolition of peremptory challenges would make juries less diverse. One argued, "If I am representing a racialized accused, I can exclude the twelfth white juror to give the next racialized juror a chance to be selected. In simple terms, the new rule will mean more all-white juries."[61]

Defence lawyer Frank Addario took a more holistic approach and criticized Bill C-75 for not addressing Indigenous under-representation among prospective jurors. He suggested, "The real heart of the work is in creating more representative juries and courtrooms in which Indigenous people are treated fairly."[62] This was a valid point and the federal government could have amended s.629 of the *Criminal Code* which limited challenges to panels of prospective jurors to cases of wilful fraud and partiality. As discussed in chapter 5, the *Criminal Code* had been interpreted so that the principles of substantive or anti-colonial equality would not be applied to the composition of panels of prospective jurors.

Defence lawyer Nader Hasan recognized that peremptory challenges could be abused by both the prosecutor and the accused, but suggested that challenges to their discriminatory use could be effective. He argued, "Just because it does not work in Alabama does not mean it won't work in Canada."[63] This was a better argument than those made by defence lawyers who simply ignored how peremptory challenges were used in the Stanley case. Nevertheless, Hasan did not address the failed attempts in Canada to challenge the alleged discriminatory use of peremptory challenges to exclude Indigenous people and other minorities. He also did not deal with the cases examined in chapter 5 that suggested defence lawyers might not be bound by the equality rights of the *Charter* and could not be required to explain why they had used a peremptory challenge.[64]

At times, the debate about peremptory challenges became heated. It is disconcerting, however, that it pitted disadvantaged racialized accused in some Canadian cities, such as Toronto, against Indigenous accused and victims. Knowledgeable observers on both sides of the debate would likely acknowledge that courts would not be likely to intervene, even in the face of significant under-representation of Indigenous and other racialized groups in panels of prospective jurors. Many defence lawyers opposed the abolition of peremptory challenges as this is one of the few tools they have in shaping juries. They are frustrated that judges continue tightly to control and limit the questions that they could ask prospective jurors as part of the challenge for cause procedure. More comprehensive and holistic reform of jury selection may have been preferable, but it would require provincial cooperation and might encounter judicial resistance if it delayed trials, infringed juror privacy, cost money, or departed from random selection.

In my view, the federal government's current proposal to eliminate peremptory challenges is a necessary first step to increase Indigenous representation on Canadian juries, but it is a small one. As Justice Iacobucci has suggested, much needs to be done to increase the willingness and ability of Indigenous people to serve on criminal juries. The Indigenous distrust of the criminal justice system that he documented has probably grown since the Stanley verdict. Even if more efforts are made to accommodate the financial, physical, linguistic, and spiritual needs of Indigenous people when they serve on juries, many may not want to be part of a justice system that fails them and has values alien to Indigenous culture and law.[65]

But juries are not going away. They are entrenched in the *Charter* and will continue to be used in the most serious cases. Bill C-75 is a partial reform that, if implemented, will remove peremptory challenges, allow judges to decide whether jurors are impartial, make minor changes to the disqualification of jurors, and provide an opportunity for judges to stand aside jurors, when necessary, to increase the representation of Indigenous and other racialized groups on juries to maintain public confidence in the administration of justice. The record to date does not provide grounds for optimism that Indigenous people and other racialized and disadvantaged minorities will be represented on Canadian juries in proportion to their population, let alone with respect to their over-representation among accused and victims. More cases with racial dynamics similar to the Stanley/Boushie case are bound to recur. As will be seen, they already have occurred.

STANLEY II?: THE PETER KHILL/JON STYRES CASE

A trial that generated polarization and an outcome similar to the Stanley case was held in Hamilton, Ontario in June 2018. Peter Khill was accused of second-degree murder for killing Jon Styres of Six Nations, a father of two, in Glanbrook, Ontario on 4 February 2016, six months before Boushie was killed. The area near Hamilton had its own history of tensions arising from Indigenous occupations in nearby Caledonia.[66] Police reported that Styres was trying to steal Khill's fifteen-year-old truck at 3:00 a.m. in the morning. Khill, who had been trained as a military reservist, left his house and shot Styres twice near his truck.

Khill was released on bail three days after the shooting with conditions similar to those imposed on Stanley such as posting $100, 000 and not having weapons or contact with the victim's family.[67] As in the Stanley case, bail was granted even though it could have been denied as necessary to maintain public confidence in the administration of justice. This raised the question of how judges should make such determinations when public opinion was polarized.

Polarized and Competing Petitions

Almost 15,000 supporters signed a petition calling for the charges to be dropped on the basis that Khill had acted in defence of his property. These petitioners would have supported the grant of bail. The petition contained comments such as: "98 per cent of the population can't be wrong. Justice has already been served"; "the right to defend your property should be paramount"; "Castle law should be in effect in Canada. Police are only a minute away when every second counts."[68] This latter comment reflected a willingness to use self-defence even when police response times were faster than in the rural context of the Stanley case.

Over 1,200 people signed a competing petition named, "Justice for Jon Styres." Many of these petitioners would have been less pleased with Khill being granted bail. They argued that "nobody has a right to kill anyone over possessions" and the petition had comments such as: "this is not allowed in Canada"; "I am signing because we must put an end to racism"; "the racist ignorant supporters who condone the death of Jon Styres simply show the ugly truth of Canada ... natives' lives matter and knowingly killing a man over a truck is murder."[69] Social polarization was by no means limited to Saskatchewan.

Challenge for Cause

The jury selection in the Khill case had two important differences from the Stanley trial. First, the prosecution applied to the judge to ask prospective jurors whether their ability to decide the case impartially on the basis of the evidence would be affected by the fact that the accused was white and the victim was Indigenous. This followed an earlier trial precedent in Ontario[70] as well as the Saskatchewan "starlight tour" case discussed in chapter 5.[71] Khill's lawyer did not challenge the question though he later argued that race played no role in the case because Khill could not identify Styres's race in the middle of the night.

The judge accepted that the question about racist bias towards the victim could be asked. The single question, however, did not address the existence of stereotypical attitudes associating Indigenous people with truck thefts in the area. Such questions combining details of crimes that may raise racist stereotypes have been allowed by trial judges in a few cases,[72] but remain a matter of the trial judge's discretion.

Although designed to root out racism, the question asked in the Khill case would also have reminded the jury that the victim was Indigenous as did the defence lawyer's closing address to the jury stressing that race was not an issue in the case. This reflects what Harvard law professor Martha Minow has recognized as the "dilemma of difference": ignoring racism, as in the Stanley trial, could perpetuate disadvantage but recognizing it in an unequal world could have the same effect.[73]

When asked, at least one prospective juror admitted that he would struggle with being impartial and was found to be unacceptable to serve on the jury. He was thanked by the judge for being honest. Another prospective juror was excused when she admitted that she lived in the same neighbourhood as the accused and had her home broken into four times and would have trouble being impartial.[74] Unlike in the Stanley case, four prospective jurors, who indicated that they had tentative views about the case (because, for example, they had been involved in a similar case or had relatives in the police or the military), were immediately excused by the trial judge.[75]

The second difference with the Stanley case was that while the defence used peremptory challenges, no concerns were reported about their use to exclude visibly Indigenous prospective jurors. This might have, however, reflected Indigenous under-representation on the Hamilton jury.[76] As discussed in chapter 5, Ontario continues to struggle with Indigenous under-representation on juries.

Six Nations Chief Ava Hill issued a press release before the trial started noting, "Indigenous People will not feel safe until there is a justice system that places value on Indigenous lives. Peaceful co-existence between Indigenous and non-Indigenous People requires a justice system that is non-discriminatory and fair. Justice is necessary if there is be any hope for reconciliation."[77] The stakes of the case were high with many making comparisons to the Stanley/Boushie case.

The Evidence

Khill testified that he left his house to confront the lone intruder without calling 911 or turning the lights on. He said, "Hey, hands up" and that "as soon as I thought he had a gun I fired." Styres had no gun, but he did have a screwdriver as well as a closed knife in his pocket.[78] Khill testified "basically it was your worst nightmare" and that he and his wife were concerned about thefts and break-ins in a rural area. Drawing on his part-time experience in the military from 2007 to 2011, Khill explained, "There was a threat outside and I did what I needed to neutralize it."[79] Some of the evidence focused on Khill's former military training.

The prosecutor stressed that Khill only called 911 after Styres was shot even though two cell phones were available in his bedroom. Medical evidence confirmed that Styres was shot twice: once in the chest and once in the shoulder with the bullets having a downward trajectory. There was, however, uncertainty about whether Styres was bent over when shot the second time and whether he was facing the truck or partially facing Khill.[80] As in the Stanley case, the forensic evidence did not provide definitive answers.

An attempt to introduce Styre's criminal record and charges that were pending at the time of his death was rejected by the trial judge. Unlike in the Stanley trial, the trial judge balanced the value of such evidence against its prejudice concluding that none of the evidence of Styre's non-violent acts would "be of any legitimate assistance to the jury in the discharge of its function. On the other hand, such evidence of past illegal acts, and past allegations of illegal behaviour could well prejudice the jury."[81] Statements that Khill made after his arrest were excluded as involuntary on the basis that he had been induced into thinking that he might not be charged or would face less serious charges if he talked to the police.[82] This was also different from the Stanley case where Stanley had tried, but failed, to convince the judge to keep his statements to the police after his arrest from the jury.[83] As in the Stanley case, however, both expert and lay evidence was offered on a critical aspect of the case. In this case, it was not about hang fire, but the effects that Khill's military training could have on his actions years later.[84]

In his closing address to the jury, the prosecutor argued, "There's not one law for ex-soldiers and one law for everyone else" and that "civilian life is not a war zone." He stressed that Khill fired two shots, including one while the victim was already dying, and that a police car was only five minutes away once 911 was called.

Khill's defence lawyer argued that even though Jon Styres did not have a gun, reasonable mistakes were permissible under the law of self-defence and that the jury should not consider manslaughter as a compromise verdict. He also argued, it was dark and Khill could not know that Styres was Indigenous. Hence, "race cannot, it does not play a role in the case."[85] He claimed that Khill acted as he had been trained to do so as a soldier and that he lived in an area without neighbours immediately nearby.

Unlike in the Stanley case, the trial judge told the jury about the 2012 law on self-defence. He explained that Khill could be mistaken about the threat of force he faced, but that his perceptions of threat, as well as his reactions to it, must be reasonable. The judge instructed the jury that Khill's military training was relevant to determining whether Khill acted in self-defence[86] and that the issue was whether Khill acted reasonably "in the circumstances as Peter Khill knew them or reasonably believed them to be" and not whether Khill "had no other course of action available to him."[87] This underlined how the 2012 law expanded self-defence by stressing the open-ended issue of reasonableness as opposed to the emphasis in the former s.34(2) of the *Criminal Code* on whether the accused believed on reasonable grounds that he could not otherwise preserve himself from death or grievous bodily harm. It also could have left the Khill jury, similar to the Stanley jury, with the impression that what mattered was subjective perceptions of "the circumstances as Peter Khill knew them." At the same time, in other parts of the charge, the judge told the jury that the accused's perceptions and any mistake about the threat he faced must be reasonable.

After starting deliberations, the jury returned to court to ask the judge whether the reasonable person was an everyday reasonable person or limited to this situation alone. The judge told the jury to consider whether it was a "reasonable reaction to the circumstances as viewed through the eyes of a person with all of Mr Khill's qualities, but taking in mind the military training but also keeping in mind that he has to obey the law."[88] This instruction left much for the jury to decide, but it may have allowed them to individualize and lower the standard of reasonable conduct for Khill.

Since 1990, courts have placed the reasonable person in the same circumstances as the accused. They have factored in characteristics such as gender, diminished intelligence, or being in prison that are relevant to the accused's perceptions and reactions. But as the prosecutor argued, Khill was not in a war zone as some battered women and prisoners find themselves in. The Supreme Court has expressed reluctance, albeit under the pre-2012 self-defence law, to extend the battered women precedent to other bullying contexts, let alone encounters between strangers.[89] Thinking about what a reasonable person with military training would have done may have had the effect of encouraging the jury to lower the standard of reasonable conduct and self-restraint required by self-defence. Khill's case was very different from the original decision that contextualized the definition of a "reasonable person" to factor in past battering in deciding whether a woman could be seen to have reasonably perceived a threat and to have responded reasonably.[90]

The jury acquitted Khill of both murder and manslaughter.[91] The prosecution has filed an appeal claiming that the trial judge erred in law by failing to instruct the jury about Khill's role and use of a weapon in the incident and by telling the jury to consider Khill's military training in determining the reasonableness of his perceptions of the threat, and his response, and admitting evidence about his military training.[92] Distinct from the Stanley case, the trial judge explained the law of self-defence to the jury thus producing possible errors of law on which to base an appeal even though the prosecutor did not object to how the trial judge answered the jury's question.

Reactions to the Acquittal

The Six Nations Council expressed shock and disappointment at the acquittal and called for the prosecution to appeal. Chief Ava Hill questioned why the Canadian justice system "fails to hold anyone accountable for the taking of a life" adding that Indigenous victims such as Jon Styres, Colten Boushie, and Tina Fontaine all had "mothers and fathers, raised as children with hopes and dreams ... it is unfathomable that their tragic deaths are unanswered by the Canadian justice system."[93] The Six Nations Council subsequently unanimously voted to ban Khill from Six Nations territory for life. One of the proponents of the motion explained, "We are that much safer without him being in our community" and another indicated, "We want to take control of our lives again."[94]

Chief Hill was sceptical that the question asked of prospective jurors about racism was enough, "How do you prove that? I can ask you if you're racist and you can say no. This whole thing is, I think, just racism rearing its ugly head."[95] This view was supported by Professor Ameil Joseph who teaches social work at McMaster and had been summoned as a juror in the Khill/Styres case and ended up serving as one of two triers of the challenge for cause in the Khill case. He later wrote, "If the question asked of potential jurors was to address implicit or unconscious bias, it did not work. What it in fact produced was a mostly male, mostly white jury who was told to deny race and racism as a fact of the case and systemically eliminate these contexts from factual analysis."[96] An approach informed by research on implicit bias would have favoured more nuanced and extensive discussion of the attitudes of prospective jurors and perhaps also judicial instructions that named and tried to prohibit the jury from relying on racist stereotypes in its deliberations.

Assembly of First Nations Grand Chief Perry Bellegarde stated that after the Stanley and Tina Fontaine verdicts, "this is the third trial verdict this year that tells First Nations that our lives do not matter, along with thirty years of documented systemic discrimination and racism in the Canadian justice system. It also sends a troubling signal to Canadians that they will not face consequences for acts of violence they commit on First Nation individuals…. It's time for all of us to stand up and say 'First Nations lives matter.'"[97]

Khill's lawyer defended the verdict stressing that it was about self-defence and not defence of property given his client's belief that Styres had a gun. This, however, ignored that, as courts have recognized, the boundaries between defence of property and self-defence are fluid.[98] It was Khill's actions, in confronting Styres with a gun when he was at his truck, that put Khill a position where he feared that Styres might shoot him.

Khill's lawyer also argued that the use of the challenge for cause to question prospective jurors was "an excellent approach to be able to dispel" any concerns about racism and one that indicated that Bill C-75's proposal to end peremptory challenges was "wrongheaded."[99] Christie Blatchford declared that "race was not a factor in Khill verdict" and suggested that anyone who suggested otherwise had not been in the court as she had.[100] At the same time, given laws that prevent interviews with jurors, it was impossible to know for sure how the jury reached its decision.

Social media reactions reflected a similar polarization as in the Stanley case. Comments such as, "Canada has become a 'Stand your Ground' country and you can murder a Native for free," were matched with "one less deadbeat criminal off the street," and "while some politicians have no problems with First Nations stealing stuff without ramifications … a jury still has the ability to think."[101] As in the Stanley case, social media was a fertile site for polarized conflict and racism.

The day after the acquittal, the spouse and two daughters of Jon Styres announced that they would sue Khill civilly for assault, battery, and negligence claiming $2 million in damages and $250,000 in punitive damages.[102] The Boushie family also subsequently sued both the Stanleys and the RCMP.[103] In both cases the Indigenous plaintiffs would only have to establish civil fault on a balance of probabilities as opposed to proving criminal fault beyond a reasonable doubt. The advantages and disadvantages of using civil lawsuits, inquiries, and inquests will be examined in the next chapter. Despite some modest improvements in jury selection and the prosecution's decision to appeal, the Khill/Styres case was quite similar to the Stanley/Boushie case.

CONCLUSION

It is difficult to be very optimistic about reform. Many saw the prime minister's and the minister of justice's "do better" tweets and comments as inappropriate. In addition, Bill C-75's proposal to abolish peremptory challenges has many opponents including defence lawyers. Its proposed reforms fall far short of the radical jury reform that may be necessary to increase Indigenous representation on juries. Even radical jury reform would not necessarily respond to broader questions of systemic and colonial discrimination that Indigenous persons suffer as both accused and crime victims or their distrust of the criminal justice system that most probably was increased by Stanley's and Khill's acquittals.

The decision made not to appeal Stanley's acquittal reflected the limited grounds for appealing acquittals on the basis of errors of law. That said, it did not discuss the failure of the prosecutor at trial to attempt to question prospective jurors about racial bias and pretrial publicity, to object to the defence's use of peremptory challenges against Indigenous prospective jurors, or to object to the admission of lay witnesses and the thirty to sixty second safety guidelines on the critical hang fire issue. It was also accompanied by a request for everyone to trust the system that ignored the larger context of systemic and colonial discrimination against Indigenous people. There was also no suggestion that Indigenous concerns about the case would be addressed through the appointment of an inquiry or a coroner's inquest to explore how Colten Boushie's death could have been prevented.

Farmers have continued to use guns to defend their property after Stanley's acquittal even though the RCMP has warned them that they may be responsible for any unreasonable use of force. When charges have been laid, as in Alberta, they have resulted in opposition and funding campaigns similar to that seen in the Stanley case. Racial tensions and the echoes of the Stanley/Boushie case continue to simmer just below the surface as the debate about rural crime and trespass laws continue.

Following a single challenge for cause question to prospective jurors about racism, a Hamilton jury acquitted Peter Khill of murder and manslaughter for firing two shots and killing Jon Styres in a case with a similar dynamic to the Stanley/Boushie case. In that case, however, the prosecutor has decided to appeal, mainly on the basis that the trial judge erred when telling the jury to factor in Khill's military training, but not his aggressive and armed role in the events that left Jon Styres dead. The Khill acquittal, combined with the decisions since the Stanley verdict not to charge farmers in Saskatchewan and Alberta who also used firearms, are signs of growing acceptance of the use of the guns to defend property and to engage in self-defence.

1 0

Can We Do Better?

INTRODUCTION

This final chapter takes up Prime Minister Justin Trudeau's controversial comments, made on the evening of Stanley's acquittal, that, "Indigenous and non-Indigenous Canadians alike know that we have to do better."[1]

But can we do better? The reformer in me suggests that we can and must do better. Moreover, the flaws in the Stanley investigation and trial are so significant that it is not difficult to do at least somewhat better. The Bill C-75 reforms announced after the verdict would prevent discriminatory use of peremptory challenges. The subsequent Peter Khill case in Hamilton affirms that prospective jurors can be questioned about racist bias towards Indigenous victims. These are relatively easy and necessary reforms.

At the same time, such reforms are far from enough. The Stanley case reveals deep problems in the RCMP, the jury, forensic science, and the ability of criminal trials to discover the truth. All of these institutions are notoriously difficult to change. They have not served Indigenous people well. The abolition of peremptory challenges or asking prospective jurors questions about racist bias may be improvements, but they do not even begin to address the legacy of colonial and systemic discrimination or the failure and distrust that Justice Iacobucci warned was the underlying disease of which Indigenous under-representation on juries was but a visible symptom.[2]

Polarization of social attitudes is also a problem. It seems impossible to bridge the gap between those who think that Gerald Stanley or Peter Khill should not even have been charged and those who believe that anything less than a murder conviction devalues the lives of the Indigenous victim. There are also questions about whether we have become too accepting of the use of guns and violent self-help and whether our perceptions about threats to ourselves and our property can ever be cleansed of racial fears and racist stereotypes. At the same time, increased regulation of guns and the reimposition of stricter standards for when a person can use force in self-defence or defence of property would encounter intense opposition because of the polarized views about these matters.

It is important to fight against discriminatory justice, but it is a defensive battle. There is a danger in focusing on providing the equal protection of the blunt and coercive instrument of the criminal law without addressing deeper social justice issues. Many people protested what they saw as discriminatory justice in the Stanley/Boushie case. Many of the calls of actions issued by the Truth and Reconciliation Commission (TRC) in 2012 addressed such issues and took aim at the gross over-representation of Indigenous people as both crime victims and prisoners in the Canadian criminal justice system. At the same time, the TRC, like the Royal Commission on Aboriginal Peoples before it, also called for the recognition of Indigenous justice systems.[3] Convicting Gerald Stanley or Peter Khill would not have brought Colten Boushie and Jon Styres back to life. It would not have changed the circumstances caused by colonialism and socio-economic conditions that had made them vulnerable to a violent death. It would not have recognized the endurance and wisdom of Indigenous laws and justice systems. Doing better in a way that is not superficial will be very difficult.

DENIAL OF HISTORY IS PART OF THE PROBLEM

As discussed in chapter 2, much can be learned from the fact that most Indigenous commentators on the Stanley/Boushie case started by considering history. Among the many broken promises of Treaty 6 was Commissioner Morris's 1876 promise that the "redcoats," today the RCMP, would provide equal protection to all. Treaty 6 is important to understanding the Stanley case, but it should not be romanticized. The misunderstanding between Commissioner Morris and the Cree Chief Big Bear about the meaning of "hanging" demonstrated that Europeans were defensive and aggressive about the primacy of their justice system from the start. The misunderstanding foreshadowed the 1885 mass hangings of the Battleford Eight after an unfair trial as well as Big Bear's own quick and unfair conviction by an all-white jury. The cases were designed, in the words of Prime Minister Macdonald, to show "the Red Man that the White Man governs."[4] Macdonald's intervention to ensure that the death penalty would be available in the Battleford cases, provides a sense of historical perspective on the somewhat exaggerated claims discussed in the last chapter that Justin Trudeau's "we must do better" sound bite was an interference with the justice system.

In the wake of the 1885 uprising and trials, the pass system was introduced and residential schools were expanded. The Stanley case was far from the first questionable verdict by all-white juries in cases involving Indigenous accused or victims. Canadians need to confront the shameful truth of this history before uttering the word reconciliation. As the TRC has written, reconciliation must be based on respectful relations and this requires "an awareness of the past, acknowledgement of the harm that has been inflicted, atonement for the causes, and action to change behaviour."[5] University of Regina political scientist Joyce Green has warned, "Legacies of historic acts of racism are often dismissed as though they were simply historic artefacts replaced by newer understandings and 'renewed relationships.' This formulation avoids questions of agency, in/justice and responsibility."[6] The Supreme Court has recently concluded that jury selection and, by implication, criminal trials are not the appropriate forum to address historical grievances and injustice.[7] But it asks too much to think that the deep grievances of the distant or near past can be ignored without consequences both for the justice system and our shared existence.

History can drive us apart and make us bitter, angry, and ashamed, but it can also result in an informed commitment to avoid past mistakes. A new courthouse in Prince Albert, Saskatchewan has a statute of Leo Lachance, the Cree trapper who had previously been treated so poorly by the Saskatchewan justice system. As discussed in chapter 3, Lachance was shot in the back by a neo-Nazi. Police and prosecutors quickly accepted that his third shot, like Stanley's, was an accident. A subsequent inquiry disputed that it was an accident. It also disputed the findings of the judge, who sentenced Carney Nerland to four years imprisonment for manslaughter, that racism had no role in the killing.[8] Honouring the life of Leo Lachance is a start to recognizing the mistakes of the past. Some day Colten

Boushie may be honoured in a similar manner. Nevertheless, recognition of past injustices will ring hollow if contemporary injustices are allowed to continue.

DENIAL OF RACISM IS PART OF THE PROBLEM

Although the use of peremptory challenges to exclude five visibly Indigenous jurors in the Stanley trial received the most media and remedial attention, the failure to question all prospective jurors about whether they could decide the case fairly without reference to the intertwined issues of pretrial publicity and racist prejudice towards Boushie is just as shocking. Prosecutor Bill Burge had persuaded a judge to allow such questions in one of the Saskatoon "starlight tours" cases and the question was asked in June 2018 in the Peter Khill case in Ontario.[9]

In the Stanley case, Burge could have pointed to Premier Brad Wall's extraordinary intervention a few days after Boushie's death as evidence that there was a racism problem. To be sure, the blunt "are you a racist" question is far from perfect. Its use in the Khill/Styres case was criticized as being inadequate to root out racism, particularly implicit bias.[10] The legal system needs to be more willing to allow detailed questions about racism. It should not dismiss more extensive questioning of prospective jurors as part of a slippery slope to an American-style questioning of prospective jurors. But asking even the one question about racism and related questions about pretrial publicity would have been better than ignoring the racism issue, one that was underlined every time the defence used a peremptory challenge to remove a visibly Indigenous juror. It was also demonstrated when the representative of the attorney general of Saskatchewan did not specifically address the concerns of Indigenous persons when announcing its decision not to appeal the acquittal. Denials of racism[11] still happen too often. Silence or denial of racism are, as Saskatoon-born writer Thomas Hayden put it, "The sound of living too comfortably with an uncomfortable truth."[12]

THE NEED FOR JURY REFORM BUT THE UNLIKELIHOOD OF RADICAL JURY REFORM

The Bill C-75 proposals to abolish peremptory challenges are responsive to Stanley's use of five peremptory challenges to remove visibly

Indigenous persons from the jury. If peremptory challenges had been abolished at the time of the Stanley trial, a more representative jury would have been selected. A jury with Indigenous people might have better appreciated the difficulties faced by the Indigenous witnesses. It might have questioned Stanley's implicit rural crime defence and his subjective fears of Boushie and his friends.

At the same time, however, Bill C-75 will not fix Indigenous under-representation on juries. It does not change the Supreme Court's 2015 Kokopenace[13] decision that requires proof of deliberate exclusion or unreasonable conduct to challenge under-representation. It stops well short of radical reforms including mixed juries or the use of volunteer jurors from Indigenous communities. As suggested in chapter 5, mixed juries of six Indigenous persons and six non-Indigenous persons are worthy of consideration even though one Saskatchewan court recently rejected that they were a Treaty right.[14] So too is the idea of volunteer jurors from Indigenous communities. Some, including the Supreme Court majority that decided Kokopenace, might argue: where does this all end? It is not possibile to have perfectly proportionate or representative juries. Nevertheless, the conditions faced by Indigenous people since colonization are distinct. They should be recognized as such.

A less radical reform, recommended by the Manitoba Aboriginal Justice Inquiry, is increased use of local juries. They are still not used in provinces so that in Ontario, Manitoba, and Saskatchewan, jury trials about events in northern Indigenous communities are still held hundreds, and even thousands, of kilometres away in Kenora, Thompson and Prince Albert. In 2002, Elder Gladys Wapass-Greyeyes stressed the importance of local trials when she asked, "Why can't we have our court days in our communities instead of becoming spectacles to the nearby communities where all our people have to go? Like most of our young people go to the court system and the justice system – that's not really fair to them. I went and I observed.... It's not very nice to go sit there and observe, but there's so many young people there that are really good kids, but they need guidance, they need people that care, to sit down with them, and talk with them."[15] The Canadian justice system should be more willing to have trials in local communities when they are invited to attend that community.

Even if a government was prepared to engage in radical jury reform by engaging in affirmative action to increase Indigenous representation on juries, it could be challenged as infringing standards of facially neutral random selection that may now be protected *Charter* rights of the accused. The courts have never applied the same standards of substantive equality and concern about non-intentional discrimination to juries that they have applied since the 1980s to every other context. Judges are defensive when it comes to juries. Radical reform must come from governments.

Another issue is whether governments should concentrate their efforts on improving Indigenous representation or include other under-represented groups. In response to the *Kokopenace* litigation, the Ontario government focused on the under-representation of Indigenous on-reserve residents in Ontario's north. Such a focus can be justified given the unique experience of colonialism that Indigenous Peoples have lived through and survived. At the same time, however, there are also concerns about the under-representation of other racialized groups.

A *Toronto Star* survey, published shortly after the Stanley verdict, found in fifty-two trials in Toronto and Brampton that only 7 per cent of jurors were Black and 7 per cent were Brown while 46 per cent of the accused were Black and 19 per cent were Brown. The survey also found that 71 per cent of the jurors were white even though visible minorities constitute 51.4 per cent of Toronto residents and 73.3 per cent of Brampton residents.[16] These results are likely caused by Ontario's continued use of property assessments as a basis for compiling jury lists, its very low pay to jurors, and requirements that jurors must be Canadian citizens as opposed to permanent residents.[17] Governments should address the under-representation of Indigenous people and others on juries, but there are likely to be limits to how representative juries will be given socio-economic and linguistic realities.

This re-enforces the need to take better steps to screen jurors for racist bias. Here again the courts have been conservative, frequently only allowing one loaded question of the "are you a racist" variety, even while recognizing that racism is complex phenomena often engrained in the implicit assumptions that many of us make. A single question was first used in Canada in 1993, the last time the Blue Jays won the World Series. It was still used twenty-five years later in the Peter Khill/Jon Styres case in Hamilton. Our understanding of implicit racial bias has improved over the last quarter of a century.[18] The law has not kept pace.

Canadian courts have resisted asking more subtle questions about racism and stereotypes to protect the privacy of prospective jurors and to avoid lengthy questioning of prospective jurors as allowed in some American cases. But just because the Americans go overboard does not mean that Canada has it right. A failure properly to confront and address racism at the start of the trial may lead to questions being legitimately asked after the verdict.

Jury selection is complex and needs to be viewed holistically. Some defence lawyers defend peremptory challenges, in part, because they can be used as a substitute for the limited questions that judges allow in challenge for cause. Some have also argued that asking prospective jurors a single question about racism in the Khill case suggests that the abolition of peremptory challenges is unnecessary and "wrongheaded."[19] This, however, raises questions about the effectiveness of the blunt question that judges have allowed and the continued under-representation of Indigenous people on juries.[20] The single question has not assuaged the legitimate distrust that many Indigenous people have of a criminal justice system that has failed them so often.[21]

Another barrier to radical reform of the Canadian jury is the old problem of divided federal-provincial jurisdiction that seems to plague every aspect of the lives of Indigenous people. Bill C-75 does not propose to amend the standard for challenging panels of prospective jurors based on intentional provincial misconduct. Such a change is warranted,[22] but it will place demands on provinces that are responsible for compiling jury lists and producing panels of prospective jurors. Bill C-75 could have been bolder. It could have contained reforms that would place more pressures on the provinces to produce representative panels of prospective jurors. If necessary, such *Criminal Code* provisions could be proclaimed in force after provinces had reformed their jury selection system. The election cycles of the federal government and the thirteen provincial and territorial governments ensure that there will always be some governments resistant to jury reform. There is a need for bolder federal leadership on this issue.

It is difficult to be optimistic about jury reform. Bill C-75 is far from radical, but it may be the best that can be done. It avoids having to prove discrimination in the use of peremptory challenges, something that many observers have concluded has failed in the US and has not been successful in the very few cases where it has been alleged in Canada. Abolition of peremptory challenges is necessary, but it will be controversial. It will require political energy and capital that is also needed for many other reforms to increase Indigenous and minority representation on juries, let alone to combat the greater problems of systemic discrimination and colonialism in our law, politics, and socio-economic relations. Juries are symptoms of much larger problems. In the end, we can do better with jury selection, but only marginally better.

ALTERNATIVES TO CRIMINAL TRIALS AND NEW POLITICAL CASES

The Stanley case was an example of a new kind of political case that emerged in the 1990s that pits the accused against both the state and the rights asserted by victims and groups disproportionately victimized by crime.[23] Another example would be the James Keegstra hate speech case which pitted his claims of freedom of expression against the equality rights of the Jewish victims of his anti-semitic hate speech.[24] When the case reached the Supreme Court of Canada, rights claimants were on both sides of the court. The court itself was closely divided about whether the offence was justified. In the end, the law was upheld and Keegstra was convicted, but he received a nominal fine. The case promoted polarization. Few on either side of the issue were pleased with the ultimate result. Nevertheless, when responding to social media about the Stanley case, Saskatchewan premier, Brad Wall stressed, "There are laws that protect citizens from this kind of hate. They will be enforced."[25] In the end, no charges were laid with respect to social media commentary about the Stanley/Boushie case. If charges had been laid, they might have only increased the polarization about the case.

The more promising aspects of Brad Wall's comments were his appeals to "Saskatchewan people ... to be the kind neighbours and fellow citizens we are reputed to be."[26] Alas, such comments had to overcome the social, economic, and political distance, examined in chapter 3, between Indigenous and non-Indigenous people. A media scan did reveal one bright spot. In April 2017, the village of Elbow, Saskatchewan located between Saskatoon and Regina signed a friendship agreement with the FSIN. The mayor of Elbow, Rod Hundeby, admitted that he grew up in rural Saskatchewan with negative stereotypes of Indigenous people. He apologized and promised to do better in the future. FSIN Chief Bobby Cameron accepted the apology and explained, "We as First Nations, as treaty people of these lands, and the non-First Nations people in this province, none of us are going anywhere, but our children and grandchildren are going to live here. What kind of legacy and foundation do we want to leave behind for our children?"[27] As will be suggested below, there are a number of issues, including policing and justice reforms and Treaty education and renewal, where there may be common ground that will not be found in criminal courts.

Criminal courts are the most polarizing of instruments in the Canadian legal system. Complainants in sexual assault trials have used civil litigation as a way to assert more power and obtain more justice.[28] A civil lawsuit has been started by both the family of Jon Styres, after Peter Khill's acquittal, and by the Boushie family after Gerald Stanley's acquittal.[29] Although the acquittals in criminal court may be used as evidence in these civil cases, Khill and Stanley will not receive the benefit of a reasonable doubt. The families will have to establish civil fault on a balance of probabilities. They will be in control of the litigation in a way that they were not in control of the prosecution. At the same time, they may still find that the victim is on trial if Khill and Stanley argue, as defendants frequently did in residential school litigation, that the life of the Indigenous victim was not particularly valuable and did not merit extensive damages.[30] Even the statement of claim, issued by the Boushie family and filed on the second anniversary of his death, may reflect this regrettable tendency to place less monetary value on Indigenous lives than other lives. It makes relatively modest claims by seeking around $500,000 in damages, including $200,000 in punitive damages from the Stanleys for Colten's death. It seeks larger sums from the RCMP for alleged mistreatment of the family when they notified them of Colten's death.[31]

Even after an OPP officer was convicted of criminal negligence causing death, the family of Indigenous protester, Dudley George, engaged in civil litigation in an attempt to reveal truths that were not produced in the criminal courtroom.[32] They stopped when the government decided to use a less adversarial legal instrument: a public inquiry. The Ipperwash Inquiry viewed the protest and the killing in a much larger context that included the history of land disputes and Indigenous claims over burial grounds. It found that a local mayor had inflamed matters by referring to the Indigenous occupiers of a provincial park as engaging in "terrorist" and "illegal activities" and that Premier Mike Harris had said, "I want the fucking Indians out of the park."[33] There have been calls for a public inquiry into the Stanley/Boushie case which might discover new information. It would also allow the Boushie family, and many others, to participate in a way that did not happen at the criminal trial.

As of yet, the Saskatchewan government has demonstrated no interest in the appointment of an inquiry. Provincial public inquiries into miscarriages of justice, including Saskatchewan's own inquiry into David Milgaard's wrongful conviction, have a poor track record in having the federal government enact their proposals for *Criminal Code* reform and this might be the case if a Saskatchewan inquiry made recommendations about jury reforms. An inquiry into the Stanley/Boushie case would also encounter claims of solicitor-client privilege if it attempted to examine defence and prosecutorial strategy. Like the Donald Marshall Jr wrongful conviction inquiry, it would be unable to question the jurors or the judge.

A more promising alternative might be a coroner's inquest into Colten Boushie's death. It could examine why Boushie and his friends found themselves on the Stanley farm on 9 August 2016. It could also examine the RCMP investigation including its treatment of the Indigenous witnesses and the Boushie family and its response to rural crime. It could examine the role of firearms in rural self-defence and defence of property and make recommendations to prevent future deaths.

Under Saskatchewan's *Coroner's Act*,[34] an inquest could be conducted with a jury designed to include Indigenous people. In his 2013 report, Justice Iacobucci commented that while some Indigenous persons are not comfortable on criminal juries that "sit in judgment of the actions of another," that "many First Nations people expressed an interest in participating in coroner's inquests, viewing the role of the coroner's jury, which does not make findings of guilt and which recommends changes to a system to prevent similar tragedies, as more aligned with their cultural understandings and ideologies."[35] Chris Murphy, who represented the Boushie family, has commented favourably on a coroner's jury of four Indigenous persons and two non-Indigenous persons in a case investigating the police-related death of a young Indigenous person.[36] Justice Michael Tulloch has stressed the important role of inquests both for the families of victims and as a means to improve police practices.[37]

A mixed Indigenous and non-Indigenous coroner's jury would draw on one of the traditional strengths of juries – the requirement for unanimous verdicts – to make recommendations that find common ground. It might also consider the relevance of Treaty 6 to the case and make recommendations designed to prevent similar deaths in the future. It could examine new and more creative ways to respond to rural crime. It could also evaluate the relevance of the Treaties, proposed changes to Saskatchewan trespass laws, gun regulations, and the 2012 changes to self-defence and defence of property to the likelihood of violent encounters in rural areas. Unfortunately, recommendations by coroners' inquests are even less likely to be implemented than those by public inquiries. Hopefully, an inquest into Colten Boushie's death would attract enough attention that the government would seriously consider and act on its recommendations about how to prevent similar needless and violent deaths in the future.

SELF-DEFENCE, STEREOTYPES, AND CRIMINAL RECORDS

Stereotypes that associate people with crime are one of the most insidious forms of racism. In 1998, the Supreme Court of Canada recognized the danger of such stereotypes in *R. v. Williams*[38] where it allowed prospective jurors to be questioned about whether stereotypes against an Indigenous accused, charged with robbery, would prevent them from deciding the case on the basis of the evidence. The case of *Williams* is admirable in its awareness and concern about racist stereotypes. But the twenty-year-old precedent is showing its age. It is underinclusive in thinking that racist stereotypes only operate against the accused or that they can be discovered and counteracted with one blunt question.

As discussed in chapter 5, there are some cases, including in Saskatchewan, that have extended the *Williams* precedent to Indigenous crime victims. It is this precedent that the prosecutor should have relied upon in the Stanley case to convince the judge to allow prospective jurors to be questioned about racism. The same stereotypes relating Indigenous people with crime and violence are relevant in cases where the accused make implicit or explicit claims of self-defence directed towards Indigenous persons. Similar issues frequently arise when police officers claim self-defence for shooting racialized or mentally disturbed individuals. One of the continuing challenges in this area is integrating equality-based reasoning in a criminal justice system that traditionally privileges the rights of the accused and clings to models of formal equality that treat everyone the same.

The introduction of Meechance's and Cross's criminal records may have played into Stanley's implicit claims of self-defence and defence of property, and triggered fears and subconscious racism in the jury that may have affected their views about Colten Boushie. These records were introduced under an oft-criticized provision that suggests that the criminal records of witnesses may be relevant to their credibility.[39] The Supreme Court partially reformed this provision in 1988 when it affirmed that trial judges have a discretion to exclude the accused's criminal record in cases where its prejudice outweighed its value in determining credibility.[40] This may explain why the prosecutor made no attempt to introduce Gerald Stanley's criminal record (which was described as dated and non-violent in the decision granting him bail)[41] when he took the stand. Nevertheless, this also created another imbalance in the trial process.

The lack of protection for witnesses such as Meechance and Cross, who were effectively placed on trial, suggests that the distinction between accused and witness can be artificial. Criminal records of Indigenous witnesses or victims may also reflect systemic discrimination against them. Their introduction may encourage juries to engage in stereotypical reasoning about crime that the Supreme Court recognized in 1998 was a potential problem for jurors.[42] The trial judge in the Khill case rightly, in my view, rejected attempts by the defence to introduce Jon Styres's criminal record.[43]

No criminal record of any witness, except perhaps for crimes such as perjury or obstruction of justice, should be introduced for the purpose of impugning their credibility. As with jury reform, we must look to Parliament. If law reform is left to the judiciary, it may be uneven and often slanted towards reforms that will benefit the accused even though stereotypical attitudes about other witnesses may also contribute to justice errors.

The criminal justice system tends to resist and marginalize rights claims made on behalf of complainants and victims. Feminist scholars and activists are only too aware of these issues and have battled against them at least since the 1970s. Much can be learned from their struggles and successes. Feminist law reform has attempted to identify, name, and prohibit commonly recurring myths and stereotypes that otherwise could escape scrutiny under the rubric of fact-finding.[44] Both the *Criminal Code* and judicial instructions

should be amended in an attempt to name and prohibit discriminatory stereotypes that may affect Indigenous people as accused,
victims, or witnesses.[45]

As discussed in chapter 8, concerns about self-defence and defence
of property permeated many aspects of the Stanley case even though
Stanley never formally raised these defences. In the end, the jury was
not given much guidance beyond being told that Gerald Stanley's
actions in retrieving his gun and firing warning shots would have
been justified on the basis of defence of property. (TT 893, 899) The
jury was left to consider if Stanley had any lawful excuse when considering whether he was guilty of manslaughter by careless use of a
firearm. The prosecutor or the trial judge should have insisted that
the jury be instructed about the necessary elements of self-defence
and defence of property once they realized that Stanley was claiming
"a self-defence factor." (TT 607) In my view, the trial judge should
have adjusted his charge to the jury to tell them that Stanley's perceptions of threats to himself and his family must be reasonable.[46]
Judges may be reluctant to do this in the absence of a request from
one of the parties, but, in this context, it was necessary to combat
stereotypes and racist fears that may have played a role as the jury
considered Stanley's fears and his actions.

The law requires that both perceptions of threats and responses
to them be reasonable in order to promote common social standards conducive to a peaceful society.[47] But as the Bernhard Goetz
subway vigilante case discussed in chapter 8 suggests, what is reasonable cannot easily be disassociated from pervasive racial fears.
In the Stanley case, these fears were manifested in the rural crime
narrative combined with Stanley's testimony that he was thinking
about a 1994 farm murder by those from the Red Pheasant reserve
and acts of terrorism as he approached Boushie just prior to the
fatal shot. (TT 687–8).

As University of Ottawa law professor Vanessa Macdonnell has
argued, the open-ended reasonableness approach, used under the
2012 changes to self-defence and defence of property, could lead to
results that are not fair to "marginalized groups" because they provide no guidance for jurors or judges to recognize the need to try to
combat biases and stereotypes.[48] It may be necessary to amend the
Code to spell out that stereotypes or "suspicion heuristics,"[49] associating identifiable groups with theft or violence, have no place in
determining what is reasonable. Such reforms could take inspiration

from a recent provocation case where the Supreme Court stated, "there can be no place" in a similar objective standard "for anti- quated beliefs such as 'adultery is the highest invasion of property.'"[50]

Jurors in California are now warned about common forms of implicit and subconscious racist bias and the need to avoid them when judging the actions of any witness or party. Others have pro- posed instructing jurors to consider whether it would make a dif- ference to their thinking if the races of the victim and the accused were switched.[51] In other words, would an Indigenous person have been acquitted of killing a white youth in the same circumstances? The time has come for Parliament and the courts clearly to state that racist and discriminatory assumptions of threats and dangers have no place in the law of self-defence or defence of property. Some may argue that such reforms will inject race into criminal trials. The Stanley/Boushie case, however, reveals that staying silent about rac- ism does not make the issue go away.

It may also be time to revisit the 2012 changes to self-defence and defence of property to see whether they have encouraged the use of guns when other less violent and more proportionate alternatives are available. Some studies have found that increased homicides have followed the introduction of American "stand your ground" expan- sions of the law of self-defence, so it is possible that highly publicized (and likely controversial) restrictions on self-defence could have the opposite effect.[52] One of the frustrations expressed by farmers at the Biggar meeting, held by the RCMP after the Stanley acquittal, is that there are no clear rules. The trial judge in the Stanley case told the jury that firing warning shots was justified by the defence of prop- erty. (TT 893, 897) This accords with statements made by the minis- ter of justice at the time of the 2012 changes, but raises the question of whether this ought to be the law.

Parliament should consider placing more emphasis on the use of no more force than necessary and proportionality between threatened and inflicted harm in both self-defence and defence of property. These concepts were stressed in prior law and law reform proposals, but were not featured in the 2012 reforms examined in chapter 3.[53] The Khill case also suggests that more work needs to be done to reconcile factoring in the accused's physical capacity and past experiences when required to apply reasonableness standards fairly without diluting the standard of restraint or encouraging unnecessary resort to violent self- help. As discussed in the last chapter, the attorney general of Ontario has appealed Khill's acquittal, in part, because of a concern that the trial judge placed too much emphasis on Khill's past military training when explaining for the jury the requirement that Khill must have reasonably perceived and reasonably responded to a threat of force from the man, Jon Styres, he killed.

Clearer distinctions should also be drawn between the violent self-help that can be justified to protect oneself and others and what is justified to protect property, including the relevance of actions by accused who perhaps unnecessarily confront potential thieves in a way that then triggers their right to self-defence. There is a danger that too easy acceptance of violent self-help can degenerate into authorization of a privatized form of punishment especially when the object of the force may be unpopular and/or engaged in illegal activities. The 2012 reforms were designed to simplify the law, but an open-ended reasonableness standard may leave too much unsaid. There is a need for clear social statements to discourage unnecessary use of force.

GUN CONTROL: "MR STANLEY HAS NO DESIRE EVER TO HOLD A GUN AGAIN."[54]

There might also be a case for setting special rules within self-defence laws to govern the use of firearms especially in relation to offences such as pointing or discharging a firearm. The use of warning shots should not be normalized. There may also need to be additional restrictions on firearms particularly with respect to handguns. Such reforms will be controversial. They will be opposed by those who believe that guns are necessary to defend rural property. Such advocates are not likely to be persuaded by arguments made by politicians or law professors who live in cities. They should, however, consider what Scott Spencer said when Gerald Stanley pled guilty to some minor firearms offences after his acquittal for murder and manslaughter and accepted a ten-year gun ban, "Mr Stanley wishes he never owned a gun ... Mr Stanley has no desire ever to hold a gun again."[55]

Changes to gun laws, proposed by the Trudeau government, have focused on adding restrictions on the purchase rather than the availability of guns including the availability of handguns such as the pistol used by Gerald Stanley. Although the studies are not without ambiguity, and Canada will always be affected by laxer American gun laws, most meta-studies have found that the introduction of severe restrictions on firearms have resulted in declines in firearm-related fatalities including not only intentional killings, but accidental shootings and suicides. In 1996, the Australian governments agreed to impose very strict gun restrictions in the wake of a mass shooting that killed thirty-five people, with Prime Minister Howard indicating that such an approach was important to avoid American patterns. Most studies have found significant declines in firearm-related deaths since that law was enacted, even though the law was very controversial when first introduced.[56] There are already predictions that both the Liberals and the Conservatives will politicize the gun issue and attempt to make it a wedge issue in the 2019 general election. There is also evidence of regional differences with much more opposition to calls for stricter gun control in Saskatchewan and Alberta than in the other provinces.[57]

Restrictions on the ability to use guns to defend property may be necessary to restrict the use of violent self-help and the escalation of situations from defence of property to self-defence. Reform may be necessary if we want to make clear that we do not live in a society where we accept people reaching for guns before calling 911. At the same time, many rural and remote residents, including some Indigenous people, may agree with Stanley's argument that 911 is much less useful in rural and remote areas than in cities. (TT 843–44) This makes the need to improve rural and remote policing especially important.

FINDING COMMON GROUND ON BROADER POLICING REFORM?

It is striking that both the Stanleys and the Boushies were equally dissatisfied with the RCMP's investigation of their case. Gerald Stanley brought a motion, denied by the trial judge, that the RCMP had violated his *Charter* rights by not retaining the grey Escape for further testing. The Boushies made a complaint against the RCMP about the investigation that, while initially denied after an internal RCMP investigation, is still being reviewed by the RCMP's civilian complaints and review agency. As is often the case, the RCMP was in a difficult position. As University of Saskatchewan law professor Glen Luther had stated, the RCMP is blamed by many farmers for underpolicing and long response times while it is also blamed for overpolicing Indigenous communities.[58]

A study of policing by the RCMP in rural and remote British Columbia, by David Eby (now the attorney general of the province), found lack of adequate consultation and troubled relations with Indigenous communities, problems with short-term officer placement, and reliance on internal investigations of complaints. He did report that many rural and remote residents appreciated the use of retired RCMP officers to create and maintain community liaisons.[59] Better relations between the RCMP and both farmers and Indigenous communities should be a priority.

As examined in chapter 2, Commissioner Morris promised Indigenous leaders, when negotiating Treaty 6, that the redcoats would protect Indigenous people from crimes committed by the European settlers. In turn, the Indigenous chiefs promised they would help keep the peace. The important role of the RCMP is symbolized by the fact that they still hand out small annual payments that First Nations people are entitled to under the Treaties. It is possible that the Treaties may still provide a foundation for building a new approach to policing that would involve the receipt of assistance and aid from Indigenous people and communities.

"why can't we have talking circles for the RCMP?"[60]

Since the 1876 Treaty, the RCMP has become a very large bureaucracy of just under 20,000 officers and one with more than its share of controversies. As discussed in chapter 2, it played a role in enforcing the pass system and residential schools for a number of generations. By 1989, concerns were raised that the RCMP was not well prepared to police Indigenous communities. Numerous reports had recommended fundamental reforms including the development of Indigenous police services. In 1991, the First Nations Policing Program was introduced to allow for self-administered Indigenous police forces and agreements with Indigenous communities, federal, and provincial governments to allow the RCMP to police Indigenous communities. The latter have outnumbered the former.[61] The RCMP has 1,500 Indigenous officers constituting 8 per cent of its officers.[62] This is promising. Nevertheless, both Indigenous and non-Indigenous RCMP officers who police Indigenous communities often do not live in those communities and often only stay at a detachment for two to three years. This prevents them from building long-term relations.

Elder Gladys Wapass-Greyeyes, in 2002, asked, "But why can't we have the RCMP living in our communities, why can't we have them taking part in our talking circles, in our AA meetings, in our community functions that we're trying to have happen for the youths? ... Why can't we have talking circles for the RCMP? Why can't they come into the classrooms and talk about the law and learn from the Elders what ways that can be utilized to help the community, the people, whether young or old, different ways they can deal with things. You know, why can't we utilize our Elders, the teachings, so that our correctional centres are not full of our people?"[63] Wapass-Greyeyes's invitation to the RCMP to be part of circles should not be taken lightly. She explained, "we got to work as a team, that's what we do in circles, we're adopting that very sacred, very sacred element of working things together in a calm way, and not to be angry at me or the person next to me."[64] As Professor Lisa Monchalin, an Indigenous criminologist, has explained, circles have special significance for many Indigenous Peoples. They stress interconnections and equality over linear thinking and hierarchy.[65] Having the RCMP or other police participate in circles could make them aware of the larger context of crime and new and creative ways to prevent crime and injury that may not involve law enforcement methods.

Governance Reform

Despite numerous reports calling for civilian democratic governance,[66] the RCMP Act still imposes a top-down governance structure with the Commissioner having control over the force subject to directions from the minister of public safety. At present, the RCMP is the least democratically accountable police service in Canada because it is subject to no board governance with community representation.

With respect to the RCMP, there is no equivalent of the recent reforms of the Ontario Police Oversight Act, 2018[67] that provide for detachment and Indigenous policing boards to give direction and advice to the Ontario Provincial Police and that allow municipal councils and band councils to develop interdisciplinary community safety and well-being plans.

A 2011 task force in the Yukon called for the creation of a six-member Yukon Police Council chaired by the deputy minister of justice that would include three people appointed by First Nations. The

Council has been created and provides a forum for both Indigenous and non-Indigenous people to make their concerns known to the RCMP who provide policing services. They provide input on the selection of detachment commanders, policing priorities, and special training to RCMP members about the Yukon context.[68]

To be sure, some RCMP detachments work closely with rural and remote communities, but officers often only stay in the community for a few years. As discussed in chapter 3, rural policing in Saskatchewan receives significantly less funding than urban policing. The Saskatchewan response so far seems fixated on creating a response force that even arms provincial transportation and conservation officers and focuses on law enforcement rather than crime prevention. Throughout all forms of publicly provided policing, there is a need to use civilians and community members in creative, cost effective, and peaceful ways.

Policing Rural Areas

The policing of rural and remote areas presents significant challenges. The Facebook group Farmers with Firearms features a constant stream of warnings and photos of stolen trucks and other valuable material taken from farms. Many Indigenous communities face serious crime and disproportionate victimization by crime, often related to intergenerational trauma, racism, addictions, mental health, gangs, and living conditions. In all rural and remote communities, there are large distances to be travelled and some evidence of higher crime rates. Federal spending on rural policing has dropped with provinces such as Saskatchewan having to absorb more costs. This has often resulted in a reduced police presence and longer response times.[69]

Partly in response to a well-publicized 1999 case, where a Norfolk farmer was convicted of murdering two burglars, the UK government provided "a budget of £30 million per year," available to police forces who could "demonstrate real improvements in the policing of rural areas." Responses included the development of local safety plans and farm watches where farmers work with designated officers.[70] There is a need to encourage partnerships between the police and the community given the high costs of public policing and the relative absence of private policing in rural areas. There is no one-size-fits-all approach. Addressing fear of crime and improving relations between Indigenous and non-Indigenous communities may be as important as addressing the actual incidence of crime. Finally, the RCMP should be part of a renewed treaty process as they were when Treaty 6 was negotiated in 1876.

Indigenous Police Services

Indigenous police services are important in responding to serious issues in many Indigenous communities. They are also a resource that can work in partnership with other police services, including the RCMP, and urban police, and help educate those police services about better ways of interacting with Indigenous people and communities. Unfortunately, Indigenous police services have faced challenges because of poor and uncertain funding. They often have inadequate facilities and not enough funds to pay or train their officers to the best standards or to provide equivalent pay or policing services. There is often inadequate involvement of the Indigenous communities in the negotiation of joint funding agreements with the provincial and federal governments. As with jury selection, Indigenous people have to get both the federal and provincial governments to agree to achieve meaningful reform. Not surprisingly given these political and fiscal challenges, twenty Indigenous police services have disbanded since 1992.[71]

There is only one Indigenous police service in Saskatchewan. It is the File Hills First Nations Police Service that provides services in a restorative and culturally sensitive manner and is subject to governance by a police service board representing its five Treaty 4 communities.[72] More Indigenous police services in Saskatchewan might improve the response to rural crime.

As in so many other areas, including health and social services, Indigenous communities have continually had to negotiate temporary funding agreements with both the federal and provincial governments. The Trudeau government has announced $281 million over five years to police 420,000 people under the First Nations Policing Program. Unfortunately, it has not announced fundamental changes to the shared-cost program under which Indigenous police services have to satisfy both federal and provincial governments, as well as Indigenous communities, to obtain continued funding. Indigenous policing has not been declared or treated as an essential, permanent service as it is in non-Indigenous communities.[73]

To respond to the under-representation of Indigenous people on juries in Ontario's north, Ontario's Debwewin Committee has, following Justice Iacobucci's report, taken a holistic approach that situates jury under-representation in a larger context. It has called for "the provision of adequate support and funding to First Nations Police Services in order to allow them to provide equivalent services to non-First Nations police services."[74] It has also recommended broader Indigenous justice reforms including "mental health, addictions and Gladue Courts/Indigenous Peoples Courts."[75]

Creative governance structures for policing might facilitate interaction between rural and Indigenous neighbours that could find common ground. Policing should not simply be about law enforcement, but should feed into other needed social, economic, health, and educational initiatives that could increase community security and well-being. Some parts of Saskatchewan have created hubs that allow the police and others to bring high risk conduct, including abuse of alcohol, to the attention of multidisciplinary teams including health, social services, and education. Some who have used a hub in First Nations communities have commented that it is a "natural fit for the values and traditions of First Nations people," because "it involves everyone in the community; is built upon the circle concept; involves sharing; offers help; engages multiple partners, and fosters humility and trust."[76] Such a multidisciplinary approach should also include Indigenous knowledge and approaches to justice issues. Indigenous communities have their own ways of peacekeeping and justice. They were a potential resource not used in the Stanley/Boushie case.

INDIGENOUS JUSTICE

Indigenous communities have long had their own legal systems. This was demonstrated when, after his acquittal by a Hamilton jury for killing Jon Styres, the Six Nations Council voted unanimously to ban Peter Khill from Six Nations territory for life. The Council explained, "Accountability is important within Haudenosaunee legal principles."[77] It elaborated on the harms that Styre's death caused to his family and community, including the community's culture, language, and land. This revealed how acquittals in Canadian criminal law, based on the reasonable doubt standard, do not always accord with broader and more communitarian Indigenous understandings of justice and accountability. Some of the proponents of the banning motion also stressed that the community would be safer. This reflects what some have observed is an emphasis on safety in Indigenous criminal justice.[78] Other proponents explained that the motion was a means to regain control of their lives.[79] Indigenous law could impose different verdicts and different sentences than Canadian law.

Indigenous law has survived many attempts by the Canadian colonial state to kill and discredit it.[80] Much important work is being done by Indigenous scholars in researching and transmitting Indigenous laws. It will be up to Indigenous communities to decide how and when Indigenous law will be applied. That said, the Canadian justice system should be more aware and respectful of the wisdom and resilience of Indigenous justice.

"We've got laws, you've got laws" [81]

Cree Elder Peter Waskahat has explained, "We had our own First Nations government: we had our life teachings on education. Even when a person had made mistakes in life, there were people who would counsel them.... It was done through the Elders ... they talked about getting that person back into a balanced life.... To become part of the family, part of their nations."[82] This understanding of justice sees it as an evolving process that is related to education and balance. It is not limited to dichotomies between good and bad men that were in Commissioner Morris's mind when negotiating Treaty 6 or the binary dichotomies between offenders and victims, justified or unjustified uses of force, truth and lies, and guilt or innocence that pervaded the Stanley trial.

At the same time, Indigenous law should not be seen as a soft form of law where there are no consequences. Treaty 6 Elder Jimmy Myo spoke to a broader view of justice when he stated, "In my law, if you do such a thing, even if no other human being is aware of it, you will always carry that for the rest of your life. Some part of it here on earth, you will pay for it, you might lose something that is more important than what you stole.... And when you die, that is when you really pay for it. That is what the law says; our law says that the amount you do not pay here on earth, when we die, we pay for it."[83] Another Elder from Treaty 6, Elder Jacob Bill of the Pelican Lake First Nation explained, "We were given justice.... If someone doesn't do something right, that is seen. That is seen. If you don't do things right, *pastahowin*, sin, things will not go right if you break the law that was given."[84] He also stated, "We're not asking anyone for a justice program, it's ours. What we want from you is help to set it up; we want you to respect our laws as we respect yours. That means get along, that Treaty-based *wahkohtowin*. We've got laws; you've got laws."[85]

An understanding of Indigenous law, that from a European perspective might be called natural or divine law, may help explain why the reactions of many Indigenous people to the Stanley verdict were so dignified. This was not Canada's Rodney King case. There was no violence or even calls for it. Indigenous people continued to treat Canada better than Canada has treated them.

Indigenous law is for Indigenous people to interpret and apply, but as a non-Indigenous person the little I have learned about it suggests that it can often be more constructive than the Canadian criminal justice system. I agree with leading Métis lawyer Jean Teillet that the Canadian criminal justice system often leaves "the victim and the community angry, hurt and feeling that the justice system is broken." She looks to an alternative informed by Indigenous justice:

What if we accepted the fact that something bad happened and we need to mend the rip in the community fabric, restore relationships and make peace, perhaps restitution? What if we acknowledged the fact that there are many Canadians our justice system does not protect – Indigenous People, women, children and people of colour – and we set about finding a process that fully embraced and protected them? What if we understood that we have built child custody, juvenile and criminal justice trains that have virtually one stop: jail. What if, instead of using an adversarial system to determine the guilt or innocence of an accused, our lawyers and juries were tasked with mending relationships? What if our juries were composed of trained peacemakers? What if their recommendations for implementing peace after the commission of a crime were mandatory?[86]

The Canadian criminal justice system does not follow such an approach and sometimes even prohibits it. At a few junctures, Scott Spencer offered the Stanley family's condolences to the Boushie family, but I could find no evidence of this happening in person. Indeed, Gerald Stanley was prohibited by his conditions of bail, from August 2016 to his acquittal in February 2018, from approaching the Red Pheasant First Nation. As Professor Lisa Monchalin has noted with respect to Cree justice, "An important part of holding the wrongdoer accountable is educating that person regarding the feelings of his or her victims.... The purpose of this visit was not to punish but rather to focus on repairing the harm done and on making sure the offender understood the consequences of his or her behaviour."[87] Although a western lawyer might argue that there is no wrong, offender, or victim until a court delivers a guilty verdict, apologies offered by a person's lawyer without such a personal encounter may ring hollow. The adversarial nature of the Canadian criminal justice system, including the bail conditions imposed on Gerald Stanley, would have prevented the use of Indigenous justice had the Boushie family and the Red Pheasant First Nation been prepared to utilize it.

> *'it's time to live a good life ... there needs to be*
> *kindness for both sides"*[88]

Some non-Indigenous people may think that Indigenous justice as described above is not really justice because it asks broader questions about prevention, well-being, and repair that are not asked in Canadian criminal courts where the focus is simply on whether guilt has been proven beyond a reasonable doubt. But the broader focus of Indigenous justice is one of its strengths. Gerald Seniuk who served as Chief Judge of the Saskatchewan Provincial Court and Professor John Borrows of the University of Victoria have written about a house of justice where courts could operate in communities. Courts would be more like hospitals or healing lodges and they would deal with issues holistically. One example would be the Tsuu T'ina First Nation Peacemaker Court that involved fifty volunteer peacemakers from those nominated by all families from the community outside of Calgary.[89]

Justice reforms, such as Bill C-75, can seem trivial compared to the broader challenges faced by Indigenous people. As Elder Isabel McNab stated in 2002, "Our people are dying. Our young people are on the street. Drugs, child prostitution; we can't sit here and dilly-dally around about justice."[90] This holistic view was also reflected in Elder Wapass-Greyeyes's statements, "You are going to have to start caring for the people around you, the work that needs to be done has to begin right at the grass roots."[91] It was also reflected in Elder Amelia Potts's inspiring statement, "It's time to work together and it's time to live a good life is what justice, understanding is all about ... there needs to be kindness from both sides as we start on our journey together."[92]

Treaties can provide a vehicle for more respectful relations and better understanding between Indigenous and non-Indigenous communities. One of the Treaty 6 concepts informed by Cree law is *miyo-wicehtowin* or getting along, having good relations. Better relations and knowledge of each other might have made it possible to think that the older Stanleys might have seen the five younger Indigenous people, who had been drinking and had a flat tire, as people that needed help to return home safely. The five young people might have acknowledged that they needed to respect the Stanleys and their vehicles and the ability of Gerald Stanley to help them with their vehicle. They might have been thankful for their help. Elder Jacob Bill of Pelican Lake First Nation Treaty 6 recalled in 2002 how his Elders told him, "You are not to fight with the white man ... remind him to remember the treaty."[93] Social distance, distrust, and mutual fear prevented good relations between Boushie and his friends and the Stanleys on 9 August 2016. It had fatal consequences. Over the next two years, the Canadian criminal justice system only aggravated this division and distrust and it did not critically examine the fear that Gerald Stanley testified he had as he approached Colten Boushie. Greater understanding and respect on both sides for the Treaty might have produced a better and more peaceful state of affairs.

Implicit and explicit appeals to the defence of private property, in both the Stanley and Khill cases, deny prior Indigenous occupation of the land. Cree Elder Peter Waskahat has explained, "The sacred earth could never be sold or given away, according to the principles of the First Nations, but it could be shared.... The earth could be shared so that everyone could peacefully co-exist."[94] Defence of property escalated quickly and violently to self-defence in both cases. Indigenous laws would likely approach defence of property very differently than Canadian laws. There likely would be more of a focus on sharing and responsibilities towards each other and to the land, water, and animals. There would be less of a focus on binary judgments about whether the use of force was justified or not.

There were only the briefest glimpses of Indigenous laws in the Stanley trial, but unfortunately they were not fully appreciated or respected. Chief Justice Popescul twice raised questions about the eagle feather, the second time on behalf of the jury and warned that it should not be waved at the accused. (TT 334–5, 703)

Stanley's lawyer, Scott Spencer, violated Cree law by asking Eric Meechance and Belinda Jackson to look at the photo of Boushie dead on the ground during cross-examination.[95] He also presented the interviews that the FSIN special investigative unit had with the Indigenous witnesses as a type of interference with the investigation even though the role of such Indigenous interlocutors was recognized first under the Treaties and now under Saskatchewan's *Police Act*.[96]

Going forward, Canadian law should aspire to be more knowledgeable and respectful of Indigenous law. One of the things that makes Canada unique is how the civilian tradition from France was preserved. Canada could also be enriched by greater awareness of, and respect for, Indigenous law.

FINDING COMMON GROUND ON PREVENTING MISCARRIAGES OF JUSTICE INCLUDING WRONGFUL ACQUITTALS

The Stanley trial demonstrates many of the same frailties in the criminal trial that are seen in wrongful convictions. As discussed in chapter 7, much of the trial depended on the facts as determined by the jury. A comparison was drawn in that chapter between the way that the three Indigenous witnesses in the Stanley case were put on trial and the way that the late Donald Marshall Jr was wrongfully convicted of murder by an all-white jury in 1971 and, subsequently, wrongfully convicted of robbery and lying by the Nova Scotia Court of Appeal in 1983. Wrongful convictions of Indigenous people in the Canadian criminal justice system continue to occur regularly.[97] This reflects their over-representation among prisoners, but it also reflects flaws in the justice system that affect all Indigenous people whether they be accused, a witness, or a crime victim.

As discussed in chapter 2, concerns were expressed when Treaty 6 was negotiated about avoiding miscarriages of justice that had happened in the US when white men went free for murdering Indigenous persons. As Professor Mary Ellen Turpel-Lafond wrote in 1994, Indigenous crime victims, such as Helen Betty Osborne, should be on a "national wall of mourning" alongside those such as Donald Marshall Jr who were wrongfully convicted.[98]

Another similarity between the Stanley case and wrongful convictions is the critical role of police investigations, including the lasting impact of police errors made at an early stage of the investigation.

The failure to cover and retain the grey Escape and the initial interview with Belinda Jackson while she was under arrest had important impacts on the eventual resolution of the Stanley trial.

The Limits of the Adversarial System

Like wrongful convictions, the Stanley case raises questions about whether an adversarial system that relies on the efforts and initiative of lawyers representing the prosecutor and the accused is best suited to discover the truth.[99] As discussed in chapter 5, neither the parties or the judge raised the question of challenge for cause on the basis of racism and pretrial publicity and no questions were asked of the prospective jurors. Similarly, no party objected to the use of peremptory challenges to exclude five visibly Indigenous jurors. A more proactive stance by the judge might have responded to these deficiencies.

In chapter 6, we examined how lay witnesses were allowed without objection from the prosecutor to testify about hang fire delays between pulling the trigger and a bullet exiting a gun of seven to twelve seconds and safety regulations of thirty to sixty seconds. The ability of the prosecutor to cross-examine these lay witnesses, in one case about a hang fire that happened forty years ago, had a limited value. Meanwhile, the articles that formed the basis for the prosecutor's expert witness opinion that experimentally induced and observed hang fires last less than a half a second were not admitted into evidence, again because none of the parties requested it. The jury was, unfortunately, not given guidance about the distinction between safety standards and the actual length of hang fires even though the courts have recognized similar distinctions between clinical and forensic uses of information in other contexts.[100] A more proactive judicial approach might have given the jury much more assistance in deciding the critical hang fire issue accurately and in a way that reflected the limited knowledge we have about hang fires.

The adversarial system looked to aggressive cross-examination of witnesses to reveal truth, but, as suggested in chapter 7, it is not clear that this works well for many Indigenous witnesses. The trial judge relied on an agreement between the prosecutor and the accused's lawyer when he instructed the jury that warning shots would have been justified by defence of property. He did not instruct the jury about the legal requirements of defence of property or self-defence presumably because neither the accused or the prosecutor asked him to do so. In my view, the jury should have been informed about both concepts to ensure that it applied the law which requires perceptions of a threat to be reasonable. As seen in many wrongful convictions including Donald Marshall Jr's, where his defence lawyer did not request disclosure or conduct independent investigations, the adversary system works until it doesn't. A more proactive approach by judges may be necessary both to protect the values of the law, including equality, and to guard against justice error.

One of the recommendations of a Saskatchewan inquiry on David Milgaard's wrongful conviction was that greater emphasis should be placed on inquisitorial investigations as a way of discovering the truth about suspected wrongful convictions.[101] Similarly, the Carney Nerland/ Leo Lachance inquiry concluded "more thorough expert examination of the physical evidence" might have helped discover whether the neo-Nazi Nerland accidentally or intentionally shot the Cree trapper.[102] Increased testing of Stanley's gun or the grey Escape might similarly have provided information that would have placed less reliance on the ability of the jurors to draw inferences from a factual scenario that raised emotional and racially charged issues and also required them to reach a conclusion about Stanley's complex hang fire defence.

"just one strong Aboriginal male or female"[103]

All-white juries and the under-representation of Indigenous people as judges affect all Indigenous people. Connie Oakes, a member of the Nekaneet First Nation, who was wrongly convicted in 2011 by an Alberta jury with no Indigenous people, has stated that with "just one strong Aboriginal male or female" on the jury, her "voice would be heard" in its deliberations.[104] The Milton Born with a Tooth case, discussed in chapter 5, suggests that such an approach places a lot of pressure on a sole Indigenous juror.[105] Nevertheless, the jury is a special institution that requires unanimity for a verdict. It is one of the few places in our democracy where minority views cannot simply be voted down.

Similar questions can be raised in the Stanley case. Would Indigenous people on the jury have made a difference? Would they have had a better understanding of the position that Belinda Jackson, Eric Meechance, and Cassidy Cross found themselves in? Would they have been more sceptical of the implicit claims of self-defence that Stanley made? It is impossible to know, but the growing research on wrongful convictions reveals how juries have made mistakes when finding facts. Such mistakes may disproportionately impact Indigenous people and other racialized minorities. We also know from growing research on implicit bias that people may rely on stereotypes and assumptions without knowing it.[106] The point is not that juries should or can be perfectly proportionate to the population, but that a jury that included Indigenous perspectives might have been better able to resist stereotypes that may have encouraged them to perceive Indigenous people as drunk, dangerousness, and responsible for a perceived epidemic of rural crime.

"Better that ten guilty people go free"?[107]

Should we be less concerned about errors in the Stanley case, where he was acquitted, than in wrongful conviction cases? The Canadian criminal justice system reflects liberal values that led William Blackstone to conclude in the 1760s that "better that ten guilty people than that one innocent party suffer."[108] This preference is built into the system including in Chief Justice Popescul's explanation to the jury that the prosecution must prove guilt beyond a reasonable doubt and that, while this does not require proof of certain guilt, it requires something much closer to certainty than probable guilt. (TT 880–1)

The reasonable doubt principle is an important component of the Canadian criminal justice system. It is also reflected in the appeal system that allows the accused, but not the prosecutor, to appeal alleging a miscarriage of justice or an unreasonable verdict. The limited right of the prosecutor only to appeal errors of law, as explained in chapter 9, essentially makes it impossible to appeal the facts that a jury finds or its conclusion that there is a reasonable doubt about guilt. The lack of prosecutorial objection to the lay evidence, or to the use of peremptory challenges, and the refusal of the judge to instruct the jury on self-defence and defence of property also meant that the trial judge made less legal decisions in the Stanley trial that could be questioned and appealed as errors of law. The Stanley case, however, raises the question about whether the prosecution's ability to appeal acquittals should be expanded to include alleged miscarriages of justice. Miscarriages of justice include unfair processes which arguably includes the Stanley trial, at least with respect to the way the jury was selected.[109]

Miscarriages of justice in Canadian law are only something an accused can allege when appealing or seeking relief from a conviction. At the same time, many in the public would conclude that wrongful acquittals can be miscarriages of justice. One of the lessons of the "innocence revolution" is that legal systems cannot always ignore lay perspectives on guilt and innocence. Much of the work done on wrongful convictions has been done by those who have refused to accept guilty verdicts as accurate or final. They have often enlisted directly affected families, often mothers,[110] science, and the media in their work.

A similar process can happen with respect to acquittals. An important example would be the Stephen Lawrence case in the United Kingdom. This involved campaigning by a Black family of a murdered seventeen-year-old that, like the Boushie family, would not accept an acquittal. This case featured advocacy by the family and media typically associated with wrongful convictions. It resulted in a series of inquiries and law reforms in the UK including the enactment of a 2003 law that allows acquittals to be reopened in situations where there is new and compelling evidence.[111] Such reforms have also inspired some Australian states to allow the accused, who claim to be wrongfully convicted, to make second appeals on a similar basis.[112] The criminal justice system could benefit from greater humility[113] and less emphasis on the finality of the verdicts of trial judges and juries.

Indigenous perspectives on miscarriages of justice might not draw the same stark divide between wrongful convictions and wrongful acquittals as does the Canadian justice system. As examined in chapter 2, the negotiations surrounding Treaty 6 demonstrated concerns about miscarriages of justice where white accused went free in the United States for killing Indigenous victims. The distinction between offenders and victims makes less sense in the Indigenous context where many offenders have also been victims. Even in the Stanley case, the witnesses, as discussed in chapter 7, were often viewed as criminals guilty of theft or assault. Colonialism has unfortunately put Indigenous people into the position where they have much more contact with the criminal justice system, as accused, victims, and witnesses, than other Canadians. The eventual answer may be found in Indigenous justice systems, but, in the meantime, there is a need to make Canadian criminal justice as accurate and non-discriminatory as possible whenever Indigenous people are involved.

Considering lay and Indigenous perspectives on miscarriages of justice opens up the possibility that wrongful acquittals can, in some cases, be understood as miscarriages of justice. Allowing prosecutors to appeal unreasonable verdicts would invite second guessing of the jury's determination of a reasonable doubt. But allowing appeals by prosecutors, alleging miscarriages of justice arising from trials that are, or appear to be, unfair,[114] may be justified. One of the messages of this book is that it may be helpful to look to growing research on wrongful convictions, notably the literature on errors and mis-understanding in forensic science, the role of racism and systemic discrimination, the problems of incentivized witnesses, and the role of fact-finding, in understanding the Stanley trial.

This is not an argument that the Canadian legal system should abolish its preference for wrongful acquittals over wrongful con-victions. Under the above proposals, the accused would still have wider appeal rights than the prosecutor and the reasonable doubt principle would still apply. But we should be concerned about all miscarriages of justice. Two of the leading legal theorists of the twentieth century, Lon Fuller[115] and Ronald Dworkin,[116] working separately on this question, agreed that society should be especially concerned if the risk of justice errors fall unevenly on particular groups. Canada needs to be more attentive about justice errors that continue to fall disproportionately on Indigenous people. If an equality and anti-colonial perspective is taken and if wrong-ful acquittals are recognized as a problem, then reasonable steps should be taken to eliminate the possibility of prejudice against Indigenous accused, victims, and witnesses. Even here, however, there are limits because even the equal protection of Indigenous people in the Canadian justice system – as necessary as it is – will not repair colonial injustice, transform socio-economic disparities, or recognize Indigenous law and justice systems.

A NECESSARY BUT DEFENSIVE BATTLE AGAINST DISCRIMINATORY JUSTICE

Cases like the Gerald Stanley case are worth protesting. Hopefully, they are worth writing a book about. We need to understand how the Canadian criminal justice system fails and discriminates against Indigenous people in multiple ways. In 1999, the Supreme Court recognized that Indigenous over-representation in prison was a national crisis.[117] Since that time, however, over-representation has become much, much worse. The most recent data, as of the summer of 2018, shows that 30 per cent of admissions to provincial custody, 27 per cent of admissions to federal custody, and 50 per cent of youth admissions are Indigenous.[118] Something is seriously, seriously wrong. As examined in chapter 3, Indigenous people are also grossly over-represented among crime victims.

> *"Our people are dying ... we can't sit here and dilly-dally*
> *around about justice."*[119]

But there are dangers in focusing only on injustices and justice reforms. It falls into a trap that, in previous work, I have called the "criminalization of politics"[120] which sees criminal law reforms and convictions as necessary responses to larger social and political problems. Equal and non-discriminatory justice is necessary, but hardly sufficient. Elder Isabel McNab did not fall into this trap when she observed in 2002, "Our people are dying ... we can't sit here and dilly-dally around about justice."[121] The Truth and Reconciliation Commission did not fall into the trap when it recommended that Canada should use the principles of the United Nations Declaration on the Rights of Indigenous Peoples as a framework to move forward.[122] That document focuses on self-determination in all aspects of life including land, resources, the environment, culture, language, education, and health, as well as justice. Indigenous justice also does not fall into the trap of a narrow focus because it asks larger questions about accountability, repair, health, well-being, and prevention that are rarely asked in the Canadian criminal justice system.

CONCLUSION

As Justice Frank Iacobucci has argued, the under-representation of Indigenous people on Canadian juries is a symptom of deeper distrust that Indigenous people have towards the Canadian criminal justice system.[123] This distrust is all the more understandable after the Stanley acquittal. Attempts to address this alienation, as well as the growing over-representation of Indigenous people as offenders and victims, have largely failed. They suggest that we need to rethink our approach to criminal justice to include Indigenous law and peacekeeping and greater use of Treaties. The Stanley/Boushie case is a warning sign of larger problems. We have ignored too many warning signs in the past.

The Stanley/Boushie case was not an aberration. It came in the wake of many similarly divisive cases discussed in chapter 3. Less than six months later, many of the features of the Stanley case were repeated when Peter Khill was acquitted by a jury of murder and manslaughter for killing Jonathan Styres. There is a toxic synergy between the win-lose dynamics of the new political case that pits the rights of the accused against the rights of crime victims and a new politics of polarization fuelled by social media and increased partisanship over criminal justice matters. The willingness of the Canadian legal system to condone the use of guns, first to defend property and then to defend self and others, seems to have increased with the 2012 changes to the law. It is time to revisit such laws, but polarization over such issues will make reform difficult.

Although the proposed abolition of peremptory challenges would have placed Indigenous people on the Stanley jury had it been law at the time of the Stanley trial, it will not result in reliably representative juries if both legal and socio-economic factors continue to hinder the participation of Indigenous people and other racialized minorities on juries. The courts have regrettably exempted the Canadian jury from concerns about colonial and systemic discrimination that they rightly recognize elsewhere. Juries are here to stay. But they need to be reformed. Alas, even with Bill C-75, we are a long way from implementing radical reforms, such as mixed or proportionate juries, that will ensure that different perspectives are considered. Even radical jury reform would not address all of the larger questions, but it might point the way.

If you conclude that Gerald Stanley should have been convicted, then you will view the case as an example of Canadian, as well as Indigenous, injustice. The Canadian system tolerates wrongful acquittals more than wrongful convictions. Nevertheless, they remain in fact, if not law, miscarriages of justice. Early investigative decisions by the police and misunderstandings of forensic issues may have played a role in the Stanley case, just as they have been significant in many wrongful convictions. The jury's decisions about facts and credibility may also have been influenced by stereotypes associating Indigenous people with crime and lies. Such stereotypes played a role in some wrongful convictions of Indigenous people including the late Donald Marshall Jr We will likely never know whether the jury actually employed stereotypes, but we do know that the jury was not screened for racist bias and that five visibly Indigenous people, who could have been on the jury, were subject to peremptory challenges by Stanley.

Even if one is inclined to accept the jury's acquittal of Stanley as a good and fair example of Canadian justice (as about 30 per cent of surveyed Canadians do), or to remain undecided (as 38 per cent of surveyed Canadians do[124]), the Stanley case should still make you think about why Canadian justice is so often experienced by Indigenous people as injustice.

In my view, it was not fair that the RCMP had a friendly conversation with Gerald Stanley after he was arrested for murder while they informed Colten Boushie's mother during a tactical search that Stanley had killed her son. It was not fair that racism was denied at the trial with jurors not being questioned about its effects or the effects of the pretrial publicity despite Premier Brad Wall recognizing that racist responses to Colten Boushie's killing were prevalent and unacceptable. It was not fair that that the defence could challenge the five visibly Indigenous people selected to serve on the jury without providing any reason and with no objection from the prosecutor or the judge. It was not fair that there were no Indigenous people on the jury in a district with a 30 per cent Indigenous-adult population. It was not fair that the jury was not given more guidance on the hang fire issue including exploration of the articles that measured hang fire delays between pulling the trigger and a bullet leaving a gun of under half a second. It was not fair that Stanley was able to make arguments based on a rural crime narrative involving defence of property and self-defence and to say he was thinking about a 1994 murder and an act of terrorism when he approached Boushie, but without the jury being told that the law required an accused's subjective fears and perceptions of threats to be reasonable and not based on racist stereotypes. It was not fair that the acquittal could not be appealed on the basis that it may have been a miscarriage of justice.

The Stanley case adds to the long list of good reasons that many Indigenous people have for not wanting to serve on Canadian juries or to be involved in a system that has failed them so grievously and so often, whether this be as accused, witnesses, or victims. It is far from the first case where Canadian justice has resulted in Indigenous injustice. It raises basic questions about our systems of justice and fairness for all of us fortunate to share this land.

Acknowledgments

I have incurred many debts in writing this book. I was honoured to be invited by Signa Daum Shanks of Osgoode Hall Law School to be part of Project Fact(a), a group of Indigenous and non-Indigenous scholars that have looked at various aspects of this case. I thank all those who participated in valuable discussions in April and June 2018. Special thanks to David Tanovich and the University of Windsor Faculty of Law for paying to make the transcripts of the preliminary hearing and trial available to all of us. Emma Cunliffe deserves special thanks for reading and making excellent suggestions on a preliminary manuscript and for attending the jury selection phase of the Peter Khill case when I was unable to do so.

Special thanks are also extended to John Borrows. He not only wrote a foreword and read an earlier version of the book, but generously provided me with his unpublished work on a blue-sky justice project undertaken with the Office of the Treaty Commissioner in Saskatchewan between 2001 and 2003. Although I still have more to learn, I gained much knowledge from the quotations from Elders included in that paper. I also continue to benefit from the kindness and wisdom of my long-time and treasured friend, John, and his entire family.

Thanks to my 2017–18 criminal law class who cheerfully allowed me to divert the class to focus on the Stanley trial as it evolved in February 2018. I thank Amanda Carling, Emma Cunliffe, Signa Daum Shanks, M.L. Friedland, Nate Gorham, Chris Murphy, Kim Murray, Jonathan Rudin, Ian Scott, Robert Sharpe, Brian Trafford and two anonymous referees for McGill-Queen's University Press for reading an earlier version of the manuscript. I also thank Jasmine

Lee and Jessie Stirling for research assistance; Nancy Bueler, my assistant, for doing her best in the futile task of keeping me organized; the staff of the Bora Laskin Law Library, especially Sooin Kim and Sufei Xu, for their excellent assistance in responding promptly to my never-ending research requests. Louise Piper provided expert copy-editing that improved the manuscript. Alexandra Peace compiled a comprehensive index. I also thank Philip Cercone, Kathleen Fraser, and all the others at McGill-Queen's University Press who worked diligently and quickly in the publishing process. Finally, thanks to my entire family and, most of all, my wife, Jan Cox, who supports and inspires me in so many ways.

I am also aware that in a book that deals, in part, with polarization, some may consider me to gravitate to one side of the poles. I represented (*pro bono*) Aboriginal Legal Services of Toronto in its intervention in the 1998 case of *R. v. Williams* that allowed an Indigenous accused in Victoria to question prospective jurors about whether their ability to decide the case impartially, on the basis of the evidence, would be affected by racism towards the accused. I also *pro bono* represented the David Asper Centre for Constitutional Rights in *R. v. Kokopenace* in the Ontario Court of Appeal when it found a *Charter* violation because of the under-representation of Indigenous person on a Kenora jury roll, a decision subsequently reversed by the Supreme Court. Undoubtedly, my approach was influenced by these experiences. I have, however, tried my best to keep an open mind and to be as fair as I could be to all involved in this case.

Notes

CHAPTER I

1 Angus Reid Institute, *The Colten Boushie Case: Canadians Divided on Jury's Verdict but Think Trudeau was Wrong to Weigh In,* February 26, 2018, http://angusreid.org/wp-content/uploads/2018/02/2018.02.23-Boushie-verdict.pdf.

2 CBC News, "Responses flood in after Sask. Premier asks for racist comments to stop after shooting," 15 August 2015, http://www.cbc.ca/news/canada/saskatchewan/responses-flood-in-after-premier-asks-for-racist-comments-to-stop-1.3721989.

3 Hon. Frank Iacobucci, *First Nations Representation on Ontario Juries,* February 2013, https://www.attorneygeneral.jus.gov.on.ca/english/about/pubs/iacobucci/First_Nations_Representation_Ontario_Juries.html.

4 *R. v. Kokopenace* [2015] 2 SCR 398 at 64, 83.

5 Tristin Hopper, "Gerald Stanley's magic gun: the extremely unlikely defence that secured his acquittal," *National Post,* 14 February 2018.

6 Hon. Frank Iacobucci, *First Nations Representation on Ontario Juries.*

7 *R. v. Kokopenace* [2015] 2 SCR 398.

8 M.L. Friedland, *The Trials of Israel Lipski* (London: Macmillan, 1984), at 204, noting "justice in theory may be blind, but in practice it has all too human a perspective.... This case shows the inherent fallibility of the trial process and the constant danger of error."

9 *Criminal Code* RSC 1985, c C-34 s 649.

10 Angus Reid Institute, *The Colten Boushie Case.*

11 Kent Roach, *Due Process and Victims' Rights: The Law and Politics of Criminal Justice* (Toronto: University of Toronto Press, 1999).

12 Mary Allen, *Police Reported Crime Statistics in Canada* (Ottawa: Centre for Criminal Justice Statistics, 2018) at https://www150.statcan.gc.ca/n1/en/pub/85-002-x/2018001/article/54974-eng.pdf?st=MR4-4naC.

13 Jean-Dennis David, *Homicide in Canada* (Ottawa: Centre for Criminal Justice Statistics, 2017), https://www150.statcan.gc.ca/n1/pub/85-002-x/2017001/article/54879-eng.htm ; Samuel Perreault, *Criminal Victimization in Canada* (Ottawa: Centre for Criminal Justice Statistics, 2015), https://www150.statcan.gc.ca/n1/pub/85-002-x/2015001/article/14241-eng.htm.

CHAPTER 2

1 Paul Seesequasis, "A Made-in-Saskatchewan Crisis: the Stanley Verdict has Deep Roots Going Back to the Signing of Treaty 6," *Globe and Mail,* 13 February 2018, 17; Darcy Lindberg, "The Myth of the Wheat King and the Killing of Colten Boushie," *Canadian Press,* 2 March 2018.

2 Jean Teillet, "To Believe in Justice We Must Probe the Sacred Cow: the System Itself," *Macleans,* 27 February 2018.

3 Gina Starblanket and Dallas Hunt, "Defending the Castle," *Globe and Mail,* 17 February 2018.

4 J.R. Miller, *Compact, Contract, Covenant: Aboriginal Treaty-Making in Canada* (Toronto: University of Toronto Press, 2009), 156.

5 James Dalchuk, *Clearing the Plains: Disease, Politics of Starvation and the Loss of Aboriginal Life* (Regina: University of Regina Press, 2014), 97–98.

6 Harold Cardinal and Walter Hildebrandt, *Treaty Elders of Saskatchewan* (Calgary: University of Calgary Press, 2000), 36.

7 Alexander Morris, *The Treaties of Canada* (Toronto: Belfords Clarke and Co., 1880), 240.

8 Morris, *The Treaties of Canada,* 240.

9 Ibid., 242.

10 Ibid., 240.

11 Ibid., 240.

12 Ibid., 240.

13 Ibid., 241.

14 Ibid., 241.

15 Ibid., 241.

16 Arthur J. Ray, Jim Miller, Frank Tough, *Bounty and Benevolence: A*

History of Saskatchewan's Treaties (Montreal: McGill-Queens University Press, 2000), 143. See generally Dalchuk, *Clearing the Plains*.

17 Jesse Archibald Barber, *Kisiskaciwan Indigenous Voices from Where the River Flows Swiftly* (Regina: University of Regina Press, 2018), 41–42.

18 Bill Waiser, "The White Man Governs: The 1885 Indian Trials," in *Canadian State Trials*, eds. Barry Wright and Susan Binnie, 3 vols. (Toronto: University of Toronto Press, 2009), 3:470.

19 Morris, *The Treaties of Canada*, 240.

20 Ibid., 234.

21 Ibid., 208.

22 Ibid., 109.

23 *Reference re Secession of Quebec*, [1998] 2 SCR 217.

24 John Borrows, *"Peace, Friendship and Respect": Indigenous Treaties in Canada* (unpublished, 30 October 2003), 114, cites *Reference re Secession of Quebec* at 219–239.

25 Robert J. Talbot, *Negotiating the Numbered Treaties An Intellectual and Political Biography of Alexander Morris* (Saskatoon: Purich Publishing, 2009), 103.

26 Morris, *The Treaties of Canada*, 234.

27 Talbot, *Negotiating the Numbered Treaties,* 108.

28 Ibid., 108.

29 Borrows, *"Peace, Friendship and Respect,"* 74, cites Elder Mayo, Symposium, at 144–5.

30 Cited in Ray, Miller, and Tough, *Bounty and Benevolence,* 131–2.

31 For an examination of how American courts started their rejection of the duty to retreat that culminated in modern "stand your ground laws" in a nineteenth-century case, which resulted in a white man being acquitted of killing a Cherokee man, see Caroline Light, *Stand Your Ground: A History of America's Love Affair with Lethal Self-Defence* (Boston: Beacon Press, 2017), chap. 3, examining *Davenport v United States* 163 U.S. 682 (1896).

32 Treaty 6, Canadian Crown and Cree, Assiniboine and Ojibwa leaders, 1876, online: http://www.aadnc-aandc.gc.ca/eng/1100100028710/1100100028783.

33 Ibid.

34 James (Sa'ke'j) Henderson, *Treaty Rights in the Constitution of Canada* (Toronto: Thomson, 2007), 551–6. See also Matthias Leonardy, *First Nations Criminal Jurisdiction in Canada* (Saskatoon: Native Law Centre, 1998), at 199–209.

35 Henderson, *Treaty Rights*, 127.

36 Elder Joe Crowe, cited in Borrows, *"Peace, Friendship and Respect,"* 75.

37 Elder Danny Musqua cited in Borrows, *"Peace, Friendship and Respect,"* 142.

38 *R. v. Cyr*, 2014 SKQB 61 at 98.

39 John Borrows "Foreword" *infra* at ix.

40 See generally Blair Stonechild and Bill Waiser, *Loyal till Death Indians and the North-west Rebellion* (Saskatoon: Fifth House, 1997).

41 Gloria Galloway, "Ottawa Moving to Exonerate First Nations Chief Convicted of Treason," *Globe and Mail*, 10 January 2018, A10 in relation to Chief Poundmaker.

42 Howard Adams, *Prison of Grass* (Saskatoon: Fifth House, 1989), 95.

43 Bill Waiser, *A World We Have Lost: Saskatchewan Before 1905* (Saskatoon: Fifth House, 2016), 540.

44 Ibid., 540.

45 Ibid., 541.

46 Barry Wright and Susan Binnie, eds. *Canadian State Trials* 3 vols. (Toronto: University of Toronto Press, 2009), 3.

47 Thomas Flanagan and Neil Watson, "The Riel Trial Revisited: Criminal Procedure and Law in 1885," *Saskatchewan History*, 34 (1981): 57.

48 M.L. Friedland, *The Case of Valentine Shortis: A True Story of Crime and Politics in Canada* (Toronto: University of Toronto Press, 1986), 35.

49 Mariane Constable, *The Law of the Other* (Chicago: University of Chicago Press, 1994), 106.

50 Jeremy Ravi Mumford, "Why was Louis Riel, a United States Citizen, Hanged as a Canadian Traitor?" *Canadian History Review*, 88 no.2 (2007): 255.

51 *R. v. Riel*, [1885] UKPC 3.

52 As cited in Bob Beal and Rod MacLeod, *Prairie Fire The 1885 North-West Rebellion* (Edmonton: Hurtig Publishers, 1984), 307.

53 Beal and MacLeod, *Prairie Fire*, 321. Waiser, *A World We Have Lost*, 565.

54 As cited in Beal and Macleod, *Prairie Fire*, 315.

55 Bob Beal and Barry Wright, "Summary and Incompetent Justice: Legal Responses to the 1885 Crisis," in Wright and Binnie, eds. *Canadian State Trials*, 3:355.

56 Bill Waiser, "The White Man Governs," 460, and "Supporting Documents," in *Canadian State Trials*, 615-17.

57 As cited in Beal and Macleod, *Prairie Fire*, 315.

58 *R. v. White Cap* in Canada, Secretary of State, *Trials in Connection with the North-west Rebellion* (Ottawa: Maclean and Roger, 1886), 27.

59 *R. v. White Cap* in Canada, Secretary of State, *Trials in Connection*, 26, online: https://archive.org/details/trialsinconnectoostatgoog, 52. Robertson in White Cap's case also asked for the jury to nullify any judicial instruction that the accused's mere presence at the scene of the crime was enough to convict. The defence lawyer appealed to the jury, "I ask you, whatever his Honour may tell you, and I appeal to you as six men of sound common sense, whatever his Honour tells you is the law, to do moral justice to that poor old man, and, if necessary override the law as you may have a right to do in these cases."

60 *R. v. White Cap* in Canada, Secretary of State, *Trials in Connection*, 27.

61 Beal and Macleod, *Prairie Fire*, 312. Waiser, "The White Man Governs," 463–464.

62 Archibald Barber, *Kisiskaciwan Indigenous Voices*, 58. (Regina: University of Regina Press, 2018), 58.

63 Beal and Macleod, *Prairie Fire*, 315.

64 Canada, Secretary of State, *Trials in Connection*, 31.

65 As cited in Ted McCoy, "Legal Ideology in the Aftermath of the Rebellion: The Convicted First Nations Participants," *Social History*, 42 no. 175 (2009): 187.

66 Ibid., 195.

67 "Judging a Judge," *Saskatchewan Herald*, 24 November 1885, online: https://commons.wikimedia.org/wiki/File:Battleford_Hangings_-_Bias_of_the_Judge,_Article_from_the_Saskatchewan_Herald,_December_14th,_1885.jpg.

68 As cited in Stonechild and Waiser, *Loyal till Death*, 211. (Saskatoon: Fifth House, 1997), 211.

69 "Judging a Judge," *Saskatchewan Herald*.

70 As cited in Beale and Macleod, *Prairie Fire*, 331.

71 Stonechild and Waiser, *Loyal till Death*, 213. Beal and McLeod, *Prairie Fire*, 331-2.

72 As cited in Beale and Macleod, *Prairie Fire*, 331.

73 Dalchuk, *Clearing the Plains*, 155–56.

74 As cited in Ted McCoy, "Legal Ideology in the Aftermath of the Rebellion," 183–84.

75 Stonechild and Waiser, *Loyal till Death*, 212.

76 Stuart Hughes, ed., *The Frog Lake 'Massacre'* (Toronto: McClelland & Stewart, 1976), 140.

77 William Cameron, *Blood Red the Sun* (Edmonton: Hurtig, 1977), 203.

78 Val Napolean and Hadley Friedland, "Indigenous Legal Traditions: Roots to Renaissance," in *Oxford Handbook on Criminal Law*, eds. Markus Drubber and Tatjana Hornle (Oxford: Oxford University Press, 2014) and Emily Snyder, Val Napolean and John Borrows, "Gender and Violence: Drawing on Indigenous Legal Resources," (2015) 48 U.B.C. Law Rev. at 593. I am grateful to John Borrows for conversations on these issues.

79 As cited in Ted McCoy, "Legal Ideology in the Aftermath of the Rebellion," 183–84.

80 Beale and Macleod, *Prairie Fire*, 213, 332.

81 McCoy, "Legal Ideology in the Aftermath of the Rebellion."

82 Stonechild and Waiser, *Loyal till Death*, 221.

83 Ibid., 199.

84 Ibid., 221.

85 Waiser, *A World We Have Lost*, 563–4.

86 Heidi Kiiwetinpinesiik Stark, "Criminal Empire: The Making of the Savage in a Lawless Land," *Theory & Event Project MUSE*, 4 no.19 (2016), online: muse.jhu.edu/article/633282.

87 As cited in Myrna Kotash, *The Frog Lake Reader* (Edmonton: NeWest Press, 2009), 170.

88 Cameron, *Blood Red the Sun*, 211.

89 Theresa Gowanlock and Theresa Delaney, *Two Months in the Camp of Big Bear* (Parkdale: Parkdale Times, 1885) in *The Frog Lake 'Massacre,'* ed. Hughes, 191, 232.

90 Kotash, *The Frog Lake Reader*, 184. See also Sarah Carter, *Aboriginal People and Colonizers of Western Canada to 1900* (Toronto: University of Toronto Press, 1999), 161.

91 Stonechild and Waiser, *Loyal till Death*, 226.

92 Ibid., 228.

93 Truth and Reconciliation Commission (hereafter TRC), *The History: Part 1 Origins to 1939*, vol. 1, part 1 (Montreal: McGill-Queen's University Press, 2015), 112.

94 Ibid., 127.

95 Ibid., 128.

96 Ibid., 221.

97 Ibid., 362.

98 Ibid., 267.

99 Ibid., 163.

100 Ibid., 602.

101 Ibid., 220.

102 TRC, *Missing Children and Unmarked Burials,* vol. 4 (Montreal: McGill-Queen's University Press, 2015), 119.

103 Joe Friesen, "The Night Colten Boushie Died," *Globe and Mail,* 20 October 2016, A8.

CHAPTER 3

1 Thomas Hayden, "This is not the Image We Have of Canada," *Globe and Mail,* 6 March 2004, F6.

2 Hon. David Wright, *Report of the Commission of Inquiry into Matters Relating to the Death of Neil Stonechild* (Regina: Government of Saskatchewan, 2004), 208.

3 "Gerald Stanley to Pay $3,900 and Receive a 10 Year Ban on Gun Ownership for Improper Storage of a Firearm," CBC *News,* 16 April 2018.

4 David Giles, "Rural Property Where Colten Boushie was Killed is up for Sale," *Global News,* 31 July 2017, online: https://globalnews.ca/news/3636764/gerald-stanley-colten-boushie-rural-property-glenside/.

5 Ian Austen, "Murder Trial Stirs Emotions about Canada's Relation with Indigenous Population," *New York Times,* 9 February 2018.

6 Joe Friesen, "The Night Colten Boushie Died," *Globe and Mail,* 20 October 2016, A8.

7 Statistics Canada, *Census Profile 2016,* online: http://www12. statcan.gc.ca/census-recensement/2016/dp-pd/prof/details/page.cfm ?B1=All&Code1=4712829&Code2=47&Data=Count&Geo1=C SD&Geo2=PR&Lang=E&SearchPR=01&SearchText=Red+Pheas ant+108&SearchType=Begins&TabID=1.

8 Statistics Canada, *Census Profile 2016,* online: http://www12.statcan. gc.ca/census-recensement/2016/dp-pd/prof/details/page. cfm?Lang=E&Geo1=CSD&Code1=4712829&Geo2=C- D&Code2=4712&Data=Count&SearchText=red%20 pheasant&SearchType=Begins&SearchPR=01&B1=All&TabID=1.

9 James Parker, "FSIN Would Push for More Native Farmers," *Saskatoon Star-Phoenix,* 25 January 2002, A3.

10 Statistics Canada, *Census Profile 2016,* online: http://www12. statcan.gc.ca/census-recensement/2016/dp-pd/prof/details/page.

cfm?Lang=E&Geo1=CSD&Code1=4712829&Geo2=CD&Code2=
4712&Data=Count&SearchText=red%20
pheasant&SearchType=Begins&SearchPR=01&B1=All&TabID=1.

11 The median household income for Saskatchewan residents was
$75,412 in 2015. Aboriginal people, however, lag behind. The
median total income for Indigenous people who do not graduate
high school was $20,291. It rose to $38,232 for those who graduated high school and $56,402 for those with a bachelor's degree.
Ibid., online: http://www12.statcan.gc.ca/census-recensement/2016/
dp-pd/dt-td/Rp-eng.cfm?TABID=2&Lang=E&APATH=3&
DETAIL=0&DIM=0&FL=A&FREE=0&GC=0&GID=1341687&
GK=0&GRP=1&PID=111819&PRID=10&PTYPE=109445&S=0&
SHOWALL=0&SUB=0&Temporal=2017&THEME=122&VID=0&
VNAMEE=&VNAMEF=&D1=0&D2=0&D3=0&D4=0&D5=
0&D6=0.

12 Statistics Canada, *Focus on Geography Series, 2016 Census*, online:
http://www12.statcan.gc.ca/census-recensement/2016/as-sa/fogs-spg/
Facts-PR-Eng.cfm?TOPIC=9&LANG=Eng&GK=PR&GC=47.

13 Ibid., online: http://www12.statcan.gc.ca/census-recensement/2016/
as-sa/fogs-spg/Facts-PR-Eng.cfm?TOPIC=6&LANG=Eng&
GK=PR&GC=47.

14 Statistics Canada, "Saskatchewan Aboriginal Peoples," based on
Census Profile 2016, 25 October 2017, online: http://publications.gov.
sk.ca/documents/15/104388-2016%20Census%20Aboriginal.pdf.

15 Bakhtiar Maazzami, *Strengthen Rural Canada: Fewer and Older:
Population and Demographic Crossroads in Rural Saskatchewan*
(Regina: Strengthening Rural Canada Initiative, 2015), 10.

16 Ibid., 68.

17 Ibid., 42.

18 Roy McGregor, "Saskatchewan's Schools Take on Province's Two
Solitudes," *Globe and Mail,* 30 December 2004, A4.

19 Sidney Harring, *White Man's Law: Native People in Nineteenth-
Century Jurisprudence* (Toronto: University of Toronto Press, 1998),
243.

20 Ibid., 245.

21 Elizabeth Thompson, "More than a Million Restricted, Prohibited
Weapons in Canada," CBC *News,* 25 May 2017.

22 Adam Cotter, "Firearms and Violent Crime in Canada," *Jurist
Bulletin Canadian Centre for Criminal Justice Statistics*, 28 June
2018.

23 Lynn Barr-Telford, "Guns and Gangs," *Summit on Gun and Gang Violence* (Ottawa), 7 March 2018, online: https://thegunblog.ca/wp-content/uploads/2018/05/Stats-Can-Lynn-Barr-Telford-Guns-and-Gangs.pdf.

24 Jean-Dennis David, "Homicide in Canada," *Juristat*, 22 November 2017.

25 Mary Allen, *Police Reported Crime Statistics 2017* (Ottawa: Canadian Centre for Criminal Justice Statistics 2018), 11. For earlier reports of higher rural homicide rates see Joyceln Francisco and Christian Chenier, "A Comparison of Large Urban, Small Urban and Rural Crimes Rates, 2005," *Juristat*, 27, 3 (June 2007).

26 Joseph Donnermayer and Walter DeKeseredy, *Rural Criminology* (London: Routledge, 2014),14.

27 Jean-Dennis David, "Homicide in Canada," *Juristat* (22 November 2017): chart 7.

28 Samuel Perreault, "Criminal Victimization in Canada, 2014," *Juristat* (23 November 2015).

29 Kent Roach, *Due Process and Victims' Rights: The New Law and Politics of Criminal Justice* (Toronto: University of Toronto Press, 1999).

30 Samuel Perreault, "Canadians Perceptions of Personal Safety and Crime," *Juristat*, 37, 1 (12 December 2017).

31 Ian McPhail, Mark Oliver and Carolyn Brooks, "Taking the Pulse: Perceptions of Crime Trends and Community Safety and Support for Crime Control Methods in the Canadian Prairies," *Journal of Community Safety and Wellbeing*, (2017), 2:2 Table III, online: https://www.journalcswb.ca/index.php/cswb/article/view/40/95.

32 Statistics Canada, *Adult and Youth Correctional Statistics in Canada 2016–7*, Canadian Centre for Criminal Justice Statistics, 19 June 2018, Tables 4, 5, 6, 9 and 13.

33 Ibid.

34 Sherene Razack, *Dying from Improvement: Inquests and Inquiries into Indigenous Deaths in Custody* (Toronto: University of Toronto Press, 2015), 199, 203.

35 McGregor, "Saskatchewan's Schools," A4.

36 Joe O'Connor, "Farmers take up Arms to Protect Property, Selves; Saskatchewan," *Edmonton Journal*, 28 September 2016: N3.

37 Ibid.

38 S.C. 2014 c.25.

39 S.C. 2015 c. 23.

40 S.C. 2012 c. 9.

41 Margaret Wente, "To Catch a Thief," *Globe and Mail,* 5 November 2009, A23.

42 Anonymous, "Charging Victim Brings Justice System into Disrepute," *Saskatoon Star Phoenix,* 26 October 2009, A8.

43 Anonymous, "Unlucky at the Moose: Thief Fortunate Chen Did not Mete out Prairie Justice," *Calgary Herald,* 9 October 2009, A14.

44 Lorne Gunter, "Canadians Never Gave up Their Right to Self-defence," *Calgary Herald,* 25 January 2011, A10. See also: Karen Sellick, "It's Time to Stop Prosecuting the Victim: Charges Should not Be Laid Against Homeowners who Arm Themselves in Self-defence," *Edmonton Journal,* 17 February 2011, A17.

45 *Criminal Code* s.494(2) as amended by S.C. 2012 c. 9 s.3. For concerns about unintended disparities created by the section see Steve Coughlan, "Citizen's Arrest, Private Property and Private Fiefdoms," *Can. Crim. L. Rev. 1,* 18 (2014).

46 *R. v. Chen et al.,* 2010 ONCJ 641 at 106. For criticism of the judge's remarks for engaging in stereotypes about the Chinese Canadian community see Anita Lam and Lily Cho, "Under the Lucky Moose: Belatedness and Citizen's Arrest in Canada," *Can.J.of Law and Society,* 30 (2015): 147.

47 Lena Carla Palacios, "Racialized and Gendered Necropower in Canadian News and Legal Discourses," *Feminist Formations,* 26, 1 (2014): 1–24.

48 "Tories, Libs, NDP Unite to Protect Thief Chasers," *Canadian Press,* 2 November 2010; "Shopkeeper Welcomes Changes to Citizen's Arrest Laws," *Globe and Mail,* 18 February 2011, A9.

49 "Manslaughter Charges Dropped," *Winnipeg Free Press,* 19 October 2011, A3.

50 *The Citizen's Arrest and Self-Defence Act.* S.C. 2012, c.9.

51 *Hansard,* 1 December 2011, per Robert Goguen.

52 Jeff Davis, "Justice Minister Slammed for Warning shot Remark," *Vancouver Sun,* 9 February 2012, B3.

53 Bruce Cheadle, "New Citizen's Arrest Law Won't Condone Vigilantes," *Canadian Press,* 7 February 2012.

54 *Hansard* 15 December 2011, at 4479, per Randy Hoback. See similar comments by: James Bezan at ibid., at 4485; Chris Warkentin, at 4488; Ryan Leef, at 4492; Rob Anders, at 3454; Kevin Sorenson, at 3886; and Blaine Calkins, at 4495 who contrasted a case where a rural property owner was sentenced to ninety days and thieves were

sentenced to forty-five days. See also *Hansard* 24 April 2012, at 7075, per Candice Hoeppner.

55 Hansard, 9 February 2012, at 5087.

56 Hansard, 24 April 2012, at 7149.

57 Hansard, 15 December 2011, at 4476.

58 Bruce Cheadle, "Efforts to Clarify Self-defence and Citizen's Arrest Raise Warning Shots," *Canadian Press*, 8 February 2012, online: https://globalnews.ca/news/209093/effort-to-clarify-self-defence-and-citizens-arrest-laws-raise-warning-shots-2/.

59 Jeff Davis, "Warning Shots a Reasonable Act of Self-defence, Justice Minister," *Montreal Gazette*, 9 February 2012, A14.

60 Caroline Light, *Stand Your Ground*, 156–162.

61 *Criminal Code* RSC 1985, cC-34, s.35 repealed by S.C. 2012 c.9 s.2. For an account of how the duty to retreat was overturned in American law including in a case where a white lawyer shot, killed, and was eventually acquitted of shooting his Cherokee tenant see: Light, *Stand Your Ground*, 68–70.

62 *R. v. Cinous,* [2002] 2 SCR 3 at 123–4.

63 *Criminal Code* ss.34(1)(c) and 35 (1) (d) as amended by S.C. 2012 c.9.

64 The old provisions were complex but frequently required that the accused use no more force than is necessary. *Criminal Code* ss.34(1), 37, 41 repealed S.C 2012 c.9 s.2. If, as in the Stanley and Khill case, the accused caused death or grievous bodily harm, an accused must "believe[s], on reasonable grounds, that he could not otherwise preserve himself from death or grievous bodily harm." Ibid., s.34(2). For assessments of the new law which acknowledge that it could be more generous than the old provisions see: Kent Roach, "A Preliminary Assessment of New Self-Defence and Defence of Property Provisions," *Can Crim. L. Rev.* 16 (2012): 275 at 297–8; David Paciocco, "The New Defence Against Force," (2013) 18 Can. Crim.Law Rev. 269 at 270, 294; Vanessa MacDonnell, "The New Self-Defence Law: Progressive Development or Status Quo?" *Can. Bar Rev.* 92 (2013): 301.

65 Marion Hammer, a former National Rifle Association President, had argued in favour of "stand your ground" laws that eliminated any duty to retreat or requirements of proportionality on the basis, "You can't expect a victim to wait before taking action to protect herself, and say: 'Excuse me, Mr Criminal, did you drag me into this alley to rape and kill me or do you just want to beat me up and steal my purse?'" as quoted in, Light, *Stand Your Ground*, 160.

66 Renee Lettow Lerner, "The Worldwide Popular Revolt Against Proportionality in Self-Defence Law," *J. L. Econ and Policy*, 2 (2006): 331.

67 Hansard, 24 April 2012, at 7075.

68 *Ending the Long Gun Registry Act*, S.C. 2012 c. 6.

69 *Reference re Firearms* [2000] 1 SCR 783.

70 Lorne Gunter, "Criminals Have More Rights than Victims," *Edmonton Journal*, 31 October 2010, A16.

71 Stephen Harper as quoted in, Phil Tank, "Harper Reassures Rural Residents on Guns," *Regina Leader Post*, 13 March 2015, A1.

72 Tank, "Harper Reassures Rural Residents on Guns." Harper also spoke before the Saskatchewan Association of Rural Municipalities (SARM) at its March 2015 convention and promised "to make the rules simpler for conscientious and responsible gun owners." His government subsequently enacted *The Common Sense Gun Licensing Act*, S.C. 2015 c.27.

73 Eric Gottardi as quoted in, Mark Kennedy, "Harper Taking Flak from Legal Experts over Rural Gun-justice Remarks," *Ottawa Citizen*, 18 March 2015.

74 Steve Rennie, "Baloney Meter: Were the Prime Minister's Comments on Guns Misinterpreted?" *The Canadian Press*, 23 Mar 2015.

75 John Geddes, "Ian Brodie Offers a Candid Case Study on Politics and Policy," *Macleans*, 27 March 2009. See generally Kent Roach, "Reforming Criminal Justice and National Security in an Age of Populism," *Criminal Law Quarterly*, 64 (2017): 286.

76 Kennedy, "Harper Taking Flak."

77 Irvin Waller and Michael Kempa, "Harper's Dangerous Advice on Guns for Rural Security," *Toronto Star*, 20 March 2015, A. 15.

78 John Gormley, "Harper's Guns and Saskatchewan's Population," *Saskatoon Star-Phoenix*, 20 March 2015, A2.

79 Ibid.

80 David Bercuson, "In Rural Canada, Harper's Gun Ownership Comments Ring True," *Globe and Mail*, 20 March 2015.

81 Mark Kennedy, "Harper Links Guns, Personal Security," *Saskatoon Star-Phoenix*, 17 March 2015, A1.

82 "Harper was Right on Guns," *National Post*, 20 March 2015, A15.

83 R. Blake Brown, "Firearm 'Rights' in Canada: Law and History in the Debates over Gun Control," *Canadian Journal of Law and Society*, 32 (2017): 97.

84 *Hudson v Canada*, 2009 SKCA 108; *Hudson v Canada*, 2011 SKQB 18.

85 A.J. Somerset, *Arms: the Culture and Credo of the Gun* (Windsor: Biblioasis, 2015), xvi.

86 "Why One Saskatchewan Man Says Farmers Need Firearms," CBC *News*, 26 March 2017, online: http://www.cbc.ca/radio/outinthe-open/what-does-colten-boushie-say-about-us-1.3923927/why-one-saskatchewan-man-says-farmers-need-fire-arms-1.3923963.

87 Online: https://www.facebook.com/pg/farmerswithfirearms/about/?ref=page_internal (accessed 17 May 2018).

88 "Why One Saskatchewan Man," CBC *News*.

89 Online: https://www.facebook.com/farmerswithfirearms/, (accessed May 17, 2018).

90 Light, *Stand Your Ground*, 9–10.

91 Online: https://www.facebook.com/farmerswithfirearms/, (accessed May 17, 2018).

92 Somerset, *Arms: the Culture and Credo of the Gun;* Light, *Stand Your Ground.*

93 TRC, *The History*, 112.

94 Online: https://www.facebook.com/farmerswithfirearms/.

95 Chris Purdy, "'It Could Have Been Me' Some Farmers Support Murder Acquittal of Gerald Stanley," *The Canadian Press*, 12 February 2018.

96 SARM Resolution, 34-17A.

97 Alex Macpherson, "You're Going to Be Punished by the Courts for Protecting Your Property – SARM Resolution Aims for Relaxed Property Defence Rights," *Saskatoon Star-Phoenix*, 14 March 2017.

98 Alex Macpherson, "RMs Want Laws Relaxed on Defence of Property; After Shooting of Colten Boushie, FSIN Is 'Disgusted' by Resolution," *Saskatoon Star-Phoenix*, 15 March 2017, A1.

99 SARM Resolution, 35-17A.

100 Alex Macpherson, "Rural Areas Might Pay More for Policing: SARM," *Saskatoon Star-Phoenix*, 21 March 2017, A1.

101 "Officers 'Enthusiastic' about Added Responsibility with Sask Rural Crime Team: Deputy Minister," CBC *News*, 25 August 2017.

102 "Province's New Rural Response Team 'a Shell Game': NDP," *Saskatoon Star Phoenix*, 22 August 2017.

103 "Plan to Arm Sask Vehicle Enforcement Officers 'Mean More Indigenous People in Jail': FSIN," CBC *News*, 23 August 2017.

104 Kyle Edwards, "In Saskatchewan, the Stanley Verdict has Re-opened Century Old Wounds," *Macleans*, 5 March 2018, online at https://

www.macleans.ca/news/canada/saskatchewan-racism-gerald
-stanley-colten-boushie/.

105 Roach, *Due Process and Victims' Rights*, chapters 8 and 9 (examining the new political case and competing due process and victims'
rights claims with respect to Aboriginal people and crime victims).

106 Peter Gzowski, "This Is Our Alabama," *Macleans*, 6 July 1963.

107 *Batary v Attorney General for Saskatchewan*, [1965] SCR 465.

108 "Three Acquitted in Fatal Beating," *Globe and Mail*, 14 May 1966,
4; "Three Glaslyn Men Acquitted in Indian Manslaughter Case,"
Saskatoon Star Phoenix, 14 May 1966, 3.

109 Hon. Ted Hughes chair, *Report of the Lachance/Nerland Inquiry*
(Regina: Queens Printer, 1993), 10–11.

110 George Oakes, "The Killing of Leo Lachance," *Toronto Star*, 27
February 1993, D1.

111 David Roberts, "The Killing of a Native Trapper by an Ayran Nations
Leader has Opened Old Wounds," *Globe and Mail*, 21 May 1991, A1.

112 *Report of the Lachance/Nerland Inquiry*, 26.

113 Ibid., 49.

114 Ibid., 17.

115 Ibid., 51.

116 Ibid., 30.

117 "Racist Views no Factor in the Killing of Native Man," *Edmonton
Journal*, 13 April 1991, G6. "Sentencing Reasons," as quoted in,
Report of the Lachance/ Nerland Inquiry, 42.

118 *Report of the Lachance/Nerland Inquiry*, 42.

119 Barb Pacholik and Jana Pruden, *Sour Milk and other Saskatchewan
Crime Stories* (Regina: Plains Research Centre, 2007), 128.

120 *Report of the Lachance/Nerland Inquiry*, 53, 67.

121 "Police Should Have Focused on Gunman's Racism, Inquiry Rules,"
Edmonton Journal, 20 November 1993, G11.

122 *Report of the Lachance/Nerland Inquiry*, 73.

123 David Roberts, "Panel Probing Shooting Death Denies RCMP
Request to Protect Operatives," *Globe and Mail*, 29 May 1992, A8.

124 *Royal Canadian Mounted Police v Saskatchewan (Commission of
Inquiry)*, 1992 CanLII 8294 (SKCA) at 13.

125 "RCMP Wants Probe of Informant's Naming," *Edmonton Journal*, 17
November 1992, A9; "RCMP Seek Probe of Informant Allegation,"
Globe and Mail, 17 November 1992, A4.

126 "The Tragic Death of Leo Lachance," *Globe and Mail*, 23 November
1993, A26.

127 Chris Wattie, "Indians Outraged White Supremacist Allowed into RCMP Protection Program," *Montreal Gazette,* 16 December 1993, B4.

128 David Roberts, "Nerland Inquiry Stymied, Critics Say," *Globe and Mail,* 17 March 1993, A8.

129 Trevor Sutter, "FSIN Chief Says Manslaughter Verdict Reinforces Belief that Justice System Has Failed Aboriginals," *Saskatoon Star Phoenix,* 23 December 1996, C1; Sherene Razack, "Gendered Racial Violence and Spatialized Justice: The Murder of Pamela George," *Canadian Journal of Law and Society,* 15 (2000): 91, 126.

130 *R. v. Kummerfield,* 1998 CanLII 12311 at 64.

131 Krista Foss, "The Cree Girl and the White Men," *Globe and Mail,* 12 November 2001, A1.

132 Jason Warick, "House Arrest – Tisdale Man Avoids Jail Time for Sexual Assault," *Saskatoon Star Phoenix,* 5 September 2003, A1.

133 Robert Gibbings, "Comments about Judge Lack Fairness, Balance," *Saskatoon Star Phoenix,* 25 September 2003, A13.

134 Jason Warick, "Acquittal of Pair in Rape of Girl Ignites Race Debate," *Windsor Star,* 28 June 2003, A18.

135 "Evidence Must Rule," *Regina Leader Post,* 28 March 2007.

136 Dale Link, "Folly to Suggest Weighted Juries for Gender, Race," *Saskatoon Star Phoenix,* 17 July 2003, A15.

137 Mike O'Brien, "Dead Man's Race Tainted Trial: Family," *Saskatoon Star Phoenix,* 10 July 2001, A4.

138 "No Detention for Miller," *Regina Leader Post,* 24 March 2000, B8.

139 "Acquittal Upsets Dead Man's Relatives," *Saskatoon Star Phoenix,* 16 June 2001, A3.

140 Les Perreaux, "All-White Jury Hears Evidence in Racially Charged Murder Case," *National Post,* 12 June 2001, A9.

141 *R. v. Yooya,* 1994 Canlii 5084 (Sask. Q.B.).

142 "RCMP Accused of Laxity in Murder of 73 Year Old," *Windsor Star,* 19 August 1992, A4.

143 Chris Wattie, "Manslaughter Verdict Causes Waves of Protest," *Ottawa Citizen,* 14 January 1993, A14.

144 Linda Unger, "Requiem for a Quiet Man," *Globe and Mail,* 28 April 1993, A24.

145 *R. v. Gordon,* 1995 CanLII 3947 (SKCA).

146 "Inmates Cry for Help Echo at Drumheller," *Calgary Herald,* 14 Dec 2001, A14.

147 *R. v. Tourangeau,* 1994 CanLII 4684 (SKCA).

148 *R. v. R.J.T.,* 1995 CanLII 4051 (SKCA).

149 *R. v. T. (R.J.)*, 1995 CanLII 6058 (SKQB).
150 Leslie Perreaux "Accident Led to Double-Murder: Caldwell," *Saskatoon Star-Phoenix*, 30 April 1997, A3.
151 Leslie Perreaux, "Five-year Sentence for Manslaughter Upsets Families on both Sides," *Saskatoon Star-Phoenix*, 10 May 1997, A1.
152 *R. v. Baptiste*, 1998 CanLII 12353 (SKCA).
153 Andrea Hill, "Boushie Family Relieved Trial Ordered," *Regina Leader Post*, 7 April 2016, A1.
154 "FSIN Backs Petition for New Prosecutor in Trial over Colten Boushie's Death," *Canadian Press*, 18 May 2017.
155 Joe Friesen, "Trial Begins for the Death of Colten Boushie," *Globe and Mail*, 29 January 2018, A1.
156 William Faulkner, *Requiem for a Nun* (New York: Random House, 1951), 92. For a somewhat similar invocation of this quote see Mark Carter, "Of Fairness and Faulkner," *Saskatchewan Law Review*, 65 (2002): 63, 70.

CHAPTER 4

1 Kristen Brown, "Somebody Poisoned the Jury Pool: Social Media Effects on Jury Impartiality," *Texas Wesleyan Law Review*, 19 (2013): 809.
2 Bruce Macfarlane, "Convicting the Innocent: A Triple Failure of the Justice System," *Manitoba Law Journal*, 31 (2006): 403.
3 Bill Waiser, *A World We Have Lost: Saskatchewan Before 1905* (Saskatoon: Fifth House, 2016), 540.
4 "Colten Boushie's Family Appeals RCMP Internal Investigation," CBC *News*, 14 February 2018.
5 Tavia Grant, "Report Submitted to Ottawa Highlights Police Abuse Against Indigenous Women," *Globe and Mail*, 19 June 2017; Human Rights Watch, "Submission to the Government of Canada on Police Abuse of Indigenous Women and Failure to Protect Indigenous Women from Violence," June 2017.
6 David Common and Chelsea Gomez, "RCMP 'Sloppy' and 'Negligent' in Investigating Colten Boushie's Death Say Independent Experts," CBC *News*, 6 March 2018, online: http://www.cbc.ca/news/canada/saskatchewan/rcmp-sloppy-and-negligent-in-investigating-colten-boushie-s-death-say-independent-experts-1.4564050.
7 Gerald Stanley's statements on 10 August 2016 as quoted in, *R. v. Stanley*, 2017 SKQB 367 at 38, 60.

8 Ibid., 32.

9 Ibid., 36.

10 Ibid., 47, 45.

11 Ibid., 47, 45.

12 Ibid., 45.

13 Ibid., 59.

14 Joe Friesen, "The Night Colten Boushie Died," *Globe and Mail*, 20 October 2016, A8.

15 Jennifer Graham, "RCMP Says no Mistreatment after Shooting of Saskatchewan Indigenous Man," *Canadian Press*, 2 November 2017. See also Friesen, "The Night Colten Boushie Died," A8 for additional detail.

16 Ibid.

17 Ibid.

18 "Boushie Family 'Disgusted' RCMP Cleared its own Officers of Misconduct," *Canadian Press*, 3 November 2017.

19 Meaghan Craig, "Racism has no Place in Saskatchewan: Premier Brad Wall Puts His Foot Down," *Global News*, 16 August 2016, online: https://globalnews.ca/news/2884368/racism-has-no -place-in-saskatchewan-premier-wall-puts-his-foot-down/.

20 FSIN News Release, 12 August 2016, online: https://www.document-cloud.org/documents/3011916-FSIN-Media-Release-RCMP-Media-Release-08-12-16.html#document/p1.

21 Graham, "RCMP Says no Mistreatment."

22 "Family Devastated after Colten Boushie Shot and Killed on Farm near Biggar Sask," *CBC News*. 11 August 2016, online: at http:// www.cbc.ca/news/canada/saskatchewan/homicide-victim-family -devastated-loved-one-shot-biggar-sask-1.3717268.

23 "Man Fatally Shot in Saskatchewan Was Looking for Help with His Flat Tire," *Canadian Press*, 12 August 2016.

24 As quoted in, Carrie Tait, "Saskatchewan's Racial Divide: The Death of a Young Man, Allegedly Shot by Gerald Stanley, has Exposed Tensions between the First Nations Communities and Their Neighbours in the Province," *Globe and Mail*, 20 August 2016, A8.

25 "Deadly Shooting near Biggar Sask Sparks Debate over Right to Defend," *CBC News*, 12 August 2016, online: http://www.cbc.ca/ news/canada/saskatoon/shooting-biggar-sask-sparks-debate -right-to-defend-1.3718700.

26 CBC Ombudsman, "Speculation as Reporting – Proceed with Caution," 27 September 2016, online: http://www.ombudsman.cbc.radio-canada.ca/en/complaint-reviews/2016/speculation-as-reporting-proceed-with-caution/.

27 Jason Warick, "Tensions Rise after Shooting Death: First Nations Criticizes RCMP over News Release in Cree Man's Death," *Edmonton Journal*, 13 August 2016, A15.

28 Colby Cosh, "A Saskatchewan Shooting, Racial Tension and a Steak Dinner," *National Post*, 16 August 2016, A9.

29 "Responses Flood in," CBC *News*.

30 Ibid.

31 Ibid.

32 Ibid.

33 Jason Warick, "Councillor Apologizes for Online Post in Boushie Death," *Regina Leader Post*, 22 August 2016, A8.

34 *R. v. Knight and MacDonald*, 2017, ONSC 6606 at 24.

35 "Bail Decision Reserved after Gerald Stanley Pleads Not Guilty in Fatal Shooting of Colten Boushie," *Saskatoon Star Phoenix*, 18 August 2016.

36 *Criminal Code* RSC 1985, c C-34 ss. 522, 515(10).

37 *R. v. Stanley*, 19 August 2016, Crim. 83 of 2016.

38 *R. v. Stanley*, 19 August 2016, Crim. 83 of 2016 at para 10.

39 *R. v. St-Cloud*, 2015 SCC 27, [2015] 2 S.C.R. 328 at 88.

40 *R. v. Stanley*, 19 August 2016, Crim. 83 of 2016 at para 8.

41 Ibid., at para 11.

42 *Criminal Code* s.515(10) (c) (iii).

43 *R. v. Stanley*, 19 August 2016, Crim. 83 of 2016 at para 10.

44 "Bail Granted to Gerald Stanley, Man Accused in Colten Boushie Shooting," CBC *News,* 19 August 2016, online: http://www.cbc.ca/news/canada/saskatoon/judge-deliberates-gerald-stanley-bail-1.3727944.

45 Joe Friesen, "High Security Surrounds Preliminary Boushie Hearing," *Globe and Mail*, 4 April 2017, A6.

46 Waiser, *A World We Have Lost*, 540.

47 Report of the Federal Provincial and Territorial Heads of Prosecution Subcommittee on the Prevention of Miscarriages of Justice, *The Path to Justice: Preventing Wrongful Convictions* (2011), chap. 4, online: http://www.ppsc-sppc.gc.ca/eng/pub/ptj-spj/toc.html.

48　See *infra* this book ch 3 at 47.

49　Cassidy Cross at PT 238.

50　*R. v. Stanley*, 2018 SKQB 27 at 31.

51　Ibid., at 28, 49.

52　Stanley factum, 16 January 2018, at para 48 available online: https://assets.documentcloud.org/documents/4378234/Stanley -Cam-Spencer.pdf.

53　Ibid.

54　David Tanovich, "How Racial Bias Likely Impacted the Stanley Verdict," *The Conversation*, 5 April 2018, online: https://theconversation.com/how-racial-bias-likely-impacted -the-stanley-verdict-94211.

55　Stanley factum, 16 January 2018, at para 11.

56　See generally Kent Roach, *Due Process and Victims' Rights: The New Law and Politics of Criminal Justice* (Toronto: University of Toronto Press, 1999), ch. 9.

57　*R. v. Stanley*, 2018 SKQB 27 at 78.

58　Nathan Gorham, "A Fair, Public Viewing of Justice: Try TV not Twitter," *Globe and Mail*, 3 February 2016, A11.

59　Kathryn Campbell, *Miscarriages of Justice in Canada* (Toronto: University of Toronto Press, 2018), 11. Ibid., Appendix A.

60　"Responses Flood in," CBC *News*.

61　*R. v. Stanley*, 2018 SKQB 27 at 31.

CHAPTER 5

1　Joe Friesen, "Family Upset as Jury Selected for Colten Boushie Trial," *Globe and Mail*, 30 January 2018, A4.

2　For a contrast between lay or non-legal understandings of justice based on discourse about suspected wrongful convictions in the media or science and legal understandings see Richard Nobles and David Schiff, *Understanding Miscarriages of Justice* (Oxford: Oxford University Press, 2000).

3　*Criminal Code*, RSC 1985, c C-34, s 638.

4　*R. v. Bitternose*, 2009 SKCA 54 at 69.

5　Angus Reid Institute, *The Colten Boushie Case*.

6　Manitoba Aboriginal Justice Inquiry, *The Death of Helen Betty Osborne* (Winnipeg: Queens Printer, 1991), chap. 8. The inquiry identified that 18 of 105 prospective jurors in the case were

Aboriginal. Aboriginal people, historically, had not been jurors, in part because they did not receive the vote in Manitoba until 1952.

7 Ibid., chap. 5.

8 *Royal Commission on the Donald Marshall Jr. Prosecution* (Halifax: Queens Printer, 1989), 177. The Commission did, however, seem aware of the potential for discriminatory use of peremptory challenges when it stated that it urged "those involved in selecting juries for trials involving Native people – both prosecutors and defence counsel – not to automatically exclude Natives simply because they are of the same race as the accused."

9 *Coroner's Act*, S.S. 1999 c. C-38.01 s.29(3).

10 *R. v. Cyr*, 2014 SKQB 118.

11 *Criminal Code*, s 649.

12 Ministry of the Attorney General, *First Nations Representation on Ontario Juries*, Hon. Frank Iacobucci, February 2013, 26, online: https://www.attorneygeneral.jus.gov.on.ca/english/about/pubs/iacobucci/First_Nations_Representation_Ontario_Juries.html.

13 Wilton Littlechild, et al., *Final Report from the Commission on First Nations and Métis Peoples and Justice Reform* (Regina: Queens Park, 2004), chap. 6.

14 Kyle Edwards, "Saskatchewan Officials Skipped a Step When They Formed Gerald Stanley's Jury," *Macleans*, 31 March 2018.

15 "'Huge' jury pool of 750 Summoned as Potential Jurors for Boushie Case," CBC *News*, 28 January 2018.

16 *The Jury Act*, S.S. 1998 c. J.4.2 s. 6(h).

17 *Criminal Code*, s 638. As will be discussed in chapter 10, Bill C-75 only proposes minor changes by moving the life time cut-off from one to two years' imprisonment.

18 *Criminal Code*, s 629. There are technical distinctions between challenging jury rolls and the array of jurors, but for clarity's sake, I will simply refer to panels of prospective jurors, in this chapter.

19 *R. v. Kokopenace*, [2015] 2 SCR 398.

20 *Criminal Code*, s 638(1)(b).

21 *R. v. Sherratt*, [1991] 1 SCR 509; *R. v. Williams*, [1998] 1 SCR 1128; *R. v. Find*, [2001] 1 SCR 863.

22 *Criminal Code*, s 634 If the accused faces less than five years' imprisonment, the parties only have four peremptory challenges and if the accused is charged with first-degree murder or high treason, they have twenty peremptory challenges.

23 Barb Pacholik, "Jury System Challenger on Trial for Assault," *Regina Leader Post*, 25 March 2014, A3.

24 One press article that diverges from other accounts admits that it is from an uncorroborated source on the panel and suggests that half of the panel was Indigenous and many expressed the view among themselves that Stanley was guilty. Candice Malcolm, "Half of Prospective Jurors Were Aboriginal, Says Member of the Jury Pool," *Toronto Sun,* 13 February 2018. Compare with Friesen, "Family Upset," *Globe and Mail,* A4. If half of the panel was indeed Indigenous, it is difficult to see how an all-white jury could have been selected with only five peremptory challenges of visibly Indigenous people.

25 Friesen, "Family Upset," A4.

26 *R. v. Kent,* (1986) 27 CCC(3d) 405 at 421 (Man. C.A.).

27 *R. v. Lamirande,* 2002 MBCA 41 at 157.

28 *R. v. Butler,* (1984) 63 CCC (3d) 243 at 27–28 (B.C.C.A.).

29 *R. v. Ironeagle,* 2012 SKQB 324; *R. v. Cyr,* 2014 SKQB 61. See generally Mark Israel, "The Under-representation of Indigenous People on Canadian Jury Panels," *Law and Policy,* (2003) 25:37.

30 *R. v. Diabo,* (1974) 27 CCC (2d) 411 at 416 (Que. C.A.).

31 *R. v. Kent,* (1986) 27 CCC (3d) 405 at 410 (Man. C.A.).

32 Ibid., 421.

33 *R. v. Lamirande,* 2002 MBCA 41 at 160, 157. See also *R. v. Teerhuis-Moar,* 2010 MBCA 102.

34 The Saskatchewan Court of Appeal reached a similar conclusion, but in more measured tones when it rejected a claim in 2009 by an Indigenous accused charged with growing marijuana "because there were no First Nations people on the jury, no one understood his customs and traditions or the healing qualities of the 'medicines' he was producing." This argument is also misplaced. Jurors are obliged to decide a case on the basis of the evidence presented at trial, not on the basis of their personal knowledge. If Mr Agecoutay or his counsel believed the jury needed to understand particular customs and traditions, it was their responsibility to put the necessary information before the trial court." *R. v. Agecoutay,* 2009 SKCA 100 at 28.

35 *R. v. Newborn,* 2016 ABQB 13 at 30–31. For strong arguments that those who have been convicted have relevant experience and should not be excluded from jury service see Michael Johnston, "The Automatic Exclusion from Juries of those with Criminal Records Should be Ruled Unconstitutional," (2014) 17 *Criminal Reports,* (7th Series), 335. For further background on the accused whose father attended residential school and a conclusion that a sentence of life imprisonment with fifteen years' ineligibility of parole was

appropriate for a beating murder on public transportation, see *R. v. Newborn*, 2018 ABQB 47.

36 *R. v. Laws*, 1998 Can LII 7157 (ON CA.) For criticism of the Court of Appeal's decision to rely on the challenge for cause procedure and not to follow the 1995 recommendations of Ontario's commission on systemic racism to abolish the citizenship requirement see David Tanovich, "The Charter of Whiteness: Twenty-Five Years of Maintaining Racial Injustice in the Canadian Criminal Justice System," *Supreme Court Law Review*, 2nd Series 655, 40 (2008): 662-3.

37 *R. v. Kokopenace*, [2015] 2 SCR 398 at 138. Of the eight, four were excused and two did not respond to the summons. Ibid., 305. One judge suggested that the adult reserve population in the Kenora district was between 21.5 per cent and 31.8 per cent, ibid., 138, while another describes the population as "approximately 30 per cent," ibid., 197. The Ontario Court of Appeal accepted even higher estimates ranging from 30.2 to 36.8 per cent. *R. v. Kokopenace*, [2013] ONCA 389 fn 4. Note that I represented the David Asper Centre for Constitutional Rights in the Ontario Court of Appeal, but not the Supreme Court case.

38 Thanks to Christian Miller who, in his research on the case using 2016 census data, has estimated about 29.5 per cent of the adult population in the Battleford judicial district was Indigenous. See Christian Miller, "Peremptory Challenges During Jury Selection as Institutional Racism," *Criminal Law Quarterly* (2019) forthcoming.

39 *R. v. Kokopenace*, 39.

40 Ibid., 93.

41 Ibid., 66.

42 Ibid., 69–76.

43 Ibid., 128.

44 Ibid., 99.

45 Ibid., 101.

46 Ibid., 75–76.

47 *R. v. Ipeelee*, [2012] 1 SCR 433 and reiterating its statements in *R. v. Gladue*, [1999] 1 S.C.R. 688 that the over-representation of Indigenous people in jail was a crisis and a result of systemic discrimination. Note that I represented Aboriginal Legal Services of Toronto in *Gladue* and the B.C. Civil Liberties Association in *Ipeelee*.

48 *R. v. Kokopenace*, 75–76.

49 Ibid., 64, 83.

50 Ibid., 73.

51 Ibid., 88.

52 Don Worme, "First Nations Perspective on Self-Government," in Gosse, Youngblood Henderson and Carter, *Continuing Poundmaker's and Riel's Quest* (Saskatoon: Purich Press, 1994).

53 *R. v. Kokopenace,* 308.

54 Ibid., 238.

55 Ibid., 231.

56 Justice Giovanna Toscana Roccamo, *Report to the Canadian Judicial Council on Jury Selection in Ontario,* May 2018, 16, online: https://www.cjc-ccm.gc.ca/cmslib/general/Study%20Leave%20Report%20 2018%20June.pdf. I am indebted to Eugene Meehan Q.C. for bringing this study to my attention.

57 Other cases in Alberta at the time had recognized that a voters' list would under-represent Indigenous people. *R. v. Nepoose,* 1991 CanLII 5968 (AB QB).

58 *R. v. Born With a Tooth,* 1993 CanLII 7066 at 14. See also *R. v. Brown,* 2006 CanLII 42683 at 22 (ON CA), disapproving of attempts to move forward African Canadian prospective jurors in panels. For a more recent case which recognizes the legitimacy of affirmative action to increase Indigenous representation on jury rolls see *R. v. Madahbee-Cywink,* 2015 ONSC 434 at 51.

59 *R. v. Born With a Tooth,* 1993 CanLII 7066 at 12. (AB QB). On the facts of the case see *R. v. Born With A Tooth,* 1994 CanLII 9151 (ABQB).

60 *R. v. Born With a Tooth,* 15.

61 "Native Activist Found Guilty after Emotional Twist," *Calgary Herald,* 15 March 1994, A1.

62 "Indian Activist Jailed 16 Months," *Montreal Gazette,* 10 September 1994, G10.

63 *R. v. Yooya,* 1994 CanLII 5084 (SKQB); *R. v. A.F.,* (1994) Can LII 1994 (ON SC); *R. v. Redhead,* (1995) 99 CCC (3d) 559 (Man Q.B.).

64 Cynthia Petersen, "Institutionalized Racism: The Need for Reform of the Jury Selection Process," *McGill Law Journal,* 38 (1993): 147.

65 The Court observed in 1989, "identical treatment may frequently produce serious inequality." *Andrews v Law Society of BC* [1989] 1 SCR 143 at 164–5; *R. v. Ewert* 2018 SCC 30 at 59. See also Vanessa MacDonnell, "The Right to a Representative Jury: Beyond Kokopenace," *Criminal Law Quarterly* 64 334 (2017): 344–5.

66 Sherley's Case 2 Dyer 144; Marianne Constable, *The Law of the*

Other: The Mixed Jury and Changing Conceptions of Citizenship, Law and Knowledge (Chicago: University of Chicago Press, 1994), 106.

67 Thomas Flanagan and Neil Watson, "The Riel Trial Revisited: Criminal Procedure and Law in 1885," *Saskatchewan History*, 34 57, (1981): 69.

68 Thomas Flanagan, *First Nations Second Thoughts* 2ⁿᵈ ed. (Montreal: McGill-Queen's University Press, 2008), 6. This book rejects the idea of unique rights and claims based on a non-literal reading of the Treaties as part of an "Aboriginal orthodoxy" that he challenges.

69 *R. v. Fowler*, 2005 BCSC 1874 at 94.

70 *Ex Parte Virginia*, 100 U.S. 339, 369 (1880). Justice Field went on to raise the spectre that a mixed jury would require "in cases affecting members of the colored race only, that juries should be composed entirely of colored persons, and that the presiding judge should be of the same race." Ibid.

71 Constable, *The Law of the Other*, 40, 143. See also Toni Massaro, "Peremptories or Peers?" *North Carolina Law Review*, 64 (1986): 591.

72 In the United States, unanimous verdicts are no longer required and the Court rejected arguments that this would allow the majority to outvote minorities on the basis that, "We simply find no proof for the notion that a majority will disregard its instructions and cast its votes for guilt or innocence based on prejudice, rather than the evidence." *Apodaca v Oregon,* 406 U.S. 404, 413–14 (1972).

73 *Peter v Kiff,* (1972) 407 U.S. 493, 503–4.

74 Constable, *The Law of the Other*, 21.

75 8 Henry 6, ch.27.

76 Constable, *The Law of the Other*, 120.

77 Daniel Van Ness, "Preserving a Community Voice: The Case for a Half and Half Jury in Racially Charged Jury Cases," *John Marshall Law Review* 1, 28 (1994): 37–39.

78 Andrew Tazlitz, "Racial Blind-Sight: The Absurdity of a Color-Blind Criminal Justice System," *Ohio State Journal of Criminal Law* 1, 5 (2007).

79 Nancy Marder, "The Interplay of Race and False Claims of Jury Nullification," *University of Michigan Journal of Law Reform*, 32 (1999): 285.

80 Katherine Hermes, "Jurisdiction in the Colonial Northeast: Algonquin, English and French Governance," *American Journal of Legal History*, 34 (1999): 52.

81 Jury Amendment Ordinance 1844 s. 1.
82 Michele Powles, "A Legal History of New Zealand Jury Service," *Victoria University at Wellington Law Review*, 29, 283 (1999): 290.
83 Ibid., 303.
84 Some object even to all-Maori juries on the basis that the jury itself is a European concept. See Neil Cameron, Susan Potter, and Warren Young, "The New Zealand Jury: Towards Reform," in *World Jury Systems*, ed. Neil Vidmar (Oxford: Oxford University Press, 2000), 196–7.
85 Samuel King, "The American Courts and the Annexation of Hawaii," *Western Legal History*, 2, 1 (1989): 9.
86 *Naturalization Act of 1870*, 33 and 34 Vict., chap. 14 s.5.
87 As quoted in, Constable, *The Law of the Other*, 145. See also Sherri Lynn Johnson, "Black Innocence and the White Jury," *Michigan Law Review*, 83 (1985): 1611.
88 *Virginia v Rives*, 100 U.S. 313, 315 (1880).
89 Caroline Light, *Stand Your Ground* (Boston: Beacon Press, 2017), 62.
90 Deborah Ramirez, "The Mixed Jury and the Ancient Custom of Trial by Jury de Mediete Linguae," *Boston University Law Review* 74, 777 (1994): 789. See also Harold McDougall, "The Case for Black Juries," *Yale Law Journal*, 79 (1970): 531.; Albert Alschuler, "Racial Quotas and the Jury," *Duke Law Journal*, 44 (1995): 704.
91 New Zealand Law Reform Commission, *Juries in Criminal Trials Report 69* (Wellington: New Zealand Law Reform Commission, 2001), para.173.
92 Caitlyn Scheer, "Chasing Democracy: The Development and Acceptance of Jury Trials in Argentina," *University of Miami Inter-American Law Review*, 47, 316 (2016): 334–5, 343. There are unlimited challenges for cause based on lack of impartiality in those Argentinian states that have adopted the jury. Ibid., 347.
93 Hiroshi Fukurai and Richard Krooth, *Race in the Jury Box Affirmative Action in Jury Selection* (New York: SUNY Press, 2004).
94 *R. v. Cyr*, 2014 SKQB 61 at 78.
95 *Constitution Act, 1982*, "The Canadian Charter of Rights and Freedoms," ss.25, 15(2).
96 John Borrows, *"Peace, Friendship and Respect": Indigenous Treaties in Canada* (unpublished, 30 October 2003), cites Elder Danny Musqua, 142.
97 *R. v. Cyr*, 2014 SKQB 61 at 98.
98 Ibid., 15. This case was also applied to an Indigenous accused who

challenged the lack of Indigenous jurors in a Yorkton trial in *R. v. Papequash*, 2014 SKQB 118.

99 *R. v. Cyr*, 2014 SKQB 61 at 177.

100 Joe Friesen, "Trial Begins in the Death of Colten Boushie, a Killing that Exposed a Racial Divide in Saskatchewan," *Globe and Mail*, 29 January 2018, A1.

101 *R. v. Find*, [2001] 1 SCR 863.

102 Molly Hayes, "Jury Selection Begins in case of Hamilton Man Charged with Indigenous Man's Second-degree Murder," *Globe and Mail*, 11 June 2018. See *infra* chapter 9 at pages 199–200 for additional discussion of the Khill case and jury selection.

103 *R. v. Williams*, [1998] 1 SCR 1128. I represented Aboriginal Legal Services of Toronto in this case.

104 *R. v. Fleury*, 1998 CanLII 13847 at 23.

105 *R. v. Horse*, 2003 SKCA 51 leave to appeal denied.

106 *R. v. Williams*, [1998] 1 SCR 1128 at 3.

107 *R. v. Spence*, [2005] 3 SCR 458 at para. 25.

108 *R. v. Parks*, [1993] 15 O.R.(3d) 324 (C.A.).

109 Carol Aylward, *Canadian Critical Race Theory* (Halifax: Fernwood Publishing, 1999), 117–118, 158–165; David Tanovich, "The Charter of Whiteness: Twenty Five Years of Maintaining Racial Injustice in the Canadian Criminal Justice System," *Supreme Court Law Review*, 2nd Series 40, 655 (2008): 665; Rakhi Ruparelia, "Erring on the Side of Ignorance: Challenge for Cause Twenty Years After Parks," *Canadian Bar Review*, 90, 267 (2013): 295; Cynthia Lee, "A New Approach to Voir Dire on Racial Bias," *University of California at Irvine Law Review*, 5, 843 (2015).

110 *R. v. Find*, [2001] 1 SCR 863.

111 *R. v. Spence*, [2005] 3 SCR 458.

112 The Court distinguished cases involving African Canadian accused and white victims noting that studies suggested that racism may be an issue "where the accused is said to have "crossed the colour line" against a victim who belongs to the white majority." Ibid., para. 3.

113 For arguments about the need for expanded challenges for cause see Kent Roach, "The Urgent Need to Reform Jury Selection after the Gerald Stanley and Colten Boushie Case," *Criminal Law Quarterly*, 65, 271 (2018): 275–6; Kent Roach, "Khill Verdict Should make Us Think Twice about Our Self-defence Law," *Globe and Mail*, 4 July 2018.

114 *R. v. Munson*, 2001 SKQB 410 at para. 2 affirmed 2003 SKCA 28.

115 Daniel Girard, "I Would Like People to Know we are not Murderers;

Suspicion Hangs over an Entire Police Force," *Toronto Star*, 11 September 2001, A03.

116 *R. v. Munson*, 2003 SKCA 28 at 23.

117 *R. v. Rogers*, [2000] 38 C.R. (5ᵗʰ) 331 at para. 6 (Ont.s.c.).

118 Ibid., para. 6 (Ont.s.c.).

119 Scott R Spencer, undated statement, online: http://s3.documentcloud. org/documents/4360813/Re-Gerald-Stanley-Trial-January-29 -2018-2.pdf.

120 Ibid.

121 "Coming Trial 'Is not a Referendum on Racism' Says Lawyer for Man Accused of Killing Colten Boushie," CBC *News*, 26 January 2018, online: http://www.cbc.ca/news/canada/saskatoon/ coming-trial-is-not-a-referendum-on-racism-says-lawyer-for-man-ac- cused-of-killing-colten-boushie-1.4506553.

122 For an Ontario case where the trial judge excused a prospective juror who admitted to bias against people who possessed handguns see *R. v. Browne*, 2017 ONSC 5795.

123 Molly Hayes, "Jury Selection Begins in Hamilton Trial of Homeowner Charged with Indigenous Man's Second-degree Murder," *Globe and Mail*, 11 June 2018.

124 Betty Ann Adam, "Night Feels Vindicated by Court Ruling," *Saskatoon Star Phoenix*, 14 March 2003, A3.

125 *R. v. Spence*, [2005] 3 SCR 458 at 1.

126 Guy Quenneville, "'Huge' Pool of 750 People Summoned as Potential Jurors for Colten Boushie Case," CBC *News*, 28 January 2018.

127 Friesen, "Family Upset," A4.

128 Debbie Baptiste as quoted in, Joe Friesen, "Trial Begins in Death of Colten Boushie, a Killing that Exposed Racial Divide in Saskatchewan," *Globe and Mail*, 29 January 2018, A1.

129 Ibid.

130 Bull Graveland, "Family of Cree Man Shot on Saskatchewan Farm Upset with Jury Selection," *Canadian Press*, 29 January 2018.

131 *Cloutier v The Queen*, [1979] 2 SCR 709 at 720; *R. v. Davey* [2012] 3 SCR 828 at [22].

132 *R. v. Piraino*, 1982 CanLII 3135 at 8 (ON SC).

133 *Batson v Kentucky*, 476 U.S. 79 (1986).

134 *Georgia v McCollom*, 505 U.S. 42 (1992).

135 Jeffrey Bellin and Junichi Semitsu, "Widening Batson's Net to Ensnare More than the Unapologetically Bigoted or Painfully

Unimaginative Attorney," *Cornell Law Review*, 96 (2011): 1075; Caren Moyers Morrison, "Negotiating Peremptory Challenges," *Journal of Criminal Law and Criminology* 1, 104 (2014).

136 *Foster v Chatman*, 578 U.S. (2016).

137 Manitoba Aboriginal Justice Inquiry, *The Justice System and Aboriginal People* (Manitoba: Queens Printer, 1991), 385.

138 Manitoba Aboriginal Justice Inquiry, *The Death of Helen Betty Osborne* (Manitoba: Queens Printer, 1991), chap. 5.

139 Iacobucci, *First Nations Representation*, 396.

140 *R. v. Lines*, 1993 O.J. no 3284 (Ont.Gen.Div.).

141 Ibid., para. 8.

142 Ibid., para. 26.

143 Tracey Tyler, "Province Contemplating Appeal of Police Officer's Acquittal," *Toronto Star*, 21 May 1993, A28.

144 *R. v. Brown*, 1999 O.J. no 4867 at paras. 6–11.

145 For two Ontario cases where discriminatory exclusion of African Canadian jurors was alleged but rejected see *R. v. Gayle*, 2001 CanLII 4447 at paras. 61–67 (ON CA) and *R. v. Amos*, 2007 ONCA 672.

146 *R. v. Biddle*, [1995] 1 SCR 761.

147 Sunny Dhillion, "First Nations Challenge Jury Representation," *Globe and Mail*, 28 February 2014, A4. In reference to the decision in *R. v. Cornell*, 2017, YKCA 12 at 18–20 leave to appeal dismissed 2018 CanLII 51170 (SCC) rejecting allegations of discrimination by the prosecutor in using peremptory challenges.

148 Carol Aylward, *Canadian Critical Race Theory: Racism and the Law* (Halifax: Fernwood Publishing, 1999), 157–8.

149 Barb Pacholik, "Jury System Challenger on Trial for Assault," *Regina Leader Post*, 25 March 2014, A3.

150 *R. v. Cyr* [2014] SKQB 61 at 98.

151 As quoted in, Barb Pacholik, "New Jury for Assault Trial," *Saskatoon Star Phoenix*, 26 March 2014, A7.

152 Chief Justice Popescul at TT 60.

153 *R. v. Stanley* [2018] SKQB 27.

CHAPTER 6

1 Tristin Hopper, "Gerald Stanley's Magic Gun: the Extremely Unlikely Defence that Secured his Acquittal," *National Post*, 14 February 2018.

2 Brandon Garrett and Peter Neufeld, "Invalid Forensic Testimony and Wrongful Convictions," *Virginia Law Review* 1, 95 (2009).

3 Hon. Ted Hughes, Peter Mackinnon and Delia Opekokow, *The Lachance/Nerland Inquiry* (Regina: Queens Printer, 1993).

4 Hon. F. Kaufman, *Report of the Inquiry on Proceedings Involving Guy Paul Morin* (Toronto: Queens Printer, 1998).

5 Hon. S. Goudge, *Report of the Inquiry into Pediatric Forensic Pathology in Ontario* (Toronto: Queens Printer, 2008), chap. 20. I was director of research for this inquiry.

6 Ibid.

7 National Academy of Science, *Strengthening Forensic Science in the United States: A Path Forward* (Washington: National Academy of Science, 2009).

8 *R. v. Trochym*, [2007] 1 SCR 579.

9 *R. v. J.L.(L).*, [2000] 2 SCR 600.

10 Gerald Stanley at TT 700.

11 Michael Plaxton, "The Stanley Verdict: Manslaughter and 'Hang Fire,'" *Globe and Mail,* 11 February 2018.

12 Question by Scott Spencer. Answer by Gregory Williams at PT 381.

13 Gregory Williams at TT 474.

14 *R. v. Marquard*, [1993] 4 SCR 223 at 251.

15 Col Jim Crossman, "Why Hang Fires Almost Never Happen," *The American Rifleman*, 32, 119 (1971): 33.

16 Ibid., 33.

17 Ibid., 33.

18 Ibid.,37.

19 Ibid., 34.

20 Lucien C. Haag, "To Create a Hang Fire," AFTE *Journal* (Association of Firearm and Toolmark Examiners), 23(2), 600 (1991): 666.

21 Ibid., 661.

22 Ibid., 666.

23 Ibid., 667.

24 Haag concluded his article with this relevant observation, "The popular warning on many boxes of ammunition to keep the gun pointed in a safe direction for some specified time after a misfire would appear to be unjustified. Rather, the prime directive to the handler and the shooter of firearms is simply to keep the gun pointed in a safe direction at *all* times." Ibid., 667 (emphasis in original).

25 Gregory Williams at TT 528.

26 Chief Justice Popescul at TT 588.

27 Sandy Ervin at TT 590.

28 Wayne Popowich at TT 616.

29 Nathan Voinorosky at TT 626.

30 *R. v. J.L.J.*, [2000] 2 S.C.R. 600 rejecting defence attempts to use results of penile plethysmography on the basis that high error rates ran the risk of distorting the fact-finding process.

31 *R. v. Trochym*, [2007] 1 S.C.R. 579 rejecting use of post-hypnosis testimony offered by the prosecution because of its unknown reliability and risk of wrongful convictions.

32 Scott Spencer at TT 846.

33 Plaxton, "The Stanley Verdict."

34 David Milward, "Justice Denied for Colten Boushie and Tina Fontaine: How their Cases Illustrate Racism in Canadian Courts," CBC *News*, 25 February 2018.

35 Emma Cunliffe, "Judging Fast and Slow: Using Decision-Making Theory to Explore Judicial Fact-Determination," *International Journal of Evidence and Proof*, 18, 139 (2014): 150.

36 Francois Truffaut, *Hitchcock/Truffaut* (New York: Simon and Schuster, 1985), 168.

CHAPTER 7

1 Hon. Fred Kaufman, *Report of the Inquiry on Proceedings Involving Guy Paul Morin* (Toronto: Queens Printer, 1998), Recommendation 52.

2 Kathryn Campbell, *Miscarriages of Justice in Canada* (Toronto: University of Toronto Press, 2018), 12 Appendix A. Another example of an incentivized witness would be an accomplice. *Vetrovec v The Queen*, [1982] 1 SCR 811. On incentivized witnesses see Christopher Sherrin, "Jailhouse Informants," *Criminal Law Quarterly*, 40 (1997): 106; Alexandra Natapoff "Beyond Unreliable: How Snitches Contribute to Wrongful Convictions," *Golden Gate Law Review*, 37 (2006): 107.

3 "Premier, RCMP Call for Respectful Behaviour as Gerald Stanley Trial end Nears," CBC *News*, 8 February 2018.

4 Naiomi Metallic, "I am a Mi'kmaq Lawyer and I Despair over Colten Boushie," *The Conversation*, 18 March 2018, online: https://theconversation.com/i-am-a-mikmaq-lawyer-and-i-despair-over-colten-boushie-93229.

5 Unnamed juror in Marshall Trial as quoted in, Alan Story, "The Tangled Trial of Donald Marshall: Racial Prejudice and Perjury Helped Put Him Behind Bars," *Toronto Star*, 9 June 1986, A8.

6 The jury withdrew at 12:40 p.m. on 5 November and returned with

its guilty verdict at 4:35 p.m. See *Her Majesty the Queen v Donald Marshall Jr*, Transcript 5 November 1971.

7 Story, "The Tangled Trial," A8. On the social context in Sydney and prejudice towards Indigenous persons see James (Sakej) Youngblood Henderson, "The Marshall Inquiry: A View of Legal Consciousness," in *Elusive Justice*, ed. Joy Manette (Halifax: Fernwood Publishing, 1992), 42.

8 *R v Pan,* [2001] 2 S.C.R. 344 at 4.

9 Ibid., 44.

10 Justice Arbour stated that challenge for cause was particularly relevant in the case where racist comments were alleged to have been made in the jury room and that "it is only at the post-verdict stage that there is a restriction on the ability to probe into allegations of bias by virtue of the operation of the common law rule of exclusion." Ibid., 94.

11 Emma Cunliffe, "Sexual Assault Prosecutions in the Supreme Court of Canada: Losing Sight of Substantive Equality," *Supreme Court Law Review*, 2nd Series, 57 (2012): 295.

12 *R. v. Marshall,* [1983] N.S.J. no 322 at 73 (C.A.).

13 *R. v. R (D.S.),* [1997] 3 S.C.R. 485. See generally Carol Aylward, *Canadian Critical Race Theory Racism and the Law* (Halifax: Fernwood Publishing, 1999), 96–111; David Tanovich, *The Colour of Justice* (Toronto: Irwin Law, 2006), 125–130.

14 *R. v. Marshall,* [1983] N.S.J. no 322 at 73 (C.A.).

15 Ibid., paras. 73, 79–81, 83.

16 Hon. A Hickman, Hon. L. Poitras, and Hon. G. Evans, *Royal Commission on the Donald Marshall Jr Prosecution* (Halifax: Queens Printer, 1989), 70, 94, 161–2.

17 Ibid., 20.

18 Ibid., 171–2.

19 Ibid., 172.

20 Statistics Canada, Indigenous and Northern Affairs Canada, "Language Characteristics," online: http://fnp-ppn.aandc-aadnc. gc.ca/fnp/Main/Search/FNLanguage.aspx?BAND_ NUMBER=346&lang=eng. CENSUS.

21 *Royal Commission on the Donald Marshall Jr Prosecution,* (Halifax: Queens Printer, 1989).

22 *Report of the Nerland/Lachance Inquiry,* 50, concluded that "the fact that Lachance was an Aboriginal is, in our opinion, one of the reasons why Nerland exhibited what at least was a lack of concern about his safety."

23 Ibid., 30.

24 Scott Spencer at TT 840.

25 Murray Sinclair, "Aboriginal Peoples, Justice and the Law," in Gosse, Youngblood, Henderson, and Carter, *Continuing Poundmaker's and Riel's Quest* (Saskatoon: Purich Press, 1994), 180.

26 Mary Ellen Turpel-Lafond "On the Question of Adapting the Canadian Criminal Justice System for Aboriginal People: Don't Fence Me In," in Royal Commission on Aboriginal Peoples *Aboriginal Peoples and the Justice System* (Ottawa: Supply and Services, 1993), 175.

27 Belinda Jackson at TT 408.

28 Scott Spencer at TT 432.

29 Belinda Jackson at PT 331.

30 Belinda Jackson at TT 429.

31 Doug Cuthand, "First Nations Traditions Tested at Stanley Trial," *National Post*, 3 February 2018. I am indebted to Professor Jeffrey Hewitt of the University of Windsor for discussions on this sensitive point.

32 Bill Burge at TT 856.

33 For an example of a court approving a prosecutor's decision not to call a witness believed to be unreliable see *R. v. Lane*, 2008 ONCA 841 at 74–5.

34 Eric Meechance at TT 321–2.

35 *R. v. Marshall* [1983] N.S. J. no 322 at para 63.

36 Cassidy Cross at TT 356, 358.

37 Erica Violet Lee as quoted in, Leyland Coco, "Canada's Indigenous Groups urge Reform after Shock of White Farmer's Acquittal," *The Guardian*, 12 February 2018.

38 Ibid.

39 Eric Meechance at TT 329.

40 "FSIN Faces the Backlash," *Regina Leader Post*, 2 April 2008, B8; "FSIN Debacle Shows the Need to Heed the Rules," *Saskatoon Star Phoenix*, 15 Sept 2011, A11.

41 *Police Act, 1990* S.S. 1990–91 c.P-15 s.38.

42 Betty Ann Adam, "FSIN Hopeful Investigation Unit Funding Secure," *Saskatoon Star Phoenix*, 28 January 2017.

43 "Women IDs Stanley as Boushie's Shooter," CBC *News*, 1 February 2018.

CHAPTER 8

1 The Supreme Court has explained, "A trial judge must put to the jury all defences that arise on the facts, whether or not they have been specifically raised by an accused. Where there is an air of reality to a defence, it should go to the jury. Second, a trial judge has a positive duty to keep from the jury defences lacking an evidential foundation. A defence that lacks an air of reality should be kept from the jury." *R. v. Cinous*, [2002] 2 S.C.R. 3 at 51.

2 Hon. A Hickman, Hon. L. Poitras, and Hon. G. Evans, *Royal Commission on the Donald Marshall Jr. Prosecution* (Halifax: Queens Printer, 1989), 7.

3 *R. v. Gladue* [1999] 1 SCR 688. I represented Aboriginal Legal Services of Toronto in this case. See generally Jonathan Rudin, *Indigenous People and the Criminal Justice System* (Toronto: Emond Montgomery, 2018) for an explanation of how *Gladue* is rooted in an appreciation of colonial and systemic discrimination against Indigenous people and applies throughout the criminal justice system and not just at sentencing.

4 Glennis Fouhy at TT 648.

5 On the role of stereotypes associating Indigenous people and particularly women with crime see Luana Ross, *Inventing the Savage: Social Construction of Native American Criminality* (Austin: University of Texas Press, 1999).

6 Gerald Stanley at TT 687.

7 On stereotypes and concerns that terrorism laws may be unfairly applied to Indigenous people see David Milward, "The Latest Chapter on Fighting Terrorism since 1492," *Criminal Law Quarterly*, 59 (2012): 278.

8 Gerald Stanley at TT 687.

9 *R. v. Baptiste*, 1998 CanLII 12353 (SKCA).

10 Scott Spencer at TT 844.

11 Scott Spencer at TT 842.

12 Gerald Stanley at TT 725.

13 Elizabeth Flock, "Trayvon Martin 'Million Hoodie March': A Short History of the Hoodie," *Washington Post*, 22 March 2012. For arguments that hoodies are seen as a sign of danger when worn by racialized men including Martin, but not by white men, see Erynn Masi de Casonova and Curtis Webb, "A Tale of Two Hoodies," *Men and Masculinities*, 20 (2017): 117.

14 Aboriginal females constitute 43 per cent of admissions to provincial custody nationally and 85 per cent of admissions in Saskatchewan in 2016–17 whereas Aboriginal males constituted 28 per cent of admissions nationally and 74 per cent in Saskatchewan. Jamil Malakieh, "Adult Correctional Statistics, 2016-17," *Juristat*, (19 June 2018): Table 6.

15 Chief Justice Popescul at TT 825 without the jury present.

16 *Criminal Code* RSC 1985 c.C-34 s.86.

17 *Criminal Code* ss.34(1)(a), 35(1) (a). In the UK, the accused's perception of threat only has to be subjective. *Criminal Justice and Immigration Act, 2008* c.4 s.76(3).

18 George Fletcher, *A Crime of Self-Defense: Bernhard Goetz and the Law on Trial* (New York: New Press, 1988), 187.

19 Ibid., 204.

20 Ibid., 206.

21 Ibid., 208.

22 Ibid., 204.

23 Ibid., 203.

24 Ibid., 206.

25 Ibid ., 206.

26 Ibid., 208. See also Cynthia Lee, "Making Race Salient: Trayvon Martin and Implicit Bias in a Not Yet Post-Racial World," *North Carolina Law Review*, 91 (2013):1555.

27 *R. v. Gunning*, [2005] 1 SCR 627; Paul Strickland, "Sentence Upsets Victim's Family," *Prince George Citizen*, 1 Feb 2007, 1.

28 Benjamin Berger, "The Abiding Presence of Conscience: Criminal Justice Against the Law and the Modern Constitutional Imagination," *University of Toronto Law Journal*, 61, 579 (2011): 596–603 and in reference to the court's decision in *R. v. Kreiger* [2006] 2 SCR 501, concluding that judges cannot direct juries to convict.

29 Alice Wooley, "An Ethical Jury? Reflections on the Acquittal of Gerald Stanley for the Murder/ Manslaughter of Colten Boushie," *Slaw*, 20 February 2018, online: http://www.slaw.ca/2018/02/20/an-ethical-jury-reflections-on-the-acquittal-of-gerald-stanley-for-the-murder-manslaughter-of-colten-boushie/.

30 *R. v. Morgentaler* [1988] 1 SCR 30 at 77. See also *R. v. Latimer*, [2001] 1 SCR 3 at paras 65–70 concluding that the accused does not have a right to jury nullification which could be encouraged by informing it of mandatory minimum sentences.

31 Robert J. Sharpe and Kent Roach, *Brian Dickson: A Judge's Journey* (Toronto: University of Toronto Press, 2003), 100.

32 "Three Acquitted in Fatal Beating," *Globe and Mail*, 14 May 1966, 4; "Three Glaslyn Men Acquitted in Indian Manslaughter Case," *Saskatoon Star Phoenix*, 14 May 1966, 3.

33 David Milward, "Justice Denied for Tina Fontaine and Colten Boushie: How their Cases Illustrate Racism in Canadian Courts," 25 February 2018, online: http://www.cbc.ca/news/canada/manitoba/tina-fontaine-colten-boushie-justice-denied-1.4549469.

34 David Tanovich, "How Racial Bias Likely Impacted the Stanley Verdict," *The Conversation*, 5 April 2018, online: https://theconversation.com/how-racial-bias-likely-impacted-the-stanley-verdict-94211.

35 Kyle Edwards, "In Saskatchewan, the Stanley Verdict Opens up Centuries-old Wounds," *Macleans*, 5 March 2018.

36 *R. v. Barton*, 2017 ABCA 216 at 162.

37 Implicit bias theory suggests that discrimination need not be intentional and can affect what jurors remember and do not remember. Justin Levinson, "Forgotten Racial Equality: Implicit Bias, Decision-Making and Misremembering," *Duke Law Journal*, 57 (2007): 345.

38 Michael Plaxton, "The Stanley Verdict: Manslaughter and "Hang Fire,'" *Globe and Mail*, 11 February 2018.

39 University of Saskatchewan criminal law professor, Tim Quigley, expressed surprise, based on forty years of law practice, that Stanley was not at least convicted of negligent manslaughter. Leyland Cecco, "Canada: Indigenous Groups urge Reform after Shock of White Farmer's Acquittal," *The Guardian*, 12 February 2018.

CHAPTER 9

1 "'The Rodney King of Western Canada': Killing of Indigenous Man Heads to Trial," *The Guardian*, 29 January 2018. This quotes a former Lutheran Minister in Battleford for the analogy to Rodney King.

2 "Gerald Stanley Trial – Complete Transcript of Public Prosecution Decision not to Appeal the Case," *Saskatoon Star Phoenix*, 8 March 2018.

3 Andrea Hill, "Farmer Cleared in Shooting," *Calgary Herald*, 10 February 2018, N1.

4 Bill Graveland, "Colten Boushie's Mother Delivers Emotional Message as Rallies Held across Canada," *Canadian Press*, 10 February 2018.

5 Joe Friesen, "Boushie Family Moves from Anger to Action in Wake of Acquittal," *Globe and Mail*, 12 February 2018, A1.

6 Doug Cuthand, "We Can Only Ask for Justice, Peace for All Concerned," *Regina Leader Post,* 10 February 2018, A9.

7 Prime Minister Justin Trudeau as quoted in, "Tories Accuse PM of 'Political Interference' after Comments on Boushie Case," CBC *News,* 11 Febraury 2018.

8 Friesen, "Boushie Family Moves from Anger to Action," A1.

9 "Tories Accuse PM." CBC *News.*

10 Ibid.

11 Bill Graveland, "Absolutely Perverse: Outrage after White Farmer Found not Guilty in Indigenous Death," *Canadian Press,* 10 February 2018.

12 "'Canada Must and Can Do Better,' Trudeau says as Controversy over Boushie Verdict hits Commons," *National Post,* 12 February 2018.

13 Christie Blatchford, "Messing with Jury System Won't Fix Indigenous Alienation from the Justice System," *National Post,* 1 March 2018.

14 Ibid.

15 Sean Fine, "Lawyers Decry PM Tweets on Stanley Trial," *Globe and Mail,* 20 February 2018, A3.

16 "Lawyers Issue Statement on Stanley Trial Reaction," *Battleford News-Optimist,* 16 February 2018, online: http://www.newsoptimist.ca/news/local-news/lawyers-issue-statement-on-stanley-trial-reaction-1.23177466.

17 Ian Austen, "A Murder Trial Stirs Emotions about Canada's Relations with Indigenous Population," *New York Times,* 9 February 2018.

18 Gabrielle Scrimshaw, "A Killing in Saskatchewan," *New York Times,* 16 February 2018, A29.

19 Leyland Coco, "Canada Murder case Prompts Rival Crowdfunding Campaigns for Killer and Victim's Family," *The Guardian,* 13 February 2018.

20 Julian Brave NoiseCat, "I am Colten Boushie. Canada is the All-white jury that Acquitted his Killer," *The Guardian,* 28 February 2018.

21 Kathleen Harris, 'Do Something: Liberals Faced Angry Backlash over Colten Boushie Case," CBC *News,* 11 May 2018.

22 "Rival Fundraisers Reveal a Country Divided Online after Stanley Verdict," CBC *News,* 15 February 2018, online: http://www.cbc.ca/news/indigenous/rival-fundraisers-country-divided-gerald-stanley-colten-boushie-1.4536395.

23 Kevin Joseph, "Racist Farmers and Thieving Indians," *Prince Albert Daily Herald,* 12 February 2018, online: https://paherald. sk.ca/2018/02/12/racist-farmers-thieving-indians/.

24 Tom Parry, "Justice Minister's Tweet on Boushie Verdict Inspired a Wave of Angry Emails and Letters," cbc *News,* 26 May 2018.

25 Andrea Hill, "Stanley Trial Sparks Emails, Letters," *Saskatoon Star Phoenix,* 26 March 2018, A1.

26 Angus Reid Institute, "The Colten Boushie Case: Canadians Divided on Jury's Verdict but Think Trudeau was Wrong to Weigh In," 28 February 2018, 3–4.

27 *Criminal Code,* rsc 1985, c C-34 s 676.

28 *R. v. Kent,* [1994] 3 s.c.r. 133; *Schuldt v The Queen,* [1985] 2 scr 592; *R. v. B.(G.,)* [1990] 2 scr 57; *R. v. J.M.H.,*[2011] 3 scr 197; *R. v. George* 2017 scc 38.

29 Nobles and Schiff, *Understanding Miscarriages of Justice* (Oxford: Oxford University Press, 2000).

30 *Criminal Justice Act,* 2003 c. 44 s.78. See generally Sir William Macpherson, *The Stephen Lawrence Inquiry,* Cmnd 4262-I (1999) at 1.12 and Recommendation 38. For arguments that such exceptions will apply in only a few cases and are symbolic see Paul Roberts, "Double Jeopardy Reform: A Criminal Justice Commentary," *Modern Law Review,* 65 (2002): 393; Ian Dennis, "Prosecution Appeals and Retrial for Serious Offences," *Criminal Law Review* (2004): 619. For arguments that wrongful acquittals should be expected more frequently given the demanding standard of proof of guilt beyond a reasonable doubt see David Hamer, "The Expectation of Wrongful Acquittals and the Potential of Double Jeopardy Exceptions," Criminal Law Review (2009): 63.

31 "Gerald Stanley Trial," *Saskatoon Star Phoenix.*

32 Ibid.

33 Ibid..

34 *R. v. Cyr,* [2014] skqb 61.

35 "Gerald Stanley Trial," *Saskatoon Star Phoenix.*

36 Joe Friesen, "Crown Says it Won't Appeal Stanley Acquittal," *Globe and Mail,* 8 March 2018, A4; David Tanovich, "With so Many Unanswered Questions, Why no Appeal?" *Globe and Mail,* 9 March 2018, A15.

37 "'There Is no Making it Right' Stanley's Lawyer Says in First Statement after Verdict," ctv *News,* 8 March 2018, online: https://

saskatoon.ctvnews.ca/there-is-no-making-it-right-stanley-s-lawyer
-says-in-first-statement-since-verdict-1.3834874.

38 "Saskatchewan Farmer Acquitted in Death of Indigenous Man
Guilty of Gun Charge," *Canadian Press*, 16 April 2018.

39 D.C. Fraser, "Rural Politicians Push for Action on Crime: Upgraded
Law on Trespassing Urged," *Saskatoon Star Phoenix*, 17 March
2018 A3.

40 Ibid.

41 Alicia Bridges, "Sask Review Considers Stricter Rules for Rural
Trespassing," CBC *News*, 7 September 2018, online: https://www.cbc.
ca/amp/1.4815756?__twitter_impression=true.

42 Government of Saskatchewan, "Review of Trespass Related
Legislation," no date but requiring public input by 1 October 2018,
online: http://publications.gov.sk.ca/documents/9/107841-Consulta-
tion%20Paper%20on%20Trespass%20to%20Property%20-%20
August%207%202018.pdf.

43 "NDP's $10M Rural Crime-fighting Plan Gets Mixed Reviews,"
Calgary Herald, 12 March 2018, A7.

44 United Conservative Party of Alberta, *A Safer Alberta: United
Conservative Strategy to Tackle the Rural Crime Crisis*, July 2018,
18, online: http://www.ucpcaucus.ca/wp-content/uploads/2018/07/
Rural-Crime-Report-FINAL.pdf.

45 Unnamed farmer quoted in, "People in Rural Saskatchewan Worried
about Crime Organize on Facebook," *Canadian Press*, 8 March 2018.

46 Karen Briere, "Farmers Take Rural Crime Fight Online" *The
Western Producer*, 12 April 2018.

47 Alex McPherson, "RCMP Gets Earful on Rural Crime from Worried
Biggar-area Residents," *Saskatchewan Star Phoenix*, 7 March 2018, A2.

48 Ibid.

49 "Rural Property Owner Who Fired Gun During Break and Enter
Won't Be Charged: RCMP," *Canadian Press*, 14 March 2018.

50 Bill Graveland, "Alberta Man Charged after Farm Shooting
Leaves Courtroom to Applause," *Globe and Mail*, 10 March 2018,
A22.

51 Meghan Grant, "Charges Dropped against Alberta Rural
Homeowner Accused of Shooting a Trespasser," CBC *News*, 22 June
2018.

52 Penny Smoke, "Father and Son Pulled over by Sask. RCMP after
Stopping on Rural Road for Bathroom Break," CBC *News*, 6 July
2018.

53 Debbie Baptiste quoted in, Joe Friesen, "Ottawa Proposes Changes to the Jury Selection Process," *Globe and Mail,* 30 March 2018, A3.

54 Stuart Thomson, "Boushie's Mother Meets with Trudeau," *National Post,* 14 February 2018.

55 Bill C-75. An act to amend the *Criminal Code.* First Reading March 29, 2018 ss.271, 274.

56 Friesen, "Ottawa Proposes Changes." *Globe and Mail.*

57 Justice Giovanna Toscana Roccamo, *Report to the Canadian Judicial Council on Jury Selection in Ontario,* May 2018 at 16 noting that 356 of 650 Indigenous people who returned jury questionnaires were disqualified in 2016 and 294 of 553 in 2017.

58 Bill C-75 s. 271.

59 Viscount Runciman, *Report of the Royal Commission on Criminal Justice, Cm 2263* (1993), paras. 63–64; Lord Justice Auld, *Review of the Criminal Courts of England and Wales,* Report (2001), 159.

60 Michael Zander, a member of the Runciman Commission, has written that he has come to view the recommendation as a mistake because it would depart from random selection of the jury, lead to demands for other forms of representation, and place jurors selected by the special procedure in a "highly uncomfortable position in the jury room." Michael Zander Q.C., *Lord Auld's Review of the Criminal Courts: A Response,* November 2001, 13, online: https://www.lse.ac.uk/collections/law/staff%20publications%20full%20text/zander/auld_response_web.pdf.

61 Michael Spratt, "Justice Bill May be Bold, but It Isn't Just," *Ottawa Citizen,* 3 April 2018, A7.

62 Friesen, "Ottawa Proposes Changes."

63 Nader Hasan, "Eliminating Peremptory Challenges Makes Trials less Fair," *Toronto Star,* 11 April 2018, A13.

64 *R. v. Lines* [1993] O.J.no 3284 (Ont. Gen. Div.); *R. v. Brown,* 1999 O.J. no 4867 at paras. 6–11 (Ont.Gen. Div.).

65 See generally Lisa Monchalin, *The Colonial Problem: An Indigenous Perspective on Crime and Injustice in Canada* (Toronto: University of Toronto Press, 2016).

66 "Tensions Flare as Caledonia Standoff Continues," CBC *News,* 22 May 2016.

67 Jon Wells, "Boushie Verdict Elevates Looming Murder Trial in Hamilton," *Hamilton Spectator,* 16 February 2018; Samantha

Craggs, "'I Feel Sick to My Stomach': Peter Khill, Charged in Death of Jon Styres Gets Bail," CBC *News,* 18 February 2016.

68   "Unconditionally Withdraw 2ⁿᵈ Degree Murder Charge against Peter Khill of Binbrook, Ontario," online: https://www.change.org/p/ madeleine-meilleur-unconditionally-withdraw-2nd-degree-murder -charge-against-peter-khill-of-binbrook-on, (accessed 8 June 2018).

69   "Justice for Jon Stryres," online: https://www.change.org/p/jus- tin-trudeau-justice-for-jon-styres?recruiter=485751394&utm_ source=share_petition&utm_medium=facebook&utm_cam- paign=autopublish&utm_term=des-lg-no_src-reason_msg&fb_ ref=Default, (accessed 8 June 2018).

70   *R. v. Rogers,* (2000) 38 C.R.(5ᵗʰ) 331 (Ont. Ct. Gen. Div.).

71   *R. v. Munson,* 2001 SKQB 410.

72   See for example *R. v. Abdullahi,* 2015 ONSC 3562; *R. v. Valentine,* 2009 CanLII 81001 (ON SC). But see *R. v. Barnes,* 1999 CanLII 3782 confirming the existence of trial judge's discretion to allow more questioning.

73   Martha Minow, *Making all the Difference* (Ithica: Cornell University Press, 1990), chap. 1.

74   Molly Hayes, "Jury Selection Begins in Hamilton Trial of Homeowner Charged with Indigenous Man's Second-degree Murder," *Globe and Mail,* 11 June 2018.

75   I am very grateful to Professor Emma Cunliffe for sharing her notes on jury selection in the case with me. Emma Cunliffe, "Notes on Jury Selection," 12 June 12 2018, (on file with the author).

76   Christie Blatchford reported "an observer at the jury pool would be hard pressed to identify anyone as 'Indigenous', let alone 'visibly Indigenous.'" Christie Blatchford, "Picking 'Representative' Jury Pool Isn't as Easy as Looking at Jury Pool," *National Post,* 11 June 2018.

77   Susan Clairmont, "'Triers of Fact' Being Chosen for Peter Khill Murder Trial," *Hamilton Spectator,* 12 June 2018.

78   "Officer Testifies Khill Told Him He Was a Soldier," CBC *News,* 12 June 2018.

79   "Why not call 911? Crown Grills Khill about the Night he Shot Jon Styres," CBC *News,* 19 June 2018; "Homeowner Testifies Military Training Kicked-in Before He Shot Truck Thief," *Canada Press,* 19 June 2018.

80   "Doctors Testify Shotgun Blasts Hit Styres at a Downward Angle," CBC *News,* 18 June 2018; Susan Clairmont, "Pathologist Describes

Shotgun Blasts that Killed Jonathan Styres," *Hamilton Spectator,* 18 June 2018.

81 *R. v. Khill,* 2018 ONSC 4149 at 30.

82 *R. v. Khill,* 2018 ONSC 4148.

83 *R. v. Stanley* [2017] SKQB 367 as discussed *infra* chapter 4 at page 73.

84 Samantha Craggs "Military Training like Peter Khill's Lasts Decades, Psychologist Says during Murder Trial," CBC *News,* 22 June 2018.

85 Dan Taekema, "'Cruel Killing or Self-defence?: Lawyers Make Closing Arguments in the Khill Case," CBC *News,* 25 June 2018.

86 R. v. Khill Transcript 26 June 2018 at 12–13. I am indebted to Sarah Dover for sharing the transcript with me.

87 Ibid., 43.

88 Ibid., 72.

89 *R. v. Charlebois,* [2000] 2 SCR 674 at 16.

90 *R. v. Lavallee,* [1990] 1 SCR 852. On the contextual standard see Kent Roach, *Criminal Law* 7th ed. (Toronto: Irwin Law, 2018), 366–78; Don Stuart, *Canadian Criminal Law* 7th ed. (Toronto: Carswell, 2014), 514–520.

91 Molly Hayes, "Hamilton Man Found Not Guilty in Shooting of Indigenous Man," *Globe and Mail,* 27 June 2018.

92 Notice of Appeal, 19 July 2018.

93 Six Nations Council, "Six Nations Elected Council Deeply Disappointed by the Canadian Justice System, Again," 27 June 2018. Online at http://www.sixnations.ca/PressRelease_SNEC_ DisappointedbyCdnJusticeSystem_Again_Re_JonathanStyres.pdf.

94 Dan Taekema, "Peter Khill Banned for Life from Six Nations Territory," CBC *News,* 13 July 2018. See also Moses Monterroza, "Chippewas Join Six Nations in Banning Peter Khill from its Territory," CBC *News,* 15 August 2018.

95 Dan Taekema, "Not Guilty Verdict for Peter Khill Shows that the Canadian Justice System is Broken, Says Chief," CBC *News,* 28 June 2018.

96 Professor Joseph argued that by asking a simple yes or no question "the process disallows (or at least strongly discourages) jurors who recognize the realities and facts of racism. These potential jurors are less likely to make it through this court's "'challenge for cause.'" Ameil Joseph, "Erasing Race but not Racism in the Peter Khill Trial," *Canada Press,* 6 July 2018.

97 "AFN National Chief: Justice Demands Action now to Show Indigenous Lives Matter," 27 June 2018, online: https://www.

newswire.ca/news-releases/afn-national-chief-justice-demands-action-now-to-show-first-nations-lives-matter-686734811.html.

98 *R. v. Cormier,* 2017 NBCA 10.

99 Christie Blatchford, "Jury Acquits Hamilton Homeowner Peter Khill of Murder in Shooting Indigenous Man Jon Styres," *National Post,* 27 June 2018.

100 Christie Blatchford, "Race not a Factor in the Khill Verdict," *National Post,* 29 June 2018, A6. See also Thomas Walkom, "Khill Acquittal Does not Prove that the Justice System is Racist," *Toronto Star,* 29 June 2018, A17.

101 Blatchford, "Jury Acquits," comments online: http://nationalpost.com/news/hamilton-area-homeowner-peter-khill-found-not-guilty-of-second-degree-murder, (accessed 27 June 2018).

102 Dan Taekema, "Family of Jon Styres Suing Man who Killed Him for $2M," CBC *News,* 28 June 2018.

103 Guy Quennville, "Family's Lawsuit Claims Gerald Stanley Recklessly Caused Colten Boushie's Death," CBC *News,* 9 August 2018.

CHAPTER 10

1 "Tories Accuse PM of 'Political Interference' after Comments on Boushie Case," CBC *News,* 11 February 2018.

2 Hon. Frank Iacobucci, *First Nations Representation on Ontario Juries* (Toronto: Attorney General of Ontario, February 2013).

3 TRC, *Calls to Action* (Winnipeg: Truth and Reconciliation Commission, 2012) Call to Action 42; Royal Commission on Aboriginal Peoples, *Bridging the Cultural Divide: A Report on Aboriginal People and Criminal Justice* (Ottawa: Supply and Services, 1996).

4 Blair Stonechild and Bill Waiser, *Loyal till Death: Indians and the North-West Rebellion* (Saskatoon: Fifth House, 1997), 221.

5 TRC, *Reconciliation,* vol. 6 (Montreal: McGill-Queen's University Press, 2015), 3.

6 Joyce Green, "From *Stonechild* to Social Cohesion: Anti-Racist Challenges for Saskatchewan" *Canadian Journal of Political Science,* 39, 507 (2006): 511.

7 *R. v. Kokopenace,* [2015] 2 SCR 398.

8 Hon. Ted Hughes, chair, *The Report of the Lachance/Nerland Inquiry* (Regina: Queens Printer, 1993).

9 *R. v. Munson,* 2011 SKQB 410 aff'd 2003 SKCA 28. See Molly

Hayes, "Jury Selection Begins in Hamilton Trial of Homeowner Charged with Indigenous Man's Second-Degree Murder," *Globe and Mail,* 11 June 2018. Elizabeth Sheehy in her detailed discussion of the transcripts of trials of battered women found that questions about racist bias were not asked in a 2006 Saskatchewan trial of an Indigenous woman and concludes that "it is difficult not to know why [defence] counsel did not seize this opportunity to pursue a fair trial." Elizabeth Sheehy, *Defending Battered Women on Trial* (Vancouver: University of British Columbia Press, 2014), 146.

10 Dan Taekema, "Not Guilty Verdict for Peter Khill Shows that the Canadian Justice System is Broken, Says Chief," cbc *News,* 28 June 2018; Ameil Joseph, "Erasing Race but not Racism in the Peter Khill Trial," *Canada Press,* 6 July 2018.

11 "rcmp Probing Report of Officer's Alleged Post on Boushie," *Globe and Mail,* 16 February 2018, A9. An extreme form of denial of racism can be found in reports of a rcmp officer serving on the Prairies who reportedly posted on a closed Facebook group that the Stanley case "should never have been allowed to be about race ... crimes were committed and a jury found the man not guilty in protecting his home and family. Too bad the kid died, but he got what he deserved."

12 Thomas Hayden, "This Is not the Image We Have of Canada," *Globe and Mail,* 6 March 2004, F6.

13 *R. v. Kokopenace,* [2015] 2 scr 398.

14 *R. v. Cyr,* 2014 skqb 61.

15 John Borrows, *"Peace, Friendship and Respect": Indigenous Treaties in Canada* (Borrows 30 October 2003), 161. Unpublished report prepared for Saskatchewan Treaty Commission.

16 Ebyan Abdigir et al, "How a Broken Jury List Makes Ontario's Justice White, Richer and Less like your Community," *Toronto Star,* 16 February 2018, online: https://www.thestar.com/news/investiga-tions/2018/02/16/how-a-broken-jury-list-makes-ontario-justice-whiter-richer-and-less-like-your-community.html.

17 *R. v. Laws,* 1998 CanLII 7157 (on ca).

18 Regina Schuller, Veronica Kazoleas, and Kerry Kawakami, "The Impact of Prejudice Screening Procedures on Racial Bias in the Courtroom," *Law and Human Behaviour,* 33 (2009): 320; Cynthia Lee, "A New Approach to Voir Dire on Racial Bias," *University of California at Irvine Law Review,* 5 (2015): 843; Carol Aylward, *Canadian Critical Race Theory: Racism and the Law* (Halifax: Fernwood Publishing, 1999), 115–25, 158–62 for criticism of the

single question approach. See also *R. v. Douse*, 2009 CanLII 34990 (ON SC) for a discussion of this issue.

19 Christie Blatchford, "Jury Acquits Hamilton Homeowner Peter Khill of Murder in Shooting Indigenous Man Jon Styres," *National Post*, 27 June 2018.

20 The juries that acquitted Raymond Cormier in respect to the death of fifteen-year-old Tina Fontaine and Peter Khill in respect to the death of Jon Styres both had visible minorities and generated less controversy than Stanley's acquittal. Kelly Malone, "Jury Chosen for Man Accused of Killing Tina Fontaine," CBC *News*, 25 January 2018. The representation of visible minorities on juries will likely increase with Canada's changing population but such changes will not remedy Indigenous under-representation.

21 Taekema, "Not Guilty Verdict."

22 Kent Roach, "The Urgent Need to Reform Jury Selection in the Wake of the Gerald Stanley and Colten Boushie Case," *Criminal Law Quarterly*, 65 (2018): 271.

23 Kent Roach, *Due Process Versus Victims' Rights: The New Law and Politics of Criminal Justice* (Toronto: University of Toronto Press, 1999).

24 *R. v. Keegstra*, [1990] 3 SCR 697.

25 "Responses Flood in after Sask. Premier asks for Racist Comments to Stop after Shooting," CBC *News*, 15 August 2016.

26 Ibid.

27 Betty Ann Adam, "FSIN Signs Reconciliation Accord with Town of Elbow," *Regina Leader Post*, 26 April 2017, A7.

28 Bruce Feldthusen, "The Civil Action for Sexual Battery: Therapeutic Jurisprudence," *Ottawa Law Review*, 25 (1993): 203.

29 Dan Taekema, "Family of Jon Styres Suing Man who Killed Him for $2M," CBC *News*, 28 June 2018.

30 For my criticisms of this approach in the residential school litigation see Kent Roach, "Blaming the Victim: Canadian Law, Causation and Residential Schools," *University of Toronto Law Journal*, 64 (2014): 566.

31 Ryan McKenna, "Family of Colten Boushie Files Lawsuit against RCMP, Gerald Stanley," *Globe and Mail*, 9 August 2018; Andrea Hill, "Family of Colten Boushie Files Lawsuit against Gerald Stanley and RCMP," *Saskatoon Star Phoenix*, 9 August 2018.

32 *George v Beaubien*, 1998 CanLII 14933 (ON SC); *George Estate v Harris*, 2001 CanLII 28235 (ON SC).

33 Hon S. Linden, *Report of the Ipperwash Inquiry Executive Summary*

(Toronto: Queens Printer, 2007), 21–22, 46, 50. I served on the research advisory committee of this inquiry.

34 *Coroner's Act*, s.s. 1999 c. 38.01, s.29(3).

35 Iacobucci, *First Nations Representation*, para. 210.

36 Charles Hamilton, "Saskatchewan Coroner's Inquest Could Become Model for Indigenous Jury Reform," CBC *News*, 9 March 2018.

37 Hon. Michael Tulloch, *Report of the Independent Police Oversight Review* (Toronto: Queens Printer, 2017).

38 *R. v. Williams*, [1998] 1 SCR 1128. I represented Aboriginal Legal Services of Toronto in this case.

39 *Canada Evidence Act*, s.12. For criticism see Anthony Doob and H.M. Kirshenbaum, "Some Empirical Evidence on the Effect of s.12 of the Canada Evidence Act upon an Accused," *Criminal Law Quarterly*, 15 (1972): 88; M.L. Friedland, "Commentary," *Canadian Bar Review*, 47 (1969): 656.

40 *R. v. Corbett*, [1988] 1 SCR 670. See generally Peter Sankoff, "The Search for a Better Understanding of Discretionary Power in Evidence Law," *Queens Law Journal*, 32, 487 (2007): 492.

41 *R. v. Stanley*, Aug 19, 2016 Crim 83 of 2016 at para 8.

42 *R. v. Williams*, [1998] 1 SCR 1128. For an argument to this effect see David Tanovich, "The Charter of Whiteness: Twenty-Five Years of Maintaining Racial Injustice in the Canadian Criminal Justice System," *Supreme Court Law Review2d*, 40, 655 (2008): 674.

43 *R. v. Khill*, 2018 ONSC 4149.

44 On the dynamic nature of matters of fact and law see Lucinda Vandervort, "Mistake of Law and Sexual Assault," *Canadian Journal of Women and the Law*, 2 (1987): 233; Christine Boyle and Marilyn MacCrimmon, "To Serve the Cause of Justice: Disciplining Fact-Determinations," *Windsor Yearbook of Access to Justice*, 20 (2001): 55.

45 *R. v. Barton*, 2017 ABCA 216 at 155–63.

46 *Criminal Code*, s 34(1)(a).

47 *R. v. Hill*, [1986] 1 SCR 313.

48 Vanessa MacDonnell, "The New Self-Defence Law: Progressive Development or Status Quo?" *Canadian Bar Review*, 92, 301 (2013): 322–5.

49 L. Song Richardson and Phillip Goff, "Self-Defence and the Suspicion Heuristic," *Iowa Law Review*, 98, 293 (2012): 318–326 arguing that mistakes about criminal threats based on racial stereotypes or suspicion heuristics should always be judged to be unreasonable even though many people might make such mistakes. Dean Richardson

and Professor Goff also propose reinstating a general duty to retreat as a way of guarding against quick use of stereotypes in self-defence situations, but also allowing an honest but unreasonable belief that the accused is acting in self-defence to reduce murder to the less serious offence of manslaughter. See also Cynthia Kwei Yung Lee, "Race and Self-Defence: Towards a Normative Conception of Reasonableness," *Minnesota Law Review*, 81, 367 (1996): 479.

50 *R. v. Tran*, [2010] 3 S.C.R. 350 at para. 34 (citations omitted).

51 Cynthia Lee, "Making Race Salient: Trayvon Martin and Implicit Bias in a not yet Post-Racial World," *North Carolina Law Review*, 91, 1555 (2013): 1598–1601.

52 A recent meta-study found that two out of three studies of American states that enacted "stand your ground" or castle laws recorded subsequent increases in homicides. Julian Santaella-Tenorio et al, "What do We Know about the Association between Firearm Legislation and Firearm Related Injuries?" *Epidemiological Review*, 38, 140 (2016): 146.

53 As discussed in Don Stuart, *Canadian Criminal Law* 5th ed. (Toronto: Carswell, 2007), 510–11 and 517; Kent Roach, *Criminal Law* 7th ed. (Toronto: Irwin Law, 2018), 384–89. Even a 2013 British law reform designed to increase a homeowner's right to self-defence provides that force will not be reasonable "if it was grossly disproportionate in the circumstances" as opposed to the usual requirement of proportionality. *Criminal Justice and Immigration Act*, 2008 c.4 s.76 (5A) and (6). At the same time, the British law of self-defence is more lenient to the accused than the Canadian law because it bases the proportionality of the accused's use of force on the accused's subjective perceptions of the threat even if they are not reasonable. Ibid., 76(3) and compare with *Criminal Code* s.34(1)(a) requiring reasonable basis for a belief in the use of force or threat of force.

54 "Gerald Stanley to Pay $3,900 and Receive a Ten-Year Ban on Gun Ownership for Improper Storage of a Firearm," CBC *News*, 16 April 2018.

55 Ibid.

56 Santaella-Tenorio, "What Do We Know," 140, 149, 151, detailing a number of studies finding declines in firearm-related deaths first in Victoria and then in rest of Australia after passage of restrictive legislation.

57 Joan Bryden, "Liberals, Tories lay Groundwork for Turning Gun Control into a Wedge Issue," *Canadian Press,* 29 April 2018. A

December 2017 poll found that 46 per cent of respondents in Alberta and 38 per cent of respondents in Saskatchewan disagreed with calls for a strict ban on guns in urban areas compared to 22 per cent of respondents in Quebec and 23 per cent of respondents in Ontario." See also, Ekos Research, "Most Canadians Want a Strict Ban on Guns in Our Cities," *Ekos Politics*, 4 December 2017, online: http://www.ekospolitics.com/index.php/2017/12/heres-a-simple-idea-most-canadians-want-a-strict-ban-on-guns-in-our-cities/.

58 Douglas Quan, "What is the Family Supposed to Think? RCMP Faces Tough Questions after Controversial Stanley Trial," *Calgary Herald*, 17 February 2018, N6.

59 David Eby, *Small Town Justice: A Report on the RCMP in Rural and Northern British Columbia* (Vancouver: British Columbia Civil Liberties Association, 2011).

60 Quoted in Borrows, *"Peace, Friendship and Respect,"* 174.

61 Nicholas Jones et al, *First Nations Policing: A Review of the Literature* (Regina: Collaborative Centre for Justice and Safety, 2014), 41.

62 Douglas Quan, "After Gerald Stanley Verdict, RCMP Faces Challenges," *National Post*, 16 February 2018.

63 Quoted in Borrows, *"Peace, Friendship and Respect,"* 174.

64 Ibid., 196.

65 Lisa Monchalin, *The Colonial Problem: An Indigenous Perspective on Crime and Injustice in Canada* (Toronto: University of Toronto Press, 2016), 26–8, 33–35.

66 Task Force on Governance and Cultural Change in the RCMP, *Rebuilding the Trust*, (Ottawa: Dept of Public Safety December 2007); Civilian Review and Complaints Commission for the RCMP, *Report into Workplace Harassment in the RCMP* (Ottawa: Civilian Review and Complaints Commission, April 2017).

67 *Ontario Police Oversight Act*, S.O. 2018 c. 3.

68 Simone Arnold, Peter Clark and Dennis Cooley, *Sharing Common Ground: Review of Yukon's Police Force* (Whitehorse: Government of Yukon, 2011).

69 Joseph F. Donnermeyer, Walter S. DeKeseredy, and Molly Dragiewicz, "Policing Rural Canada and the United States," in *Rural Policing and Policing the Rural*, ed. Rob Mawby (London: Routledge, 2010).

70 Richard Yarwood, "Policing Policy and Rural Policing," in *New Labour's Countryside: Rural Policy in Britain since 1997*, ed. Mike Woods (Bristol: Policy Press, 2008).

71 Auditor General of Canada, *Spring 2014 Report,* chap. 5; Savvas Lithopoulos, *Lifecycle of First Nations Administered Police Services in Canada* (Ottawa: Public Safety, 2016), 8.

72 File Hills First Nations Police Service, "About Us," online: http://www.filehillspolice.ca/about.html (accessed 15 September 2018).

73 "Federal Government to Spend $291 Million over Five Years to Improve First Nations Policing," CBC *News,* 10 January 2018; "Chiefs Want First Nations Policing Declared an Essential Service," CBC *News,* 30 October 2017.

74 Ministry of the Attorney General, *Debwewin Jury Review Implementation Committee Final Report,* April 2018, online: https://www.attorneygeneral.jus.gov.on.ca/english/about/pubs/debwewin/.

75 Ibid.

76 Chad Nilson, "Canada's Hub Model: Calling for Perceptions and Feedback from Clients at the Focus of a Colloborative Risk-Driven Intervention," *Journal of Community Safety and Well-Being,* 1(3) (2016): 58; Chad Nilson, *Collaborative Risk-Driven Initiatives: A Study of the Samson Cree Nation's Application of the Hub Model* (Ottawa: Public Safety, 2016), 41.

77 Six Nations Elected Council, "Six Nations Elected Council Deeply Disappointed by the Canadian Justice System, Again," 27 June 2018, online: http://www.sixnations.ca/PressRelease_SNEC_DisappointedbyCdnJusticeSystem_Again_Re_JonathanStyres.pdf (accessed 15 September 2018).

78 Hadley Friedland, "Navigating through Narratives of Despair: Making Space for the Cree Reasonable Person in the Canadian Justice System," *University of New Brunswick Law Journal,* 67 (2016): 269.

79 Dan Taekema, "Peter Khill Banned for Life from Six Nations Territory," CBC *News,* 13 July 2018.

80 Robert Cover, "Foreword: Nomos and Narrative," *Harvard Law Review,* 97, 4 (1983): 11, 31, 41, stressing the ability of cultures collectively to produce laws and nomos with or without state actions. For my own arguments that Cover's approach may overestimate how the officially enforced verdicts of courts can kill alternative legal systems, and especially civil society exonerations of those who have been wrongfully convicted, see Kent Roach, "Reform and Resistance: Criminal Justice and the Tragically Hip," *Manitoba Law Journal* 1, 40(3) (2017): 45ff. The ability of Indigenous law to survive alternative state verdicts and dispositions may be even greater, in part, because of its lengthy traditions.

81 Quoted in Borrows, *"Peace, Friendship and Respect,"* 168–9.

82 Harold Cardinal and Walter Hildebrandt, *Treaty Elders of Saskatchewan* (Calgary: University of Calgary Press, 2000), 16.

83 Ibid., 8.

84 Quoted in Borrows, *"Peace, Friendship and Respect,"* 110.

85 Ibid., 168–9.

86 Jean Teillet, "To Believe in Justice, We Must Question the Sacred Cow, the Justice System Itself," *Macleans,* 27 February 2018.

87 Monchalin, *The Colonial Problem,* 54. On the importance of visiting to Cree forms of justice and its ability to adapt to urban contexts see Anna Flaminio, *Urban Indigenous Kinship Visiting* (unpublished SJD thesis: University of Toronto, 2018).

88 Quoted in Borrows, *"Peace, Friendship and Respect,"* 165.

89 Gerald Seniuk and John Borrows, "The House of Justice: A Single Trial Court," *Criminal Law Quarterly,* 48 (2003): 126.

90 Quoted in Borrows, *"Peace, Friendship and Respect,"* 102.

91 Ibid., 103.

92 Ibid., 165.

93 Ibid., 202–3.

94 Cardinal and Hildebrandt, *Treaty Elders,* 31.

95 I am indebted to Jeff Hewitt for explaining and sharing this point with me.

96 *Police Act,* s.s. P-15.1 s.38.

97 Kent Roach, "The Wrongful Conviction of Indigenous People in Australia and Canada," *Flinders Law Journal,* 17 (2015): 203; Malini Vijaykumar, "A Crisis of Conscience: Miscarriages of Justice and Indigenous Defendants in Canada," *University of British Columbia Law Review,* 51 (2018): 160.

98 Mary Ellen Turpel-Lafond, "Reflections on Thinking Concretely about Criminal Justice Reform," in Gosse, Youngblood Henderson, and Carter, *Continuing Poundmaker's and Riel's Quest* (Saskatoon: Purich Publishing, 1994), 211.

99 Keith Finlay, "Towards a New Paradigm of Criminal Justice: How the Innocence Movement Merges Crime Control and Due Process," *Texas Tech Law Review* 1, 41 (2009); Kent Roach, "Wrongful Convictions: Adversarial and Inquisitorial Themes," *North Carolina Journal of International Law and Commercial Regulation,* 35 (2010): 387.

100 *Trochym v The Queen,* [2007] 1 SCR 239; *R. v. J.L.J.,* [2000] 2 S.C.R. 600.

101 Hon. E. MacCallum, *Inquiry into the Wrongful Conviction of David Milgaard* (Regina: Queens Printer, 2007), chap. 6.

102 *Lachance/Nerland Inquiry*, 49.

103 Connie Oakes quoted in Claire Theobald, "Lack of Indigenous Jurors Undermine Faith in the Justice System," *Toronto Star*, 22 May 2018.

104 Theobald, "Lack of Indigenous Jurors." *Toronto Star*.

105 As discussed in chapter 5 at pages 102–3, there was one Indigenous person on the jury in Milton Born with a Tooth's trial. She initially told the court she did not agree with the verdict, but eventually agreed with the guilty verdict.

106 David Tanovich, "How Racial Bias Likely Influenced the Stanley Verdict," *The Conversation*, 5 April 2018, online: https://theconversation.com/how-racial-bias-likely-impacted-the -stanley-verdict-94211.

107 William Blackstone, *Commentaries on the Law of England*, 9th ed. vol 4, book 4 (Oxford: Clarendon Press, 1765-1769), chap. 27.

108 Ibid.

109 Professor Clive Walker has argued for an even broader understanding of miscarriages of justice as occurring "whenever the rights of others are not effectively or proportionately protected or vindicated by State action against wrongdoers." Clive Walker, "Miscarriages of Justice in Principle and Practice," in Clive Walker and Keir Starmer, eds. *Miscarriages of Justice: A Review of Justice in Error* (London: Blackwell, 1999), 33. See also Savage, Poysner and Grieve, "Putting Wrongs to Rights: Campaigns Against Miscarriages of Justice," *Criminology and Criminal Justice*, 7(1) (2007): 83; Kent Roach, "The Meaning of Miscarriages of Justice in a Post 9/11 World," in G. Lennon, C. King, and C. McCarthy, eds. *Counter-Terrorism, Constitutionalism and Miscarriages of Justice: A Festschrift for Professor Clive Walker* (London: Hart Publishing, 2018).

110 Sarah Charman and Stephen Savage, "Mothers for Justice? Gender and Campaigns against Miscarriages of Justice," *British Journal of Criminology*, 49 (2009): 900.

111 Stephen Savage, John Grieve, and John Poysner, "Stephen Lawrence as a Miscarriage of Justice," in Nathan Hall, John Grieve, and Stephen Savage, eds. *Policing and the Legacy of Stephen Lawrence* (London: Willan, 2009). Many changes have been made in the UK, but concerns persist that killings of racial minorities can be underinvestigated by the police and racism by white attackers has too often been defined

by police and courts as self-defence. Harmit Athwal and Jon Burnett, "Investigated or Ignored? An Analysis of Race-Related Deaths since the Macpherson Report," *Race and Class*, 56 (2014): 22.

112 South Australian Legislative Review Committee, *Report on Criminal Cases Review Commission Bill 2010* (Adelaide: Legislative Assembly of South Australia, 2012), 82–83. For criticisms of the analogy but support for allowing second appeals by accused see Bibi Sangha and Robert Moles, *Miscarriage of Justice: Criminal Appeals and the Rule of Law* (Australia: LexisNexis, 2015), 6.5., 10.

113 I am indebted to my colleague, Amanda Carling, for discussing the importance of humility as reflected in the Anishinaabe seven grandfather teachings in understanding and combatting miscarriages of justice. See more generally John Borrows, *Law's Indigenous Ethics* (Toronto: University of Toronto Press, forthcoming).

114 *R. v. Khan* [2001] 3 SCR 823 at [69]; *Reference Re Truscott* [2007] ONCA 575 [110].

115 Lon Fuller, *The Morality of Law* 2nd ed. (New Haven: Yale University, 1969), 179–180.

116 Ronald Dworkin, *A Matter of Principle* (Cambridge: Harvard University Press, 1985), chap. 3.

117 *R. v. Gladue*, [1999] 1 SCR 688. I represented Aboriginal Legal Services of Toronto in this case. On subsequent developments see Jonathan Rudin, *Indigenous People and the Criminal Justice System* (Toronto: Emond Montgomery, 2018).

118 Jamil Malakieh, *Adult and Youth Correctional Statistics in Canada, 2016–2017* (Ottawa: Statistics Canada, 2018).

119 Quoted in Borrows, *"Peace, Friendship and Respect,"* 102.

120 Roach, *Due Process and Crime Control*, 313.

121 Quoted in Borrows, *"Peace, Friendship and Respect,"* 102.

122 TRC, *Reconciliation*, vol. 6 (Montreal: McGill-Queen's University Press, 2015).

123 Hon. Frank Iacobucci, *First Nations Representation on Ontario Juries*, February 2013, online: https://www.attorneygeneral.jus.gov. on.ca/english/about/pubs/iacobucci/First_Nations_Representation_ Ontario_Juries.html.

124 Angus Reid Institute, *The Colten Boushie Case*.

Index